First Ladies

Also by Catherine Breslin

Unholy Child
The Mistress Condition

First Ladies

A Novel by
Catherine Breslin

McGRAW-HILL BOOK COMPANY

New York   St. Louis   San Francisco   Auckland
Bogotá   Hamburg   Madrid   Mexico   Milan
Montreal   Panama   Paris   São Paulo   Singapore
Sydney   Tokyo   Toronto

1 2 3 4 5 6 7 8 9 DOCDOC 8 7

ISBN 0-07-007648-0

LIBRARY OF CONGRESS CATALOGING-IN-PUBLICATION DATA

Breslin, Catherine.
  First ladies.

  I. Title.
PS3552.R388F57 1987   813'.54   86-27677
ISBN 0-07-007648-0

Book design by Kathryn Parise

To my sister Susie, who saved the day one more time. . .

and to Cambodia.

Acknowledgments

It's never possible to cobble up adequate thanks for all the help rendered with a book seven years in the brewing. But some people in their own ways left their own special stamps on how it turned out.

For that gift, I'm particularly grateful to Valerie Harper, Joyce De Villez and Gloria Steinem. . . Denis Cameron, Chhang Song and Tara Cameron. . . Timothy Allman (for his wisdom and his silver, both priceless), Frank Sieverts and Wendy Chamberlain. . . Stephen Rosenfeld and Myra MacPherson of the *Washington Post*, Bill Maynes of *Foreign Policy* and Bill Garrett of *National Geographic*. . . Dr. Arlon Tussing, Jerry Brady and Dick Drayne. . . Marty and Joan LaVor, Celia Eckhardt and Gloria Emerson. . . House mavens like Hyde Murray and former Congressmen Bill Ayres and Bob Eckhardt, 'the Hon. Bob' . . . a trio of parliamentarians: the Senate's Robert Dove; the House Deputy, Charles Johnson; and Floyd Riddick. . . Jim Ketchum, the Senate Historian, and George White, the Architect of the Capitol. . . Clem Conger's White House Staff. . . Prince Norodom Sihanouk and Princess Monique. . . Moune and Perry Steiglitz, Ann Zill, Ambassador Kishore Mahbubani. . . Patrick Brogan, Peter Kiernan. . . David Blundy and Ron Hall of the *Sunday Times of London*. . . Kitty Kelley and Larry Leamer and Kathy Hammer. . . Grace Lichtenstein, Elizabeth Wynhausen, Claire Foudraine. . . Stephanie Stern, Bill Martin, Leremy Berger. . . Judith Daniels, Roberta Ashley and Helen Brown. . . Tonika Bailey, Makeba Wilson, Debra Wilson Bailey. . . George McNeill, Dr. Bert Rosen, Leon Wolfers and Arthur 'Frog' Collins. . . Ken Cummins, Ron and Jan Schoenberg, Barry and Karen Jagoda, and Esmeralda Cumes. . . Tom Victor, magic-maker. . . Catherine McDonald, Donald Cheung and Dawn Leonard. . . Bill Campbell, former Radio Shack wizard. . . my indefatigable researcher, John Davis. . . my tenacious agent, Wendy Weil Trossman. . . my diligent editor, Tom Miller, and McGraw-Hill Editorial Director, Gladys Justin Carr. And Diane Keitt, who chased me down for deadlines.

Warmest thanks to you all, and to a few hundred others I haven't space enough to mention.

First Ladies

CHAPTER ONE /

March 14, 1979

Robin

If he was flying up to 'chew a few things over' with her on a freezing winter Wednesday afternoon, that had to mean something major, something probably quite unpleasant, was heading into her fan.

She picked up a rental car to meet him at the Eastern shuttle. Dizzy with dread, she saw him lope into the corral near the head of the herd, squeezing past the few who'd beaten him off the plane. Tie loose, briefcase tilted aggressively, looking full of himself and loaded for bear.

Spotting her, he popped a wary, seductive smile. "Hey, Robin." He touched her sleeve, dropped a grazing peck on her cheek. "Thanks for, ah, coming by. Let's get the hell out of here, go someplace private."

At the car he took the wheel, of course, and suggested they maybe take a spin out to Jones Beach. Hearing a distinct splot onto fan blades, she said all right, fine, whatever he was up for.

On the drive to the shore they talked skittishly of the kids, and his flight up from D.C. Maddeningly coy for once, he wouldn't tell her why he'd come. "Lemme clear my head with some salt air first, Rob."

The waiting sawed a bit on her raw nerves, but she probably wouldn't like what she heard anyway. Leery of him, of his mood, she switched to her calming deep breathing, perked to alert against his well-worn bag of tricks.

A derelict stone gas station along the highway jiggled loose a memory of the first time she'd met him, the fatal Block Island lobster roast. Dancing in the sand, groping in the firelight. . . . Now Jones Beach.

In a sudden flash she realized he might've flown up here to talk about. . . their getting back together. *Ouff!*

She wished she had time to figure out what she thought about that but he was driving too fast, white lines ripping distractingly through her field of vision. Anyway she was busy holding up her end of the dicey conversational minuet. "So, um, how's your mother been lately?"

Finally, perched in the dunes, he sprang it: What did she think about the idea of his running in the primaries against Roy Bob Talbott?

She felt herself tumble off the cliff she'd always known was waiting for her, blown away by that ticker in the Devlin package. *God help me, he's going to run!* Yet the good-girl part of her clapped hands, whistled with polite surprise: "Larry! You're really going to do it? Fat into fire?"

His eyes fixed on her, he said well, that depended on a few things. He looked suety but still handsome, mopishly solemn, somehow sweaty with sincerity even in the cold March wind.

Mouth shaping a smile, she said congratulations, she guessed, she just couldn't believe he was actually going to take on a sitting president of his own party. Feeling like she was drowning in his bit of news, this horrendous gamble that could be the death of her.

She'd learned that much at least from three years of Alcoholics Anonymous—enough to know the mortal trouble she'd be in trying to live through another of those bedlam campaigns. But here he was stroking her with his honey Irish smile, running on about the encouraging soundings he'd been taking. Confessing his seat-of-the-pants hunch that if Roy Bob kept on screwing up like he was, the Democrats wouldn't have a prayer of a chance in '80 and this country would be in one hell of a fix.

Sprawled beside him in the sand, she wanted to touch his face—but then he'd feel her ice-cold fear even through her gloves. He cocked his head and said shit, Rob, if he didn't have the balls to make a run of it they might get stuck with some Republican bozo like Cowboy Dan Sterling for president; now how would she like that?

She smiled and groaned, said oh, come on, don't kid around. President Dan? He said well, that was one way the ball could bounce.

Ripped with apprehension, she grasped at a straw, pointing out that Larry didn't need her approval to run, let alone her poor help campaigning. But he said no, no, he'd already decided he wouldn't go for it unless she was in there with him: "Don't let that influence your decision, Robin—you go with what feels right for you. You can write your own ticket, do as much or as little as you want. I'm only after what's best for you, you know that." Two-beat pause. "But the way things are, I wouldn't try to make a run like this unless you agreed to go along."

She looked out at the sea, cold, grey as her insides, and said well, she'd need a while to think that over. Talk to her doctors, her AA people and so on. He said sure, sure, of course, take as long as she wanted, her health and welfare were absolutely the prime number one consideration here.

Yet all along they both knew she wouldn't have guts enough not to cave in and play along. If her alternative was being held responsible for his bugging out. . . one more campaign was only another campaign, after all. How could that be any worse to live with than trashing his claim to the Family Destiny?

Curly hair plastered to his face by flying sand, he kept on talking, running out the campaign numbers she heard as measurements of how deep he was in this already. She watched it kindling on his ruddy, animated face, firing up for the Game of Games. But how could she ever on god's green earth manage one-day-at-a-time of that. . .

After a while he wanted to stretch his legs, so they hiked down to the shoreline. He skipped stones in amazing leaps over the whitecaps, somehow driving them through the whipping froth. He wheeled toward her, exulting into the wind, "Shit, Rob, I can't do any worse than them!" Singing out over the waves like Canute, so cocky then, so pure with the dare he was finally taking. Heart leaping with alarm, she wondered if "them" meant his brothers too. *Oh lord, he's going to run and that'll maybe do me in for good.*

Her panic snuffed suddenly on a thought rolling in like a healing wave of deliverance: *But he won't make it anyway! No way in hell he'd win.*

CHAPTER TWO /

January 9, 1981

Robin

The ringing phone dislodged an unexpected shred of memory, seashell slid from the pockets of her head: *All along you never reckoned he'd win.* That first disloyal hunch Robin had mislaid in the tumult of breaking news lately, Larry staying alive through upset after upset to all those cries of bravo, terrific, she cheering like the rest of them. She'd never wish he wouldn't make it but. . . .

You never really believed he could. Back at the reluctant start, that condescending private intuition had pulled her through. Well, so much for her pol-wife smarts: He'd gotten the VP slot instead, as a consolation prize, and now by some awful fluke the hung election would have to be decided in the Congress. In this roaring constitutional crisis, the Senate was voting today for a VP who would maybe wind up. . . .

Let the damn phone ring. Whatever the news was, she didn't really want to hear it. She'd long ago cured her bad habit of leaping to snatch every call on that private line as if it were a screaming baby. A ticking bomb. At 1:18 on the murmuring TV, CBS was still running a soap. *Maybe it's a reprieve. . . .*

"Oh, Mrs. Devlin." Arnstein's breathless, euphoric tone said it all. "The Senator asked me to tell you the final head count's holding at fifty-one."

She covered her wince by tugging the sweater over her jeans, saying faintly, "Well, that's great news, Sally."

Giddy laugh. "Sure thing. Of course we expected it, but it'll be great to have it official." Sliding into her usual voice, crisp, busy-important: "So the Senator says he'll call you as soon as he can after the vote."

"Fine. Are the boys watching the debate?"

"Yes, they're up in the gallery with their aunts."

Robin thanked her for calling: "I won't keep you, I know you're all terribly busy right now."

Laying the phone back on the old pine desk, she watched the tiny rainbows sun-kindled from the crystal ashtray. She kept waiting, wistful, reluctant, for a clarifying moment to match that trick of light. One clear focus on the vaporous madness all around her, fanned out in bright, perfect rainbow arcs. To somehow make sense of this impossible thing that was apparently going to happen after all.

It occurred to her now that Arnstein's call might be as close as she'd get. Tuning her gut gyros to that dismaying fact, she shivered down into a lotus tuck against the living-room wall, easing her pelvis open, loose. Then rolled up into a headstand, brain gorging on the bloodrush. Colors spinning, concentration tightening behind her closed eyelids, she felt herself tumbling down a glittery No-Exit rabbit hole. Crazy Alice might've survived the fall, but how many others could?

Dan Rather came on with a bulletin: The next act of the political drama touched off by the failure of the Electoral College to elect a president would be this afternoon's Senate vote for a vice president according to the Twenty-fifth Amendment. She was hearing Larry's promise at Jones Beach, to shanghai her into his campaign: "Just come along for the ride, Rob, you can bail out any time you want."

Huddled with her in the dunes that day, he'd looked almost like a kid, hair dancing wildly in the gusts, eyes hungry for the prize she'd always known he'd go for sooner or later. And she'd talked herself into believing him, believing she could handle it. If he just hadn't said he wouldn't make the run without her. "But that's no skin off your nose, Rob, I only want you to do what's best for you."

She'd forgotten how much that counting on him not to win had eased her through the horrendous weeks after he'd announced. Roller-coaster all the way. Now, two years and too much risky business wiser, she watched Phil Jones upside down in a Senate hall, droning on about party ranks unbroken in three hours of intense partisan debate over this unprecedented veepship: in this corner Republican Congressman Jesse St. Claire, former DJ, ex-Baptist minister, versus Democratic Senator Laurence Devlin, brother of the late great President Michael Devlin.

She felt the adrenaline rush of a last whiff of escape: *Get out while you still can, getoutgetout.* . . .

The phone rang again. She froze, gut clenched. . . then flipped to her feet, woozy with apprehension. But it was only Tish Varner, running late from her closing and now stuck on Sutton Place, no cabs in sight.

Oddly appropriate to be stood up by her AA sponsor on this pivotal afternoon. Hugging, calming her flutter, she realized she'd been fundamentally alone all through this crowded, rocky trip, whether she knew it or not.

In the Philadelphia honeymoon apartment she'd been left mostly to herself—because Larry was so busy on Michael's presidential run, she thought then. But things hadn't changed in the little Georgetown house after Melissa was born. Later the big Potomac riverfront house had always seemed bursting with kids, animals, strangers, friends. Yet there she'd been more isolated than ever—there, and in the drying-out sans he'd finally shipped her off to.

She drifted over to the tenth-floor window. The Central Park view used to work on her like Valium, but now she saw only the network trucks parked down in the street. Patient scavenger birds waiting her out. *If they just knew how I was up here stewing by my lonesome.* Her throat was tight, dry, aching for a drink. Voice hissed like a radiator: *Too much, too much to handle, don't try it on your own. . .*

She flipped down on the rug, breathing deeply, telling herself sternly, *It's okay, you're okay!* Her fear pumped adrenaline like a vodka river in her veins, the fix she couldn't walk away from. But she'd need more than that to face the storm building outside this nest. *Just a hit to stabilize you, who's to know. . . .*

Therebutforthegraceofgod, THEREBUTFORTHEGRACEOFGOD. . . .

She felt like she was about to barf. On the TV someone said the odds favored Devlin if party lines held, but votes, like chickens, were best counted after they'd hatched. She muttered amen to that, and took her juice pitcher to the kitchen for a refill.

She'd decided days earlier to wait out the Senate vote in New York, but was flayed by guilty second thoughts now. She should be up in the gallery with Sean and Jason doing the pol-wife ritual bit, leading the cheers for Larry's big moment. Instead the kids were there with his family, and here she was hiding out with a cranberry-papaya fix.

Of course she wanted him to get it. She couldn't, wouldn't begrudge him that. But she never imagined it could, let alone would, happen *this* way. The god-awful mess still didn't make one bit of sense to her.

En route to the bathroom she passed the extra bedroom, her hideaway painting room, commandeered and demolished into a Secret Service command post—one more rude reminder that she'd run out of time to put this thing together.

She peed and powdered her nose, shiny with anticipation. Tish kept telling her to remember the surgery she was going through was good news, there was no malignancy; but it didn't feel benign right now. She squirted lotion onto her crinkled hands. She kept trying to organize, make lists, but always wound up in the bathroom where too many showers had turned her into a pink prune. So now she'd taken to soaking in oil before and after but still couldn't stay out of the john, the only place she had any privacy left.

On its newsbreak, NBC said the Senate vote might decide more than the vice presidency, since if the House of Representatives fell short of a majority vote for one of the three presidential candidates, either Devlin or St. Claire would be sworn in January 20th as the first acting president. She stiffened, hugging the fear flowing through her like acid. *There's the rub. . . .*

She still couldn't believe Roy Bob Talbott, a Democratic incumbent with a Democratic majority, wouldn't pull off the House vote. Especially if Larry sailed through the Senate this fast. But as she fussed over her hanging plants, ripping off dead leaves, she forced herself to acknowledge that a week earlier she'd been saying no way would the Electoral College deadlock. . . then no way would the Senate go for Larry over St. Claire. . . .

Yet here he was getting it, in just three days—which blew her mind. She thought the Senate should at least give the House a chance to pick the president first, and anyway how could they ignore Sterling's two-million-vote edge—which showed how much political smarts she'd picked up in twenty-three long, tough years.

The panic she'd been fending off with headstands, showers and closet clean-outs fluttered to roost. Yet she couldn't walk way from what was happening, she was headed smack into the storm. She chattered, "I don't care, I can handle it, I'll work it out." But the singsong mantra didn't help.

For five touch-and-go years the magic word crutches that had carried her through were *Don't project, take it one day at a time.* Now, when she most needed that good advice, she was hearing *Don't spin your wheels. Quit playing these shell games. Better look ahead to some overall plan and be damn straight about what's coming down.*

She pulled off a yellowed leaf. Never did decide if these dead leaves came from too much watering or too little. The book said it worked both ways, Tweedledee Tweedledum. If she couldn't figure out her own plants, how could she hope to cope with the swarming craziness closing in on her?

Somebody was saying the Senate's job was less complicated than the House's, since the senators would vote as individuals, not state delegations, and on only two candidates. But the Senate Democrats had only a two-vote majority, so if any conservative Democrat broke ranks, the tie-breaking vote would have to come from the man Devlin ousted from the ticket last August, outgoing Vice President William Hillyard.

She groaned and crossed fingers, praying it wouldn't come to that. Bill Hillyard was still so pissed he'd rather chew off his hand than vote Larry into the job.

Sitting cross-legged against the overstuffed chair, she mused on the firestorm that would explode if the House couldn't come up with a president. The whole country'd go nuts, right-wingers especially. Sterling's crowd. If it worked out that way they'd crucify Larry—if it was him in their way—and she'd be caught in the middle. Like wearing your underwear into a cyclone.

She wished the damn Senate would stop blathering and get it over with. There'd be no verdict anyway today on what she wanted most to know: Would Larry wind up. . .

Acting President. She could barely squeeze the words from her head. She'd tried so hard lately to convince anybody who asked—anybody but Tish, the only one she could really open up to—that all this wouldn't faze her a bit. Water off the old duck and so on. But that acting president bit scared her out of her wits.

It might be easier not knowing what she'd in fact be up against— bliss in ignorance, qué será será. But she'd seen too much already, too close up—what it had done to Michael, and Stephen, all puffed out of shape by the power and the glory. Larry too, little brother snacking on the leftovers. When she'd been sweet-talked into agreeing to Larry's presidential run, she'd forgotten how those Devlin boys had been then, what they'd been becoming.

But she remembered now. Remembered Michael and Alexis, Alex layering her White House existence like a Chinese dowager empress, sealing herself off from the embarrassing divertissements that trailed in Michael's wake, handy for his sampling. Both pretty much blinded, finally, by the strobe light they lived in. Beginning to believe their own myths, their own self-inventions.

If Larry got dumped in there now, it'd be even tougher. He'd be the glitch in the system, the president who was never supposed to happen. God, the flak he'd get. . .

And that big house, Pamper Palace, servants waiting on you hand and foot, anything you wanted at the crook of your pinky. Suddenly it reminded her of the drying-out farms, loony bins Larry used to ship her off to when she went around the bend. Same zippy staff and perks that never stopped—but you were still locked up in a gold-plated funny farm.

She floated a vision of Birch Woods as the White House, silvery Dr. Godsden steeple-fingered in a gold Oval Office egg, peering into her guilty soul. She'd spent half her life trying to get out of those places. Now that she'd finally done it, thanks to AA and Tish, they were maneuvering to send her *back in there*?

She punched up CBS, where Dan Rather was saying the Senate would vote to elect a vice president within minutes.

No matter how many ways she'd tried to get ready for this, none worked. She huddled on the rug, patting down her butterflies, muttering, "Okay, here goes nothing."

Rather was off on a minuet about the Republican ticket of Sterling-St. Claire winning the popular vote in the 1980 presidential election by more than two million votes, blue and red graphics flashing:

POPULAR VOTE

Sterling-St. Claire (R)	42,176,219 (49%)
Talbott-Devlin (D)	39,966,514 (46%)
Balch-Fenster (I)	4,681,291 (5%)

"But they failed to get the 270 Electoral College votes required for a majority when the Alaska and Massachusetts electors cast their ballots for the Independent Party candidates, who'd narrowly won the popular vote of those states. . . ."

More graphics:

ELECTORAL COLLEGE VOTE

Sterling-St. Claire (R)	267
Talbott-Devlin (D)	251
Balch-Fenster (I)	17
Needed for majority	270

Rather said anyone who found that confusing had plenty of company around the country and in the halls of Congress. "Since no candidate won in the Electoral College, the Twelfth Amendment to the Constitution provides that 'the House of Representatives shall choose immediately, by ballot, the President' from the leading candidates, 'not exceeding three,' each state having a single vote. The Senate elects a vice president by simple majority 'from the two highest numbers on the list,' in this case, Devlin and St. Claire."

From a jammed hallway Phil Jones said informed Senate sources anticipated a narrow victory for Devlin as "one of their own. The vice presidency has been called 'the forgotten office,' but that may be about to change. If a majority of House delegations fails to elect a president by January 20th, the vice president-elect would assume full powers as acting president. If I could follow your lead, Dan, in quoting from the Twentieth Amendment: 'If a President shall not have been chosen before the time fixed for the beginning of his term. . . then the Vice President elect shall act as President until a President shall have qualified.' "

Robin switched channels distractedly. *That toot again*. She hoped they were only belaboring the point because they *wanted* so for that juicy news twist to happen.

For the off camera vote, NBC superimposed a running count on campaign vignettes. At 2:42—over a clip of Rob Bob Talbott launching the bombshell that he'd picked Larry as his running mate—the score was Devlin 10, St. Claire 12.

At 2:51—over Dan Sterling's memorable election-night claim of "what seems to be a victory here" before late Alaska returns snatched it away—Devlin 22, St. Claire 21. "Twenty-two minutes into the vote, party lines are still holding—good news for Laurence Devlin."

She crouched on her knees, stress venting in low moans. Finally: "Sixty-six days after November's general election America at last has a vice president-elect, Laurence. . . ."

She scrambled to her feet in a daze, hands clapping, screen blurred by tears. Distant cheers from the extra bedroom. "Devlin was elected by a 51 to 49 vote of the Senate, sitting in extraordinary session after the Electoral College deadlocked last Tuesday. . . ."

She whispered, "Bravo, Dev. Bravo." Her panic-kinked emotions loosened with the fait accompli. Vigil done, fat into fire—now what?

The play-by-play focus was already shifting to the House, where Talbott reportedly "hopes to match his running mate's victory. The magic number there will be twenty-six—the number of state delegations needed for a majority by one of the three presidential candidates. Doug Balch, the Independent, is generally regarded as the spoiler in the race between incumbent Democratic President Talbott and former Governor Daniel Sterling, the Republican challenger. . . ."

Red and blue flashing:

HOUSE DELEGATIONS

Democratic	23
Republican	17
Independent	1

Tied   9

Needed for majority   26

Off on the critical deadlock in the nine equally divided states: "If no candidate gets a majority by noon on January 20th, Vice President-elect Devlin in a dramatic break with precedent will be sworn in as our first acting. . . ."

She stabbed up another channel, muttering, "C'mon, where are you, Dev. . . ?"

Suddenly Larry was smiling gravely at a battery of mikes, big as life, victory glowing through his ceremonial crust. She scrambled closer, grounding instantly on his slightly stunned face. Her raw mood calmed in his steady triumphant light. *Made it, babe!*

He laid on ritual strokes for his Senate cohorts: "And since the vice president also presides over that body, I look forward to four years of continued service with them." She pressed the screen, framing his head. Up close he was a grid of fine lines, moving color strips, but still giving off that devilish spark she remembered from Jones Beach when she hadn't dared touch him like this.

She crooned, "Dev, you made it!"

Gold sweat beaded his brow, laugh lines danced at his eyes. Tiny tics of ecstasy tugged his mouth when he was asked about four years as acting president if the House deadlocked. His eyes straight to hers, dancing, but his voice was firm with rebuke. "I'm confident the House will act promptly to reelect President Roy Bob Talbott."

If Dan Sterling won, would he resign to make way for a Republican vice president? One gleam shot out before he snuffed his astonishment at the question. "Certainly not." His face was shifting, glimmering, feeling the wind of this win like he had the run two years back. Gut satisfaction in, "I intend to carry out the responsibility that has been entrusted to me for the next four years."

How could a Democrat vice president hope to function with a Republican president if Sterling won? He declined comment on hypotheticals. From the babble, he took a question on whether the Senate had "unjustly overturned" the 42-million-vote Sterling-St. Claire mandate. He said calmly, "Over the 200-year history of our republic we have periodically, with great care and national debate, refined the process of presidential elections to ensure continuity of government. Today the Senate held a fair election according to that constitutional process, and I'm confident the American people will judge it as such. Now if you'll excuse me. . . ."

He stepped away into a bobbing crowd, ignoring a shout on a Supreme Court challenge of the vote. Robin flexed backward over the rug, moaning with edgy relief. *The Court, oh god, never thought of that. . . but he made it!*

He'd done fine in the crossfire. Terrific, in fact. Which didn't alter the fact that nobody had a clue what was going on in this unholy mess, or what anyone was really up against, including herself.

Especially herself. Except that she sure was into, as the TV wise men liked to say, a whole new ballgame.

Roy Bob Talbott popped up in the Rose Garden, crowing over the Senate vote, fully confident the House would promptly follow suit. She barely listened, thinking fretfully, *She said he'd call after the vote.*

A crib on Van Buren's veep, elected by the Senate in 1837, was interrupted for "Governor Daniel Sterling, with a statement from his home in Middleburg, Virginia." Robin bolted up to catch him striding jauntily, hand in hand with his wife Priscilla, across their photogenic barnyard.

The small brown-haired woman in the pale-blue coat was such a genius at the smoothie pol-wife bit she made it look easy. Tougher job than anybody'd think, and nobody did it better than Prilla. Who else could make that joined-at-the-knuckles Siamese-twin routine look almost natural?

Yet Robin blinked at the close-up of Prilla moving toward the camera. Her look was somehow askew, unfocused. Not the usual worshipful glaze, dished out like relish to her husband's hot-dog speeches.

Might take one to know one. . . . Robin wondered if anyone besides herself could see clear as ice that Prilla was cracking apart.

CHAPTER THREE /

January 9th

Prilla

Bong. Bong.

The tolling grandfather clock went off like a cannon behind Priscilla's back, shot through the thin tuning fork of her body. *Ask not for whom*. . . . She sprang away from it, heart thundering, head skidding with alarm, scrambling to remember if a tolling clock was bad luck.

But how much worse could their luck get than the call she strained to hear from Dan's end. "Yes, sure. I'd hope so." She should've got on the extension, for heaven's sake. Couldn't tell much from his troubled scowl, wary voice. "Right. Well, let's take it from here and see how it goes. Anyway, Prilla and I want to extend our congratulations."

Her teeth snapped shut on that ritual message. As he hung up he smiled at the sound, nodding as if to applause. "Okay, let's get this over with. Pril, you all set?"

"Sure." They marched through a swirl of staff to the kitchen door. He paused to glance at his cue cards, frowning, lips moving as he stashed the lines for instant recall. His face strained, pouchy with fatigue. She thought numbly, *He's still stunned, off edge*. . . .

As he slid the cards in his pocket, she reached for his hand. He lit a tired smile. "Ready for the lions, Mommie?"

Brightly: "You bet." She straightened his tie, her good-luck touch, and held his eyes, willing her strength into him. "Break a leg, sweetie. You'll be terrific."

The ritual kiss dropped softly on her cheek. He nodded to the Secret Service agent standing at the door.

Now!

Switch-on like an electric jolt. Head lifted, shoulders squared, serene on-stage smile snapped into place, she walked beside him out into the camera eyes.

They were a swarming army today, tethered behind ropes. She caught voice-over snatches as she crossed the yard: "Coatless despite the below-freezing. . . ." "His prospects overshadowed now by Vice President-elect Devlin's upset victory. . . ."

Lights burned the chill from her skin, burned off the winter gloom. She swam in the shimmering electric-white blaze, still blank with shock. *What happens now? Who'll save him, salvage this?*

One big light shone right in her eyes, bright as sun. Like those enormous kliegs at the old Hollywood premieres, nights when the town turned inside out with magic. Like the premiere of that ghastly movie *Sugar and Spice*, when the studio wanted Dan to take Sheila Golden, that ditsy young blonde she'd known even then was a nobody going nowhere.

☆

Danny didn't *have* to take that girl, he could've gotten out of it with a graceful, diplomatic no. He said yeah but he shouldn't turn them down, he wasn't getting much work offered lately, better not rock their boat. Tiptoeing on eggshells, she purred, honey, that doesn't mean you have to jump to their beck and call; they'd respect you more if you stood up for what *you* want.

All that weekend at his ranch she watched, waited for the right moment to bring it up. She'd need perfect timing, couldn't, mustn't get it wrong. Coming in from their ride he was so happy, so horny and het up—right after their rides was usually the best time to broach anything as delicate as Sheila Golden.

So she maneuvered him into a rassle in the barn hayloft. Tumbled in those spikey bales, back bent practically in two, straw raking like needles through her shirt, she seized the moment to unload every sweet, uncomplaining bit of ammunition she could shake from her frantic head—daring, risking the whisper, "Besides, why go with her when I love you better than aaannybody else ever could?"

Finally he said, by gosh, he guessed she was right, and shut her up with a kiss. They never made it out of the barn that time. . . just as well, since she'd left her diaphragm back home in her dresser drawer again that weekend. So later, if she had to, she could always say but you remember that time in the hayloft. . . .

She thought then that it was all settled. But he didn't call for ten days and then she saw in *Variety* he was taking Golden after all. She called Joe Schatzberg, Daddy Braxton's friend, the MGM vice president, trying to make him take her. Joe wouldn't, but he fixed her up with a young New York actor.

Oh, that ghastly, awful night. She wore a dotted pink organza that looked like somebody's bedroom curtains. The boy was a pansy with muscles, at least five years younger than she. Constantly spraying his throat, moaning about how L.A. was ruining his voice. She ignored him, head swiveling, looking everywhere for Dan. *Ah, there!*

Lights spilled around him and that tall girl all in gold, poured into a gold lamé sheath, gold sprinkles sprayed in her cotton-candy blonde hair. Hanging so prettily on his arm, breathing in his face. Dan laughing, head cocked to listen. Bulbs popping as he slid his arm around that teensy waist.

He'd thrown her over, and she'd probably die from the disgrace. Transfixed with pain, Priscilla's anguish combusted into a prayer of desperation.

Oh god, please god, if I can only have him I'll never ever make him sorry. I'll make him the happiest man on earth. Just let me prove how much I love him and I'll never ask for anything again, only make it me there on his arm.

☆

"Good afternoon." With a start she homed back on Dan, jaunty and brisk at the mikes of the barnwood platform. "A few minutes ago I spoke with Senator Devlin and extended congratulations from Prilla and myself for his success in the Senate vote."

Now why on earth was she thinking of Sheila Golden? Of course she'd won him after all, *she'd* been the one on his arm, by his side through the whole amazing trip. But no way, no way, was it supposed to turn out like this.

"As I told him, I'm confident we can work together in a bipartisan spirit of national unity after the House elects me as president." Golden of all people. Maybe she'd harked back to that because she hadn't felt so hopeless and floundering, so utterly lost since that awful time.

Face frozen, locked on him, she listened with resistant disbelief, amazed to be hearing: ". . . I foresee no difficulty working with Senator Devlin. He comes from a patriotic family long involved in public service. . . ."

Nauseous ripple at the idea that the most he could look forward to now was having Larry Devlin as his veep. Danny had *won* that election, by two million votes. No matter how they tried to explain away what was happening, she locked on that root truth: *They're trying to steal it from my Dan. . . .*

Hard to remember how she'd fed on those triumphant, roaring crowds, waiting out the fairy-tale finish. Now bone-tired, drained, she tasted panic like dry chalk.

". . . few specific constitutional duties for the Vice President, but I'm sure Devlin can make a fine contribution to my administration." *Don't crack, don't cry.* She dipped her eyes, avoiding the cameras lined up like machine guns.

Avoiding, but never forgetting. At this very instant infinite images of her and Dan were being sucked into those lenses and shot out to millions of TV screens. So strange to think of those splintered reflections whizzing through the air she breathed, filling up miles of videotape. . . .

In their first year as governor, when it all seemed such fun, like a Christmas present she'd never expected to get, she hadn't realized quite how much all that image business counted. His knack for acting, for using the media, seemed then like a handy plus. It took her a while to see it was practically the whole game.

This Senate shocker stirred dark, sharp fears in her—the whole mess was pitching out of control, she herself might splinter right before the camera eyes. Most of the massive campaign machine spinning out from Dan—PACs, polls, computers, phone-banks, commercials—was only remotely real to her. But she was always acutely tuned to the only part that could kill them off in one careless minute: the sprawling red-eyed dragon.

She'd considered it friendly when the campaign was cranking up; she'd even joked with Dan about how to exploit it even more brilliantly, projecting his magic across the country, conjuring the world they all wanted, that he promised to deliver.

But as the campaign unwound, the dragon had grown bolder. Like living with some electronic movie monster that dominated their lives, always scrambling after them, raucously demanding its daily feed. She'd thought for a while that Dan's master strokes could tame it, but she knew better now. She knew it hungered mainly for a fatal 'mistake,' an off-the-cuff slip that could finish them off.

Look what had happened to Romney. Or Muskie. Both bumped off with a chance remark. That's all it took, one off moment caught on those wretched tapes. So far Dan had lucked out, no fluffs played longer than two days. He was better at TV than movies even, but it took constant vigilance and hard, hard work to keep that luck rolling.

All this while they'd been full-time partners on the trail. She'd teased him that she could hardly help but pick up some of his knack, but now she needed every bit of it to get her through this afternoon. Above all, slip no hint to the beast that their carefully crafted step-by-step triumph might be coming apart in their hands.

". . . and I urge the House to reaffirm the mandate voted by forty-two million Americans last November 4th."

She had a terrifying, icy-clear realization that all the rules were broken now. The sudden-death jeopardy they'd lived with for so long was intensified now; from here on they'd be winging it, working without a script.

Oh god, she was afraid.

Questions hurtled after his statement: Had he talked to St. Claire? Did the Senate vote diminish his chances in the House? Would he accept Devlin as acting president if the House deadlocked?

He waved them off. "Sorry, folks, no comment." As he turned from the mikes, she slipped her hand in his, smiling radiantly into the lights.

They scrambled around him all the way back to the house, firing questions as she tried to hurry him along. When someone asked if the Senate vote was a repudiation of his running mate he wheeled around. "Certainly not. Jesse St. Clair is one of the finest public servants I've been privileged to know. Obviously the Senate took the easy way out and voted strictly on party lines." She yanked imperceptibly on his hand. *No, no, not that!*

Too late, he added lamely, "But I'm confident the House will rise above partisan considerations and respond to the mandate of the American voters."

Smile locked on, glance averted from the red eyes, she drew his steel to her magnet, tugging him back to their precarious refuge.

CHAPTER FOUR /

January 9th

Robin

Ben Boylan, elated: "Mrs. Devlin, please hold for the Senator."

"Oh! Sure thing, Ben." Nervous, rusty-wheel squeak.

Larry's voice trailed distantly over the phone. ". . . put him on tap, tell Gil to work it in."

Old eddies swirling, she snapped, "Larry, are you there?"

"Oh, Robin?" Buoyant. Almost boyish. "How're you doing?"

"Terrific. How about you?"

His laugh exploded pleasure. "No, um, complaints on this end."

She cleared her throat. "Hey, big fat congratulations, Mr. Veep."

"Thanks." Fresh victory surged in his voice. "Funny how much better that sounds than it used to."

Receiver to her ear, she drifted to the window. Two more trucks below. "So welcome to the funeral business. Bravo and all that good stuff." Dry swallow. "I'm just a bit surprised it went so fast. What happened to the famous two million two mandate?"

He said he guessed the number that counted was fifty-one Democrats. "Okay, so listen, are you coming down here?"

"Yes, sure." She plucked absently, fretfully at her jeans pocket, picking up the brisk nag-toward-duty vibes she usually got from his calls. "What about the House vote, then? Will Talbott get it on first ballot too?"

"Sure, chances are." His tone nettled, remote.

She reached for lightness. "Well, how soon, d'you think, Dev?"

Impatiently: "In a couple of days, Rob. When they finish gassing on the floor. Hold on a second." Muffled snatches. Then, "Robin? Things are getting a little hectic around here. So Gil's laying on a plane for you at Butler and I'll see you out at the house, okay?"

"No, wait a minute, Larry." Twisting the cord, searching out the words, she ignored the distant doorbell. "Look, I'd better stick around here for a few days. Till the Talbott vote comes in."

Her words hit Larry like a kick in the gut. With the Senate cloakroom still rackety with the celebration of his coup, Robin slammed him back down to earth, rambling on about how she wasn't awfully good at cliff-hanging, as he ought to know, and all this deadlock talk she heard. . . .

She trailed off. For one rash moment he thought maybe she'd say okay, never mind, she'd be down in a few hours. Instead: "Larry, how good are the chances Talbott won't get this thing out of the House?"

"Damn good, I hope." She hadn't brought that subject up for weeks—which he'd thought meant she was over it, was finally ready to roll with the punches. But he realized now from her quavery voice that she'd probably just been too chicken to mention it. "Look, I've got no time now for. . . ."

"Sure, understood. I just think I should hang in here for a bit, till we know what the agenda is. So I get my act together before I stroll down into—whatever. If you follow my drift." Prodded by his chill silence, she added, "I mean, there's a big difference between those two jobs, Dev."

A jammed cloakroom was no place to be holding this conversation. Back turned to the crowd, he pleaded in a hushed, confiding voice, "Look, if it works out that way, it'll probably only be for a couple of days. Christ, we can just have some fun with it, Rob."

She promised they would, if that was how it worked out.

So she was going to buck him all the way. Cross him up, rain on his parade. He said tightly, flatly, "Okay. Play it your own way."

"For sure I'll come, Dev. I just need a bit more time if you can manage without me." Stacked deck in that terminology: She knew he'd never say he couldn't manage without her.

"Mmph," he said curtly. "Catch you later, then."

He may have squeaked through this vote, but, by god, that didn't mean he could control his own wife. He hung up, choked with angry dread, praying she wouldn't—once again—bring it all down on his head.

Shivering at her own boldness, Robin went to see about that doorbell.

Perched on the foyer chair, Tish Varner was unzipping her boots, laughing with Jim Connerty, a Secret Service agent. As he ducked discreetly toward the spare bedroom, Robin said, "By the way, Jim, I won't fly out for a few more days. So batten down the hatches here, okay?"

"No problem, Mrs. D." Tugging at his powder-blue double-knit lapels, he blurted, "I'd like to take this opportunity to congratulate you and your family."

She tried on a good-scout smile. "Thanks, Jim. That's very kind of you." When he closed the bedroom door, she turned to Tish and slipped with a low cry into her strong, fortifying embrace.

On the subway coming over here Tish had spotted a guy scouring the *Daily Racing Form*. The irrepressible horseplayer in her immediately shook out eight-to-five odds against Robin coming through this in one piece.

Now as Robin pulled her into the living room, chattering about how she'd found the guts to tell Larry she was staying put for a few days till this Talbott thing got unfogged, Tish watched the dimples of stress roving that lovely, drawn face and revised the odds to eight to three.

Tish said mildly, noncommittally, "You don't have to do it, you know. . . go down there at all."

For an instant Robin cocked her head, seeming to size up that way out. Then she veered off in a snit of pique: "You're years late for that. I promised I'd go down there if it came to that, and you went along with it. So don't pull the rug out on me now."

Tish reminded herself not to try that tack again. Robin was already skimming close to the edge. Look at her cowering by the TV up in this virginal white-and-gold apartment, hiding out from the vicious reporter pack. Brooding over how pissed off Larry was about her not coming, so that would be "one more thing to make amends for."

As if Robin hadn't spent most of her star-crossed life trying to make amends, to husbands, kids, parents, even husband's clan. Turning handsprings of guilt that were never enough.

Tish had tried hard to be fair to that family, since she basically considered them a collection of shitheads. So she allowed they'd had considerable provocation from Robin's end. After agreeing to be her AA sponsor, Tish had got her own dose of that—weepy confessional calls from her charge far into the night, binges and disappearances, blurted fears and urges and long-dead sins.

Finally she'd soundproofed the den walls in her Houston Street loft and added a ceiling, so she could at least field those calls in privacy from her gentlemen friends. Her Robin Devlin Memorial Room, she called it. From the look of things today, it had some hard use coming up.

The trick was trying to minimize the damage ahead. For a long time now she really hadn't been leveling with Robin. It wasn't her place to say don't. And anyway who could expect Robin to walk away from the wild possibilities opening up—First Lady by fluke. My god, who wouldn't go for that!

So Robin wasn't quite like the rest of her fellow healing drunks any more. She wasn't allowed to be as crazy as the others. Yet only her external circumstances had changed—the woman herself was a healing fawn, trembling, still sniffing the wind for danger. All those hellish nights still in there skittering behind that pretty put-together skin, regardless of the strange new dance Larry was pressing on her.

What benefit-of-personal-experience guidance could Tish offer for *that*? All she had to work with were old nostrums about sticking tight to the program, going to meetings. And here was Robin talking flag and duty, thumping Uncle Sam's tub. Tish heard much of that as smoke screen, alcoholic grandiosity, can't-do-without-me bull. But right now it was damn hard to make a case for that.

As if picking up her wavelength, Robin started in on how she wouldn't let herself get boxed in or overtired. "I'm not ignoring any of the risks, Tish. I'll take it easy, turn it over, first things first." Babbling on about watching her HALTs and keeping the schedule light, as if that would somehow shield her from the meteor hail down there.

Tish wasn't concerned about the tea parties. She mainly worried about how to handle Robin's craziness, that potentially fatal illness ticking in her like a time bomb. And she knew by now that nothing made Robin crazier than prolonged exposure to her husband.

Larry the Rat with Women, Tish thought of him. A rakish good-looker with charm to burn when he chose to use it, and more brains than she'd expected. But he also had a casual brutality in the way he dealt with any woman who wasn't his mother. A special, sporadic brutality for his wife.

Some people excused that as endemic to the game of politics. Tish didn't give him that much of an out; she saw the same type all over business and law. Offhand, she didn't especially blame him for it; some unlucky men just turned out that way. But the quality was like an acid pool in him that the pellets of Robin's craziness could drop into any time.

Abruptly, Tish asked Robin how long she'd been clean and dry. Robin waved crossed fingers: "Three years, four months, twenty days." A glance at the clock. "And about six hours."

Remembering how touch-and-go so much of that pressure-cooked campaign had been, Tish decided to be cheered by that statistic. "Well, that sounds like a pretty good head start. Now if you can just manage to keep your brains unscrambled. . . ." She added in sudden, awkward blurt, "In case I haven't mentioned this lately, I'm damn proud of the way you've been holding up your end in all this."

With a shy, wary smile, Robin tugged her foot onto her thigh. Not sure how to take that rare Tish compliment, she muttered that the vote of confidence might be premature.

"No, I mean it, you're doing fine, amiga." Tish was a tumble of lean Modigliani bones on the white couch, her salt-and-pepper topknot like a silvery little wheel, bright as a leftover chemical rainbow. "So far, so good."

Robin was trying to tune out Jesse St. Claire's claim that the great American Constitution was never designed to steal an election, just what they'd seen happen today. But Tish grinned: "There's my favorite, the ex-preacher DJ. This thing gets crazier by the minute."

"Mm hmm." Even in the weird, uncharted trip ahead, Tish was still her safest guide for sifting reactions. Still the only one who understood *her* craziness.

She caught Barbara Walters taking "a look back at the man who'll be our new vice president, the senior senator from Pennsylvania, Laurence Devlin." Images flashed like peeks from a family album: Larry at 6 in a starchy Devlin lineup. At 15 winning a sailboat race. With his brothers on Michael's first congressional campaign.

Suddenly she saw herself with him on the screen, Barbie-doll bride clinging to his arm, the little plastic couple on the wedding cake. Like fun-house mirrors throwing back twisted glimpses: Hugely pregnant on a beach, trying to control squirmy Melissa while Larry testily 'relaxed.' Holding Sean in the four-foot Devlin christening dress, Melissa clinging to her sleeve, Jason drooling on her knee. "But this idyllic family image was shattered when the senator's wife's personal problems became public knowledge. . . ."

With a bruising shock she recognized the glazed, disheveled woman being hustled from the scene of a car accident. "Oh, my god," she whispered, watching herself leave a police station, flinching from the cameras, Larry grim at her side. Close-up at a Main Line fund-raiser, face ravaged, staring vacantly.

She ducked her head, eyes blinked shut to the accusing images. Coughing, patting her chest, feeling punched in the belly. Tish took the TV controls, doused the sound.

Silence. Tish said angrily: "Okay, there's one surprise out of the way. Now you know those bastards are going to run any garbage they find in their files. So what?"

She shook her head, still shrinking from the glimpses. "I don't know, Tish. I just—lord, they won't ever leave it alone, you know?"

Tish talked rapidly, urgently about what a different woman Robin was today from the one carousing on those benders. How she had the tools now to keep that from happening again, to deal sanely and soberly with whatever came up.

"Well, shoot." She stretched out on the rug. "We're talking ancient history anyway. But I wish they didn't have so much of it on tape."

Suddenly, from Tish: "Related subject: Did you and Larry work out any conditions for your going back? Is this flat-out reconciliation, you move back into his bedroom?"

Robin glanced up at that beaky, inquisitive look. By tacit agreement they usually skirted the prickly details of her life with Larry. Tish's mouth would make an unconscious little pucker whenever she talked about him, yet she readily conceded that Robin was the one married to the guy, the only one whose gut instincts mattered.

The question spun in her head. That one she hadn't quite confronted. . . . *But his undertow's too strong; sooner or later he'd pull me under again.*

Moment of truth, she blurted, "No, no, not a reconciliation as if nothing ever. . . I'm not zipping back to his bed, Tish. I couldn't go at all if I thought for one minute I was back to stay; I can't live with him that way again."

Tish's relief lapped against her own. Tish dutifully supposed that if Robin kept an open mind, played it by ear, she might be pleasantly surprised. Possibly these damned peculiar circumstances could give them a fresh start?

Robin shook her head wistfully, saying she couldn't afford that one-and-only fantasy any more. "I've changed so much, Tish—*you* know that. And he can't. Won't. Doesn't even try. It's hard enough to stay dry around him, with all that old shit. But if I turn into his yo-yo again. . . ."

Frowning, wary, Tish said she'd better make that crystal clear to Larry as soon as she could: "I'm concerned enough about you getting kicked into that mess down there. Now add to that you can't live with your husband. . . ."

Robin argued doggedly that she wouldn't necessarily have to. "If he's just the veep, I can commute from here. All I really promised was I'd live in the White House if he wound up there, and I still don't think it'll come to that."

Tish made her promise to call at least every day, "Even just to say hello. I don't want us separated. And any time you need to see me, you holler. Ditto for Ron or Shirley. The shuttle goes every hour."

Robin thanked her for the offer, devoutly hoping she wouldn't have to take her up on it.

Before they left for dinner at Shirley's, Alexis Devlin came on the TV, trim and gorgeous, throatily commending the senators' wise choice. "Damn, I'm late for my stand-up," Robin fretted. "Come on, let's blow the bunker."

Tish grinned. "Attagirl."

Robin walked through the apartment lobby inside a tight envelope of agents, TV lights kindling a blaze of welcome. Blinking through the steely-white haze, she could barely see the walls of mikes and cameras, and rickety sawhorse barricades reinforced by blue-coated cops.

She slowed to wave blindly, field some of the pelting questions: "Of course, I'm thrilled. . . . Yes, I'll be going to Washington very soon. I just have a few things to take care of here first. . . ."

Like wasp swarms, massing, buzzing, stinging. "I talked to him several times today. And the children too. Of course, they're very pleased and proud of their dad. . . ."

Jim hustled her safely through the rat pack, bustled her to the refuge of the Secret Service car idling at the curb. Even so, she was shivering as the blue Dodge gunned off down the street.

CHAPTER FIVE /

January 9th
Prilla

There she was, bold as brass: "I talked to him several times today. And the children too. Of course, they're very pleased and proud of their dad."

Priscilla yanked at the belt of her robe. "Listen to that." Mincing imitation: " 'I talked to him several times.' She didn't even have the decency to put in an appearance for that vote."

Edgy chuckle from Dan. "Yep, I guess."

She stared at that fresh, photogenic face, tumbling red-gold hair, hands jammed in the pockets of the dark mink tossed on over jeans like an old trench coat. Even in the grainy CBS news coming in early from Baltimore she looked so young, so. . . unconcerned. Asked if she expected to move into the White House, the woman gushed, "Heavens, I haven't a clue. I'm still trying to get used to the idea my husband will be vice president."

Priscilla snapped, "I'll just bet you are, lady."

Close-up on that face, saying softly, ". . . so I guess we'll have to help each other get adjusted to this situation. Because it's brand new to us all, really, isn't it?"

Walter Cronkite thought that should stand as "the last word on this extraordinary day, coming from Robin Swann Devlin, the lovely young woman who last week was a hardworking art student in New York City, and eleven days from now may become our first 'acting' First Lady."

Anh! That again. . . .

Spine ramrod straight, Priscilla stalked to her closet, muttering, "Unbelievable, just unbelievable. She can barely recognize her own family, let alone what's going on with this mess. But she still has the brass to waltz out for those cameras as if she *belonged* there."

For so long the nemesis had been Norleen Talbott. Now, suddenly, that flighty redhead. At best the hippie gypsy would be Second Lady. At worst. . . .

Dan said mildly she shouldn't let it get her goat. But to be toppled from her rightful place by Robin Devlin, of all people. No, no, too cruel, too unfair.

She fumed, "And that ridiculous vote! I can't believe the Senate can actually get away with that." She yanked out a silk blouse, checking for wrinkles. "Those Democrats can whine about constitutions till they're blue in the face, but I know highway robbery when I see it."

She'd been off on this toot since the darn vote had come in. Dan guessed she'd never actually seen it coming, though his gyros picked it up two days ago.

He sure wished she'd get over it. She was his main gyro, the one constant that held all the rest together for him. When she veered off on a tear like this he felt like he was listing, running aground.

The only way he knew how to get through this thing was keep walking straight ahead, one foot in front of the other, and act like a winner. Act like he never expected for one minute he wouldn't make it.

He'd never been much good at poker back in his Hollywood stag days when he'd get roped into an occasional game, often enough to keep his old-boy standing. But he'd sure picked up a few tricks since. Looking back over the last few years, he wished he had a dime for every time he thought for sure he was up the creek, goose cooked. And damned if he hadn't bluffed his way through every time. A little sweet talk, a little soft-shoe shuffle wrapped up in some red, white and blue, and, by gosh, they'd wind up cheering down the roof.

But he'd need the footwork now more than ever. He hadn't yet let himself say it out loud—especially to her—but he knew they stood one heck of a good chance of seeing this whole thing fizzle out like a box-office bomb.

Only way he knew to stop that from happening was act like it couldn't. He tended to believe that anyway; he'd come too far on luck and accidents of timing to play the doubter now. But by golly, he was human too, and finding it damn tough to hold up his end in this when everything around him was falling apart.

If he had any shot at all at turning it around, he'd need her to be there for him. She was the mirror that reflected back his carefully constructed world, the one he'd put together out of baling wire and campaign promises and durable imagination. The way she was carrying on now, fuming, hissing, tossing clothes around like a kid having a tantrum, all he could think was: *She blames it all on me.*

He said hesitantly, "Hon, don't you be upset." Hearing his own ragged voice, he lifted his hands in a weary, pleading gesture. She looked up, thunderstruck, like she'd been slapped. "We'll handle this like all the rest, Pril, and I swear it won't matter in the long run. All we've gotta care about is the House, and it'll sure be a different story there, I promise you."

For a long minute she just stared at him, rooted to the spot. "Oh, of course it will, sweetie!" She threw down the clothes and rushed into his arms, crooning that she'd never doubted that for a single minute, he was always first in her thoughts, her heart—her life.

As her wiry arms pressed like steel around his back, he felt her turmoil dissolve into a powerful intensity. Felt her strength flow into him. She whispered fiercely in his ear, "You'll make it. No matter how they try to take it away from you, Daniel Sterling, you *will be* president."

Jauntier now, more like himself: "Damn right. We'll win this thing yet, Pril."

"Sure we will," she murmured, a little choked. "You can count on that, hon."

He sat on the bed and switched to NBC news, Chancellor leading with the darn Senate vote: "Devlin won his narrow victory when all fifty-one Democrats voted for one of their own. . . ." She cuddled beside him, hugging his chest, distracting him with soft, peckish kisses while Devlin crowed about the victory for continuity in American leadership.

Then Roy Bob Talbott, insisting the House in its wisdom would shortly reunite the Talbott-Devlin ticket. She purred sarcastically, "Howdy Doody's Rose Garden routine."

Dan chuckled. Chancellor continued, "Meanwhile Daniel Sterling, the Republican presidential candidate, denies his own prospects are hindered by. . . ."

As they came on-screen, she started, nails sharp in his ribs, murmuring, "Oh, I look awful." He said loyally, "Come on, hon, you're gorgeous as ever." She did look a bit fuzzy, a little blue and peaky against the upbeat look he was pulling off. Her washed-out blue coat didn't help, but he guessed they oughtn't look like they were celebrating anyway.

". . . congratulate Senator Devlin, and I look forward to having him serve in my administration. . . ."

She squeezed him, murmuring, "And if you believe that, Jack, I've got a spare bridge you can buy."

He laughed over his own "certainly some disappointment for my running mate. . . ." *Gotta remember to scratch Jesse from the script.* "But I'm confident the House will affirm the mandate entrusted to me by a clear majority of the American voters last November 4th."

Somebody asked if him working with a Democratic vice president wouldn't be like putting Menachem Begin in harness with Yasir Arafat. She stiffened, making a wordless sound he translated as yes, exactly.

He parried: "We're all Americans first and foremost. I'm sure I'll find many useful roles for Senator Devlin in the great work of moving this country into the national recovery which is the goal of all Americans."

"Oh, good hit, Danny! Right on the nose."

He snuggled her closer against him. She leaned into the hollow of his shoulder, her fragile nearness somehow making him feel solid and alive. She often told him she drew on his strength like a dry sponge touched to water, but sometimes he thought it worked the other way around.

Chancellor got into the heated horse trading on Capitol Hill, the crisis atmosphere with "little chance of a first-ballot victory, with nine state delegations neutralized by an even split between Democrats and Republicans. . . ."

Abruptly, she peeled loose, stood up, and headed for her dressing table. He watched her arched, rigid back, her snappish moves. Feeling some of the starch bleed out of him again, he said bleakly, stubbornly, "Pril, I promise you we're going to win this thing."

She switched on the portable makeup mirror, one more cheap gizmo she was using to survive in this drafty old farmhouse. She knew he wanted more comforting, more reassurance, but right now she was flat out of both.

Briskly slapping moisturizer onto her spiderwebbed face, she said dryly, "Tell that to the idiots who wrote that Twenty-fifth Amendment. What on earth they were thinking of? Didn't they *know* about those split delegations?"

Bruised, pummeled by this brutal day, she felt the tiredness rooting in pits of pain through her body, harder and harder to shake off. But she tried not to let him see how much anger she was tamping down. How much heartache. . . .

That still didn't blot out his need for her, huge as the earth. His utter need for her to shield him, tend and second-guess him, be his 'everything.' She'd always wanted it that way, of course, but now he held her to it. Sometimes reminded her with a look passed between them: *Okay, lady, you got me into this.* . . .

Two beeps sounded on their private line, the answering service alert to approved calls. Reflex moved her to answer, but he picked it up first.

"Okay, put him through." She peered at him, mouthing, "Who?" He smiled coyly. Boomed heartily, "Phil, how're you doing, fella?"

Phil Laubert, anchorman in the 'kitchen cabinet' of self-made millionaires who'd launched and bankrolled Dan's political career. This made six days in a row Phil had called—every day since he'd zeroed in on the numbers predicted for the House vote.

Phil used to wait for Dan to call.

Scowling with concentration, she rubbed white pigment over the dark bags under her eyes. She watched him sharply in the mirror, locked onto his end of the call. "Well, sure. That Senate vote was no surprise to us, Phil." No, no, no, she *had not* expected it—never.

And neither had Phil.

Now they were talking numbers, those appalling numbers projected for the first House vote: twenty-three or twenty-four for Talbott, seventeen for Dan—*the seventeen states they already had!* Dan was frowning now as he told Phil to remember this thing was winnable with a shift of just nine votes in the target delegations.

Phil was about as horrified as she was at those numbers. When she'd asked Elliott how long a win would take from such a dismal start, he brought up the 1801 Jefferson-Burr deadlock that had gone thirty-six ballots. Said this one might last for nine, ten weeks. *Two or three months!*

She persuaded Dan not to pass *those* numbers along to Phil, the ruthless tycoon so used to having things his own way, so baffled and enraged by "that blasted weenie roast on the Hill." Dan was listening now, scratching his ear. . . still listening. She spun around and caught his eye, telegraphing encouragement. He threw her a grimace, saying warily, "Well, now, that's pretty hard to nail down yet, Phil. We'll have a better grip on the timetable after the first vote."

The miserable truth was *no one* knew how long it would take—or how to pull it off. And they needed to find out *now*. Right now, yesterday, last week!

"I'll tell you, Phil, this situation kinda reminds me of the boy who woke up Christmas morning and found a shovel and a roomful of horse manure. . . ."

The blasted pony joke again. Phil wasn't asking for *that* with these drawling updates, with his talk about playing hardball, rolling up momentum. She wondered what Phil thought about Dave Elliott, if he was onto Elliott's game.

She and Phil were alike in one way, always counting. And maybe in one other: Offhand, she couldn't conceive of a mortal thing she wouldn't do to get this over with, get them where they deserved to be, where they belonged.

" 'By gosh, there's gotta be a pony in here somewhere!' " The talk moved onto money, campaign funds. Dan chuckled that fifty mill ought to hold them for a while, he guessed.

She used to be thrilled out of her wits hearing big round figures like that—just a fraction of what Dan was worth now. Yet she didn't trust the money anymore. How could she? Two hundred million they'd blown already on the campaign, and all it got them was bogged down in this mess.

"Sure thing, you bet, Phil. And I think we might just shake a few more votes loose before Monday."

He'd be at it again tonight, wearing out the phones, Elliott at his elbow, coaching, feeding him cues. Individualized pitches aimed at one pigeon after another. Nobody did that kind of stroking better than Dan. But all the rah-rah hadn't gotten them a win.

He hung up smiling. She burst out, "Well?"

"Phil says we've got fifty million in the war chest. And they could double that in a week if they had to. The FEC funding rules after a hung election are so fuzzy Phil figures this thing will be over with before they dope out what applies."

"Wonderful, hon! What else did he say?"

"Not much. He mostly wanted to sound off on the House."

Watching him carefully in the mirror, she said, "Well, you can hardly blame him for that."

"Nope." He went to the bathroom for a touch-up shave, talking through the open door about Mort ragging Phil about the blasted FEC red tape. "He can't believe how many ways they've cooked up to keep you from spending your own bucks."

She patted on a shower of powder, painted her spidery eyes. Phil needed watching, tending. Mustn't have any slippage now from the kitchen crew. But she mainly worried about the new men crowding into the act around Dan, edging her out of the focus. Elliott especially, so glib and slick in his double-breasteds and patent-leather hair.

In the postelection panic she'd thought Dan must need what these 'experts' could deliver. But look where it had gotten them—Elliott squeezing her out of his meetings with Dan, always watching her in that startled what-are-*you*-doing-here way. She didn't for one minute trust him to pull this off. But if not him, who?

She felt like she was lurching through a nightmare, praying for somebody, somebodies who knew what to do next. Praying she wouldn't have to be the one to find them.

He came out of the john. "Pril, how're you doing?"

"Fine, almost ready." Quick dabs of lipstick, three squirts of perfume. She leaned toward the mirror. *There! Back to my real face.*

CHAPTER SIX /

January 19th
Robin

Dennis Darien riffled through Robin's walk-in closet. "You're leaving the magenta silk? Darling, you must take the magenta silk."

Wearily jamming a sweater into the suitcase spread on her bed, she said she was taking too much junk already.

"Nonsense!" He dragged her to the mirror and held the dress against her, beaming. "Oh, yes, yes, darling, a definite yes. Look how that gorgeous color picks up your hair."

"Oh, lord." Avoiding the bleak, strained face staring back at her, she tried to visualize this rag at a White House do. "What would I wear it to?"

"Any of the receptions, darling. Dinners, it would do beautifully for a short-skirt dinner."

"All right, then." She tossed it onto the heap on the bed as jumbled as her head. "But that's *it*, Den."

He flew to the closet, chirping his dismay. "Not the gold satin?" He whipped it off the rack. "You must take the gold satin. I love you in this, dear."

She said with all this mess she should dress very understatedly. Nothing too gala or upstagey, the veep's wife shouldn't preempt the number one. He crooned delightedly, "But darling, you'll *be* the number one. Mrs. President!"

She winced, still resisting that looming fluke. "Says you. Anyway, I still think Talbott might—"

"Just listen!" He pointed dramatically at the bedroom TV, which was droning, ". . . this third House vote. Despite official optimism in the Talbott camp, continuing deadlock seems likely. In which case Laurence Devlin will be inaugurated tomorrow as our first—"

"See, even Roger Mudd says so!"

Resisting an impulse to knock him head over heels into the pile on the bed, she snarled, "I don't give a damn what Roger Mudd says."

"Now, darling," he purred, "we want you to look golden, to upstage Mrs. Tacky and Mrs. Frump"—his names for Prilla Sterling and Norleen Talbott—"which you'll certainly do anyway, you gorgeous young stunner."

"Boy, some help you are, Dennis." She snatched the dress from him. "All right, I'll take it, but that's it, not one stitch more. I told you, only two suitcases."

Wringing his hands, he said if she wouldn't let him whip up something appropriate for this amazing occasion, the least she could do was take enough for last-minute leeway. That peahen coat was a *dreadful* choice for the Inaugural. At least the lilac didn't look like a meter-maid uniform.

Goaded by his flutter, she lashed back, "Okay, I'll take the lilac if that'll stop your nattering."

He stiffened. Injured, he murmured, "Well, excuse *me*. I only thought—"

"Den, I know you're trying to help, but—you're not." She pushed the dresses into the bulging garment bag. "How many times do I have to tell you? This isn't like a regular Inaugural—just listen to that TV you always throw at me. The balls and hoopla are on hold. There'll just be a quick swearing in and a few receptions. If Larry does fill in, it'll only be for a few days, max."

He said that wasn't the way he'd heard it.

"When he finds out what a veep actually does, he's going to hate this job." She heard her singsong quaver with weird detachment, as if it came from someone else. "Anyway, I'll just commute. So two suit-cases will do it."

He said softly, "Dear, it's quite normal to feel a tiny bit over-whelmed when you're about to become the First Lady, you know. They all reacted the same—Eleanor Roosevelt, Bess Truman. Pat Nixon, Betty Ford, even your dear Alexis. They started off shaking in their boots, so don't you—"

She shut him up with shrill indignation: "I'm not overwhelmed, I just don't think it's going to happen. Since when are you the big expert, anyway?"

He said he'd been boning up. He thought it might help her to know she wasn't the only one who'd felt this way.

She looked away from his moon-eyed gaze, fighting off a prick of tears. At this point empathy did her in quicker than nagging, and she couldn't afford to let go now. Swallowing hard, ignoring his concern, she tugged at the zipper. "Look, Dennis. This damn thing won't even close."

"Here, let me do it." He bustled her away from the bed. "But you mustn't leave the mink, darling, in this polar-bear weather. I won't let you go without that nice little mink."

She yanked a round bag from the closet shelf and rolled the coat into it. Cry of protest: "That *hatbox*? You're squishing that lovely coat into a pathetic little—"

"Enough! I'm not kidding, Den."

He zipped up the bags somehow, pausing to ogle a tall blond man in a wolfskin parka being chased up the Capitol's marble steps.

"Den, turn that off."

"Ssshh, listen."

Someone called out, "Congressman Kittyhawk, will your one-man Alaska delegation still hang in with Balch?"

Kittyhawk turned, sunlight glinting on the fur framing his face. "That's for me to know, and you to find out."

Hot pursuit up the steps. Had President Talbott offered any deals over the White House breakfast? Kittyhawk's answer tossed over his shoulder: "Surprisingly bad eggs they serve in that place."

Dennis clapped. "He'll stick! I'm sure of it—that gorgeous hunk will stick with the Independent." He broke into a jig. "Imagine that, it's actually going to happen—our own dear Robin one of the White House queens, tripping in Martha's shoes!"

She recoiled, muttering, "Footsteps, not shoes."

"Whatever, dear. *She* didn't want the job any more than you do, by the way."

Dennis was trying to think who Kittyhawk reminded him of, sashaying up those steps like Paul Bunyan without the ox. Pretty, pretty, who was it, now?

Of course: Larry. The well-named about-to-be President of Vice. The resemblance wasn't so much in the good looks as in their rat-ass rake-hell style. A hint of reflex thumb-in-your-eye while they ran off with the game.

Or played their own game, first to last. He picked up a whiff of utter cynicism from them both, two tough promoters of Numero Uno. Those cookies wouldn't stop at much. A pair of swordsmen, he'd bet the rent. Used to having *that* their own way too. He wondered who Larry was dicking lately. Or how many.

The young rawbone signed off with ". . . and you folks around here better get your act together." Larry was conspicuously nimbler at ritual pieties and doublespeak, of course; Kittyhawk's virgin rudeness was a blast of fresh air from the D.C. miasma pits.

To which poor dear Robin was being abruptly dispatched. Little red harbinger of spring flying down into that nest of eagles, hawks, whatever—mostly vultures, he supposed. So here they were, packing up the few pitiful feathers she was taking down as armor for the root-a-toot.

Fretful with concern, he spotted a nightie on her top shelf, creamy old satin, bell sleeves dripping lace. Like an heirloom from a horny grandma, just right for. . . . He squeezed it into her case.

Part of him was ecstatic, demented at this news. He'd have a ringside seat at the best circus of the year. Maybe a scribble in the guest book of history. He could hardly ask for a better giggle than that.

Yet he also brooded and fussed for his friend. She wasn't the strongest woman in the world and didn't function at her best down there. Of course, the whole whoop-de-doo was every girl's fantasy come true: Presto chango, you wake up First Lady. But Robin had said she'd bloody much prefer to pass.

He knew she meant that. So he was a little bothered that she *wasn't* passing, of course; she was hell-bent determined to stick it out, see it through. And he'd scraped her off the floor, held her head enough times to realize that if it turned out much rougher than she was bargaining for, there might be rather dicey times ahead.

When she emerged from the john, makeup retouched, he was into her jewelry box. "Dear, you're not leaving the garnet lavaliere?" Car ad on the TV.

She switched it off as he blurted, "It's a marvel how calm you are. I won't sleep a wink till I see you up there holding the Bible for your darling—"

She called down the hall irritably, "Jim? Let's get this show on the road."

To avoid the sidewalk rat pack, fatter with each day's postponed departure—even the stuffy *New York Times* was predicting she might duck the Inaugural—the agents had worked out a secret escape route, down a back alley to a nearby garage. The waiting Secret Service cars gunned up the driveway and down the block. She peered incredulously out the window. "Lord, Jim! Don't tell me we got away with it?"

Connerty broke off a radio exchange to flash his Indian-corn teeth. "Looks like it, Mrs. D."

A cop escort picked them up at Columbus Avenue, but no press vans. *Good omen*, she decided firmly, taking a nostalgic peek at her spikey island from the Triborough Bridge. Her refuge-to-come-home-to when this detour was done.

On the Butler Aviation tarmac she saw the crowd near a small jet and realized her luck had run out. The agents leaped out, Jim opening her door. She slid out with prescribed skirt-control moves, armored with her on-the-job smile.

Six agents instantly circled around her. But with no sawhorses, the press gang rushed up, firing:

"Mrs. Devlin, do you plan to move into the White House?"

"Will your husband become Acting President?"

"How do you feel about being First Lady?"

Lots more than she expected—maybe ten video crews, plus a horde of scrambling photographers. She kept smiling, murmuring, "Really, I've nothing to say."

Agents and cops struggled to push out a path: "Okay, let's move it, please. Back up!" As two photographers scuffled, the protective circle around her suddenly broke. Surging past her bodyguards with a sharp whoosh, the press swarm trapped her, shouting behind the thrusting artillery, cameras, lights:

"Why'd you stay away so long?"

"Have you talked to your husband, Robin?"

"Are you up to taking on the job of First Lady?"

She tried to smile as agents shoved and wrestled. Jim shouted, "Move back! Give us room here!" but still they jostled against her, pelting questions:

"Will you stay in D.C.?"

"What's your reaction to the House deadlock?"

"Robin, does this mean your separation's off?"

A heavy foot tromped on her toes. Her terror flipped to rage: All those agents hovering all those months—where were they now? Suddenly a tall young man punched an arm aggressively past the cameras. Recognizing a nephew—"Kevin!"—she grabbed his hand and yanked him through.

"Hey, Robin, great to see you." Arm clamped chivalrously on her shoulder, he announced loudly, authoritatively, "Okay now, Mrs. Devlin has a plane to catch. If you'll be good enough to get out of the way. . . ."

Finally the waves parted for a jolting, chaotic escape to the plane. Shrugging off Jim's distressed apologies for the snafu, she buckled her seatbelt. She was trembling, still feeling the assault. Her mouth tight, dry. Whisper in her ear: *You know you'd get through this so much better with just one little nip. . .*

She overrode it, gut wrenching: *There but for the grace of god. . . help me, help me hold on!*

She aimed a shaky smile at her 25-year-old nephew, one of the nine kids half-orphaned when Stephen was killed on a fact-finding mission to Vietnam. "Lord, Kev, I've never been so glad to see you." She told him about her back-alley escape. "But we ran out of strategy till you popped up to save the day."

"Glad to help. I wasn't sure I could catch your plane, but it worked out okay." She recognized that animated, exultant Devlin look, the look that went along with a big win. "Damn, what a great day. Uncle Larry makes it all the way after all."

"Maybe. And anyway, just pro tem. He says it'll just be for a few days, you know. So don't plan to move in."

That Devlin look troubled her. Something about these kids always seemed so—strange, even in her own children. That oddness of being born American royal. Often she had no idea what they were thinking. But at times like this, the big win they were raised to go for, she understood only too well.

☆

That summer she was trying to decide whether to stay with Larry —before she realized it would take more courage to leave than to stay, more courage than she had at that point—she spent her days building sand castles at Bar Harbor with Kevin and Melissa. Melissa, barely 2, was no help at all. But Kevin was 5 and took it very seriously.

He'd been squeezed out of his house by too many babies, and she was trying her damnedest to avoid the rat's nest of Devlins all around. So every day they worked at their splendid concoctions of moats and ramparts, towers and flying buttresses, chains of castles sprawled along the high-water line where the next tide would wash them away.

She remembered his little face puckered with concentration as he built a stick bridge, remembered thinking, *So many secrets you don't know yet.* While she debated whether the raw, broken pieces of whatever she and Larry shared could fit together again, Kevin's innocence was somehow a healing presence. But by now he had generational, personal secrets of his own—plus he probably knew most of the guilty ones his elders had squirreled away. One thing about those Devlins, they always knew more secrets than she did.

Come to think of it, Kevin may've even had that edge on her back when they were building their castles.

☆

Sally Arnstein had no trouble recognizing Robin's transparent dismay that her plane had been met by Sally instead of the kids. Sally was nursing her own dismay that she was back to baby-sitting the Bird, missing out on all the real action back in Larry's office. She explained to Robin that the kids were waiting at the house. "With all that's going on, we just couldn't coordinate. . . ."

"That's fine. What else is happening?"

Sally complained that the Secret Service had kept the press too far back for good coverage of the arrival. She unlimbered a thin, sarcastic smile: "Which is really a shame, Mrs. Devlin, since we've been counting the days till you came."

That poke got no reaction from the Bird. Sally segued into a schedule update for the next day, assuming no surprises from the overnight House session: 8 a.m. family Mass at Saint Brigid's, 9:35 motorcade from Greensleeves. "There's some confusion about whether you'll have the traditional White House coffee with the Talbotts or proceed directly to the Capitol. . . ."

One more briefing among the many since Sally was plucked from the overworked crew in Larry's office for the less-than-prime assignment of riding herd on his wife. She used to wonder how a man with so much going for him ever got tied down with such a self-destructive loser in the first place. But when she got to know him better, she learned to be grateful for that. The ideal pol-wife, after all, was mainly one who wasn't underfoot, making petulant demands on her husband's time— and in that sense, at least, Robin filled the bill quite nicely.

As Sally zipped through the long list of Inaugural rites, she caught Robin frowning, obviously worried about taking it all in. On to the billetings: Mrs. Devlin Senior with the Rourkes in Georgetown, Alexis and daughters with her brother in Virginia. Robin interrupted: "Who's staying at Greensleeves?"

"Oh, just the immediate family. The Senator thought there'd be enough confusion as it was."

The Bird's small sigh of relief echoed Sally's own reaction. *That's right, lady—you get the guest room.*

That one bit, at least, Sally couldn't've planned better herself.

Eyes locked on the red flashers ahead, Robin tried to focus on the details Sally was spouting. All so remote. Surreal. But her job was to stay calm and organized. Do it as well as she could. No goofs this time around.

She rolled down her window as the car turned up the long, curved drive. The boys burst from the house and ran along the car, grabbing her hands, drumming a rowdy fender welcome. Even laughing, she felt that heartflip always triggered by her kids.

Jason pulled her out in a noisy bear hug, swirling her off her feet as Sean thumped exuberantly on her shoulders. "We made it, Mom! We're making it all the way!"

For the first time in a long while, she felt this might turn out okay after all. She pulled their heads down to bump foreheads, private gesture from the days they were still little enough to pick up but big enough to duck kisses—a Devlin habit. She flashed that brutal day—god, only five years ago!—when she'd 'bumped goodby' leaving for New York. Sean was only 10, much shorter then, and oh, how he'd cried.

Now their heads angled awkwardly down to hers—her babies grown into gangling Devlin men. She said huskily, "Hey, troops. It's awful good to see you."

Sean was jubilant. "Hey, watcha think, Mom?"

"I think it's terrific, of course." Her smile was luminous, wide. "I'm real glad for everybody. Especially Daddy."

Jason said, yeah, he'd be home soon. "He bet me ten bucks at breakfast that Talbott would get more than twenty-three votes. I'm gonna make sure he pays up."

Saying that was one bet Daddy wouldn't mind losing, she spotted a skulking camera crew. "Ah boy, look who's here. Shall we give them a tap dance?" They turned politely toward the big blue lens; she waved, and Jason lifted his arms in a V.

In the entry hall Jason helped her off with her coat—a rare, startling flourish of chivalry from her 17-year-old—and filled in what she'd been missing: mainly waiting for Dad, horsing around with Tim, Andy and some of the cousins. Melissa was due in soon from college. "She wanted Thad to pick her up at Dulles. Aunt Cecily's around somewhere. In the kitchen with Delia, I think."

Robin watched intently as he talked, feeling her gut-knots easing. "Then you're doing all right, you guys? No problems? Everything okay?"

"Yanh, sure, Mom."

Sean grabbed her shoulder for a light, pivoting leap. "Everything's terrific, Mum."

She'd planned a vague apology for staying so long in New York. But the kids didn't seem to need it, so she trailed them into the rambling old house already raucous with celebration. A handful of cousins—two Devlins, two Talleys and a Rourke—tripped over Sally and other staffers in seething, festive chaos. Kilkenny barked at her as if she were a stranger, a trespasser—which was exactly how she felt.

☆

Like the first time she came here, nineteen years ago. These half-empty rooms in a September gloom, the P Street furniture looking tatty, out of place. Larry nervously led the tour. "Real good buy, Rob. Wait'll you see the grounds."

She'd loved that old P Street house—till the July afternoon she'd flown back early from Maine and found Larry in bed, not alone. She spent the rest of the summer mostly incommunicado at the family compound, guarding her own secret. Ducking his calls, building those glorious castles.

In his panic of reparation he traded in the dear little house for big, sprawling Greensleeves, without even asking her. When she found out she refused to go see it. Told him, "Do what you want. Like you always do anyway." So he moved by himself, and brought her and Melissa "home" after Labor Day. A new house so beautiful was hard not to like, yet she wandered through the empty-barn rooms thinking, *This place will never feel like home to me.*

☆

It still didn't, even overflowing with celebration. Yet the jubilant mood hoisted her spirits as she moved through the noisy congratulations to the kitchen.

Delia was in the back pantry, head bent with Cecily, the most prolific of the in-laws. No small claim. Cecily babbled that they hadn't heard her come in, and apologized with a leathery cheek peck. Delia chimed in: "You sure have missed some big times around here, Mrs. Devlin."

"So I gather," she smiled.

Delia had come with the house, one more item in Larry's damage-control blitz. He'd hired her after the boss of the House men's room described how his cousin had rescued a pickup stalled in mud. When Larry first introduced her to Robin, Delia was standing, arms akimbo, in the big old kitchen, already defending her turf. Robin had no trouble believing this woman could lift trucks.

In the bad old days the sisters-in-law had huddled with Delia as often as they could, rooting for pay dirt. Now, welcome home: Delia was hunkering with Cecily.

Robin told Cecily she'd dropped Kevin at the airport. "I think he's home looking for you." Cecily lamely explained she'd come by to see if Delia needed help with supplies.

Leaping to her own defense, Delia rattled off the hams and pies she'd baked, the cakes and casseroles neighbors had dropped off. *Like a funeral*, Robin thought, fighting off the daze. She asked if she could help. Delia's crisp dismissal poked her aside: "No thanks, Mrs. Devlin. We've got everything under control here. . . as usual." Tacit reminder of who ran this house, fed the kids, tracked the phone calls and dental appointments. And now Cecily was muscling in on the groceries.

Robin felt her gyros tilt. She poured a mug of coffee, remembering when she used to spike it from her secret vodka stash, right under the nose of her bloodhound keeper. She smiled guiltily at Delia, and congratulated Cecily for the news: "I'm so pleased for you and all the family."

That got her a belated, wiry-energetic hug. "Oh, my! Congratulations to you, too, Robin. I meant to tell you how thrilled we are for you, of course." Tiny payback in that penitent embrace: *One bit she'd done better than they had.* . . .

She fled the kitchen-turf war as soon as she could; she'd lost that one years ago anyway. Now she needed quiet time to reconnect with her kids, hug and fuss over them. But Jason was in a ping-pong match, back to his clan games. And the rec room reminded her of the day the decorator hanging those chintz drapes had stepped around her, passed out on the rug, the sort of memory that wasn't at all helpful today.

She found Sean at the breezeway fridge, popping open a Pepsi, and asked if he was all set for tomorrow. He guessed he'd wear the grey suit Daddy'd given him for Christmas. Did she want to see it? She beamed. "You bet I do."

They slipped upstairs, where she helped pick out a blue shirt and Princeton tie, crooning, "You'll make me so proud of my big, handsome son." He usually resisted this much fussing. Might be humoring her now, by letting her play Mom. Yet he might also need her reassurance, this child who most resembled her—not just the freckles and red curls, but the thin-skin sensibility mixed in his Devlin ways.

Seized with concern for him, she straightened his collar, asking what he thought about it all. He lit up an ear-to-ear grin. "Boy, it's terrific." Pet all-purpose Devlin description.

"Well, sure. But it means big changes for you guys."

"Yeah. Dad says we'll really like the White House." His eyes averted. "Are you, um, staying in New York?"

She said probably not; she hadn't worked it out with Daddy yet, but she figured she'd camp in there with them.

Pure rapture: "Hey, that's great, Mum!"

She said quickly, "Now that probably won't be for long, you know." Stung by his blistering wish to have his parents back together. "So don't. . . make any big plans or anything."

Subdued, he mumbled, "Okay." Then Tim Rourke called him to the phone and he was off, bounding on coltish legs.

At the stairs she heard the zoo below in full swing, kids whooping, wrestling, Sally arguing on the phone. . . .

Abruptly, she fled to the odd-shaped little room off the master bedroom, a sort of cupola with long, low windows overlooking gardens. The "baby room," strewn now with jock gear—sailbags, unstrung rackets, mitts, balls. On the wall hung a faded watercolor she'd painted before Melissa was born—"Womb with a View"—like something left behind in a dusty attic.

She sank into the rocking chair, feeling time slip away to a great stillness. That first day Larry had shown her this room, she'd known instantly someone had built it for a chair just like this, with a cradle rocking beside it, rafting together through the waving branches just outside.

So she'd seized the moment, huddling into the nook of that odd-shaped wall as she told him she was three months pregnant. Making herself stare right at him, to read his face. If she saw what she was afraid of, she'd grab Melissa, call a cab and leave him to this rattling-empty barn.

But in his reaction, she'd read amazement. Right after that—joy, maybe. Relief. Delight. Victory. Hard to call, but she recognized it as his own peculiar kind of love. So she'd stayed.

Might've been better all around if she *had* left then, but no second-guessing now. Down below in the winter-bleak gardens was the lonely little playhouse where Melissa used to spin out fantasies for hours on end, singsong scolds piping out over the flowerbeds. Then suddenly, at 11 or so, Melissa wouldn't go near the place. Robin never knew why. One more mystery of her inscrutable daughter she'd never puzzled out.

Now her magic room was his jock garage. Stepping over hockey litter, sensing her invasion of his privacy, she slipped uninvited through the bedroom door. Through the wall of time, moth to flame, swirling with memory.

Amazing how little had changed since she'd moved out. The drapes were more sun-bleached maybe. Her chintz-ruffled dressing table strewn with family pics, mostly moments she hadn't shared. She choked up over a blowup of Larry and Sean in a cockpit, peering at sails, drenched, windblown, Larry's arm around Sean. The kid's face was awed, exulting, leaning into his father's shelter. *Get a copy!*

Delia's touch was obvious in the neatly made bed. Left to himself, he was tidy as garbage in a tornado.

Idle wonder who was sharing his sheets these days. Delia used to have amazing radar for that, when any of his ladies came around—as they often did. Delia adored her Mr. Larry but didn't hold with "bob-cattin' around," so she tipped her hand with furious mutterings, bashing of pots. Thinking the Missus was too soused to pick that up. Robin worked hard at being a good, canny drunk, taking every edge she could skate on. So she never discussed that with Delia, though she got very good at recognizing the skillet choruses that announced the new Lay of the Month.

Everywhere, flood of memory from the days when they were still trying to live with each other's craziness. That bed she took to after her baby—Michaela, dear Michaela—had died in the delivery room. Stillborn, they said. But they wouldn't let her see her, hold her. A nun said she was with baby Jesus. Robin said go to hell, Sister.

Back home, she'd burrowed into her bed, fleeing from the pain. He'd sat on the foot of that bed, telling her, "We'll have another, Rob. It doesn't matter." But it did, it had.

That death hung over them, even after the boys were safely born. The doctor said nobody knew why it happened. "Don't be hard on yourself, Robin. Sometimes they just can't take that first big step into life." As if that child had been *dead* all those months inside her.

In retrospect they hadn't handled their grief any better than the rest of it. Something had broken between them, some fragile filament of trust, but neither one had sense enough to get it fixed. He numbed himself with work and god knows what else; she discovered helpful nips in the afternoon.

A cracked mirror on one closet door, from the night she keeled over trying to dress for a party. That shiny john where she used to heave her guts into the blue porcelain bowl. She remembered him once standing over her, saying through her wavering haze, "I can't take any more. Are you getting this, Robin? Am I getting through? Because I've flat had it."

The metallic drone she barely noticed shifted to eggbeater rhythm. Helicopters overhead meant Larry was coming home. Soft winter duskiness filled the room, intensifying the chopper sound. She trembled in the pulsing beat, choking on the urge to flee. *Before it's too late. . . .*

Siren wails chimed in. From the window she saw the blue flashers of his motorcade explode like a blinking dragon tail up the curved drive. She shrank behind the curtain as the cars screamed to a halt. Agents sprinted to the limo, but Larry stepped out before they got there.

He waved his arms, silhouette-etched in white TV glare. As he turned she caught a flash-freeze of his face, chin jutting, kindled with a look she hadn't seen for so long.

So alive, so alight.

Sean and Jason popped through the crowd into the light. Larry touched them in that easy, natural way he never used with her. Jason's face fierce with worship. *Oh my. . . .*

Realizing with a guilty start she should be down there too, she rushed to the stairs. Cecily was glaring up, bellowing, "Robin! Where are you?"

"Oh, sorry, Cecily." She ran down the steps.

Cecily said for goodness sake they'd been looking all over for her. "Hurry up, Larry's already here!"

As she let herself be grabbed, she said calmly, "I know, I saw him come."

"Well, good heavens, they're shooting the immediate family out there. You can still. . . ."

She said let the boys do it, they'd get plenty of her later. Cecily's hand jerked free as she took in that alien notion. "Oh! If that's how you feel. . . I just thought you might want to let them see you're finally here."

Robin let that pass, and trailed Cecily down the long hall full of people staring raptly at the door. A fresh wave of agents bristled in, their tight glances raking the room. Then Bing McCarthy, the family photographer, oh no—

And there he was.

Larry come home. Filling the doorway, ruddy, triumphant in his victory glow. Moving inside, he lay on hands in obscure benediction, booming, "Fred, how're you doing? Cecily, thanks for coming by." As he shook one hand, slapped an arm, his eyes darted ahead, speed-reading the crowd.

Your move, now!

Larry was laughing at some remark when he saw her.

Ouff. He froze in midmove, froze the moment. He'd thought he was braced against that collision with her eyes. Yet in this spun-out instant she filled the room.

Long, skipped beat. Then, "Hey, Robin. Nice to see you." Blood thundered in his ears.

He took a few steps toward her as she moved into the DMZ opening between them. He rarely kissed her in public, but this time there seemed no graceful out. Muttering, "Hey, how're you doing?" he touched her elbows, brushed dry lips to her cheek while eyes popped around the whole damn room.

"Nice to be here," she mumbled. Blushing even. "I see you're holding up pretty well."

"Thanks." She looked real good, at least, for what that was worth. Blooming, fresh. Still lots of little Miss Swann, Marymount girl in that face. "I hear you got quite a reception at Butler."

"Oh, it wasn't so bad."

Already others were crowding between them with chirps of congratulation. He let himself be nudged, tugged away from her. He wasn't jumping to her string just because she'd finally shown up.

He worked a trail of handshakes toward the den, aides magnetized around him. He knew without looking she was trailing in his wake, bobbing in the hullabaloo. In the den he took his briefcase from Gil and stood, back to the door, rattling off more speech lines.

When he heard her quietly ask Ben if there was any chance of getting five minutes with Himself, the seething he hadn't acknowledged as anger fizzled into guilt. He spun around. "Ah, Robin." His smile felt odd, tight. "So how's, ah, things with you?"

"Fine. A-one. But I wouldn't mind a private word. . . ."

"Right." He checked his watch. "I'm heading for the shower, if you want to talk upstairs."

"Terrific."

They took the back stairs through a gauntlet of glances, she trailing him. In the hall she caught up and shot him a little smile. First clue she was glad to see him. "So what goes on here, babe?" she asked. "How're you doing, really?"

He said actually it was looking pretty good. "Cross fingers and spit in the wind, but I think we might get a whack at doing something here." He flicked on the bedroom light and kicked the door shut. Rump leaned on a dresser, he crossed his arms and peered guardedly at her, saying as flatly as he could, "Well, nice of you to show up."

Opening shot for the next round of marital war.

She smiled warily, eyes flicking to him, then skittering off. Standing tilted, as if he were tugging her off balance. "Now what's that supposed to mean?"

He shrugged, anger sparking behind his tight face. She said she wasn't ever *not* coming: "I'm sorry if the delay pissed you off or whatever, Dev, but I told you I'd come. I can't help what those bastards make news out of."

He itched to tell her to go straight to hell. Instead, he picked his words with barbed care. "Okay. But at the risk of 'invading your space' or whatever you're calling it these days, I'd like to know right now how long you plan to stick around. Now that you're finally here."

She said she'd try for the duration of this acting presidency thing, anyway. "If you want me to."

"Sure I do. This whole New York deal wasn't my idea, if you recall."

She nodded, gulped. "Okay, then I'll stick." His mood soared on relief so strong it took him by surprise. The last damn thing he wanted was to need anything from her. "For as long as I can. . . provided it doesn't. . . if I can handle it."

He crashed back down to earth. She was looking away from him, babbling in a tinny voice as if she knew this wasn't what he wanted to hear, saying anyway, "Tish doesn't think it's such a good idea for me to be here, you know. I told her I'd promised to give it a try, but you and I both know it could be hell on wheels out there, Larry."

Invoking that damn AA lawyer friend of hers again, like his mother used to rattle rosary beads. He wondered what in hell really went on between those two. From the first time he'd met Varner, she was on his case, fixing him with a don't-mess-with-me-buddy glare. Good looker for her age, long and skinny as a snake. Lots of juice in her too, but the type he wouldn't go near with a 2-foot stick. Yet for some reason he'd never fathomed, Robin would hardly piss in the morning unless Tish agreed she should.

"Of course, if you're right that it turns out to be just a couple of days. . . ."

"Hey, hold on." He yanked his tie loose. "I can't guarantee that."

"I know, Dev. Look, I'll give it my best shot. But I want it on record I'm not signing up for a four-year hitch."

He let out a wary laugh as he popped his shirt buttons. "Okay, fair enough."

She waved him off, saying so go take his shower and then they could have another run at this conversation.

He took her up on that. Fiddling with the bathtub taps, he remembered that night he'd found her in the garage, passed out in the back of her wagon with a half-dead vodka bottle.

That's when he realized she was smack out of control. He told Delia to leave her alone, leave her right where she was. All night, the whole next morning he left her there. Every time he came out to check on her, she'd've moved around but was still conked out.

By noontime he went wild. Carried her up there and threw her clothes and all into the tub, reaming her out, pleading, threatening, unloading all his guns. She cried and apologized—which she didn't often do by then—and promised to shape up. He'd believed her because at that point he was still believing what he wanted to hear.

He stepped into the stream and lathered his head, wishing he could wash her out of his hair as easily as shampoo. All he knew for sure was that he'd come home tonight flying high on the top of the world, and right now he felt like a hostage again.

Outside the half-open john door she kicked off her shoes and switched off the bedside phone, trying to sift out a tight agenda for the few minutes she might snatch before Gil or Ben pushed in here on some business, bumping her from the bedroom. Her usual welcome home.

While he was underwater she paddled rapidly around the rug, fighting the tug of his undertow on her scrambled head. When his mask had slipped, briefly, she'd seen the anger she expected—but overlaid with fear. And relief. Stabbed with astonishment, she realized he might even need her now.

Yet he could still reel her sea anchor into his gut from across a room. Already she was telling him what she knew he wanted to hear, and she needed to somehow make him understand that his whole package was the antithesis of what she should do to protect against her disease. That he was asking her to risk her life, her sanity. That if she crashed again she might not make it back. . . .

He never did understand that, of course. He seemed to have no idea how terrified she was of him—not of what he was, but of what he could do to her. Tish said once he was lucky he had never woken up with 8 inches of steel in his chest, especially when Robin was sobering up. Robin mentioned they hadn't been together much since, and Tish said ah, yes, well, that explained it.

She knew what he wanted: the same old wife, sober. The docile chameleon she'd been as a good, canny drunk, only without the booze and the guilts. But she was someone else now, someone ripped apart by the nightmares and mood swings and free-floating anxiety of second-year sobriety. Someone skating on constant fear. Monstrously self-absorbed.

Angry beyond belief at having to compromise—jeopardize—everything for a man she wasn't sure she even liked.

When he shut off the water she paced outside the door, eyes averted as he talked with jovial incredulity about how Talbott was, true to form, still screwing up: "Goddam, who'd believe it? With a forty-six-vote Democratic majority and a shitload of deals he's trying to peddle, Roy Bob's still shooting up his foot all over the Hill."

She grimaced. "Lord, I almost feel sorry for him."

"Hey, don't waste your nickel. That guy has a damn genius for self-destruct."

He came out pushing back his wet hair, strutting self-consciously to his dresser, towel tucked around his puffy waist. Rare modesty in deference to their separation, she supposed. Thinking of the vast weight about to be laid on those sloping shoulders, she hoped to god he was up to this.

"So what's on your mind, Rob?"

She said she'd like it understood they weren't just rolling back the clock here. "Nothing's really changed with our. . . situation, Larry. I mean, one of these days I wish you'd make some time so we can talk about where we. . . ."

She trailed off under his indignant glare. He shored up the towel as he pulled shorts from the top drawer, snapping, "Robin, do you mind? I've had a hell of a day."

"Yes, sure." A shade too late, she realized her timing was, as usual, completely off. "That can wait, no problem." She looked away as he shed the towel. "I guess mainly I just want to hear what's. . . going to happen. From here on out."

He thought Sally had filled her in on the schedule. She said she meant, "what's *really* happening. I'm trying to avoid any big surprises, hold the stress down to where I can handle it. You know the basic AA drill."

Sprawled on the bedspread in his baggy white shorts, he froze at that mention of AA. Socks in hand, he watched her with that pained, slightly baffled expression he used when she talked about things like the booze.

"So the point is—look, I just need to hear from you what's going to happen, Larry. What I should expect."

His eyes dropped, his flushed face suddenly looking weary, harrassed. "Well, like I told you, Rob—it looks like the acting presidency's going to take. For a while, anyway. But I can't guarantee it, if that's what you want."

She hissed her irritation. "I'm not asking for guarantees, Larry. I just need a better grip on what I'm getting into. And right now I don't understand this thing *at all*."

Snapping on a sock, his frown shifting to exasperation, he said if she put it that way, he guessed he wasn't sure what the hell was going on either: "Except I finally get a whack at the presidency. Sorry if that's not what you wanted to hear but, Christ, give me a break, will you, Robin?"

In a rush of contrition, she realized he was right: She was, once more for auld lang syne's sake, demanding things he couldn't possibly deliver. Like certitude, or sweet reason. She knew her problems seemed trivial and self-absorbed to him; he couldn't get "life-threatening" through his head. And if he hadn't yet grasped what she was going through trying to control her disease, he wasn't about to start now.

She quickly babbled, "Right, right. I'm awfully proud and happy for you, babe, that you've finally got your shot at it. And I'm feeling fine lately, you know, so don't worry about. . . that." She bent toward him. "Okay, Dev?"

He said suddenly, distractedly, blue knit sliding up his leg, "I'd do that for you if I could, you know, Rob. Give you some goddam guarantees. I realize you're getting dragged headfirst into something I said was no way going to happen. But what the hell, Robin. . . ."

She pushed away her questions, doubts. "I know, Larry. We'll just have a bloody good time of it, babe, I swear."

Eyes wide, vulnerable, he asked if she remembered what she'd said before their Stratton ski weekend in '58.

Her irritation snagged on that evidence of his tidy, disembodied memory: Stratton weekend in '58. Not something closer to the bone, like three weeks after they'd become engaged, when she finally decided it was up to him if they slept together—so of course they did. "Well, not the words, verbatim. But I certainly. . . ."

"You said sometimes you thought we were flying off a cliff, and we'd wind up in a jillion pieces."

CHAPTER SEVEN

January 19th
Prilla

When the TV roll call started with a guy in a stars-and-stripes tie declaring Alabama's vote for President Talbott, Dan Sterling realized his wife was missing. As Dave Elliott, his House expert, was pointing out they might pick up a swing in that one-vote-margin state, Dan called out, "Pril, you're gonna miss the show."

"On my way, hon," she trilled from the kitchen.

Dave hissed into his ear, "Now Hank Farley's a good old Alabama conservative who may not run again, Governor. And Jack Treen supports your beefing up the national defense."

All of a sudden Prilla was there on the porch, toting a loaded tray, announcing in a pained voice, "Fresh coffee and tuna melts, gentlemen."

Dan jumped up. "Whups, Pril, let me help with that!" The insider team sprang right behind him, babbling thanks. Chet Stagg, their troubleshooter, got to the tray first.

She spurned a sandwich, sitting on Dan's left flank. Dave Elliott picked up his running commentary, chuckling over Wayne Kittyhawk's booming announcement from three screens that the sovereign state of Alaska voted for the Independent Party candidate, Douglas Balch: "There's that handsome pup kicking ass again. Now Talbott pulled out all the stops on these one-man delegations—especially Kittyhawk, an Independent who called himself a liberal Democrat before he switched to Libertarian."

Dan said he was a salty young cuss at least, give him that much. He was already getting an uneasy sense of how goldarn complex and contradictory this House was, although Dave had a knack for packaging it into snappy nuggets. Yet Dave had put in thirty good years as a Congressman from Oklahoma, six more as a Hill lobbyist—and he said *he* was still getting a handle on that anthill himself. His bottom-line advice was if Dan didn't get a lasso wrapped around that House situation pretty quick, he wouldn't swear it could be done at all.

Dave hissed that Roy Bob Talbott had dangled federal loan guarantees for the Alaska natural gas pipeline: "Now there's a deal could be worth eighty billion, but Kittyhawk turned him down flat."

Dan grunted with surprise. "By gosh, if every man has his price, you'd think eighty billion would do the trick."

Dave said nah, that wet-eared freshman probably had his own agenda for the hardball he was playing: "But don't you write him off just yet, Governor."

Arkansas was tied again. Chet Stagg pointed out that Dan had a lot of conservative support down there; if that tie broke, it'd likely be in his direction.

As Dan was agreeing with that, Dave chipped in: "That chap's Ken Mosher, a Baptist preacher and good old boy from a Moral Majority constituency. He's one of my leading candidates for delivering the dynamite turnaround speech that could trigger your landslide, Governor. So we might give some thought to turning your legendary salesmanship loose on him. . . ."

Priscilla glared indignantly at the so-called 'House expert,' who seemed quite unaware he'd interrupted Dan.

She sensed a tilt, an off-balance in the feisty, upbeat mood on the porch. Dan's whole inside team, the seven who'd been with him over the sixteen-year haul and for better or worse had gotten him where he was today, sat lined up like a bunch of wallflowers. They'd all earned plenty of black marks in her book. Paul Tighe as campaign manager was probably more responsible than anyone else for this unholy mess, although Chet and Ezra certainly shared the blame.

But at least they *belonged* here—unlike the interloper who had Dan's ear, so suave and chatty, hissing his inside tips about Talbott's deals. Sometimes she thought Elliott passed along any shred of malarkey that popped into his head, just to get a rise out of Dan.

The lot of them should still be working to turn this vote around, not watching it on TV like Monday night football. But their combative spirits were warming Dan's mood. He'd got up that morning grumpy, wrung out with frustration. She'd bucked him up as well as she could, but he was hard to reassure these days—which unsettled her as much as anything else. So if this gung-ho bunch could snap him out of it, maybe. . . .

Cheers on the porch for California's "former Governor and the next President." Elliott cackled that Roy Bob had no easy pickings there, but with a one-vote lead they'd best keep close tabs on that delegation.

Barely catching the commentary through his babble, she watched

ABC's montage whenever she and Dan popped up on it, but she kept homing back to the gloomy stage set of the House. She was still bowled over that they could do this to Dan. Look at those slick, preening pols, parading up one after another, trying to snatch back what he'd rightfully won. If they could get away with that, the whole country must be coming unstuck.

Reflexively, she critiqued the TV image of Dan and herself emerging from this morning's meeting with Republican brass: too stiff, her smile too glazed. *Loosen up out there, lady.* Next, some kind of airport riot around Robin Devlin. *So she's coming, finally.* . . .

When Dan got Minnesota, Elliott said hold your hat for Talbott's own Mississippi. She caught a hiss about "that sweet little sugar-beet arrangement I clued you into, Governor."

Dan said, "Yep, sure enough." Mississippi hung in with him. The men crowed. She wondered hotly how many other "arrangements" Elliott had with Dan, what else they were up to behind her back.

Sitting here biting on her tongue, she finally zeroed in on what troubled her most about Elliott: He talked as if *he* called the shots. As if his judgments were better than those of the man who would be President. Dan and his team could hardly get a word edgewise into Elliott's ramblings, as if the House were his private clubhouse, and only *he* could unravel why holding at seventeen was the best they could hope for—and no wonder they were stuck there, with Dan letting himself be monopolized by a slick old gasbag like this.

Dan knew she was ticked off, but there wasn't a heck of a lot he could do about it. What she really wanted was for this vote to come out different. In other words, a miracle.

But he was more of a realist, maybe, in his own way. He'd listened enough to Dave and the rest of them to realize they'd be lucky just to survive the day with no slippage in the count, so he was mainly concentrating on putting the best face on it he could.

A distinguished old gent with a purple bow tie from West Virginia profoundly regretted it could not comply with its constitutional duty to vote for a president, due to a deadlock in the delegation. Dave said that was Harley Richmond, the Foreign Affairs Committee chair and an eminent constitutional scholar: "He tells me he's having a devil of a time trying to reconcile the House mandate to 'choose immediately' with the hang-up of the split delegations."

For some reason the courtly old gent reminded Dan of his first football coach at Thermopolis High. The face, not the manner. Coach Squirek moved like a bull patrolling his pasture.

☆

When he made that team, it was the first damn thing he'd belonged to that made him feel good. Like a family that worked. That first season he mostly sat it out on the bench next to gabby Jackie Bunz, who talked out every play. That's how he learned the game—that, and watching the coach, steady as a rock, always there for his boys.

Up to then he'd mainly focused on trying to make out like everything was okay. Never thought in terms of his life going anywhere—he was too busy getting through each day, maneuvering around his father's "spells," wondering if tonight would be one of the nights Momma sent him out to look for him. Those trips he hated, into the bars, into the dark city night. The worst part was finding him and trying to talk him into coming home. One night he skipped the bars, told Momma he wasn't around. Then Poppa made it back to the front yard, passed out, and pretty near froze to death.

He remembered almost wishing the cold had done its job—but of course that would've been his fault, for not scraping him off the barstool first. Momma was a saint, strong as nails, always putting the best face on it, around the kids at least. But they had to live with her pinched, angry hurt, her frantic waiting when Poppa was off on a spell.

Sometimes it was almost worse when he was home and you'd *wait* for him to go off, feel it coming like a summer storm. Momma made them ask in their night prayers, please keep us a happy family together. But the worry was always there like a background hum. Sometimes it was almost relief when he disappeared again.

First time he started to feel things might go right for him after all was when Coach Squirek put him, a scrawny, overeager freshman pup, on the team. Coack Squirek—now *there* was a man you could look up to, count on to come through for you.

Even with not much chance to play, he plumb loved the game. He'd sit there listening to Jackie Bunz run his mouth. Praying they'd win it for Coach, for the hugs and shouts and ecstatic camaraderie of victory.

☆

When Wisconsin tied at 4-4-1, Dan remarked there was one more Independent Talbott didn't bag. Dave jumped in: "Right you are,

Governor, but that Morinski fellow reacted quite strongly when Talbott tried to sweet-talk him on milk subsidies. He's dean of a Lutheran college out in Oshkosh, brand new to this politics game, you know. So I'd be very straight in any approaches your PAC boys make to him."

Prilla leaned forward and craned her neck right at Dave. Dan ducked her eyes, but reached out to pat her hand. After Wyoming went for him, the final tally flashed: Talbott 23, Sterling 17, Balch 1, Tied 9. *Good as a win*, he told himself firmly, groping for the old thrill as the boys on the porch broke into applause. "Way to go, Governor!" Chet boomed. "Talbott's raiders didn't pick off any of our guys."

"Hear, hear," from Ezra. "You've just licked a sitting president with heavy guns on his side, Governor, and that calls for some celebrating."

Celebrating being left alive on the cliff. . . .

Priscilla stood up and bent to kiss Dan, trilling, "Congratulations, sweetie! That's a big, *big* victory for you."

"Thanks, hon." He grabbed her hand, pressed it to his shoulder, saying okay, so back to the showers for Roy Bob.

Elliott lit off into how Talbott had just run out leverage, but mind you he was a persistent cuss, he'd fight down to the wire through the overnight session. "But I wouldn't lose any sleep over that if I were you, Governor."

She stiffened at that "if I were you." So casual, so crass. *Somebody should straighten this joker out.*

But he was rolling on a locker-room spiel: After a few easy switches like the New Jersey recount or the Kentucky by-election, Talbott's horse-trading deals would be leaking, no way they wouldn't. Then Dan could make his move. "You just talk over some wavering Democrat like Ken Mosher or Jack Treen, Governor. Let that fellow deliver a hellfire speech challenging the House to rise above the infernal bickering and rally in patriotic national unity around your flag. If he hits it right, we could stampede you into that Oval Office before the night was out."

Dan was beaming, wringing her hand. "By gosh, that's one scenario I like the sound of."

Paul reminded them that Senator Norris, the Inaugural Committee chair, would call Dan at four o'clock "to formalize your invitation to tomorrow's swearing in."

Feeling those words like north wind, Priscilla watched the hurt behind Dan's wry grin. "Well, by gosh, I hope we won't be buried in a back-row seat."

"No, sir!" Fat-faced gloom instantly lifted. "Our staff consulted on all the protocol, and the three presidential candidates will be in leather armchairs in the front row."

Somehow those leather chairs snapped her controls. Ruffling his hair, she murmured, "Danny, if you don't need me, I think I'll get back to. . . ."

"Yes, sure, Mommie." Distracted concern in those tired eyes. "You okay, then?"

Brightly, falsely: "Fine and dandy!"

Chet handed him the phone. Minority Leader Whittaker. Dan's voice trailed behind her: "Frank, I want to commend the fine job you did holding our troops. . . ."

Walking shakily to their room, she couldn't scrub that strutting parade from her head. Such a normal assortment: fat, thin, bald. . . . threatening as an Elks convention. *But they could kill it for Dan.*

Those idiots whooping up his "big victory" seemed to have no idea how much he was hurting. How much pride he had to swallow to take what was being done to him, robbing what he'd already won. And tomorrow would be worse. Sheer ordeal, playing spear-carriers for those Devlins.

Trying not to stew in her dread, she went to the bathroom and appeased her queasy tummy with some Maalox. The puffy mirror face looked almost like she'd been crying, but her eyes were dry as burnt coals. She pressed a cold washcloth to her face, sifting out small, distracting chores: *Wash out your pantyhose. . . iron your dress. . . .*

Two buzzes on the phone. She blotted her hands and picked up the bathroom extension. The operator asked if she wanted to talk to her daughter Natalie.

"Will you hold for your mother, please, Miss Sterling?"

"Oh! Yes, sure." When the call came through the service, Natalie got those few seconds, at least, to brace herself—but unfortunately not enough warning to get a good reinforcing buzz on before she went to the mat with Mother.

"Natalie, darling," voice reedy with forced warmth. "I'm sorry I didn't get back to you sooner, but things've been pretty frantic around here. How are you doing?"

She said okay, but she wouldn't mind if somebody took the time once in a while to clue her in to what was going on. "D'you want us there for that thing tomorrow, or what?"

Mother said no, no, there wasn't any point in that. "Your father's only putting in a token appearance, you know, so there's no reason to fuss. It doesn't help to have you overreacting and flying off the handle, Natalie."

She snapped back, "I'm not flying off any handle, Mother, thank you very much." Sometimes she thought her parents should've settled for having dogs instead of kids, so they could just parade them out on pink leashes and not have to worry about their talking back. "Yvonne said she thought you expected us to show up. If you don't, then we won't."

She should've known they didn't want her, or some secretary would've called before this. She'd asked Yvonne once if it ever bothered her that their parents would apparently rather have a hundred flunkies flapping around them on the trail than have their own daughters there. Yvonne said no, not one bit—count yourself lucky, kiddo.

But Natalie didn't share that relief. While her parents were wrapped up in the big story of the year, she was left home to watch soaps and baby-sit an empty house. Like they were ashamed of her, almost. Leery of having her around.

Now Mother was into her song-and-dance about how full their hands were right now. "So I hope we can count on you to just keep on an even keel, Gnat, and hold things together at the house."

Gloomy sigh. "Okay. D'you want me to tell Yvonne?"

"Yes, dear, would you do that, please? And the boys too, if you talk to them." Natalie heard the snappish irritation in that carefully filtered voice. "Explain this won't be a family event, because it's not your father's show—not quite yet. We'll have our turn soon enough."

They were afraid she'd go haywire again. Scratch the itch of her boredom with some bad old habits. They just never seemed to give any credit at all to the fact that she knew they were in the fight of their lives and she was trying her damnedest to help out any way she could. But she was maybe too much like her mother, not awfully good at forgive and forget. She said all right, she got the message, and asked how Daddy was taking all this: "Is he okay?"

"Yes, sure. But awfully busy, of course." Translation: *Stay off their backs.*

Okay, she'd try. But she hoped Mother would remember that too much push could lead to shove. "Well, just tell him I called and wished him all the best, okay?"

All through the call Priscilla heard veiled threat. Trouble dead ahead. One thing they *didn't* need around right now was moody, unpredictable Natalie, spouting back off kilter when she felt bored or neglected. Priscilla trembled to recall the tantrums, bloody scenes—and sensed one building now, when she was least able to deal with it.

"Fine, dear. We'll talk to you very soon. But for now, can we count on you to hold the fort out there, Natalie?"

She hung up, queasy with regret for not having been more supportive. Wasn't easy for the poor kid stuck in that empty house. But she had to set some limits to the extraordinary demands, the drains on what scant energy she had left. That call dipped out a new bottom, and planted worries about Natalie heading for another blowup. *Now,* of all times.

At her crammed closet she pulled out a pumpkin-colored Nipon coat. Her Inaugural outfit was a lovely hot-pink Adolfo, her signature color, inspired by some Duchess of Windsor classics. But her best friend Ginny Hibbing said don't waste it on this dress rehearsal. Her alternatives were the Nipon or a kelly-green Galanos. She wanted something bright enough to signal confidence, but muted to suit the dismal circumstances.

Ginny said the Galanos would just encourage the Irish clambake angle, didn't she think. Of course, dead right, the green was out. And the Nipon had a nice little matching pumpkin hat, so that settled that.

When Ginny mentioned that the outfit was probably headed straight for the Smithsonian, Priscilla wondered if Ginny remembered the first time they'd ever talked about that museum. She didn't dare ask, in case that would remind Ginny.

☆

Every detail of that crystal moment was etched in Priscilla's head. Cruising I. Magnin's ballgowns, scouting for Ginny's trip to London after Ike's '53 inaugural, they saw a copy of Mamie's gown on display—pink peau de soie with long pink gloves, V neck, and gathered skirt embroidered with two thousand rhinestones. Ginny called it bridesmaidy; Priscilla thought it looked like a tinseled Georgia-Peach queen.

But behind it, in a photo mural, Ike and Mamie waltzed at the ball, skimming on glory, swamped with glowing fans.

Bam! The idea lit, bolt from the blue. She tucked her arm through Ginny's, sighing, "Oh, wouldn't that be the best fun ever, to move into the White House!"

Ginny instantly picked it up: "The *parties*, darling, think what glorious parties you could have. And the Smithsonian would be begging you to send over your old clothes."

So it started as a joke, but Priscilla quickly nursed it into a private game. They tickled the fantasy, shuffled the possibilities—as if it could happen to either one of them. One day, not entirely by accident, Phil Laubert happened to overhear. Six months later he and Mort Hibbing talked to Dan about possibly running for governor. The ball hadn't stopped rolling since, but Priscilla always had that tiny worry rattling in her head, that some day Ginny might mention to some reporter how the whole presidential idea began.

☆

An hour later Priscilla was bent awkwardly over the bathtub, a sopping towel pressed to her face as Jean-Marc, her pinch-hit hairdresser, rinsed her out. "How's that? Not too hot?" he asked anxiously.

Muffled through the towel: "It's fine."

"There now, that should do it." He swathed her head in a dry towel, rubbing roughly as she arched her spine, kneading out the stiffness. She knew she courted back sprain every time she risked one of these ridiculous tub shampoos—one more hazard of the increasingly treacherous road.

He led her to the padded chair pulled up at the bedroom dressing table. She closed her eyes as he combed her out, still seeing that executioners' parade of pols.

". . . so delighted when you called. . . always honored to help out our *real* First Lady. . . ."

Healing thoughts floated loose from her fatigue. As soon as they got to the White House she'd have a professional sink and chair installed —and a professional dryer—so she could do this like a civilized human being.

"Every single soul I've talked to, bar none, is shocked at how that Congress is defying the vote of the people. . . ."

But the voice in her head was Dave Elliott's, saying, *maybe two or three months.*

CHAPTER EIGHT

January 20th
Robin and Prilla

Crowd noise fell away as the Devlin limo rolled into the heavily secured Capitol grounds, past empty parking lots and rows of rifles at attention. A pop tune rattled in Robin's head: *Help me make it through the night.* . . .

In the sudden hush Melissa muttered that if she heard "historic first" once more she was going to barf. Mother Devlin piped up, "Now remember to pray for your father, children." Larry checked his watch: "Okay, one minute late for launch time, troops." Robin pressed one hand discreetly on her stomach. *Hello, little butterflies. My old friends.*

At the East Front Law Library entrance the Escort Committee waited, poker-backed formation against a massed blob of press and security. She stepped from the car into the rumply bear hug of House Speaker Charlie Whalen, who boomed in a voice big as his belly: "Robin, my dear, you're a lovely sight for these old eyes."

No starch in *his* protocol, at least. She smiled. "Charlie, it's always grand to see you."

Finito the unscripted niceties: She marched briskly at Larry's side down the white marble hall. With no normal traffic, it seemed empty, deserted—except for the spit-polished military honor guard frozen 10 feet apart, TV lights glinting off naked bayonets. *Almost like an execution squad and my god, we're the show.*

Fifty feet down the hall, Larry and his committee peeled away, too abruptly for parting words except Sean's blurted, "Good luck, Dad." With Mother Devlin somehow managing the brisk pace, the rest marched past a locked souvenir stand, around the huge columns of this wedding-cake building.

The old lady'd had her big moment already at the family breakfast table, when Barbara Walters interrupted the bickering over bacon with a replay of their foray to Mass, tiny Mother Devlin leading her triumphant flock with tall, handsome Larry. Lots of breathless stuff about the remarkable, indomitable 86-year-old matriarch, first American to see two sons sworn in as president—proud, dignified Pauline Devlin who'd raised her large family for public service, now seeing her lone surviving son succeed to the office sometimes called the Devlin Family Destiny.

Canonized by Barbara Walters, at least, with honeyed words not lost on Mother Devlin, who instantly purred a call for more prayers for Larry: "And ask the dear Lord's blessing on his presidency." Robin was all the while trying hard not to make an anniversary out of this first time she'd seen Mother Devlin since the well-recalled eight-second birthday party—which she'd rashly shown up for a year after her move to New York. To help mend family fences, she'd told herself, she'd had two glasses of toasting champagne because it seemed too weird not to. Over the next three days, she congratulated herself for not touching another drop. By by week's end she'd bought a bottle. Two weeks later she woke up in St. Vincent's. . . .

Enough! Anyway that crash wasn't Pauline's fault.

At the crypt area, Robin's escort peeled her into a right-hand turn. She threw a quick, bravado wave to the kids. Jason called out, "Break a leg, Mum."

Down another hall a gold-braided guard opened a door with DISTINGUISHED LADIES taped below S.142. Inside was Arlette Norris, wife of the Inaugural Committee chair, reaching out in welcome—and Ranking Wife Norleen Talbott. Riveted by those steely Talbott eyes, Robin barely heard Arlette's effusive greeting. "Hello, Arlette. So good to see you. Norleen, how are you?"

Icy, controlled: "Very well, thank you, Robin." Hand cold as those grey eyes. Up close you saw tiny pancaked pits, souvenirs of the acne craters long since sandblasted from Norleen's cheeks. But the pain so transparent on TV showed less now than the rage glinting through that plastic mask. "A bit of business, if you don't mind. I've arranged with Chief Usher Fletcher to leave our family furniture in the White House, if you don't object. Since we may move back soon, it might economize on the moving bills."

"Oh, fine. Of course, Norleen," she said, bewilderedly as a lace-trimmed maid tugged off her coat. "Whatever's. . . easiest for everybody."

Jerky nod. "Yes, that's the general idea."

The "hostess wives" of the Inaugural Committee fluttered up. Robin hugged the ones she knew, like Gertie Whalen, shook the others' hands. In the sprinkling of stony pretend-I'm-not-here security men and white-gloved military aides, the tight-faced trio of candidates' wives made no move toward her. Elaine Hillyard was wanly remote. Judy Balch picked at her nails. Prilla Sterling wore a goalie mask like Norleen's.

Tougher already than she'd bargained on. This ritual coffee better be loaded with caffeine, because right now she badly needed something wet and sharp to pierce the velvet fog of her numb panic.

Norleen was still babbling about the furniture, how her sons and their wives would spend the night packing up personal belongings: "Mr. Fletcher's arranging accommodations for you and your husband, but if you could keep the children and your other, ah, relatives out of the family quarters until tomorrow morning. . . ."

Robin said certainly, but the staffs had already worked that out, hadn't they? She wondered why Norleen was harping so on this. But of course Norleen was still in shellshock, one minute running half the world through her henpecked husband, then presto chango, out on her buns in a flukey run of luck. Maybe the furniture was all her bruised head could handle right now.

Norleen said coldly, "So I'm told. But of course I wanted to confirm it with you."

Robin said glad to help any way they could: "For whatever it's worth, I did suggest we stay at our house, to simplify things. But that idea didn't get far, I'm afraid."

Norleen said no, she understood the Secret Service preferred to have Larry in residence there tonight. She looked like she'd been hit by a sledgehammer from behind, and was trying to figure out how on earth it had happened.

Robin covered her confusion by fussing with her gloves. The maid brought her lukewarm coffee without much caffeine jolt. Trying not to watch her violet coat rerunning on the TV against the back wall, she furiously ransacked her head for small talk to fit this ghoulish scene.

She knew from bitter experience it was tough enough to force a good-loser performance while still hemorrhaging from a defeat. But thrown face to face with the winners, doubletough. It finally dawned on her that as about-to-be ranking wife, it was her job to greet the also-rans. Stepping up to Hillyard, she couldn't say what she felt: *I know how lousy you feel. Just please don't take it personally.* So she settled for, "Good to see you, Elaine. You're looking well."

Hillyard, who hadn't looked her square in the eye since Talbott had dumped her husband to make room for Larry, said distantly, "Thank you. And congratulations, Robin."

"Judy, so nice to meet you, finally."

Balch, with mild sarcasm: "And so nice to finally meet *you*, Robin."

She moved on, determinedly pleasant, hand outstretched. "Prilla, we haven't run into each other for a while." This cookie was one of the rare, proud old breed like Mother Devlin. Sixty if she was a day, young as face-lifts could make her, not a dyed hair out of place. "How are you?"

Hand limp and cool as a dead perch. "Very well, thank you, Robin." Sparks of disdain in those carefully made-up eyes. "And you?"

"Oh, fine and dandy, thanks."

Unstrung by that brief ceremonial round, she escaped to the bathroom off this ornate holding pen.

Priscilla took in every detail of the woman's flouncing entrance. *As if she belonged in this room. Probably fresh from the beds of her New York lovers.* But fairly calm and self-possessed in that perky lilac coat. It might help some that she was such an out-and-out political nitwit. Priscilla doubted whether Robin even knew enough about the whole cave-in going on around them to be as scared as she ought to. But of course, she *was* getting the House. . . .

Even with her chorus-girl hair decently pinned up for a change, the woman had a flighty quality about her. Priscilla never had the remotest idea what to expect from her next. Except it wouldn't be remorse for her abandoned children. Or her discarded husband, who anyway seemed to share her alley-cat morals. Not that any of this bothered those Congress wives rushing to fawn and twitter over her like a bunch of bridesmaids. Even cold-fish Norleen cozying up. Raving about furniture, for heaven's sake. *Winner take all.* . . .

Steeling herself as Devlin came toward her, Priscilla was struck by the piercing blue eyes, like Paul Newman's. Brief exchange, chill but polite: "Nice to see you," "Fine and dandy." The rigid self-control she prided herself on carried her through, damming the grief she tasted like bile.

She'd somehow expected Devlin to be a bit more unstrung, more flibbertigibbet. She realized now this woman she'd virtually ignored all these months could shape up as a more dangerous rival than Norleen ever had.

On the ride in from the country she'd tried to focus on the banners, homemade signs, bed sheets tacked to porches: CONGRESS: GIVE US BACK OUR PRESIDENT DAN! PRILLA FOR FIRST LADY OF THE WORLD. She'd told Dan she'd settle for the U.S.A. But the city sidewalks sprouted nastier banners. To distract him from one about President Devlin saving America from tarnished Sterling, she pointed to a red sign against a high black fence, saying there was one she hoped the TV boys picked up on: CONGRESS DON'T ABORT OUR GREAT NEW BEGINNING. ELECT DAN STERLING.

He blanched, apologized, said he'd just have to make this up to her. Choking on chagrin, she recognized the big white house behind the fence. Squeezing his hand, she said right to those tired, hurt eyes, "Now you listen to me, Daniel Sterling, we'll be in there before you know it."

He said sure they would: "That's a promise, Mommie." In the windshield's postcard view, the Capitol festively cascaded red, white, and blue Inaugural bunting. *Should be black crepe, for what they're doing to my Dan.*

Not for an instant would she let him know what she was really thinking: This *was not* how they should be coming to claim this strange town that had haunted their schemes and pipe dreams for so many years. They should be riding in triumph, cheered by parades and marching bands, not slipping through cold, anonymous streets. Yet she didn't—couldn't—blame Dan. Never. Those others like Tighe and Elliott were responsible.

This town would still belong to them. Priscilla would see to that soon enough, whatever way it took.

Stiff with grief, she watched Norleen turn aside for a furtive swipe at her cheeks. *One down, at least. . . .*

When she noticed Robin slip off to the bathroom, she quietly set down her cup and followed.

Over the sound of flushing, she nodded to the maid in starched apron and cap, glancing over the cosmetics and beauty aids spread out on the marble sinks. *Shame to leave those pretty little colognes behind. . . .* As Robin came out from a cubicle, smoothing down her skirt, Priscilla retrieved her compact from her purse.

"Hello again, Prilla. You're looking awfully well." Wry smile. "Been a rough few weeks, hasn't it?"

Dryly: "I've had better, yes."

From her surprise at the array on the sinks, you'd think she'd never set foot in a first-class ladies' room. "Heavens, it looks like they expected us to stay all night. Look, a hair dryer. And panty hose. As a matter of fact. . . ."

Robin kicked off one shoe, peering at her foot. Smiling sheepishly into the mirror, she said she'd thought she was starting to run: "But I guess it was just my toes feeling nervous."

Priscilla leaned forward and pinned those eyes in the glass, asking sweetly, solicitously, "Tell me, Robin, are you planning to stay long on this little visit?"

The question slipped through Robin's defenses like a slap. Even flinching, she held Sterling's eyes. "Matter of fact, I'm staying for the duration, Prilla. Assuming that's what you meant to ask." *Bitch, damn bitch!* The sheer gall, cyanide-sweet behind silk ruffles and an angel-wing hairdo fingernails could break on. "Just between us, I'm looking forward to it. Washington's become such an interesting town lately, don't you think?"

"Mm-hmm." Prilla snapped her compact shut. "Well, won't that be nice for a while. . . for the children especially."

Robin stalked out and helped herself to a tiny eclair. Seeing that harpy pol-wife chorus, she'd felt fairly merciful to what they were going through, all so much more desperate for the job than she was. But Prilla's crack reminded her any pity was pissed away.

John Chancellor was marking the countdown on TV: ". . . Inaugural podium where eighteen minutes from now Laurence Devlin will become the first vice president-elect ever to take two oaths of office in immediate succession. . . ." Tension hummed in the holding pen, aides, scuttling to radio cues, congressional wives slipping out to the platform. *Five little Indians, standing on the shelf. . . .*

Last-minute flutter of coats, combs, and powder puffs as aides whisked off Elaine. Robin waited out her cue, hushed, steeling for the show. *Four little Indians. . . .*

As Prilla and Judy were led out, Robin saw Elaine on the screen, moving down to her seat on the arm of a beefy Marine. *Two little Indians. . . .* Jim Connerty slipped up behind her, murmuring, "Best of luck, Mrs. D."

"Thanks, Jim." She patted nervously at the waist of her coat, Talbott stony by her side. She blurted, "My, don't you hate this waiting business, Norleen?"

No answer. A gold-braid lieutenant murmured, "Mrs. Talbott, Mrs. Devlin. . . ." They marched out, flanked by a small platoon. Down the echoing hall, following the shiny bayonet line. Through the crowd at the platform entrance, Robin saw Prilla and Judy move down the steps, sharing the arms of a single escort. Washed with dismay, she realized she and Norleen would also be doubled up on one usher. *Good lord. Like a Bobbsey twins quadruple wedding.*

On a hissed cue she set off down the red carpet, dimly aware of the long-range TV guns, hoping she didn't look as ridiculous as she felt, doing a bridal march with Old Stoneface hanging on Daddy's other elbow. Pattered applause along the aisle. She smiled blankly, searching for the kids. There, down front, cheering their heads off.

At her aisle seat next to Norleen and Elaine, she turned jauntily toward the kids. "How's it going, troops?"

"Terrific, Mum," from Melissa.

Gorgeous Alexis was sitting with her daughters, Shelley and Frances, next to Mother Devlin—an arrangement guaranteed not to please either woman. Robin tossed an empathetic smile to Alexis, and asked if her mother-in-law was "warm enough back there." The old lady waved her off indignantly.

Oh well, same to you, then. She turned back to the huge crowd filling the stands, spilling over the lawns, down along the Mall. The view, at least, was as majestic as the rhetoric soon to be piped down that expanse.

Bill Hillyard was hustled down the steps by his Committee escorts, followed by the presidential also-rans, Balch and Sterling. The Marine Band swung into "Hail to the Chief," a last hurrah for Roy Bob Talbott, who bounded down looking as if he were about to cry.

Now Larry, face grave, moved in on tumultuous applause like breaking surf. Waiting tensely for her cue, she heard little of Jim Norris's emcee-welcome except profuse mentions of the also-rans, sandwiched between repeats of "this historic moment. . . ." Butterflies swarmed through "America the Beautiful" and Cardinal Riley's blessing.

Now! On a crooked-finger signal, she moved next to Larry. As Chief Justice Welch lumbered across the platform, Larry muttered sotto voce, "Last chance to bail out, Rob."

Smiling, she whispered, "Too late, babe." Someone handed her the gilt-edged family Bible. She watched his face as he echoed the magic words, felt his trembling hand on the book as he swore his two oaths—the veep's first, oddly enough much longer and wordier than the next, the one that mattered.

Done! So quickly, somehow. . . .

She took the Bible back to her seat as Larry began his Inaugural Address. On inspired afterthought, she passed the Bible to Mother Devlin, mouthing, "for safekeeping." Ten brownie points in the old lady's twinkle.

Her reeling brain couldn't absorb the words of his speech. But she sensed the forceful cadences building as he hit his stride, drawing waves of applause. He finished with a ringing, "Now, with the faith and courage of those who came before us, let us dedicate ourselves once again to discovering the hidden promise of the American dream."

The cheers poured in, swelling to a roar when Larry motioned the also-rans to join him for the lifted handclasp. Tumult was still building when he waved the wives forward.

She moved through the familiar choreography on automatic pilot, dazedly tuning her gestures to his. For endless minutes they rode that jubilant ovation, that epiphany for the country's pro tem rescuer.

Closing benediction and "Star-Spangled Banner." As Larry headed up the steps into a sea of celebration, a white-gloved Marine offered his elbow to Robin.

Enough! She waved him off and followed Larry, acknowledging the shouted congratulations: "Thank you. . . thanks very much." Numbly she told herself, *So that's it.*

The idea had no shape or feel to it yet, but this man she was trailing up the stairs, her once and present husband, was now President of the United States.

Alexis Devlin decided the scaled-down Inaugural luncheon, squeezed into the Old Senate Chamber, was nicely symbolic of the whole event—impromptu, compromised, nothing like the real thing. But closer to it than she'd ever expected dear old Laurence to get.

Hard not to think of him as Little Brother Goof-Up, trying on his big brother's shoes for size. But she must admit he did a grand job on the speech. If talk was all the presidency was about, he'd be off to a fine start. Of course, with the rat's nest he was headed into, he'd need more to work with than a way with words. She somehow doubted he was up to the job, but she hoped for once she'd be proved wrong.

He'd best not expect much help from his poor wife, who seemed to be wobbling rather close to the edge. Robin was trotting through her paces more or less on cue, but with a certain glaze about the eyes. Alexis wouldn't count on her for much.

But she *looked* fine, at least. In fact, rather good. Alexis always thought those pinup-girl looks wouldn't hold up, but she seemed wrong about that. Maybe all those years Robin was pickling her system had some good effect after all.

A memory flitted from the weekend Michael had dragged Alexis up to Bryn Mawr to butter up his father, when Michael was having it out with the old man about making himself scarce on the presidential campaign.

☆

The day was fraught, needless to say. Willie kept roaring, "So you want your own father to butt out." Michael tried to stroke him with no Dad that's not it, but of course that *was* it, exactly.

And in the midst of that, Laurence popped up with little Miss Swann, announcing that they'd just gotten engaged. A total shock, and not a particularly welcome one. Alexis had only met the girl once before, had no opinion about her, really. Except that Laurence had been quite smart not to bring her around much, considering her trite good looks. Willie had a nasty habit of going after his sons' girlfriends when they looked like that, and the poor girl didn't seem quite up to dealing with *that*.

Alexis hung around eavesdropping while dear old Pauline gave Robin the royal grilling, asking to be "refreshed" on the Swann family background and so on. The only parts that seemed to charm her were the bits about Iron Jack, Robin's rowdy grandfather, who'd built ships in Brooklyn.

Alexis's own opinion was that the girl seemed sweet but a little anxious, rather breathless. Mousy under the surface flash, and altogether too obliging. Good little Marymount girl, who happened to look like a Rockette. Of course, a Mother Devlin grilling could reduce anyone to mush, but Alexis certainly didn't sense that Robin had the grit and stuffing she'd need to hold her own with *this* bunch. And if Robin couldn't find the spunk to stand up to the family—like Alexis herself had—they'd run her over with a 2-ton truck.

In the end it turned out to be worse than trucks. Yet for all the ups and downs, she'd made it this far at least. *Goes to show, one never knows. . .*

☆

Alexis watched her take a hug from courtly old Harley Richmond, a House institution in his trademark purple bow tie. While Harley rumbled something about this being a remarkable day for the soothsayers, Robin sighed, "Oh, Harley, isn't it just?" Shivering, she sank into his chest like she wanted to crawl into his watch pocket.

Well, god knows Alexis could sympathize with that. Nothing really *could* get you ready for the job Robin was about to take on, but one could hardly envy her going into it cold turkey.

Turning away from Harley, Robin's glance snagged on the military aide dripping medals, carrying "the football." Cute macho euphemism for the nuclear codes. She stiffened as she recognized it, eyes glazing again.

Alexis glided up behind her and murmured, "Hang tough, dear. The fun's just beginning."

In the armored stretch limo gliding down Pennsylvania Avenue, presidential fender-flags flapping in the obliging wind, House Speaker Charlie Whalen rolled a cigar, preparing to joust over the crowd size.

Eighty thousand, Senate Majority Leader Jim Norris said. Looked more like a hundred to Jake Kenzer, the Senate president pro tem. Robin said oh, surely not so many.

Charlie unplugged his cigar and growled, "One sixty, Ma'am, according to Chief Morrison not five minutes ago." Goddam Senate still licking their gums over getting out the vote on their side, leaving the heavy artillery trained on the House. At least he could get the damn crowd size right.

Robin mentioned surprise at such a big turnout with no parade. Charlie rumbled in reflex blarney that *she* was the parade, pointing to a crudely lettered WE LOVE ROBIN! banner. "I've seen a bunch of those. You've got some fans out there, girl."

Never thought he'd be riding this holy mile with the Devlin kid brother. Good-for-nothing baby of the family, not worth six pinches of his older brother. But here was Philly's own Larry Devlin getting a one-man Pennsylvania Avenue parade, at a time when the whole goddam government was coming unstuck.

Bottom line for putting it back together was Charlie damn well had to get that vote out of his House, get Roy Bob Talbott back on the job. . . before they found out how many more kidney punches the poor old Constitution could take. He hoped to god Larry Devlin understood what a hell of a fix they were all in till this thing got resolved. What a delicate, dangerous, national spot. . . .

Every time he wrapped his mouth around "Mr. President" to this one, his gravelly tone said don't unpack yet. But good god, if the alternative was squiring the old Hollywood cowboy down the avenue for a four-year run—now how bad could a Devlin be, as a veep sitting in? Long as he didn't get too big for his pants. And that sweet little woman of his, now she'd had some hard times but she was a good girl, Iron Jack Swann's granddaughter. Bloodlines would tell.

As the stiff, coded talk battled back and forth in the car, shaded by the pitched battle just waged over the Inaugural arrangements, Charlie watched Larry eyeing the sun-roof latch, itching to pop his head out for a few rounds of Julius Caesar. Glowing, euphoric, like he'd won the World Series. . . which maybe he had. Pro tem, anyway.

Till Charlie got out his vote.

When they rolled up to the White House fence, Larry finally couldn't hold back. He ordered the car stopped, then plunged out through the alarmed agents into the crowd.

Little Robin plowed right in after him. Charlie hung behind her like an avenging shepherd, trying to reach ahead to punch out a route for her. Even with agents bobbing all around, they swam through shrieks and clutches. A hysterical, almost sexual swarm, women fighting for a touch of Larry. *By god, like Michael's old campaigns.* . . .

The kids caught up with them somewhere in that crazy mob, and at the tall black gate they all suddenly popped free. Tramping up the long, curved drive, Robin linked arms with Sean and Melissa, laughing into the winter sunshine.

The building loomed much bigger than she remembered. Gleaming, unreal. *Disneyland, D.C.* Front-door welcome squad of butlers, Marines, and Chief Usher Alexander Fletcher, plus his six flunkies.

In the cavernous entry hall, butlers leaped to peel off coats. Fletcher led on to the Blue Room for tea, a ceremonial swill laid on to make up for the morning's coffee.

Larry made short work of it. Charlie Whalen had barely finished a rambling story about his first visit here—for some of Harry Truman's arm-twisting—when Larry rattled his cup back to saucer. "Speaking of getting on with the job. . . ."

The escorts beat a quick retreat, chorusing, "Good luck," "Godspeed, Mr. President." Larry turned to the kids with a luminous grin. "Anybody want to check out the office?"

Rhetorical question. The Chief Usher led the gallop to the Oval Office. Jason pointed out family photos along the walls, on hooks barely cool from the Talbotts, but Larry urged them impatiently on. *Like he's on magnets.* . . .

The West Wing foyer was jammed with a "spontaneous" staff party, mostly Larry's people, some of Talbott's. Larry climbed on a chair and plugged for continued support in this transition period, hoping to benefit from "your valuable experience in serving President Talbott. Let's show

how well this integrated team can work to keep the ship of state afloat." Translation: *Stay as long as you want, all you Roy Bob moles. Or till Larry's guys pry your hands off the doorknobs.*

On to the sanctum sanctorum, hushing instinctively to whispers and tiptoes. Robin sank into a seat by the fireplace, awed, amazed through the blur of her exhaustion.

The room looked oddly empty—bare walls and shelves, as if somebody'd grabbed the good stuff when the fire alarm went off. She noted cheap brown linoleum rimming the gold-and-blue carpet. Useful observation for the memory box: *All is not what it seems in this place.*

The kids quickly shucked their shyness, peering and poking. Sean tried out the swivel chair behind the big carved desk. Jason staked out the marble mantelpiece for the family sailboat model he and Larry had built. Melissa produced a shady memory of her last visit here, at Shelley's sixth birthday party, when Uncle Mike had invited them for cake and ice cream.

Larry prowled the room, raking in every detail, face etched with incredulity. As his eyes crossed hers, she telegraphed, *Right, babe, it's real. You made it.*

He smiled, rubbed his belly: "Yep, sure enough."

Bing McCarthy's assistant delivered 8-by-10 proofs of the Inaugural. The kids promptly strewed the stack across the desk, hooting and howling while Bing clicked off the next batch. But Larry cut the ego orgy short: "Clear out, troops. I've got a Cabinet meeting in ten minutes."

Good lord, he's settled in already.

Fletcher waited outside to divert the kids onto a tour of the recreational facilities and to steer Robin and Sally Arnstein to the Red Room "to confer on the evening's arrangements." Robin thanked him for a splendid welcome. As he launched his consider-this-your-home-as-well-as-the-nation's speech, her mislaid nervousness flapped back to roost.

He slid into a briefing: "At five o'clock you and President Devlin will receive the Congressional leadership and wives in the Blue Room. At 5:20, the Cabinet and wives in the Red Room. . . Supreme Court, Dean of the Diplomatic Service. . . members of Congress and spouses, in the East Room. The President will speak briefly. . . ."

"Good heavens, Mr. Fletcher!" The ornate silk-and-gilt room shrank before her eyes, Alice-in-Wonderland. "That must be almost a thousand people. How can you possibly squeeze them all in?"

He chuckled reassuring. "One thousand one hundred thirty-eight,

Mrs. Devlin. Not counting staff, family and friends, who will be received more informally in the West Wing."

Sally pointed out that Congress was invited in two shifts, since President Devlin was "anxious to include them all, as a gesture of national unity."

Already she felt the soreness of that ordeal-by-handshake. "Look, whatever's planned is fine with me. But that sounds like a very. . . elaborate event." By the way, could he make sure no one served her alcohol, in drink or food?

"But of course, Mrs. Devlin!" Seeming pained that she'd felt it necessary to mention that, Fletcher suggested he might walk her through tonight's event.

They tramped around the movie-set rooms of rickety antiques and marble busts. A man in a blue blazer was on his knees, laying cueing tapes on the Orientals. She tried dutifully to absorb the rat-a-tat instructions: ". . . front of the fireplace for a group photo. . . process through to the Grand Hall. . . ." But all she remembered was afternoon sunlight shafting through the hand-blown glass of the balcony door.

She asked him to tell the aides to poke her if she got confused, and gratefully accepted his suggestion of a pit stop in the Queens' Bedroom, her billet for the night.

When she saw the silky, dusty-pink room with the huge old four-poster canopied bed, she felt sure she'd checked into the wrong hotel. But since it was too late to do anything about that now, she shooed out the three maids, kicked off her shoes, and slid under the satin bedspread.

She blinked at the pink silk cocoon overhead. Much too keyed up to sleep, but maybe rest her eyes. . . .

CHAPTER NINE /

January 20th
Prilla

Just getting into the Sterlings' suite at the Carlton was like trying to break into Fort Knox, even for Prilla's dearest friend. At one point Ginny Hibbing hissed indignantly to her husband, Mort, "You'd think we were after the family silver." Of course that's the way it went around

Prilla and Dan these days, layers of pomp and security that would dazzle an emperor.

Ginny really wanted to be downstairs where Dan and Prilla were glad-handing blue-chip contributors. She coveted every minute she could squeeze with Prilla lately. Wouldn't even mind watching their dog-and-pony show. But Prilla'd said, "Darling, you'd be so bored, and we're so rushed. . . ."

Ginny recognized a brush-off when she heard it. But she couldn't really blame Prilla, with the awful pressure they were under. All so unexpected. Every day one doozie complication after another. Mort said by gosh, if he'd had any idea how tricky it was to elect a president in this damn country these days he'd've tried to take over Wall Street instead.

But Prilla couldn't brush them off completely, since the Hibbings had arranged tonight's gala "consolation" dinner dance at the home of their dear friends the Montagues. So Prilla had invited them to come by to "help us dress."

That certainly seemed a little ho-hum, can't the maids do that. But once she and Mort actually got into the suite, alone except for a few staffers flitting in and out, Ginny realized what a prize this was. That fireplace, for instance, she knew almost as well as her own; day after day on TV Dan held court around it. Yet now she saw it was only *faux bois* ornamental—so much for the Carlton!

When Mort dropped cigar ashes on the rug, she snapped, "For heaven's sake, don't set the place on fire!" Now how long had it been since she'd ragged at him over something like that—but they were waiting around for Dan and Prilla, after all. Not just Dan and Prilla their dear old pals, but about to become the most important people on earth.

The thought took her breath away still. And felt a bit strange, like a dress that didn't fit. For so many years, after all, Prilla'd sort of danced around Ginny's maypole, not vice versa. The first few times they'd even joked about somebody running for president, Ginny thought they were talking about Mort. That's how she remembered it, anyway.

Of course, Dan turned out to be much the better choice. She couldn't imagine Mort being *anybody's* darling, let alone the darling of millions upon millions of people. She just wished they could get this awful, endless, in-between time over with, and get on with the main event.

At 6:30 some agents hustled in, and right after them. . . .

Prilla was hanging on Dan's arm, head down, eyes half-closed. She looked bruised, almost. Utterly exhausted. Covering her shock, Ginny swished across the carpet, chirping, "Prilla dear! I thought you'd never get here."

Instant transformation: Prilla's head lifted, face lighting, smile locking on. Like somebody'd yanked her strings. She laughed. "Me too. Darling, don't you look lovely!" They hugged, patted cheeks, ritual greeting of the Group. A cooler hug for Mort, Prilla saying how grand it was to see him "on the ramparts with us."

Ginny'd just never for one minute thought of it turning out like *this*—and neither had Prilla. The poor darling was bearing up like a horse, turning in a great performance. Ginny couldn't imagine how she did it.

Or how much longer she could keep it up.

Over drinks in the living room, Mort asked how the fat-cat do had gone. Dan said, "Top-notch. Don't you think, Pril?"

She said oh yes, and it was so good to see their loyal old friends. But something in the tinny, too-hearty way she said that made Ginny think maybe it hadn't gone fine at all.

Mort hoped the gathering "shook a few greenbacks into the collection plate." Prilla looked at Dan, head tilted. She seemed to want to hear more of that, but Ginny felt like a kid who'd waited up all night to open presents—and she certainly hadn't waited for more of that boring money talk.

She whispered excitedly, "Darling, it's such fun to *see* you, finally. We've got so much to catch up on!"

Prilla blinked at her. . . then grabbed Ginny's hand. "Right. Leave the boys to their business. Come tell me what you think of my dress."

When her numb brain finally focused on what Ginny was hissing, Priscilla suddenly realized her own exhaustion: *Get out of these clothes. Hot shower.* She led Ginny to the master bedroom Dan had vacated in deference to Ginny's visit.

She'd kill right now for an hour's nap in fresh sheets. Instead she'd have a blast of Ginny's unquenchable optimism, which might do more at this point to perk her draggled spirits. But she also needed a clear readout on how the Group was reacting to that House mess. Ginny's flighty, breathless manner might come across as devious to others, yet Priscilla read her—always had in their thirty-year friendship—like a clear glass pane.

First she had to flip back onto Ginny's wavelength. The wives who were her entrée into the Group never mixed in the work part of these powerful men's lives. They knew it was different for her, of course, but she always downplayed that around Ginny. Ginny loved to feel a part of "this enormous, wonderful thing that's happening," as long as that didn't include anything so boring as campaign business.

So Priscilla showed her the Galanos hanging in the closet, pink chiffon with a beaded top. She interrupted the flow—"Those *exquisite* seed pearls!"—to remark on Ginny's dress. "Gorgeous! Champagne's your perfect color."

Ginny preened before the mirror. "Thanks, dear. Of course it's not my *real* Inaugural gown, but that one will keep." Poking a cigarette into her long gold holder, she demanded, "Now, darling, tell all."

"Ah, that's quite an order." Priscilla stripped to her slip, saying of course they'd been awfully busy, but she couldn't help thinking it wasn't supposed to happen this way.

"Yes, of course. But darling, look at the bright side. Now Talbott's fallen on his face, right where he belongs, it won't be long till we're ringing in the Sterling administration in proper style."

Forcing a jaunty chuckle, she said Ginny sounded almost as rosy as Dan, who was betting his boots this would turn around soon. She never, ever let herself forget that any slip to Ginny could go straight to Mort: "And I'm sure you're both absolutely right."

"Of course we are, darling. Honestly, you should hear Mort sounding off. Of course he's absolutely *furious* at that House, but he hasn't any doubt Dan's going to—"

Priscilla said she hoped Mort understood that none of this was Dan's fault.

"Of course not, darling!" Ginny flipped her hand indignantly. "Nobody would even *think* that. It's just like Dan's been saying all along, that old rats' nest of a Congress needs a good housecleaning from attic to sewer."

She smiled. "Yes, that's so true. I'm so glad you all understand that. . . ."

"Prilla dear, it's *you* I'm most concerned about. I keep thinking how beastly all this must be for you. But I must say you're bearing up as gorgeously as ever." Wincing at that transparent lie, Priscilla creamed off makeup while Ginny raved on: "Everyone who's anyone will be there. . . ."

Prilla excused herself to take the hottest shower she could stand, to melt the strain from that ghastly charade on the Congress porch, torture by freezing, on live TV. And the fund-raiser downstairs—tough sledding, full of yellow alerts. The same men who'd treated Dan like Moses come down from the mountain were pressing inside tips to get at key congressmen. Giving off contagious anxiety, panic in the ranks.

Now matching rumbles from Ginny. One more thing to juggle. For years their girl talks had spun on what it would be like when Dan won "the big one." Yet when they'd met as Junior League volunteers, Ginny was the quintessential rich man's wife, elegant, exquisitely dressed, pampered crown princess with wealth-and-power perks—while Priscilla was just a housewife to a struggling actor past his prime, making do on iffy income from TV and product promotion. Shirt ads, my lord.

She'd worked at cultivating Ginny's friendship, drawing Dan into that magic circle. Often feeling like the match girl, nose pressed to a glittery window. Then Mort and Phil finally saw Dan's political potential, persuaded him as "one who shares our interests" to run for governor, and arranged insider tips to make him almost as wealthy as they were. Almost. But never quite their equal. Once when she'd thanked Phil for cutting them in on one lucrative deal, he said it was the least they could do for the man they hoped would steer their flagship all the way to the top.

Their flagship. Yet they'd all come so far since. . . to the cruel hard choices bearing down on them. She wondered who'd wind up choosing first, Phil or. . . herself.

Phil, surely. Here *she* was, furiously toweling her spidery skin, still feeling like a nervous schoolgirl around Ginny, anxious to please and mind her manners. To somehow still *earn* this friendship—such an asinine trip to lay on herself!

Coming out of the bathroom in her velvet robe, she did feel a tweak of matchgirl still, watching Ginny flip her diamond-and-emerald rope. But this pampered grande dame was also her best friend and most loyal fan. Ginny's prattle almost *did* make her believe she'd dance soon in. . . .

She smiled warmly across the room. "Gin, I'm so glad you came over early. You make it a party already."

Ginny beamed, champagne glass lifted in toast: "Prilla, I can't *tell* you how much I've missed you, dear."

In the minutes before Jean-Marc came by, Ginny pranced and gabbed, ". . . quite thrilled with who's coming to our pre-Inaugural gala. All the elegant Washington people you and Dan should know, from the Supreme Court down to the BOTs. Georgetown's Beautiful Old Things, dear. Once you meet them, you'll be amazed how useful they'll be to you in the Big House." She fended off Priscilla's dry glance with a wagging finger. "You'll see, darling. You'll just see. Any day now."

For one giddy, reckless moment, Priscilla almost believed her. She took odd comfort in Ginny's familiar ramblings on family and friends. As if nothing had really changed. . . yet.

When Jean-Marc turned up with his bulging cases to do her hair and makeup, Ginny amused them with yarns about the day's events. Like the woman dressed in photos of Priscilla—"Hat to boots, darling, I swear. And her boyfriend wore a cowboy hat and a rubber mask of Dan. . . ." Both raved over her Galanos, the finishing touch to her party mood. They floated out to meet the men in the living room, almost as if they had something to celebrate.

The motorcade rolled off to the Montagues' rambling red-brick Georgetown mansion, sirens wailing, Ginny still chattering. The house gleamed with old silver and Old Masters, tables in pink moire—"What else but your signature color, darling?" Ginny gushed—sprinkled through the solarium and the library. From the jewels and flowers to guest-list titles, it all looked like a White House production: practically perfect.

Yet with her meticulous eye for detail, Priscilla wondered why some men wore business suits instead of black tie. Like the Arizona congressman introduced as one of Dan's leading field generals in the House. A few minutes later she heard Frank Whittaker ask him, "No time to change, eh?"

He said nah, he'd got hung up with Devlin's number two. Hadn't got out of the East Room till fifteen minutes ago. Whittaker said they'd changed in the car. "Janey says if we do that much more she wants a Winnebago with an inboard john."

Instantly, instinctively, she pivoted between them and Dan. *Shield him, somehow.* . . . They were all around him now, men he couldn't trust as far as he could spit. Even some who called themselves his generals, but paid court to those damn Devlins before coming here tonight.

It hit her like brick slide: In this whole strange town, who could you trust? Even the ones who came and kissed your hand, boosted you and wrote out checks—you couldn't count on their loyalty to Dan. Outside his own tight circle, the rest were mainly whores who'd go with whoever won.

They led the glittery procession in to dinner behind a Scottish piper, applause swelling over the strange, lovely wail. She smiled and twinkled, and wondered how many more snakes were out there, cheering them on.

CHAPTER TEN

January 20th
Robin

Melissa mused on how weird it was to see her mother sleeping like a little kid in the big old bed, mouth open, dribbling spit on the starched pillowcase. Looking so defenseless. Like she'd never harmed a fly.

Melissa gingerly nudged her shoulder. "Hey, Mom, up and at 'em." She grunted, burrowed deeper into the covers. "C'mon, lady. It's dress-up time again."

Yawning, heaving up on one elbow, Mom said groggily, "Hi there. Don't tell me I actually slept."

"Like a log. Nice digs you've got here, by the way." Melissa peeked into the adjoining sitting room. Awed whisper: "Chee-sus! They've laid out our dresses. Ironed, even."

Her mother said drowsily don't get used to it, and asked how the tour had gone. Melissa said the big hit was the movie theater, with pool tables and bowling alley a close second.

Getting ready, they squealed and showered and primped like bridesmaids put up in a fancy hotel. Mom reassured her about the green silk tunic, the safest thing Melissa had in her closet and right now she couldn't bear to shop for anything else. Mom said she knew just what she meant.

Melissa'd forgotten how much fun Mom could be when she was as freaked as you were. Long time since they'd laughed like that together, till their ribs ached. Both a little punchy with nerves, Melissa guessed, but it beat breaking out with hives.

Mom was at the sink, rolling her eyes like Charlie Chaplin as she gargled a load of mouthwash. Suddenly she dipped forward and spat it out. Just something about the way she did that, wiping her mouth on the back of her hand, reminded Melissa of the times she used to catch her throwing up. The bad days when she'd say she had the flu.

Instantly a snowstorm of memories blew back. Painful snaps of the times she'd worked so hard to forget. Melissa got quiet and still, guarding her tongue. Guarding her hurt.

Her mother noticed that—kept on chattering, but with silences in between, as if she was cranking up to ask what was going on. Melissa had *no Mum, nothing's the matter* ready and waiting on her tongue. No way, no way was she getting into that.

Rap on the bedroom door, muffled, "Three minutes, Mrs. Devlin."

"Thank you," she called out, voice high and wavery as a piccolo. "Hon, can you zip me?"

Saved by the knock. Melissa obligingly zipped, sighing over the skinny-minny waist under her hands. If she were marooned for a year on an iceberg, she still couldn't whip herself into that kind of shape. "You look terrific, Mum. What color is this anyway, electric grape?"

Robin chuckled, flashing Dennis. "Magenta, magenta. Thanks, Missy, you do, too." She patted her tummy, feeling like Marie Antoinette on her way to. . . .

She swept that thought into the storage bin, along with her concern for whatever was going on with Melissa—one minute her tender, funny old self, the next cold and tight as a clam. She reached out and crushed the dear child into a hug, rumpling silks together, and whispered, "Darling, I'm so happy to be with you."

Melissa echoed the squeeze, then pulled away. Eyes smiling like they had a secret between them. Robin patted her daughter's arms, laughing for courage. "Okay, Missy, let's go do it to it."

Larry and the boys, plus assorted aides and ringmasters, already waited in the broad hallway, Sean peeking around the Chinese screens blocking off the family rooms. Robin hissed, "Sean!" and pointed him back.

A white-gloved Marine maneuvered them into proper ranks at the stairway door. He murmured a reminder: "Please pause for a photo opportunity on the landing, Mr. President."

Larry nodded, clearing his throat. Robin knitted her trembling fingers. *Breathe slow, deep.* . . .

The door swung open as "Ruffles and Flourishes" piped from the floor below. She tucked her hand into Larry's elbow and paced down the red carpet, praying that she wouldn't trip.

TV lights hit her legs like sunlamp heat as the band swung into

"Hail to the Chief." Four more steps and her eyes caught the glare. But she couldn't see the applauding crowd until they'd maneuvered past the awkward end of the stairs and turned to pause on the landing.

Stunned, half-blinded by the strobes, the floating faces. *Dear god. Like a thousand already.* . . .

☆

Somehow the handshaking marathon went better than she was braced for. The well-oiled White House party machine slid her through so smoothly her old dog paddle kept her afloat. In fact she was surprised by how quickly they got ceremonially piped out of the last reception at 9:36.

The chief usher still hovered, waiting to escort them to the family party rollicking in the West Wing. Larry was instantly swallowed in the uproar; she warily circled the rim. This was her first contact with so many massed Devlins since the Mother Devlin birthday disaster. The only one she really wanted to talk to was Alexis, who'd long since flown the coop. So she put her guttering energies into touchdowns with in-laws: "Great day for the family, wasn't it?. . ."

☆

At eleven she realized the kids should get home to bed. But the boys wanted a goodnight from their dad. Her patience fraying, she looked for Larry. Kevin Devlin thumbed her toward the Cabinet Room.

She rapped and opened in a single irritated move. In shirtsleeves at the long table, Larry huddled with Ben Boylan and a few top strategists. As he glanced up like a kid caught behind the barn, she knew instantly that he was plotting how to hold this top-of-the-mountain turf for as long as he could. *Forget that "few weeks at the most, Rob."*

She snapped, "Excuse the interruption, Larry."

"That's okay. What's up?"

She said the children wanted to say goodnight. When he came out to the hallway she was struck by the reverential stir around "Mr. President." Even his own kids were tongue-tied with deference.

They saw the kids into the waiting limo with hugs and admonitions to be back in time for breakfast, seven-thirty sharp. Then Larry headed back to the party. Fletcher and two agents instantly materialized to escort her to the mansion, where a maid in lacy apron and cap waited outside her bedroom door. *Lord, I'll be lucky if they let me go to the john alone around here.* . . .

She dispatched Fletcher with a 6:30 wake-up call, but the maid trailed her into the room, which somehow looked a little smaller than before. Her ivory-satin nightgown was fanned out on the turned-down sheets of the canopied four-poster. *Score one for Dennis. Stratton souvenir nightie makes it to the big time. . . .*

The maid offered to help her undress. Robin laughed embarrassedly, "Thanks very much, but I do that quite well by myself." *Definitely* the wrong hotel.

Pat, pat on the plumped pillows. "Now if you need anything during the night, Mrs. Devlin, you just pick up the phone. And President Devlin"—eyes discreetly averted—"will be right across the hall in the Lincoln Bedroom."

She thanked her again, too profusely, wanting only to be left alone. To sleep.

When the woman finally left, she stripped off her makeup and clothes and slipped on the gown, like poured cream. She slid between crisp sheets. . . wide awake now, random memories of this amazing day firing in her head.

Groaning with dismay, she got up to do fifty sit-ups on the rose-and-gold Oriental rug. . . until she noticed the fragile old gown was tearing a bit around the hand-stitched seams. Fingering the soft lace that spilled down her arm, she cooed remorse for working out in such an antique.

Grandma Swann's, she thought. From the attic trunk. She'd brought it to Stratton because it seemed she and Larry were finally going to Do It, and she wanted something a little bridey and special to set the mood. Talk about full circle. Or was it 180 degrees? Anyway, she loved to think of Grandma wearing it for Iron Jack. Shame they couldn't know how far it had come!

She stood up and cased the shelves of the spindly secretary for something to read herself to sleep with. Dismal assortment. She settled for *The Living White House.*

Tucked back in bed, she pored dutifully over pics of her predecessors—Grace Coolidge cutting a cake, Alexis parading to dinner with the Shah, Betty Ford dancing with Prince Philip. A rap on the door interrupted.

Startled, she dropped the book, called out, "Yes, come."

Larry asked through the open door, "Rob? You still up?"

She said matter of fact, yes. "I'm doing some late homework." She was perched up in that behemoth of a bed, hands fluttering from a book to her hair. Blushing a little, smiling. He decided she was glad to see him.

He came in grinning, juggling two long-stemmed glasses and a silver ice bucket nesting a large bottle of Perrier. "I thought what the hell, we could stand one more toast. Considering it's been a hell of a night."

She chuckled as he awkwardly nudged the door shut. "Sheer inspiration, Dev."

"Glad you think so." He set his load down on the bedside table and poured out his oblation, offered with a bobbled half bow. He raised his glass: "Here's to you, Rob."

Clink. She said, "A grand welcome to the hot seat, my boyo." She had on something that reminded him of their first time together. It struck him she'd changed amazingly little since then. Longer hair, a little riper, but in some ways even prettier. Still the same soft, undefended glow.

"Yeah, well. We'll give it a good shot, anyway. Maybe get a few things moving." Nobody'd say that about him, god knows. But looking around him, still lit with the sheer joy of his win, he guessed he hadn't felt so peaceful, so eased in as long as he could remember. "Damn, Rob. We made it."

She beamed. "Yep. Sure enough, Dev."

Yanking his tie loose, he asked what the homework was. She waved the White House cover at him. "Real inspirational stuff. Flo Harding shakes hands with her dog, Mamie waves to bald old Ike. You get the picture."

He asked if she remembered the shit fit Mamie'd thrown after Alexis had moved into this room in '61, when her decorators were loose in the house. "Come on. You forgot Mamie telling the press the Queens' Bedroom was supposed to be saved for *real* queens?"

Pealing laugh. "Oh, god. Alexis must've loved that."

"Well, Alex always had her own ideas about who rated the royal rug." He shucked his jacket, hung it on the door handle, watching her curled in pillows like a tiger cat.

The lit fuse that had propelled him through the day was sputtering now. He was a bit startled to find himself *here* for the winding down, but then he'd been surprised for years by Rob. And today was an incredible kind of high, a giant strung-out come he was maybe leery about floating down from. If the fabulous parachute ride had to end. . . do it on home ground. Safe ground.

She asked if he'd thought much about Michael today.

Her question scratched open the part he'd been ducking. Slowly: "Oh, yeah. Sure. You too?" She nodded. He added softly, looking away, "Him and Stephen both. I couldn't help thinking—damn, wouldn't it be. . . ."

Beyond that wistful fantasy was the bottomless pit of his essential loneliness. The isolation he couldn't bear to look at, today of all days. Once as a kid he'd traipsed a beach with Michael, striding in his damp footprints. But Michael got pissed about something and dropped a load of wet sand down Larry's suit. "Just remember you don't fill my shoes, twerp."

Wondering if the surprise etched on her face mirrored his own, he abruptly changed the subject. "By the way, you did real good today, Rob."

Those rare compliments always jigged her off balance. She murmured, "Well, thanks. You did pretty good yourself."

Fingers dancing in the drapery fringe, he asked what she thought of the day. She squirmed contentedly, giving in to a smile. He laughed, his eyes touching hers, nudging reminder of old, private understandings. Old lacerations, too, and missed connections. Too many, finally, to be healed. But she was amazed and touched to realize he'd chosen her to help him wind down on this astonishing night. As if no one else could do it quite the same way.

He spilled random impressions: Cowboy Dan, teeth gritted, rising to the occasion. Roy Bob crying in his beer.

"Well, you can hardly blame Roy, he's still got to live with Norleen. Can't you see him trying to explain. . . ."

"God, yes. Ten years from now he'll still be spinning her new alibis." He slapped his gut. "Well, stuff it. He lost the job fair and square, because he didn't have a piss ant's idea how to do it right." Roaming back to the door, he dropped his tie over the jacket, unbuttoning his shirt in his shed-the-day reflex.

Reminding him that Roy was only three votes short, she said please don't count on an elephant's pregnancy, babe.

Out came the shirttails. "Shit, if that's anywhere near two years, I might settle for that."

When she asked how the day had gone for him, he kicked a chair closer to her bed and sank into it with an impish, amazingly boyish smile. "I guess. . . spectacular. God, all these years I've thought about it, decided to go for it, *went* for it. . . just getting there, even without the four-year lease, it was. . . worth the trip."

The whole cast of characters danced in his quick, exuberant bursts, but she was startled to hear so much about Charlie Whalen. How Charlie'd said he "better damn well enjoy this honeymoon, because it's going to last about thirty-six hours." How Charlie seemed to be boning up on Woodrow Wilson's crackpot ideas for a U.S. parliamentary system with the House Speaker playing Prime Minister.

Not mentioning what Charlie'd once told him in a blowup years ago: He wasn't worth six pinches of Mike.

"Charlie's ass is in the sling over this vote, and he's damn well jockeying to get me in there with him. You know the first thing he asked me today?" She shook her head. "How much help Roy Bob will get out of me."

She tried not to smile. "Good question, babe. . . ."

He said listen, he'd do what was right. But Charlie Whalen had decided an acting president wasn't the real thing: "He thinks *he's* the top Democrat now. Did you notice he picked up Secret Service protection?" Astonished, she asked why. "Because he's next in line to the throne till he gets out that vote. Way he sees it, he's got the power and I've got the real estate—on temporary loan. But our esteemed Speaker is about to get set straight. I'll give Charlie a run for his money. . . ."

She was astonished at the fretful rancor. So much for shared Philly blood. ". . . let's just say Charlie's interests and mine aren't identical. He's got all eyes on the House now. Catbird seat. But Charlie's got his dick out on this one and he's got to come up with a vote."

She chuckled softly. "Live it up while you can, babe."

He said that was just what he had in mind. "We'll see who's running the show here, dammit. . . ."

His face was animated, shifting in the loose flow of his thoughts. For so long she'd mostly seen a brooding sourness in him, a jowly haggardness, too many scotches cushioning his tired eyes. But tonight he seemed redeemed, renewed. And quite beautiful to her, carried through his drivenness to some place of resolution.

As he talked in jerky marital shorthand, she didn't resist the old closeness tugging her. Watching him jab the air, she realized he had magic fingers now—suddenly consecrated, priestlike. One magic finger at least, that fit the button inside the football. *They're lucky it's him, a good man who'll give it all he can and then some.*

Back on his feet, he prowled restlessly, pent-up energy escaping in staccato bursts. "Charlie says I'll be lucky to get a Flag Day resolution through the House. But Harley Richmond thinks he's full of shit. Harley says one beauty of our system is how it turns up leaders to fit its critical times, and he thinks I may be just what the doctor ordered. . . ."

Ah, such a night this was for him. She shared his amazement, if not all the rest. And after this raw-meat day, his unwinding seemed almost unfinished, somehow, without. . . .

Droit de seigneur, they used to call it. Not such a big deal, after all those years. At least not since his upset New York primary win when they'd tumbled into bed back at her place in a kind of accident of celebration.

☆

But that night at Stratton, now, he was *le vrai seigneur*. So courtly and slow, so sweetly unfolding her petals. They played it like a classic wedding night, tacitly assuming a virgin bride. He'd never actually asked her if she'd slept with any other boys, she supposed in order to let him play this rite of passage by the book. So she never mentioned the other three or four, who hadn't amounted to much anyway. She just wrapped herself in Grandma Nellie's satin, burying the others at sea, in her wakening head.

Oh, he was such a dear lover that night, so deliberate and tender. She thought holy moley, look what she'd been holding off for three years. But by next morning he was already back into what she came to recognize as his normal-speed rate: rapid transit. Grab the locomotive quick or you'd miss even the caboose.

Even so, that one night at least, she'd been properly wooed and seduced.

☆

She watched him quietly, rolling the thought, feeling it in the charged field between them. Waiting for him to make the move. Yet he kept walking and talking, like a music box refusing to wind down. "At least three guys called me President Talbott. Force of habit, I guess, although one seemed pretty deliberate. . . ."

Lord, but they'd had some good times, awful good times, steaming and whistling across the sheets when she'd grabbed his caboose. She wavered, uncertainly libidinous, reasoning through shy confusion that he must've had that idea, too, when he came in here.

It took her a while to realize he might be feeling too vulnerable just now to broach it. *Up to you, then.* . . .

Daring for once, she broke a brief silence with, "Well, listen. Seeing as we've got such a lot to celebrate, why don't you take your pants off and stay for a while."

He sat on the bed, rubbing her knee through the blankets, wind whistling through his parachute cords. A grin shaped his whisper. "Hey, Rob. That's the best idea I've heard tonight."

He leaned over her, arms framing her shoulders, feeling her heat. She ran light fingers over his face. "Love your laugh lines."

"Absolutely the best."

He yanked the blankets back and slid his hands over her old-satin body. She arched to the touch, pulled his head down beside hers. Glancing, quivery connection, her mouth flitting from his, hummingbird. He rolled down beside her on the mattress, tugging the bedclothes loose, rolling his body up against hers, falling free.

Suddenly she flipped her head to embrace his face, his kiss. Their mouths locked as if in slipstream, firing at the touch, moving on his pent-up pulse. He gripped her silky ass, slid her crotch over his bursting dick. *Ahhh yesss.* . . .

She willed herself to float out on the cadence of those familiar moves, that ballet of their many couplings. Thrusting kisses now, tongue reaching to her throat. Bodies slipping, sliding. Hand pushing hers to his swollen pants.

Squeezing through the cloth oh yes she wanted this wild new feel of him inside her. He sucked in a gasp, arching away from her. She found the zipper, awkwardly tugged, reached in. Out sprang that hard shaft, soft lip. . . .

"Aaahhhh!" He flexed upward, whipping his clothes off with spare, well-remembered moves as she peeled off Grandma Nellie's gown. Low, vibrant whisper: "Great idea, Rob."

He was already moving in his own rhythm as she embraced his urgency. A shade too late, she wondered if the room was bugged. She took him in and molded to his lunge, wrapping her creamy core around him. Milking his ride, sucking at his soul. Suddenly he reared up, cried out, clamped her butt around his explosion—

Done, and she'd only begun.

CHAPTER ELEVEN

January 21st

Robin

Jolting awake around two thirty, Larry heard a light, whiffling snore blending with the creaks of the house. She was sleeping on her back, mouth gaping, arm flung out. He slid carefully out of bed and gathered his clothes, watching to see if she'd stir, hoping she wouldn't. He needed to get clear of her, clear of them all, to hear himself think.

Dim hall outside wrapped in quiet, though snatches of talk drifted from the other end of the house. He tiptoed across, muffling his heartthud in the armload of clothes, feeling like a kid exploring way, way out of bounds.

In the Lincoln Bedroom, a globe lamp threw eerie light on the tortuous carving of the high, gloomy old bed. His pajamas were laid out on the folded-back sheets. He dropped his load on a sofa and pulled out his half-smoked cigar, firing it up in nervous reflex.

It tasted like old tires soaked in stale booze. He stubbed it out and put on his rarely worn pj's—in case that was the way things were done around here, though he'd heard Winston Churchill went buck-naked even in front of the maids.

He prowled the room, strutting a little, maybe to fend off any unwelcome second thoughts. If this wasn't the top of the heap, where the hell would you find it?

For some reason he couldn't recall, Churchill never liked staying in this room. Maybe it was the ghosts. Anyway he ducked the honor when he could. But no wonder, it looked like a turn-of-the-century Omaha railroad hotel. A sad-sack profile of young Abe stared at the bed—like a dare. If you didn't yet believe in his ghost, stick around a while.

Maybe Churchill didn't like the stiff, lumpy mattress. Antique too, you could bet. He didn't sense Abe's ghost. Or anybody else's. But he did wonder if his queasy gut could still be alibied by first-day jitters. Wondered if once he'd settled in, shaking down a little, he might some time sack out in this holy temple of a room without feeling like a cat burglar come in over the roof.

By damn, I made it!

Bravado reminder to chase away the doubts and shadows sifting into him like a bad hangover. He kept thinking of a bullfight he'd once seen in Barcelona. Guy walked out with a bunch of cloth and a blade skinny as a knife and faked out that bull. Two tons of riled-up trouble on the hoof, and the guy'd even turned his back on that animal, turned and walked away because he'd pulled it off.

Now he had his shot. Maybe.

He sat gingerly on the mattress, kneading its lumps. All the ways he'd reckoned over the years on how best to get here, all those constantly shifting grids of possibility—he'd just never figured on this.

He stretched out, pulled the sheet over his chest. "Acting President" wasn't exactly a driver's license. He'd just have to walk out there with it, see what he could do.

Goddam. . . .

Hesitantly, he picked up the bedside phone. A wide-awake male voice instantly snapped: "Yes, sir, Mr. President."

He aimed a cocky grin up at young Abe and asked for a 6 a.m. wake-up call.

When Robin woke he was gone. As if he'd never been there, except for the feel of his body stamped on her bones.

She flipped the bedcovers and found a stain on the bottom sheet, leftover from their mingled juices. She smiled, fighting off flicks of dismay. Feeling more of his juice in her sensitized crotch, still swollen with workout afterglow.

Trying not to feel dumped, abandoned. So maybe she'd hoped for another go this morning, bang-bang start on another busy day, grab the merry-go-round while you can. So what? Better this way, she supposed. She didn't plan to make a habit of him. And she wasn't much up for a rerun of last night—which was all she'd likely get.

Damn odd to climb *down* from a bed. She slipped on her negligee, opened the door and peered down the long, broad hall dimly traced by dawn light. Clear view now to the huge arched window. Before the kids landed, she needed to snatch some sense of where she might fit in here. She slid timidly into that forbidding terrain that suddenly seemed utterly unfamiliar.

Like the yellow Oval Room, her favorate once. Now it looked as welcoming as a Chippendale warehouse. In the master bedroom, the massive four-poster was smothered in glitzy gold drapes. Andy Jackson's old bed, the one Alexis had hauled out of mothballs for Michael.

Larry's room, obviously. Helpful orientation. For her own turf she'd need a quiet corner, preferably as far from here as she could find.

"Can I help you, Mrs. Devlin?"

She spun around on a white-jacketed butler gazing tactfully at his polished shoes. Clutching the neck of her negligee, she babbled oh, no, thank you. "Is it all right to just. . . look around a bit?"

He said surely, ma'am, whatever she wished. She said she meant was she disturbing any Talbotts? He said no ma'am, Mr. George and Mr. Sam had left the house.

"Well, thank you. I woke up early, and I thought. . . ." Already explaining herself to the hired help. Oh, this would be a long, tough day.

Blandly grave, he ordered coffee or tea. She picked coffee and, resisting an urge to run, cruised with stately speed back to her room. She managed to be made up and dressed in a suit by the time a maid brought a tray. "Thanks so much," she chattered, eyeing two small, perfect, pink roses in a silver bud vase. "Put it by the window, please. Oh good, you brought the papers too."

"Yes, ma'am, Mrs. Devlin." With brisk ceremonial moves, the maid simultaneously unfolded the *Washington Post* and poured from a silver pot. "Cream and sugar, ma'am?"

"A little cream, please." Family pics spread over the page. Melissa would love the one of their march up the White House drive, where she looked ravishingly svelte.

The maid hovered, oozing solicitude, asking if she'd slept well. "Yes, thanks. I'm sorry, I don't think I remember your name. . . ."

"Carmen, ma'am. Anything else I can do for you now?" A shy smile lit up the fresh, youngish face, curious eyes behind the granny glasses, tight-bun hairdo.

She asked to be alerted when the children arrived.

☆

She was waiting in the hall when Kilkenny led the boisterous swirl off the elevator. "Hey, Mom, how's it going?" "Jeez, this place isn't as big as I thought." "Where's Daddy?"

"Right here, Mel," he called out, coming down the hall. Wet hair raked to his skull, he looked pretty good for such a morning after. He embraced the kids, saying welcome home, nice to see them on the button for a change. He flipped a wave in her direction—and a cryptic smile. "Morning to you, Rob." His tone briskly cordial, somehow neutral. The sound of a man who'd skipped out in the wee hours.

"Morning yourself, Dev."

They trooped to the dining room, where the festive mood sank under a squad of servants toting silver platters. When Larry made the introductions, she recognized Chief Butler Hamilton from her early-morning foray down the hallway. "Hamilton's the head man around here, so watch your P's and Q's," Larry warned the kids. Hamilton introduced an assistant butler and two maids.

Robin's appetite shrank in the chill realization that they'd seen their last shred of privacy for a while. *But who could live like this?* The kids listened, cowed, silent, as Larry drew Hamilton out about "the normal routine."

She caught Larry's irritated frown when he waved off a third offer of eggs. As he primed the kids with a parting bulletin—". . . regular school day tomorrow, so make the most of today's goof-off time"—his head seemed somewhere else. Off on the high-stakes game he was crashing, she supposed.

He walked out in a flurry of bowing and scraping, muted bells signaling that he was on the move. She opened with, "All right now, kids. Please remember we're guests in this house. I expect you to keep your feet off the furniture and—"

"Sure, Mum," from Jason. "Can we be excused?"

Forget it. She sighed, "Yes, all right."

Clatter of feet, flutter of napkins as the kids instantly vacated the table. She sat there blinking at the fusty old military wallpaper, listening to them pound up and down the hall, wondering if she was already in over her head. . . .

Wondering *since* she was already in over her head, where and when her rescue would turn up.

Presto chango: Hamilton glided back in to ask if she cared to receive the chief usher.

Alexander Fletcher turned up at the family quarters as soon as he decently could after the bells had cued him to the presidential departure—specifically, two minutes. In that brief period the boys were already rampaging like rutting cattle, flinging doors open, calling out dibs on rooms. Their mother welcomed him with a moan: "Oh, Mr. Fletcher, just in the nick of time."

This lot would clearly be no picnic, he thought. Two galloping adolescent boys and a noisy, scrambling dog with claws just right for gouging the parquet. The plump older daughter seemed a trifle shy and withdrawn, although one never knew with girls that age; of course she'd generally be away at college, *deo volente*. . . . And then the wife, an enigma wrapped in mystery wrapped in Irish coloring, all freckles and wild red hair. Reminded him somewhat of Maureen O'Sullivan playing John Wayne's young colleen.

Wheezy with concern, she asked if he had any suggestions on room assignments—precisely what he'd turned up to provide, of course. He quickly steered the boys toward the matching front rooms overlooking Lafayette Park, "used by the Johnson and Nixon girls." The young one picked first—Luci Johnson's old suite. Two minutes later they were arguing over which one had a better view.

Fletcher suggested that the daughter might find more privacy in the smaller rooms on the third floor. Girls these days could be more trouble than boys, but if they had any sense at all, they at least tried to keep their comings and goings clear of the fishbowl glare of the second floor.

The daughter didn't seem to know what she wanted, one way or the other. She kept muttering sotto voce that she wouldn't be here much anyway, so what did it matter.

His main concern was with the mother. An earnest young thing, quite appealing really, her striking cornflower eyes still doing 180-degree sweeps, taking it all in. No Empress Theodora airs to this one; in fact, she had rather a brown-mouse way about her. Unusual for a Devlin. But that sort of humble pie never lasted long around here in any case.

It'd be no bed of roses breaking in this one. He'd start by finding out if she and her husband cared to share a bedroom, or were last night's arrangements the modus vivendi. Rule one for running this house: When in doubt, assume nothing.

He tried a delicate probe: Would the President in all likelihood select the room with Stonewall Jackson's bed? She nodded, "Oh, yes, I think so." No mention of the royal we. No "this will do us nicely."

So he led her down the hall, leaking proprietary pride. "Now several of our First Ladies, including Mrs. Alexis Devlin, as I'm sure you recall, chose this bedroom adjoining the President's." Frowning, she peered into the room, now a den cluttered with Talbott chairs. She shook her head, mouth puckered into a rosebud of distaste, murmuring no no no.

He pressed on, improvising. "Of course, some, like the second Mrs. Roosevelt, preferred the southwest-corner room, which is smaller but well lit, since it has two exposures."

No sale. Meanwhile the boys discovered the third floor and Cupid's bed, a gloriously rococo bow-and-arrow-trimmed four-poster, which they noisily dared their sister to claim. Suddenly the mother called out from the small southeast corner suite, "Mr. Fletcher, are these rooms taken?"

He galloped over, appalled to see she'd lit on the space he joshingly called the attic. The tuxedo couch and armchair were Truman leftovers; the dark buffaloes-and-swans escritoire seemed to fill the tiny sitting room. In the adjoining bedroom old lavender-ribboned wallpaper twined around the pine headboard of an odd-sized bed.

He tried to explain that these third-floor suites were generally utilized for semitransient residents, not suitable for a First Lady. Even the younger boy piped up with dismay, "But this is just a dinky maid's room, Mom."

She called it "quaint," plenty big enough for her. Said she loved the old-fashioned wallpaper and the view of the monuments, right to the river—ignoring the tarpaper roof.

Twangy with distress, Fletcher felt obliged to instruct her a bit on the long-standing tradition of the second floor, insisting he had "no wish to impede your decision, of course, Mrs. Devlin, yet I would—"

Stabbing him with those extraordinary blue eyes, she said, "But of course, Mr. Fletcher." Looking calm and somehow older, not so green. "Thanks for your concern. So please have my things moved up here as soon as it's convenient."

That might be fine and dandy for *her*, but it made a good deal of trouble for Fletcher. Each new family arrived here like an invading horde, spewing chaos, dislodging the delicate harmonies that made this house tick. He must patch the transitions as quickly as he could, weave the functioning of the house back into the seamless garment it must be.

He'd been trying to make her understand since she came into his hands yesterday that the wise course of action now was *try not to disrupt the house*. Yet here was her first decision—a doozie. This bizarre move to upstairs Siberia was bound to stir up talk. Even the mothers-in-law usually lived on the second floor, after all.

So he was perhaps a little harsh on her, a little unrelenting when they sat down for a first working session. Her sharp-nosed assistant, another greenhorn, took notes for her. Like a head counselor breaking in the new camper with a 5-mile hike, he prodded a blitz of decisions from her concerning the boys' schedules, coordinating the carpool, the Secret Service and so on.

He described in some detail their daily consultations, liaison with

the East Wing and kitchen staffs, as well as with the chief butler, and
the systemized bilateral bookkeeping. Delia, the family housekeeper,
would be retained as cook in the second-floor kitchen. A valet would be
provided for the President from the naval staff; the same man could
"serve as masseur to the President and yourself."

Quailing, she said that wasn't a high priority. He pressed. "None-
theless, that beneficial service is available. And if you do not have a
personal maid, I could recommend several candidates from the staff."

"Goodness, I won't need. . . ."

"I think you'll find that service more helpful than you might presently suppose, Mrs. Devlin. Particularly in the care and organization of
your wardrobe and so forth."

He'd tossed her a line through the storm, at least. If she had wits
enough to snatch it.

Suddenly a face floated out of Robin's bewilderment—Carmen, who'd
brought her morning coffee, probably auditioning for the job. Anyway,
the only maid's name she could remember.

With a smile meant to convey yielding, she said she'd bow to his
advice. Perhaps they could try Carmen? He beamed approval. "An
excellent choice, Mrs. Devlin."

She knew he'd been signaling her since yesterday: Make no waves,
madam; stick to the trodden path. She meant to go along as much as
she could, but Alexis had called this guy a magic-maker, gloriously
resourceful, had promised he'd make her life livable in the madhouse.
Yet sitting between him and Sally, Robin felt pummeled from both
sides.

After Fletcher finally left, Sally insisted that Robin show her flag in
the East Wing by touring the First Lady's offices. Robin brought Sean
along for moral support. Coming off the elevator downstairs, they found
Jim Connerty and Brian Ramner waiting like old-buddy guard dogs.

As they marched down the hall, Sally crammed in a briefing on
Norleen Talbott's staff resignations. But Robin was tuned to the questions Sean jabbered at Jim: "Who sleeps here besides us? Who picks
the movies?"

Inside a big office, two dozen women lined up, a patchwork color
guard pit-a-patting wary applause. Filing numbly down the row of hands,
Robin caught few names and fewer titles. Norleen's "girls" looked as
raw and tense as she felt. Must be no treat to see your boss kissed off
with such abrupt dispatch. So Robin put on her Irish wake face, grave,

condoling. But when someone finally blurted, did she by any chance plan on immediate staff changes, Robin realized *that* was the root distress—not nostalgia for Norleen, just panic over the paycheck.

She said dryly that the only thing she'd planned so far was a hot shower before she went to bed.

☆

Back upstairs Robin walked into a domestic tableau in the Oval Room: Melissa leaning over the couch arm, talking to Jason, who was down on the rug wrestling the dog.

Too late, halfway into the suddenly silent room, she caught the vibes. *They're talking about you.* Trapped, honking with embarrassment, she threw herself into a chair. "Gadzooks! Alone at last, away from the madding crowd."

Melissa threw her a withering glance. "Come on, Mother. You don't have to make such a dramatic deal out of this." Jason silent behind an angry, hostile smile.

She sprang up and headed out. There were all too many reasons for her children's unrelenting disapproval, but she couldn't deal with them today. Melissa called guiltily, "Wait up, Mom. How'd it go downstairs?"

She flipped her hand in a later, later gesture.

Up in her corner suite, so much nicer than the gilded barn downstairs, she found her crisply ironed clothes already hanging in the closet. Cosmetics laid out on bathroom shelves; lingerie tucked into dresser drawers. Her address book sat by the sitting-room phone. Anemones, her favorite flower, bloomed on the coffee table. She smiled at that silent evidence of an impeccable house. *As if you'd rubbed a magic lamp.* . . .

The phone rang. An operator asked if she'd take a call from Mrs. Alexis Devlin. Good old Alexis, purring in that throaty, boarding-school drawl, "I just wanted to welcome you to the madhouse. Has Hamilton thrown any tantrums yet?"

Suddenly it all seemed much more manageable. They dipped briefly into yesterday. Alexis had vivid, sarcastic vignettes, mostly about other Devlins, but she wanted mainly to hear about the house. Robin didn't mean to mention her third-floor bedroom, but somehow it slipped out. Alexis zinged back tartly with, "Oh, good stroke, I wish I'd thought of that." She even remembered Carmen, said that must be Carmen Caldwell who used to scrub in the downstairs kitchen. Alexis thought she'd run off to Okinawa with one of the gorgeous Marines, but if she'd been around that long she might make an ideal pipeline for Robin, "Because *that's* what you need right now, dear. Don't fret the budgets and the parties, Mr. Fletcher will see to all that. You mainly have to be concerned with the things he won't ever tell you."

Lord knows Robin agreed with that. Alexis suggested bluntly that she "have a little chat with Carmen some time soon. And meanwhile don't let them make you do a single thing you don't want to. I guarantee you *I* never did."

Robin felt much better after that spark of support from Alexis, the iceberg queen of the in-laws. Face it: Nobody knew what she was going through right now better than Alex.

Feeling like a kid exploring Granny's attic, she poked into the sitting-room cupboards and drawers. All empty, dusted clean. Tugging the string of her curiosity, she roamed out to the solarium, opened a built-in cabinet. . . .

Full quart of J&B, half-empty Gilbey's gin.

She froze, staring at the bottles, hearing a thundering duet:

Just a quickie so you won't come apart.

Shut the door NOW. Just walk away!

Come on back, nobody's looking. Can't manage without your old friend. . . .

One drink could trigger the whole package, instantly consume you. And when did you ever have just one drink?

It'll go much better with just one little pop. . . .

She slammed the door and leaned against it, fighting overwhelming longing. *Help me, lord. There but for the grace of god, therebutforthegraceofgod. . . help me hold on!* Teetering on the cliff edge, in the roaring slipstream. *Just one, just one, so much easier with just one.* . . .

She forced her feet to step away, leaden, tripping on the rug. She made them move toward her sitting room, fighting a riptide: *Come back, come back, your lucky chance.* . . .

She stood at the phone, wondering how to call out on this thing, smoothing her hair with trembling hands. Voices crooned to her hesitation, *Hold off. Not yet. Just a quickie to clear your head.* . . .

She snatched up the receiver. An operator asked if she could help. "Please. I want to call New York. Do I dial direct?"

Disembodied cheer: "Just give me the number, Mrs. Devlin. And welcome to the White House. We're very pleased to have you here."

She rattled off Tish Varner's office number. Static in her head said sit down, relax, but the arched bow of her body stood frozen at attention, circuits scrambled, heart pounding in its tight-drum cage. *Quick quick, come back.* . . .

Strong voice boomed on the phone. "Robin? You there?"

The bow loosened. "Yeah." Her rubber knees collapsed her into a chair. "Tish, I'm so glad you're there."

Tish knew instantly that the shrill, reedy voice came from the high wire. *Already!* Quiet with fear, she asked, "Robin, where are you? Did you slip?"

She said no no, look, she was in her room. "But I just found two bottles out in the solarium."

Frantically weighing the danger level in those few blurted words, Tish asked calmly if she'd opened them.

"No, but I sure *wanted* to. A good stiff belt. . . ." Shaky, gasping from the near miss. "What stopped me was remembering our deal that I call you first."

The nightmare Tish had rehearsed so many times was coming real on the other end of the phone. Barely landed down there, Robin was already head over heels, spun out of control, on the edge fighting off a slip. But for crying out loud, no way, *no way* was this going to work out.

Tish wished she could hug away some of that scared hurt right this minute, tell the poor kid just come back home and forget about that lunacy down there. Instead she got quick whiffley breaths over the phone, as if from a cornered dog.

Hands clenched together as if they were gripping Robin's, Tish looked at the blowup of her on the desk and talked right to those eyes. Briskly, cheerfully, she told her everything was going to be okay. "You're all right, Robin. You stopped yourself and you reached out." Talking her down from the wire, touch light as fingertips. "You did right. You're turning it over. You didn't slip."

"Real close, Tish." Timbre picking up. "But I didn't."

Tish said okay, now would she please put down the phone and get someone to lock up the bottles. "Or dump them down the sink, but I'd rather you didn't get that close."

She said right, she'd do that right after this call. "Really, I'm okay now. Just hearing your voice does the trick."

Those two bottles were hardly a splash in the ocean of booze down there, but they'd do for a start. "Do it *now*, Robin."

Robin carefully put down the receiver and found Carmen gliding down the hall. She said, "Carmen, there are two liquor bottles out in the solarium that shouldn't be lying around. Could you please put them where they ought to be?"

Back on the phone, curled up shoeless on the couch, she apologized for not having called yesterday when so much was going on. Tish said she was more interested in today. "Now look, how're you doing? And give it to me straight."

Robin managed a tight laugh, feeling her body rhythms flow back. "Better, now that I'm talking to you. I heard you debating the demon voices, by the way, thanks very much."

Tish asked what was going on before she'd found the bottles.

She turned the day over in her head like a lit-up globe, finding it "all quite—strange. . . with a few rough moments." She skimmed a mention of "the huge *office* I'm supposed to run." And of her brief run-in with Melissa. "All part of the package, I suppose. But Alexis called and was a big help. Mostly it's gone pretty well, knock on wood. I didn't fall on my buns yet, anyway."

Tish asked if she could get out to an AA meeting. She said she didn't think so. "The whole. . . it's so complicated. I can't go anywhere without. . . well, you know."

Tish made her promise she'd at least make sure *today* that she was properly plugged back into the Chevy Chase ladies' group. Then she added casually it happened she was free as a bird tonight, would Robin like her to pop down?

She said no no, Tish was too busy for that. "Anyway I'm over the hump now, so I really don't need you to bother."

Tish said cut that polite-girl crap, there was nothing higher on her agenda than helping Robin through this. "Have you got that straight, Red?"

She laughed from the gut. "God, Tish. I'm so glad you're there."

Tish grunted that was more like it. The shuttle went every hour; she'd come now if that would help. The one thing she didn't want was Robin toughing this out on her own.

"No, really, I'm fine. Just talking to you helps lots."

"All right. Call any time, day or night. I'll leave forwarding numbers if I'm out. Or call Ron Mathis or Shirley if you can't reach me. Meanwhile remember the most important thing in your world is that you didn't take a drink today."

They traded parting homilies: "Stay in the now."

"Just get through tonight. . . ."

"Right. Don't worry, Tish. I'm okay. I'll get through this in one piece, you bet."

Just to prove it, she called Dennis and asked him to send on the rest of her clothes. Then she called Carmen in for a chat.

CHAPTER TWELVE /

January 21st

Prilla

The *L.A. Times* woman had a lipstick smear on her front tooth. And dog breath that drifted between the two seats—just the sort of thing Priscilla detested about these elbow-to-elbow interviews on the plane. When Dan was president she wouldn't do another airborne interview, except in facing seats, with a table between to fence off the reporter.

Right now beggars couldn't be choosers, so she was doing fifteen minutes with that bitchy L.A. blonde, Deanna Robert. A nemesis since Dan's governor days. It showed how bad things were for them that Priscilla'd even agreed to a sit-down with Robert, after all the wicked hatchet jobs she'd done on them.

Yet now even the home base needed shoring up. So here they were jousting away with lines they both had down pat. Yes, Priscilla was confident that her husband's support around the country was strong as ever. ". . . stronger, if anything. We've had such extraordinary response, such a heartwarming flood of calls and letters." No, it wasn't difficult for her to see someone else take over the First Lady role. "The only title that interests me is Mrs. Daniel Sterling."

The trick was to keep the exchange bland as milk. But with this tootsie you could never trust what she'd do with what she got. Like that goring she'd given Priscilla's hairdressers, and her friends—the whole Group had been in shock for a week. Or the one she'd never, ever forgive: Robert ridiculing the idea of love-at-first-sight for Priscilla and Dan by profiling "a few" of the other women he'd dated after they'd met, in those two and a half years mostly blotted from her mind. *Watch out watchout. . . .*

Robert's face was a flat moon of sympathy today, her voice low with condolence. "To find yourself still working the trail so long after you expected the campaign to be finished," recorder poking closer, crowding Priscilla's narrow space, "that must be quite tiresome for you, Mrs. Sterling."

Tiresome! That pitying word detonated her rage. She struggled not to react, fear reining in her dangerous anger, shielding her from this predatory blondie, all claws behind the feathers. *Tiresome, you say!*

She snapped back, "Of course I'm disappointed, Deanna. Mostly for the country's sake. But any day I spend by my husband's side is a good day for me." In the nick of time, a press aide came down the aisle to bail her out. "Now if you'll excuse me, I think he may need me up front."

Dan finished his own interviews a few minutes later and joined her in their front-row seats, gripping her hand as they came down at Lexington, helping her override the whipsaw anxiety still lashing her at takeoffs and landings, even after all these years in the air. . . .

Tiresome, she thinks!

Robert's unexpected dab of pity, L.A. Blondie feeling sorry for *her*, focused a cruel reality for Priscilla: A day after that criminal farce on the Capitol steps, here they were, flying off to campaign in *Kentucky*. As if any two-bit corner of the country would do for them now. An idiotic bit of scheduling intended to show Dan "back in the saddle again," too late to be changed by the time she'd found out.

The motorcade pulled up at a horse farm famous for Kentucky Derby winners. Talk about sublime to ridiculous. . . . Dan lit up at the sight of "those magnificent animals"; she brooded on Robert's crack.

A half hour later, on the Lexington courthouse steps with a motley bunch of blue-grass fiddlers and elephant cutouts, she took in Dan's pep talk to a thin noontime crowd: "Jonas Pryor's the man I need with me in Washington to help out with a real barn cleaning in that Congress." Already back on the road, back at the white-knuckle flights, ignoring the empty press seats in the 707. Plumping for the two-bit lawyer trying to beat the widow of a drunken Congressman run over on Christmas Eve. "And you know what gets carried out on those shovels. . . ."

Few laughs from the gawkers. The whole trip was an idiotic waste of Dan's time. He should be back in Washington, working on that stalled vote!

Pryor maneuvered him over to the lawn to meet some local brass. Priscilla was tapped by Pryor's drab little wife, popping the buttons on her pea-green coat, and a bunch of twittering women: ". . . just about your biggest fans in Sideview!" "So thrilled to meet you right in person, even prettier than your pictures. . . ." One said she'd kept a scrapbook on her and Dan for "more'n thirty years now." Priscilla purred that he'd be so tickled to hear that.

In fact, she found it horribly depressing to think they'd been at it that long. But there was good political capital in the starlight glow reflected on those faces. One woman murmured, "Such a shining example to our young folks of how a good marriage should work. . . ."

More hope than envy in those liquid, adoring eyes. As if wives of lesser men could feed off her myth, steal some of her magic to pump fresh life into their own withered happy-ever-after fantasies. She knew that was her big hold on them: She was the one it'd all come true for, the one who'd got it all. But this was hard work on three hours' sleep.

She edged back to Dan, compass homing on true north. She nudged him free of the glad-handers, into camera range.

Upstairs in the hotel he did a dozen local-media interviews before a Chamber of Commerce lunch. She stayed in the room for his three-minute radio bits. He was in fine form, hitting his new lines bang on, pitching for "a congressman who'll work that House for the good of the country, not just a handful of Washington politicians."

For the TV takes he sat under a Lincoln portrait, next to a blue vase of red and white roses. The first interview was a remote, questions piped to his earpiece from a Louisville studio. But he couldn't hear them. The sound engineer scrambled as Dan sat in his interview stance, entertaining two print-pool reporters with a reminiscence of '50's live TV: "By gosh, one night my trousers split up the back seam four minutes before we went live coast to coast." *That one again.*

"So I dropped my pants, and the seamstress rushed up with a needle and thread."

Dan stayed cocked for action, smiling at the blue lens, hands gripping the chair. But he let his spirits stretch in these few minutes away from grueling routine. On any unexpected break, his head could slide happily off to ramble through the old yarns he loved to tell. The Gnat said once they came out a bit more polished every time. She might be right about that, but he let them come any way they wanted, and it felt like running in a field of flowers, sun warm on your back.

Sometimes he thought all it would take to make him happy was a constant audience and enough time to spin out every story that was in him. "Touch and go there for a while, you'll excuse the expression, and my director was having a heart attack on offstage right." Fresh embroidery there, but it fit. "I got 'em zipped up again just a few seconds before the red light went on. . . ."

He must have a thousand great yarns from the days of those old live-TV dramas. Relived in the telling, they somehow seemed like the best times of his life. Not one to down-peddle a good thing, he knew by now those nostalgic old yarns added some to his own myth.

That wasn't why he told 'em, though. He did it because he loved to, nothing he loved better, and now somebody was always listening. He could spin those anecdotes Paul called "cockle-warmers" from any period of his life: The football teams. The summer lifeguarding. His first job, on Wyoming radio. The first lucky breaks in Hollywood. The live-TV stuff just happened to be a personal favorite, because so many wacky, unexpected things happened then, and darn if that didn't add up to the best stories.

Crackles like ancient thunder in his earpiece. "Whups! Governor, I think we have it. Can you hear me now?"

Glitch fixed, Priscilla blew him a kiss for luck and went out to the hall. In her own interviews they always tried to ambush her with that golden oldie: How could she possibly be all *that* fascinated, hearing him do the same speech, same stories she'd heard so many times before? She always answered by the book, that she *was* very interested in what her husband said because she learned so much listening to his sound, workable solutions and so on. But she wished just once she could fire back, "I'd sure rather hear his old songs than yours, cookie."

Down the hall Chet Stagg talked to two junior aides. Lightning rod for her sparking anxieties. Impulsively, she beckoned. He came instantly to her side: "Mrs. Sterling. That went well this morning, don't you think?"

She said coldly, "No, I don't. It didn't get us an inch closer to where we ought to be, and I'd like to know how soon something's going to get done about that, Chet."

There it was—the opening Chet had been waiting for. Hushing her with wary agreement, he led her to an empty room where they could talk. Since he'd come aboard for the first gubernatorial run, crackerjack ad man recruited by Phil Laubert, he figured sooner or later she'd come to him.

He just never knew when. Or for what.

She nodded agreement to his closing the door. Hand on the knob, he tried a noncommital feint: "Bit tough to be stuck on the sidelines in this, isn't it, Mrs. Sterling?"

She snapped back, "Of course, that's not the point. What's going on with this highway robbery in the House?"

He'd recognized in his first week on the job, sixteen years back, that she had most of the raw guts in this family. The old man was a good yarner, great on the stump, amazing old guy in many ways, but when it came to fire in the belly the missus had it all over him.

The jam now called for fire and then some. Still he hesitated, weighing his moves. *Don't blow the shot.* . . .

He said cautiously that her husband was getting a lot of conflicting advice: "Every Tom, Dick and Harry's into the act." Her birdy eyes were right on him, drilling. Searching out the answers she'd burn to get. "But that doesn't add up to real muscle on the logjam."

She stared. Suddenly he burst out, "You want my frank opinion? I don't feel we've got a hand on the throttle here." He was talking too much, not listening enough to *her*; but he'd waited so long for this signal, the backup poured out: "We're in a maximum tight spot, and we're not doing everything we could to salvage the Governor's win."

She winced at that "salvage," grabbed at her throat. She never did know just what Chet was thinking. She could count on one hand the times she'd seen real emotion on that blandly handsome face, his permanent tan stretched tight over sharp-angled bones. But she liked his ex-Marine ways, right down to his overgrown blond crewcut. And the military precision he used going after his objectives.

In this long pressure-cooker campaign Chet was one of the few national staffers without a black mark in her book. She hadn't forgotten how he'd squashed a brewing scandal over a nest of pansies on their gubernatorial staff—cleaned that nastiness right out, and the best part was they never had found out how he did it.

The press hadn't found out, either. Sometimes she thought the less they understood Chet, the better off they'd be. The point was he understood her and Dan, better than any of those others. She implicitly trusted him to be absolutely loyal. To do his flat-out level best for Dan.

So she fixed on those cold tiger-eyes, telegraphing her trust. Telegraphing her need. "Well now, somebody'd better start doing something about this mess pretty quick, don't you think, Chet?"

CHAPTER THIRTEEN /
January 22nd
Robin

Robin finally stood up to the Secret Service.

They'd been telling her what to do and how to do it for so long now that she didn't often fight back. But this morning when she'd tried to jog around the White House grounds and discovered they wanted her kept inside like a potted palm, she drew the line: She'd have her run, like it or not.

Jim Connerty had fought on for a while, Boston Irish goat. "Too many crazies and Bombniks out there, Mrs. D." So she agreed to avoid the bare-fenced front lawn. Out in the "back yard," she crunched wide figure-eights in the drifts among the trees behind Larry's office. Finding her rhythm, reaching for ecstasy, she tried to ignore the three agents lumbering in her crisp prints.

She found the tennis court hidden in the pines, winter-lonely in its cold wire lace. She circled it and broke out across the lawn, zigzagging broken-field to the fountain belching graceful antifreeze into the overcast. *Blow, baby, blow!*

Past the spouter she sprinted, long, noisy leaps into virgin crust. Slalom into the trees along the east fence, darting, twinkling around the trunks. Where was John Quincy Adams's old American elm? There at the fork of the drive, huge, towering, its branches rattling a gusty welcome.

Breathless with the beauty of this place, she took a cool-down stroll through the Rose Garden, peeking over at Larry's empty office windows. Behind her, Jim wheezed that if she should be so inclined as to try this again, she'd have to stagger her timing to avoid setting a pattern.

She jabbed his arm, pealing laughter. "Jim, you sly dog. Why didn't you tell me that's such a gorgeous run?"

Still damp from her shower, she personally toted to her East Wing office, over Jim's grumpy protests, a few art works brought in from the house with the boys' jock and electronic gear. "Decided to perk up my walls a bit," she explained lamely to Sally Arnstein.

Sally peered at the red-and-gold temple dancers and elephants marching across black silk. "Very nice, Mrs. Devlin." Politely dubious, as in good god, what next?

"Yes, it really is," Robin agreed, finding a nail for the wood strip anchoring the 4-foot hanging. Should come up with a better way to mount it. Must be lots more valuable now than when she'd discovered it in a Phnom Penh marketplace. "What's so unusual is each thread's dyed separately before the piece is woven. An old Cambodian woman told me it's like the days of a person's life, each one different but made to harmonize with the rest."

Sally dutifully inquired when she'd been in Cambodia. In '63, Robin said, "on an official visit for President Devlin. Just a few weeks before he. . . died."

Face quick-freezing lugubrious regret, Sally said that was "sort of before my time, unfortunately."

Sure, kid. Rub it in, why don't you?

Sally seemed to consider the weaving. . . peculiar. Par for the course. She couldn't see it as a miracle relic of a Shangri La country ravaged since by war, pestilence, starvation—all the awful stuff Sally's head was well trained not to grasp. Yet the silk parade made that distant, magical place a shade more real to Robin at least. She hung up two more gleanings from the same trip, a Balinese batik and a primitive Indonesian oil. The effect was patchy, but her stamp to the room. "Okay, enough decorating. What's up today?"

Sally proposed combining two items: action footage for NBC on a Devlin White House feature and the chef's request of a menu review before tomorrow's diplomatic reception. Taping her meeting with the chef might "fill the bill nicely."

Robin questioned such a contrived setup, said she never trusted eavesdropping cameras. But Sally insisted the NBC piece was "a top priority for the President. As long as you're declining interviews, the kitchen tour might satisfy NBC. President Devlin's eager to project a reassuring image of continuity and leadership in the White House."

Robin noted how easily "President Devlin" rolled from that mouth. How in hell did a kitchen look-see convey "the Devlin administration firmly in charge"?

Yet an hour later she came to the cavernous kitchen in a swirl of agents and staff, TV lights blazing on white tile walls. Sally introduced

Shana Locke, a Barbie blonde with hard-coal eyes who "understands the ground rules, Mrs. Devlin. No questions, they'll just roll tape."

Pearson, the porky head chef, in crackling starched whites from head to foot, trotted her around his turf like a Vegas pit boss, playing to the cameras—spinning copper bowls on marble counters, flicking knives like fencing swords, boasting about the garden party once prepared for 300 ABA-convention lawyers, "but President Eisenhower brought two thousand home with him instead. That was one occasion when the kitchen ran short of food. . . ."

She hated pretend-the-camera's-not-there, but Pearson had his tour down pat and didn't mind hogging the lines. She trailed him awkwardly, asking lame questions as he pressed tastings on her—a sliver of paté, a puffy hors d'oeuvre "which I might recommend for the diplomatic reception."

Grabbing her cue, she asked shyly what else he'd suggest for that event. He snapped off a salute, sucking in wind. "If you'll permit me, Mrs. Devlin. . . ."

It came out like a soaring *Fidelio* aria. When he stretched the single breath all the way to "strawberries Romanoff and *coupe marron glacé* with petit fours sec," she broke into applause. "Bravo, Mr. Pearson!"

He tossed off sotto voce that dishes would also be available "as Mr. Bill Wilson preferred." The AA code name, which she devoutly hoped wouldn't go coast to coast. Now he was riffing on various First Ladies' buffet-menu favorites: "Mrs. Johnson liked steamship rounds of beef and whole hams. . . jelly molds for Mrs. Eisenhower. . . I'm told Mrs. Truman was partial to cake, cookies, chocolates and punch."

Flashing on old Bess Truman's Secret Service detail in Independence, she looked across the room—and saw Jim Connerty. Those shadowing guards she'd have now for. . . the rest of her life.

Hurtled through a trapdoor, tumbling, voices shrieking: *DRINK! You need a drink! Can't get through THIS without your old friend's help. Never, never make it. . . .*

CAMERAS ON; REMEMBER THE CAMERAS!

Panicked into overdrive, she numbed enough of her shock to keep her moving, face locked on freeze, praying she'd get out of this without unraveling. Fighting for calm, choking on the urge for blotto blotto BLOTTO, she waited out her exit lines, a windup round of handshakes and thanks: "Good to meet you. . . so grateful. . . ." *Off, enough, turn them off!*

At the waiting elevator, gasping with release, she waved off Sally and rode up by herself, huddled against the wall. Nauseous, woozy with thirst, muttering her mantra to drown out the crackling: *Just one, who's counting, you know how much you need it. Just one little nip. . . .*

She snatched up her sitting-room phone to call New York. "Tish? Oh god, it happened again and I'm coming apart, I can't stop, Tish, I want it so bad. . . ."

Tish took in that shrill, keening wail about a trapdoor, who could live a whole life like this. . . .

Twelve-nineteen on her watch. If she left right now, with luck she might catch the one o'clock. "Robin, now calm down and listen to me. Just tell me what happened."

She got the gist of the babbling: SOS, crash dead ahead. If she left now it would take two hours minimum to get there, and Robin needed someone with her right now, this minute. Tish tuned to the frantic teetering in that voice. "Robin, you're all right. You'll be all right. Slow down and catch your breath, you're okay, buddy." Maybe Shirley or Ron could hold her on the line, keep her talking until Tish got there.

Sounding suddenly much calmer, Robin asked, "Tish, did you mean it that you could fly down tonight after work? Because I. . . just really want to see you."

Tish cravenly decided she could salvage her afternoon appointments and still play hero on the six o'clock shuttle. Rapping her desk with crossed fingers, she said good enough, just hang in there, kiddo, she'd be down in a few hours.

The voices were gone when Robin hung up the phone. They always went quiet around Tish. But her gut was still ripped. Not quite drink signals, but churnings, lashings—terror. Anxiety. Rage. Agitated, she paced the room, slapping her thighs, looking out on the tarpaper view. *Trapped.*

Smack-dab, utterly trapped. And unbearably alone. Abruptly unplugged from the life she knew, marooned with all her fears for company.

A face floated in her head. An old Marymount classmate, now a *Washington Post* reporter. She'd noticed Stephanie buried in the press pack a few times; her impulse always was to call her over for a hoot about the whole business. Loaded idea, which she dutifully pushed from her mind. *Blotto, blotto, who's got the blotto. . . .*

Yet maybe if she reached past these damn walls to ground her fears, reconnect with someone from the life she'd lost. . . . She sifted her agitation, trying to heft the dangers in that idea. *Dammit, why not?*

Stephanie Mayo's beeper went off as she drove over the Q Street bridge. She double-parked and called in on the pay phone screwed to a deli wall, feet stamping against the cold. The *Post* operator said, "Okay, Mrs. Mayo, hang on for the White House," and patched her through.

Seconds later: "Stephanie? Hi, lady, how're you doing?"

She sagged against the wall, limp with disbelieving ecstasy. Saying as casually as she could, "Hey, great to hear from you! Congratulations and all that."

Robin said the congratulations belonged to somebody else, but anyway thanks for the thought.

No clue to why she'd called. In the racket of a passing truck Stephanie blurted impetuously, "How's this for coincidence, I was just on my way to your old P Street house to see if I could poke out a story." All she could think to add was so let's get together, but that would blow her whole hand. She tried instead, "So how're you doing, anyway?"

"Well, I thought maybe we might talk about that. . . ." The hesitant voice picked up briskly. "So why don't you drop by for a spot of tea, or whatever."

Stephanie managed to say calmly, "A smashing idea, which I do believe I could fit in." She drove hammer-down to 1600 Pennsylvania, patching her makeup at the red lights. *Get in and take your chance, before Robin thinks twice.*

The East Gate guards already had her name. As she set off the metal detector, she realized she and Robin had started out more or less as campus equals, peers, although Robin was even then cruising in Larry Devlin's hot red Olds '88 convertible, while Stephanie was dating Mario, the Sicilian bartender who parked his motorcycle in his bedroom.

Granted, it must've been no picnic being married to an annual contender for Swordsman of the Senate, that brutally-competed-for honor. But a few good perks came along with the deal, at least, starting with this latest change of address. *Family elevator!* She'd been trying since LBJ's reign to get a ride in this odd little box.

The doors opened on a freckled, peanut-butter-colored butler, bowing, reeking of suspicion. And behind him, Robin in slacks and a sweater that matched her eyes—laughing, shaking her head as if to ask why in blazes she was doing this, saying, "Stephanie, so good to see you."

Robin's hearty handshake was meant to fend off the sticky familiarity of an old-school embrace. As their hands pumped, she wondered if her visitor picked up on that.

"Good of you to have me, thanks," Stephanie said jauntily. Trim little bundle of energy, looks holding up nicely. Snazzy dresser, lumberjack reflexes in Ann Taylor suits. "Actually I've seen quite a lot of you lately. But. . . ."

"From the pack. Righto, let's not count that." They shared a nervous, tentative laugh, Stephanie making 360-degree sweeps of the hall as Hamilton peeled off her coat. They agreed it was nice to be able to *talk* for a change.

Robin took her to the small den tucked above the portico, the least pretentious nook she could find. But Stephanie muttered oh, this must be Norleen Talbott's upstairs office.

She bristled warily. "Well, it's nobody's office now." Poke of warning on Mayo's grasp of details: *Assume there's zip she doesn't notice.*

With shy, ice-breaking chatter about their kids, they wove in strands of all they'd been through together, school to babies to marital splits. At college they'd moved in different crowds—dormmates, not buddies. But since Robin had come to D.C., they'd lunched occasionally, trading insights on what Mayo called "this uniquely whacked-out town." Robin sometimes teased her, called her the Keeper of the Keys; Stephanie thought Reader of the Chicken Guts put it better.

By the ground rules Stephanie always respected, they talked first as friends before going "on record." Even when Robin was boozing, half-ripped when they talked, Stephanie was fair in what she wrote, thank god. For instance she never mentioned that she'd brought Robin to her first AA meeting, on Capitol Hill. It didn't take, but at least Steph had tried—and kept her mouth shut.

When Stephanie finally steered the talk back to the present circumstances, Robin muttered vaguely that this place "turns you into some kind of totem, some nun. All this First Lady, First Family flapdoodle they lay on you—you might as well live in the cloister."

Whatever Stephanie'd come up here expecting to hear, it wasn't nun talk. Robin looked pretty good, looser, easier than when she was out swimming against the pack. Yet she seemed a bit—dizzy. Spacey, her smile bent. Lonely. Jittery.

Stephanie brought up the last time they'd gotten together like this, in February for a *Redbook* interview in Robin's apartment, and how articulately, even movingly Robin had talked then about "that rough campaign and all that."

Robin moaned. "Was that when the ghastly one-liner. . . ?"

"You mean, 'If you think maybe your—'?"

"Yes! Right!" Robin snapped, obviously not caring to hear the whole chorus about husbands playing around. "You know, that damn thing's still being quoted. You owe me a big one for that, Stephanie."

It pissed Robin off to see that mollifying smirk. The laugh was certainly on her; they both knew she couldn't offload any blame for the pearls rashly spilled in these "talks." Yet here she was back at the risky jousting, fending off Mayo's disarming flattery: "But we all thought you were a star performer on the trail. Very self-assured, very together, not just about the campaigning but—"

"But how I felt about my husband's alleged philandering, for instance. And was *that* why I drank—which I certainly shouldn't've talked about on record, Steph."

Stephanie tried to insist that showed terrific guts, not to mention insight.

"Hardly!" Robin waved off that bit of sop. "One thing you learn when you really sober up, you know, is to stop using handy excuses to comfort yourself with one more drink. Because we've all got excuses, and they're not why you drink. You drink 'cause you're a drunk: simple as that."

Stephanie said how much she'd always admired Robin for talking up with more guts than any other political wife in town. Shaking her head, Robin called that one more bad habit she'd like to break: "I wish now I'd never said lots of those things—especially when I was still drinking. But once it's out, as *you* know, they never let you forget."

As Mayo rehashed how proudly, even eloquently Robin had defended Larry and the issues he was fighting for, Robin got up and moved to the window, incredulous she'd been so naive, so taken in. Outside more pickets were parading than yesterday. One banner read, PRESIDENT DAN STERLING'S WHITE HOUSE.

Quietly, fiercely, she said, "Steph, there's some kind of fire-storm building out there. I don't know what, but I feel it so strongly, some breaking apart." She wheeled around. "This is strictly off the record, understood?"

"Of course!"

"Well, you make sure. Anyway, I think it's happening all over, not just in this country. But it's as if nobody. . . they just stand up for the cameras rattling off the old speeches, sermons. Gassing on 'the issues.' As if that could stop it from coming."

"Ah, yes."

"God, don't misunderstand what I'm saying." She glimpsed herself in a fish-eye mirror, bulging, mushroom faced. "The point is—I have great respect for Larry. I think he's more likely to come up with answers, if there are any, than men like Talbott. Or, heaven help us, Sterling." Smouldering glance. "Stephanie, so help me, if you quote me. . . ."

Coconspirator smile. "Perish the thought."

"Anyway, with all that's happened, I don't want to find myself turned into some starry-eyed media princess. If I can help it, I'd like very much for that not to happen."

Stephanie said, at the risk of sounding crassly insensitive, did it matter, really, *how* they painted her? "Because it's all just sideshow anyway, isn't it? A little First Lady do-wop to go with the main act."

"Yes, it does matter. To me," she said flatly. For a moment she wavered, dead reckoning. Then, trusting her instinct, she plunged: "By the way, we can go on record if you want. I trust you not to twist anything I say, use it out of context. And clear any direct quotes with me first."

Startled, Stephanie pulled out her recorder. "Thanks. Agreed." She gulped. "Ahh—what's it like?"

Robin veered skittishly off into the legendarily marvelous White House staff, that really did make you feel "like part of some enormous family."

Sly interruption: "Speaking of family, last time you waffled on whether you and your husband were over the separation. All you said was you'd live here if he won."

"Well, as you can see. . . ." She waved at the walls.

Stephanie said despite the presumed happy reunion, one had to wonder if that wasn't maybe more geography than. . . .

Robin knew the easy answer was a quick denial: "Obviously we're back together." Easy, safe. Expected. Yet. . . . She looked at the ashtray, bristling gold presidential seal. If Larry proved right about "just a couple of days," she knew she'd regret this tea party. But she had no faith in her imminent deliverance—and she still had to live with herself.

Quietly: "I did promise that I'd live here if he won. And that's the promise I'm keeping."

"You mean, you're, in effect, still separated?"

"I mean just what I said. I'm here because I'm keeping that promise."

Stephanie asked if she found "all this alleged romance revived by the heady White House air somewhat—offensive?"

"Inaccurate, at least. An inaccurate description of our present circumstances."

CHAPTER FOURTEEN /

January 22nd

Prilla

As Phil Laubert's Caddie hardtop rolled up the drive, he saw Prilla at the barn door, flagging him down, pointing him to a parking space by the barn while she waved off a pair of agents bearing down on him.

He unfolded his long frame from behind the wheel with slow, stiff moves meant to communicate the discomfort of his drive. Standing firm by the door, she trilled, "Philip, dear, so good of you to drop by!"

Turf war going on here, he assumed. He hesitated, swaying slightly toward the house, as if tugged to Dan. Then he drawled, "Pleasure's entirely mine, Prilla, as usual," ambling over to deliver a stiff embrace.

Good old Prilla, running true to form. He wondered how much finagling it took her to set up this "accidental" collision. Fact is, he wanted a few words with the old gal himself. He knew pretty much to the bottom line what he'd get from his session with Dan: corny jokes and some rambling yarns, wrapped in a booster dose of we-can-do-it. But Prilla tended to see things with a more acid, more brutally pragmatic eye, if you could get her to admit it.

That acid view was what interested Phil right now. He told her she looked lovely as ever. Wincing, sighing at that bald lie, she dabbed self-consciously at her hair. "Aren't you sweet to say so. And how's your darling Suzy?"

"Bearing up well, all things considered, and she sends her love."

"Well, you be sure to tell her how much I miss her." She tucked her arm into his, maneuvering him into the tackroom, saying she was so glad to have this chance to talk to him before he saw Dan. Nervous, fluttery as a Georgia belle, although his private name for her was Mrs. Steel.

She asked if he'd heard the good news about their man winning the New Jersey recount. He said he'd caught it on the car radio, good news indeed. His eyes heavy with reproach as he added dryly, "One down, eight to go, Prilla."

Chin jutting, she said well, it broke the darn logjam, anyway, and they were trying to get the new man sworn in before this afternoon's vote. He grunted, pipe poked between his teeth, and asked if she had anything else on her mind. Not altogether sure he wanted to hear it.

She said as a matter of fact she did. "Not that I mean to butt in, Phil, but I'm just so terribly concerned. . . ."

"As are we all, Prilla." Prickly with dread, he waved her on with an impatient gesture: She'd say Dan was out of it, couldn't hack the pressures, the jig was up. . . .

She said she thought maybe he and Dan might get around to discussing staff changes.

Staff changes! Hell's bells, that bullshit!

And he'd been about braced for World War III.

She caught the slight flicker of disdain rippling over the stone face. Let him sneer, let him sniff. Dan would be president, after all. Why for pity's sake should she still tiptoe around Phil Laubert, so fearful of crossing him?

Yet she needed something from him now: her ticket back into the game. For once her timing had worked just right when she caught him driving up. But Phil didn't make it easy. . . .

She patted her chest and plunged on: Surely some kind of staff shake-up was overdue. Lately she'd questioned some of Paul Tighe's judgment calls. Maybe Paul had outlived his usefulness. But she was mainly troubled by the whole business about Dave Elliott—all the time Dan was spending with him, all the one-sided input he was getting.

Perk of interest. "Oh, yes? How so?"

She shrugged. "Phil, I just don't know how far we can trust that man. I'm not sure he has Dan's best interests at heart. He's not one of us, doesn't talk our language. Oh, he's great on House yarns and all that, but where's his bottom-line loyalty in all this. . . mess?"

Point well taken, he allowed.

She said all she wanted was for Dan to find the right people, right strategies to straighten out that blasted Congress. "But I'm not at all sure Elliott can pull that off, even in the three months he says it'll take."

He watched her closely, arms folded, pipe twitching in his jaw. Always playing his cards so close to the vest she wouldn't know for sure what he was thinking. But she did know she needed him with her on this.

She asked how confident he was they were getting the best possible input on the House. He hedged. "Well now, Prilla, if you've got a better mousetrap in mind. . . ."

She said the approach they needed was to use a real loyalist, someone who knew Dan's thinking A to Z, knew how to use his strengths. They needed a team perspective. "So we can trust what we hear about what's going on there, Phil. Before we lose any more time!"

He knocked his pipe, scattering dry ashes. "Matter of fact, Prilla, I've had questions myself on that score. You're right to speak out, and I value your confidence."

She spilled her relief in grateful purrs. "Phil, you know how loyal Dan is to his people. Maybe *too* loyal sometimes. But we can't afford any more slipups. We need the best damage control available, bar none, the A-one best."

He asked if she had anyone in mind to fill the bill. She said well, maybe someone like Chet Stagg. "Someone from 'the family.' If you're familiar with how Chet's come through for us in every pinch, never once let us down—well, of course you are! He's your man, after all, isn't he, Phil?"

Teeth bared in a smile, he agreed Stagg was "one of my original recruits, at least." That was the gamble, weak link in her plan: Chet was Phil's boy first—and maybe last. She couldn't count on undivided loyalty; Phil never let go of his people. Tricky sharing, but in the present mess she'd have to take her chances.

"He sure was! So we have you to thank for his sixteen good years of troubleshooting." She reminded Phil it had been *his* idea to turn Chet loose on that nasty little nest of gays in Dan's gubernatorial office, and look how beautifully that got handled. She'd like to see Chet have a bigger piece of this critical action now, didn't Phil think?

He made a noncommittal rumble.

She blurted rashly, urgently, "I don't even know what's happening to us, Phil. We need someone like Chet in place to find out. We can't let this slip away now."

Crisply, Phil said as he headed for the door, "Rest assured, my dear, I've no intention of letting that occur."

☆

Dan and Phil spent a few hours closeted in the den. She stayed out of it; she'd said her piece already to the powerful, enigmatic man who was her prime rival as Dan's number-one adviser. She didn't entirely trust Phil Laubert—didn't trust his perceptions of her. But she'd use him any way she could, to fit her own intricate needs.

After Phil left she trailed Dan to their bedroom, knowing he'd decide to "catch forty winks." Knowing he'd ask, "You joining me, hon?"

"Yes, all right." He hated to nap by himself. As he kicked off his boots, she asked how the talk with Phil had gone.

Pretty good, he yawned, rambling on about the direct mailings and the soft-money drive. Then: "Phil thinks maybe we're relying too much on Dave Elliott. He'd like some of our own fellows more involved in that House situation."

Aha. . . .

Shaking the extra blanket over him, she said carefully, now there was an idea, what did he think?

"Well, I dunno." He stirred restlessly. "By gosh, Dave's sure a team player. Got a darn fine head on him, and he's been a good ambassador to that three-ring circus on the Hill." He liked that line he'd coined about Elliott so much that by now he was fighting the Washington bureaucracy with "loyal ambassadors" spread around town.

"But he's not the only one, don't forget." Head tucked in his shoulder, she stroked his chest. "It might be time for a new approach, now that we're finally moving. Danny, I'm so happy about New Jersey!"

Drowsy chuckle. "Yep, that's sure good news. But I don't much like changing horses in midstream. . . ."

Minutes later she slipped slowly, carefully from his flaccid embrace and went back to her desk. "Dear General and Mrs. Trent, Dan and I were so pleased by your telegram. . . ."

Timing. So much was timing now. And momentum. That wasn't cutting Dan's way either. They'd counted so much on New Jersey, it was already discounted, and nothing else was breaking for them. Control unraveling more every day. . . .

She woke him in time for the evening news, rattling a rum collins next to his ear. He said groggily, "Thanks, sweetie. That hits the spot."

She perched on the bed, stirring her ice cubes, watching him rub the sleep from his tired face. "Good nap?"

"Yep, I guess." Distracted musing: "Maybe Phil's right about counting too much on Dave. Might stir up the organizational pot a little. . . ."

Decided, then! "That's fine, Danny," she said brightly. "Dave can still work with the team—you just don't need to spend so much time with him." She'd see to *that*. Elliott would be eased out with breakneck speed. "You don't want him to go away mad, but I'm all for a fresh approach."

She asked who he was considering for the slot. He said maybe Chet was worth thinking about. She lit on that. "Oh, good idea, let's get Chet in there pitching. He's utterly loyal—look at the big financial sacrifice he's made to stay with us so long. And he knows advertising, he knows media and politics. I think he's got some good ideas for moving on that House."

They watched the news with Paul and Ezra, NBC leading with the New Jersey recount: Kent Braithwait, a 47-year-old insurance broker from Bayonne, newcomer to national politics, "squeaked through this contested election on the Sterling coattails." She stood behind Dan's chair, kneading his shoulders as Braithwait came on, puffy-proud, claiming "high honor and privilege to cast my first vote for the man who'll lead this great nation back to strength and prosperity. . . ."

Dan said happily, "By gosh, I want to call that fella and thank him personally. Paul, can you get on that?"

"Yes, sir, Governor. Right away."

As Paul grabbed the phone, Roger Mudd said from the screen, "Now for a contemporary version of a true-life Cinderella story, here's Shana Locke at the White House with our first 'acting' First Lady, America's new sweetheart, Robin Devlin. . . ."

CHAPTER FIFTEEN /

January 22nd
Robin

As the novelty of the setting wore off, Tish Varner's worries fluttered home to roost.

Arriving at the fusty gilded barn, she was enormously relieved to find Robin looking like her breezy old self, flipping out jokes about "all the starch and flapdoodle." Obviously not *en pleine crise*. When they holed up with a juice pitcher in an egg-shaped room furnished like a small museum, Robin promptly sat in front of the lit fire and flexed her hamstrings. Seeing her splayed out in this postcard setting, so natural and nonchalant, somehow defused the worst of Tish's qualms. So the queen also shits on Sundays and Robin had moved to the big house. So what else was new?

On Tish's urging, Robin ran down on the day's events. The kitchen episode struck her as legitimately disturbing but no huge deal. Nothing Robin wasn't already aware of. Tish wasn't troubled by tricks of perception so much as by the reality of the shark pool in which Robin presently floated.

Hearing about the chat with the reporter friend, Tish prickled alarm. In Robin's present fix, a chat with Stephanie Mayo was courting major trouble—yet she'd invited her here almost casually, Jaws to the fishbowl.

Robin tossed her head. "She asked if I had any First Lady projects in mind, how's that for originality." Robin was into her hoity-toity Empress Josephine routine, acting unique, fantasizing control of an uncontrollable situation. "But I certainly wouldn't take on anything like Norleen. So organized, I mean."

"Mm-huh." Josephine à la Catherine the Great, flying high on grandiosity. Tish asked mildly, "Did she, for instance, ask if you and your husband are acey-deucey again?"

Robin resisted the stringing of the beads. Yes, Stephanie had pried a bit into the split. Robin said she hadn't expected that. Prodded by Tish's glare, she added, "Okay, so I should've known she would." More faintly: "Or maybe I did know, up front. . . ."

Tish slapped the couch, saying she wished she had a tape of this, if Robin could just hear herself—"Do you realize you're kiting on a dry-drunk right now?"

Flinching from the accusation, Robin said come on, don't make a federal case out of one lousy interview.

"Robin, I recognize your sound. Like an emotional voiceprint. And I hear an angry, volatile, self-centered woman coming on like a drunk." Tish ticked off the alcoholic reflexes at work: flying off the handle at situations, acting grandiose, less than honest—with herself or anyone else.

Hotly: "You think I'm lying to you? Dammit—"

"Yes, to me, but more important, to yourself. Just mull over why you chose to unburden yourself to a *Post* reporter, of all people. You think it helps your situation to splash your marriage problems all over the press?"

Robin muttered that after NBC's hose job on her tonight, Cinderella in the big house, she was almost glad she'd talked to Stephanie: "It's hard enough holding this together without a fantasy romance wrapped around my neck. So Mayo got my version of this Wonderland scenario. You give me crap for thinking I'm unique, but dammit, Tish, this whole mess is unique. And I'm just trying to keep my head above water."

Tish reminded her how much her sobriety had cost her—mad years of pain, withdrawal, crying jags. Daymares, nightmares, endless overnights with the shakes and jeebies. That horrific night-blinding she once got driving back from Philly. If she slipped, she'd have to go through all that again. "Take my word for it, your disease is progressing right alongside your sobriety. It'll be that much harder to come back. Do you need to hear the tapes?"

Tapes rescued from Tish's answering machine, the desperate calls from Robin's slip three years ago: "Can't stop. I tried and tried and I can't. . . ." "Robin! Slow down and listen. Just listen to me. Ask the bartender where you are." Strangled weeping. "Oh god, I can't stop. . . ."

No, she did not want to hear the tapes. Or the rest of Tish's nag. She knew she'd never survive another drying out—the boozing, maybe, but not the sobering up.

Her long face sculpting concern, Tish suggested that she consider whether she'd put herself in a risky situation beyond her grasp. "Maybe you're not able to *be* the wife of a president, Robin. If you're endangering your sobriety, you not only have the right to leave, you *have* to do it."

That again!

"No, no, no." Flexing backward on the curl of that unwelcome thought, she said she couldn't bug out now, she'd promised Larry she'd stick for the duration. Assuming he still wanted her around after. . . . Anyway, despite the SOS call, she hadn't thought about a drink for hours.

Tish asked about present stresses, especially "the social obligation bit." Robin wandered into rumination on how often she'd tried to crank up for some event by taking a few belts, sometimes passing out wherever she fell. "A few times in the kids' rooms. God, what I put them through. . . ."

"Look, I don't have to ask if you want a drink right now."

Sad smile. "Yeah, but this is the hardest since a long time, Tish." She *knew* she might be dead today without AA. She accepted that she couldn't ever drink again. "But when the heat's on, how can I cope, that snake's still hissing in my ear: Why not one little quickie?"

She'd go to the Chevy Chase meeting tomorrow. "But I can't talk to those nice dimply ladies like to you, Tish. I can't drop my guard, open up at all." Tish said go anyway and she'd be there for backup.

They talked briefly about Melissa, the fragile, clinging child once so close to Robin that her family nickname was Shadow. Now a porky, anxious young woman, full of pain, conversing with her mother in "polite jokes. Always skating the thin ice between us." She'd caught a look from her today. "I swear she was almost. . . afraid of me, somehow."

Tish steered her back to the functioning of the house, the reassuring routine. Robin passed along Alexis's advice on the must-do First Lady duties. "She wound up doing exactly what she wanted. She says don't forget you can always say no."

"Damn right!" Tish beamed. "That goes for the whole package. If you can't cut it here, get the hell out."

Chin out. "I'm not quitting, Tish."

Then, short of walking, she had alternatives. "Structure your days. Only schedule X and Y, that's it."

Robin looked into that chiseled, caring face, her lifeline out of the long nightmares. Gut knot loosened, somehow manageable, she sighed, "Tish—thanks. For everything."

Tish grunted. "Okay, that's more like it. And remember, I'm as close as the nearest phone."

Before the kids came home to shatter the mood, she took Tish out on the Truman balcony to sample the rare view of the monuments— lit-up flags dancing around George's dappled needle, Tom snug under his dome. Shivering, Robin mused about how often she'd driven past those memorials, "never thinking I'd ever be living with this view of them. But here we are. . . ."

Palms pressed to the cold rail, she looked down at the fountains spouting, glowing on the darkened grounds. *Rapunzel, Rapunzel, let down your hair. . . .*

Tish had it all wrong: She was safer in here. She couldn't leave this refuge now without screaming sirens, TV, all the rest. She'd be a prisoner of this mythic fortress till the siege was done—but outside would be worse.

Abruptly, she said maybe she'd "try to make something of this, somehow. Instead of just—muddling through."

Tish hugged her brusquely, pounding warmth back into her cold arms. "If you say so, Josephine. But first let's make it through the night."

CHAPTER SIXTEEN /
January 23rd
Prilla

The script of the rush commercial called for Priscilla and Dan to hold hands on the couch by a crackling fire. Whoever came up with that lulu hadn't reckoned on the heat of flaming logs and TV lights in an old-barn house with no air conditioning, so they sweltered while Dan sawed away at lines from a second-rate civics-class lecture: ". . . don't intend to let this handful of partisan politicians challenge the sacred legitimacy of our electoral process. . . ."

No time for rewrite before the saturation airing tomorrow night, so she swallowed her objections. She was doing a lot of that lately, declining to point out stupidities or miscalls she'd've pounced on a few months ago. Just when she most needed it, she'd lost her sure instinct for how they should move. All she sensed were nagging worries, fretful doubts—the pinpricks she tried so hard to keep from Dan.

He grumbled that his lines "read like a mouthful of cabbage." She squeezed his hand and told him never mind, he'd give it that old magic touch.

He did fine in the run-through, but on the first take he fluffed "sabotaging." She purred encouragement as they set up again: "You'll zip through like butter this time, hon."

In this supposedly wintry scene her face prickled with heat from the roasting blaze. *Got to crank up that staff! No more sloppy third-rate work, inexcusable.* . . . Nothing seemed to go right these days, not one blasted thing.

The second take he aced down to the closing pitch, to "let those

Congressmen know by your calls, cards and telephones that you—darn! Did I just goof again?"

Inane discussion over "telephones" versus "telegrams" while the makeup man blotted their shine. Waiting out their cue again, she whispered fiercely, "Break a leg. This time you'll get it perfect, sweetie!"

Hum of tension in his grunt. She gripped his hand, willing sixty perfect seconds. "Good evening, my fellow Americans. . . ."

CHAPTER SEVENTEEN /
January 23rd
Robin

Robin was startled by the rush, squirt of pleasure tickling through her as Jim Connerty drove a blessedly anonymous blue Ford through the West Gate into traffic, two unmarked Secret Service cars riding shotgun fore and aft. She breathed deeply, gulping in free air, looking out on the feast of ordinary streets. *But is this trip really necessary?*

It felt like first-day-back-to-kindergarten after having the measles. Or mumps. She fought off a fit of jitters, like she always did going to Bella's. She'd even trade this glorious ride if she could wriggle out of it, but Tish said don't you dare. . . .

At a red light the skinny man parked beside them did a double take on her. He gestured, mouthing, Are you really?

Smiling, she waggled her fingers. Nodded slightly.

Jim said edgily, "Hey please, Mrs. D."

She sighed. "Yes, boss." A random memory: Bella Spelvin in red satin at a Senate do, old Dixie belle hissing an invitation to a "meeting." Knocked for a loop when it dawned on her Bella meant a meeting for *drunks.* That shocked her into another resolution to definitely cut back, tamp down her boozing for a while. But go spill her guts in Bella's fuddy parlor? Not bloody likely.

Bella's husband Walt was still an Oregon senator then, so Robin kept bumping into them, and Bella kept inviting her to drop by and check out the pol-wife group. One night when Robin had keeled over into an elaborate bank of French Embassy flowers, Larry'd told her later he'd been ready then and there to take off and leave her in the plants, give up on her for good. But Walt picked that moment to tell him she'd come out of it "when she's ready, same as Bella did."

He threw that up to her later, when she was busy throwing up herself, into the blue john. Somehow that odd bit of insight penetrated her fog. Or maybe she just realized that Larry meant it, this was his last stab at shaping her up. . . .

Anyway she went to a meeting. Not as bad as she expected, so she went back a few times a month. Didn't dent her drinking much, or persuade her she had a permanent, disabling disease like polio. But it did set the hook. When she moved to New York that fall Bella passed her on to Tish's group. Later, much later, after Robin had finally broken through her own walls, Tish told her she could probably thank Bella and the pol-wives for that crucial start.

So in a real way this did feel like coming home. Her jitters peaked as she spotted the yellow stucco sprawled behind high hedges, Bella waving from the back porch, calling, "Y'all welcome back!"

Poop-deck bosoms under a riot of blue curls. If Robin could invent her own grandmother, she'd want one just like Bella. She ran up the steps, laughing, "Hello there, lady, fancy meeting you here."

"Robin darlin', it's so good to see y'all again," Bella crooned, folding her into the pillowy tits. Nudging her reassuringly toward the kitchen door, she said, "Now y'all should remember most of us, I think. . . ."

Robin only recognized three of the nine women in Bella's paneled library. A younger mix now, not so much blue hair. All trying very hard not to make a fuss.

Her nerves steadied with the opening prayer: God grant me the serenity to accept the things I cannot change, the courage to change the things that I can, and the wisdom to know the difference.

Her alternative Mass, Larry called it. A curiously intimate yet impersonal rite. She tried to focus on *that* instead of the strange new odd lot of pilgrims she was tucking in with. Or her pesky recollection of the third meeting Bella had coaxed her to, when she'd stopped off after in a Wisconsin Avenue bar. That time she hadn't made it home till. . . next day, more or less. Those awful times, amazing she'd gotten through them at all.

A woman named Janet doing the drunkalogue. Wire-thin with a stark grey bob. And a garden-variety history of suburban boozing—car accidents, supermarket blackouts, bottles stashed with helpful neighbors. *There but for. . . .* Janet's teenage son was a drinker and doper. "I told him he can't stay home if he goes on like that, but he won't come into the program."

Sylvia, an ex-congressman's wife, said she sure empathized with anyone being driven nuts by her kids, but the boy had his own higher power "and you're not it. But you can set some rules, like 'under no circumstances will you drink or drug in this house.' " Others chimed in ritual offerings: "Easy does it," "Turn it over." The kyrie eléisons of AA.

A tranquilizing empathy seeped through her. Familiar words seemed to loosen the knots of her obsessions, to heal. Melt the resistance that still fizzled in her—though not so furiously as before.

Pearl, a new mother in elasticized slacks, brought up the drink signals she got nursing her baby. Dotty talked of nodding out at her mother-in-law's family dinners. Somehow it all seemed to fit. When they joined hands for the closing prayer Robin was soothed, serene, her demons tamed. *There but for the grace of god. . . . One day, one thing at a time. . . .*

Good for Tish to've prodded her back. Right now, right here, Robin felt strong and calm enough to climb mountains.

CHAPTER EIGHTEEN /

January 24th

Robin

"Whups. 'Nother dead soldier." "No sweat, got another case here. . . ." Robin spilled awake, gasping, heart thudding in panic, thinking the dream was real.

God knows it *felt* real. In a locked-up bar with Kevin Devlin of all people. They'd magically got at the bottles, knocked 'em off one by one, wallowing, stinking. . . . She made herself limp on the mattress, unkinking with deliberate yoga breaths. Sliding from one bad dream to another—Stephanie's article, which she'd cravenly avoided last night.

Carmen's knock poked her up into the pillows. She waited out the ritual fussings, the morning alert. "Nice sunny day, but colder than it looks. . . ."

Carmen finally left.

She snatched up the *Post* Style section, wincing at the splashy FIRST

OF TWO ARTICLES. "Robin Swann Devlin, the unexpected First Lady named for two plucky, graceful birds not unlike herself. . . ."

A quick skim brought no great shocks. The quotes seemed. . . accurate, at least. Including, "She declined to comment on the state of their separation: 'I mean just what I said. I'm here because I'm keeping that promise.' "

What would that cold print say to strangers? Impossible to imagine. But considering the tricky dips of the interview, she probably came out better than she deserved.

In any case, water over dam. Downstairs, Larry's sizzling glare alerted her he'd seen Stephanie's piece, but he didn't mention it. God knows *she* wouldn't bring it up.

To catch up on the backlog, he'd declared this Saturday a regular workday. After he left for his office, Sally Arnstein arrived with a foot-high paper-stack. "Lord, Sally," she groaned, "do you have to haul it all in at once?"

Unamused laugh. Sally said if they spent the day at it they might make some headway. Spreading her wares, she purred about Mayo's "quite favorable profile, didn't you think?"

Curtly: "I guess. What else is cooking?"

The latest media wish list included *Nightline*; *Good Morning, America*; and *Today*. Jane Pauley wanted a White House remote, "live if possible, but they're flexible. And Barbara Walters called about building a special around you. That's a traditional vehicle for a First Lady's first in-depth—"

"No more interviews," she said flatly. "And no more kitchen look-sees, either."

Sally felt "obliged to point out this coverage could be useful to President Devlin in this indefinite—"

"This isn't a discussion, Sally. I'm just telling you I want no more interviews."

Sniffing, Arnstein handed over drafts of "appropriate mail response" for Robin's okay.

She skimmed: "Thank you for writing. . . . Pleased to send you this enclosed photograph of (*a*) the Devlin family; (*b*) the White House." She said she didn't want those idiotic form letters going out over her signature. "Leave that for now, I'll get back to it."

Another rush priority: the dinner for the Spanish royal visit. "One hundred and two names left to be cut from the guest list. More, if you and the President want to add any."

Butterflies in full revolt, she said she'd ask the chief usher about that on Monday. Frowning, Sally brought up the dinner entertainment, table decorations. . . .

She waved them away. "Save that for Mr. Fletcher too." Ridiculous, this "executive role" they were foisting on her! Years of pol-wife teas and women's-page chats were no defense against a paper-flood like this. She'd been trained in smile and make-nice—now they wanted her to run an army.

After five hours, Sally's stack barely dented, Robin begged off to run ten laps around the grounds. When Larry hadn't turned up by 7:30 she told Hamilton to serve dinner, since there was no telling how late he'd be, and she wanted the boys kept on some kind of schedule.

Halfway through, bells signaled that Larry was on the move. They looked up expectantly as he loomed at the door—beside him a tall, lanky man, ambling like a ghost from her past. "Evening, troops, sorry I'm late. Hamilton, can you throw on another plate? Robin, you remember. . . ."

"Cal Farragut, of course!" Rumpled blond hair shot with silver now, but the rest a scrapbook snapshot, face gaunt, composed, a bit more broken in. She got up and hugged him, saying how could she forget the man who'd introduced them. "Over a Block Island lobster pot. Cal, I'm afraid to think how long it's been since I saw you."

He lit a wry smile. "Ah, shoot. I was hoping you'd remember, Robin."

A maid scurried to set a place. Larry muttered distractedly, "Rob's the one who gives out the interviews around here." *Ah boy, you haven't heard the last of that one. . . .*

He introduced Cal to the boys as his long-gone Hotchkiss roommate. She prompted, "An usher at our wedding too." Cal said well, an accidental usher, after Billy Considine broke his leg. She chuckled, "Oh, bull. You were always my first choice, Cal."

Catching the slip of her double entendre, she tipped a blush. But no reaction from Cal. Impossible to tell if he'd flipped the same memory.

Heart of the heart of the beast drummed in Cal's head as he warily reconnoitered each new move. Now the beauty inside the beast, pink with surprise at the sight of him.

She never came across right in photos. Sometimes he wouldn't recognize her, flipping magazines, but face to face she'd changed very little. Sharper focus to her expression, maybe. Squint lines sprouting by the eyes. But even hostessing this glitzy Versailles mess hall, she had a sassy bloom, a dead-game curiosity peeking through her party manners.

You could tell right off the bat that time had bent this pair in different directions. Even back at Hotchkiss he'd known the years would accumulate on Larry Devlin with fatty excess, and sure enough, the guy looked gorged, overblown by too much too soon but still piling it on, pigging out. But Robin was. . . just Robin. Cal supposed that was how she'd survived in that pack, by floating on her own little jet streams.

He shrugged off his blazer, dropped it over the back of the chair. The butler made a slight gagging noise and tried to peel it off the chair. Cal grabbed it back. As they skirmished, the guy stared at the gaping elbows in Cal's sweater.

The jacket stayed where Cal had planted it. Turning back to the table, he caught Robin smiling behind her hand. Somehow he'd thought of her as fragile, easy to break. It struck him now she was about as delicate as hammered brass.

As the men tucked into their asparagus soup, she said she gave up. "Cal, when was the last time we saw you?" His grey eyes prodded, haunting cues. Then it came to her: "Of course—Cambodia, wasn't it? In '63."

Warning edge in Larry's casual, "That's right."

For some reason she smiled at Jason and said out of the blue, "You don't remember that trip, but you were along, sort of—that's where you got started."

Jason blushed, goggled. Nobody else paid much attention. Larry said he'd kept track of Cal mainly through his *Life* covers during the Vietnam war. Where'd he been since? Mostly overseas, odd jobs out of Paris, most recently Oxfam.

Robin hadn't reacted much to this sudden reappearance—didn't dare to, not here, not yet. So she focused instead on how odd it was to see these two back together. Cal had been only a fringe element in the pack Larry'd run with, but she'd always been amazed they were friends at all—cocky, pampered-rich Younger Brother and lean, oddly tuned Yankee ascetic. Yet watching them play to each other now, Larry moving, talking in ways that echoed years back, she decided this visit might do *him* some good, at least. Cal was the first guy she'd seen all week who seemed oblivious to the presidential flap.

She asked what stroke of luck had brought him here, after such a long silence. Larry answered for him: "He talked his way past my schedulers and hit me up for a free meal, that's what. If you kids want to be excused, by the way. . . ."

As Larry expected, they jumped at the offer. Cleared out in a minute flat. He told Hamilton and the maids to leave the food on the sideboard, thanks, that would do for tonight. Nose in the air, Hamilton banged enough platters on his way out to convey his huff. Left Robin chewing her lip.

Hell with that. Larry knocked the table to get her attention. "Rob, you understand what we're getting into here goes no further than this room." She said oh, all right, sure, her eyes ballooning with surprise.

He knew it was nothing, probably. Dogshit, pipedream. But he wanted to try the idea out on her, watch for sparks. He said, "Cal, tell her what you're doing here."

Cal explained that he'd just brought her husband "a bit of business. Or a shot at it, anyway." Larry saw Robin's jelling bewilderment as she heard about Le Anh, Cal's friend from junior year at the Sorbonne, a poly-sci student from Hanoi "who I figured was probably a Communist. And sure enough, years later I found him in Geneva reporting for North Vietnam's news service, which meant he was doubling as a spy."

Sure, it was crackpot. Fifth-rate James Bond. Bad TV pilot. So why could he taste it already in his gut, like a dark forbidden pleasure?

"Two months ago we met again at UNESCO in Paris and picked up the threads—as much as you can with those guys. I told him I was consulting for Oxfam and working on a project of my own. I didn't say what. He had me to dinner, so I invited him back. While I was in the kitchen, he cased my living room and saw the wedding photo."

She asked blankly what wedding photo.

Cal smiled and said hers, of course. He'd taken to hanging it up, the past few years: "For the rise it gets out of people, I guess. Le recognized the three Devlin boys—and me. That's when he about peed on the rug."

She cracked up over that one: No, no, too good.

Damn right, too good. Larry knew he mustn't let the built-in impossibles in this job goad him into some way-out flyer, some swan dive into the wild blue yonder. Cal said yep, score one for auld lang syne. "This week he turned up for lunch. Asked if I could contact Larry. I said why should I. He said to find out if President Devlin was interested in doing something of mutual benefit to both our countries."

Her saucer eyes rolled back to Larry. "Dev, for heaven's sake. What's that—a feeler from Hanoi?"

He shrugged. "Who knows? In deference to my long-lost friend here we'll check it out, but don't hold your breath."

Cal said he'd asked Le Anh "the obvious—if he meant normalizing relations between the two countries. 'A fruitful area for discussion,' he said. I took the liberty of saying Larry certainly wouldn't bite unless the Vietnamese were ready to end their military occupation of Cambodia, and he said again that 'could be discussed.'"

He tried to explain to Robin how the arrogant, devious, secretive Vietnamese, operating on their own historic-imperative agendas, might actually be trying to hand Larry a diplomatic opening that could end five decades of war and give the United States a major strategic advantage vis-à-vis the Soviets and Chinese. He smiled slyly at Larry. "Not to mention a Nobel Peace Prize for you, of course."

Bingo....

Odd how off that idea sounded, out loud. His bubble popped, Larry speared a forkful of steak and suggested they stick to the facts. "Two guys sitting over a Paris beer don't add up to zip, much less a substantive peace feeler. Come back down out of the clouds, hey, buddy."

Cal's head was gradually tuning to the serves, like eyes adjusting to jungle nightlight. *Tread soft, look sharp....* Behind a shell of calm his mind was trigger-sharp, alert with the desperation of nothing-left-to-lose.

A grim joke that they'd combed him over with their metal detectors coming in here, patted him down for guns and grenades. Yet they'd missed even a whiff of the explosive notion he'd smuggled in, ticking like a bomb in his gut, the one thing he'd gladly kill for.

He lobbed a few arguments back at Larry: If Le Anh's signal was more than a free-lance probe—"and bet your socks it is, those guys don't fool around on their own"—it could indicate a split in the Hanoi Politburo, old gerontocrats versus younger war vets. If they were willing to budge on Cambodia, Larry might get "a unique opportunity to haul some kind of victory out of the bloody ash pile over there. Forget who 'won' or 'lost' the war, Dev. What counts is *who wins the peace*. Go check out the balance sheets for England, Germany and Japan and tell me who really won World War II."

Larry frowned, shook his head. Yet that hook was in him, working on his ruddy face as Cal insisted, "If you play this right, Dev, the big winner could be the U.S."

Robin asked how good the chances were this might work out. Larry sniffed: "Realistically? Zero, zip."

They sawed back and forth, Larry the wary devil's advocate, Cal ransacking his wits, his swamp of memory for enough shreds of commonality to rig a bridge to this guy's overloaded mind. Trying to decode how much the former wise guy who'd sloughed off on all his history courses understood of the ancient, infinitely complex antagonisms of Indochina.

Larry kept harping back to Vietnam as the big little international pauper, running the world's fourth-largest army with piss-all foreign aid except three million Russian bucks a day. Cal pointed out that was thanks to "you and your pound-of-flesh embargo, by the way. Whether it serves any useful purpose is beside the point, of course."

Larry said he declined to dignify that with a response; anyway, there were six dozen ways they could be trying to fry American ass with this cockamamie 'olive branch.' "Jesus Christ, Cal, you think if they were for one minute serious about a feeler they'd work it through *you?*"

His hopes shriveled like a beached fish. *Forget it, kiss it off, the guy's got as much imagination as a roach.*

Cold with disappointment, Cal said he'd assumed Larry was aware that the Vietnamese, like most Asians, put more weight on family and friendship ties than on Western bureaucratic channels, "which are as mysterious to them as the East is to us. I find their way of thinking a good deal wiser than ours. Le approached me as a friend of yours"— gesture flipped between them—"on the basis of our Sorbonne relationship, plus my ties to Cambodia. The trick here is to fathom the logic behind that delicate move."

Robin leaned into the silence, frowning with concern, and asked Cal why he was so involved with Cambodia.

Forget Larry: Robin was the weak link. Come to think of it, she always had been.

Cal peered at her, talking softly, hypnotically about the extraordinary, dreamlike country where for twelve years he felt he'd "come home, to where I belonged." The Enchanted Kingdom, outsiders called it, where graceful Khmers with enigmatic smiles moved like dancers through a perfumed, dozing countryside. His words stirred memories in her, of a gold-roofed fairyland carved from lush jungle. "Ah, Cal."

He started. "Of course, you were there, Robin—you saw for yourself. Somehow I keep forgetting that."

She said lord, they were only galloping through, they hadn't got anywhere near the feel for it that he had.

"Well, that's a pity." He mused about rivers swarming with fish, trees heavy with fruit, rice fields spilling out two or three crops a year. Almost a paradise where no one ever needed to go hungry—which made what happened all the more ironic. Despite their deep distrust of foreigners, rooted in centuries of invasions, the Cambodians had "a naive faith in us, their blue-eyed American allies. And we left them with empty guns to fight off those utterly ruthless Khmer Rouge—our last, worst Asian betrayal."

No, no, he must be wrong, I don't remember that! Yet Larry, frowning, tight-faced, offered no rebuttal.

Arm flung over his chair, Cal talked about a college kid on the plane from Paris asking him who Pol Pot was. He'd rashly supposed the American memory span ran longer than a few years, but that earnest frat boy'd never heard of the criminal, mass-murdering madman who took over Cambodia after we turned tail and bugged out in '75.

They debated how many millions had died under Pol Pot. Cal said two to three, Larry's "more reliable estimate" was one and a half. Larry was in his bulldog mood, aggressive as usual, yet she sensed his resisted appetite for the deal.

Cal pointed out that a lot had died from sickness and starvation, as well as from the hoe, a preferred tool of execution—cheaper than bullets. Staring at his twisted face, she realized he was telling them what had become of the Enchanted Kingdom. "God, Cal. What a terrible time that must've been."

Haunted eyes turned on her. Flatly, softly: "It was the most godawful tragedy you could imagine. Even Genghis Khan didn't put his own people's children in mass graves. And for four years we stood by, turned our backs. Did nothing while those Khmer Rouge butchers killed thousands every day."

Why were they arguing statistics anyway? The numbers were incomprehensible; the reality was "a field with 38,000 skulls bleaching in the sun like a harvest of cabbages. And for every field like that, hundreds more will never be dug up." The reality was that the dying continued. "But you may have a chance to do something about that, Larry. It's a fortunate man that gets that kind of shot."

A startled look moved over Larry's face. He said nobody was holding any brief for Pol Pot, but—

"Come on, Larry!" Cal claimed the U.S. had lobbied like Boston ward heelers to keep the Khmer Rouge in Cambodia's U.N. seat, and was still backing them today. Larry said dammit, we weren't backing Pol Pot. They argued what Cal called the "diplomatic alibi" of denying that seat to the puppet government of the land-grabbing Viets. Cal insisted that, in point of fact, *we were still backing Pol Pot*, still funneling arms to the forty thousand troops he had left in the border jungles. "And I swear to god, Larry, if the American people only realized what kind of monstrous mass murderers we're doing business with, they wouldn't stand for it. Not for a minute. It's like Adolf Hitler was still holed up in the Alps, with Stalin and the U.S. promoting him at the U.N."

"Christ, what d'you want, Cal?" Larry snapped. "You'd rather we rubber-stamp the Vietnamese occupation?"

"No, no. *They* also stood watching the massacres, by the way. When Pol's gang killed enough Cambodians to suit them, their tanks took the land they'd been after for centuries. If they stay, they'll slowly assimilate any they don't kill." Cal's gaze burned across the table. "Larry, get your head straight out on the bottom line here. It's not get-even with the Viets. It's the survival of a nation. Of a unique people."

With a sly smile, Larry slipped a Xerox from his pocket and handed it to Cal, who glanced at it and grunted. "Huh. I wish I'd known you said that."

"Hey, no fair," Robin protested. "Let me see that."

Cal passed it over: a press release dated April 2, 1979—"three months after the Viets invaded." In it Larry called for an international conference on Indochina, with the goal of obtaining a cease-fire and establishing peace, neutrality, and independence for Cambodia. "The depth of suffering of the Cambodian people is one of the great human tragedies of the twentieth century. They face today a brutal choice of torture and murder by rival government forces or slow death by hunger and disease. Neither the United States nor the international community can ignore their cries for help."

Flush with fresh respect, she beamed at Larry, who was relishing the one-up. As usual, he'd been way ahead of her.

Cal wished he could smack that smug, satisfied grin right off Larry's face. The dork had been bogged so long in Washington bureaucracy he actually seemed to think waving a PR release at a problem was tantamount to solving it.

Tamping his disgust, he let Larry assume that this approach, "if that's what this goddam vague signal consists of," was made in the context of that statement. His terms remained the same: diplomatic recognition and trade relations in exchange for total withdrawal from Cambodia.

At least he was right about that. Cal asked what response he'd gotten to the release. Nothing from Vietnam, Larry said, but he'd discussed it with Prince Oudong.

Cal glowered. "Ah, sure. That profiteering old war criminal would love to ride your coattails back to his royal hot seat, but he deserves to be lined up and shot with Pol Pot."

Larry snapped back that Oudong would be essential to any potential opening, since he was the only Cambodian leader with international credibility, dammit. Reluctantly, Cal agreed. The long odds against any workable solution were what had brought him here with his begging bowl, after all.

In all the talk about chessboard pieces, Ours versus Theirs, what mainly stuck in Robin's head was Cal's rumination on the differences between the militaristic Vietnamese and the mystical, creative Cambodians. "So in some ways it was art versus war. Even their simplest implements—a plow, a hoe, a wooden spoon—have the form and elegance of a work of art." Cal moved his hands like brushes in the air. "They're amazingly talented. Oh, just extraordinary. Unique, like the whales. And we're killing them both off."

She mentioned the hanging in her office—"amazing, like you said, Cal. Each thread dyed separately and woven into such a lovely, lyric piece. . . ." He told her wryly to hang onto it, since the Khmer Rouge had also destroyed all that.

That somehow shook her more than the massacres and skulls. With resisting horror, she heard how Pol Pot had obliterated "whole cities, stone by stone. Most of the Buddhist monasteries, plus the monks. Also the written record of a remarkable 1200-year history—all the books, all the art. So it was cultural genocide, too, on the soul of an extraordinary civilization. In his mad, ambitious delusions of grandeur, Pol almost succeeded in transforming Cambodia into a society of ghosts and psychotic children."

She burst out, "Oh, Cal. I'm so sorry."

Jolted from his reverie, he told her he'd brought along the project he'd been working on, a short film that "tells better than I can what it was like living—and dying—in the hell Pol Pot made of that place."

Larry pushed aside his plate, saying he realized those people had been through hell. "What I can't get a handle on, Cal, is what your Hanoi friend expects *me* to do about it."

Watching, catlike, Cal said that Larry might get a chance to pull off a diplomatic coup "of great potential value to yourself. But it'll never work unless you guarantee the Cambodians don't get screwed in the deal like so many times before. I want to be sure you understand that, Larry."

Larry rubbed his neck, stress tip-off. "In any case, with the, ah, domestic political situation right now, there's zero chance any initiative like that would fly."

"Larry!" she blurted. "If there's any chance to undo some of that ghastly war, of course you've got to—"

"But why're the Viets moving on this *now*?" Cal cut in eagerly. "Because you're the glitch in the system, the President who was never supposed to happen. And they'd rather take a chance on you than wait for President Dan."

Bristling at that name, Larry reluctantly brought up "a distinction I don't like to dwell on, but my job happens to be *acting* president. The heavy-duty shit you're talking about—no way could an acting president take it on."

That confession of his impotence was one more revelation. *God, he's having a tougher time of this than I thought. . . .*

Cal calmly waved aside the objection. "At least you didn't have to hock your political ass to get here—and you're the only President they've got. So for as long as the job lasts, you've got a rare kind of freedom. A unique opportunity to pull off some creative diplomacy and act like a statesman instead of a bought-and-sold vote whore." Pause. "So *use* it, man."

Exasperated: "Boy, you never quit. I'll say that much for you, pal."

A discreet rap on the door. Hamilton glided in and murmured to Larry. Larry said fine, show them to the Treaty Room. Back in his crisp, take-charge Presidential Mode: "Okay, Cal, it's put-up or shut-up time. I've invited a few guys over to blow holes in your boat."

Who, she asked. Koenig and Lessard. Cal's feeler was at least getting full-dress treatment—National Security Adviser and Secretary of State. Larry shrugged on his jacket, heading out. She murmured, "Cal, lots of luck."

"Thanks, Robin. Hang in there, kid." He trailed serenely after Larry, shiny old blazer slung over one shoulder.

Usually she left pol talk at the table like a doused electric light, but tonight Cal's unspeakable visions crowded her mind, flitting like his Khmer ghosts. *Unique, like the whales. And we're killing them both off.* . . . Beanpole Farragut, that rangy, one-of-a-kind Protestant saint—relaying a major diplomatic signal? Curiouser and curiouser!

Up in her suite she flipped through phone messages: "Mrs. Devlin Senior, third call." "Friends" she couldn't recall. A Wall Street broker she'd gone out with twice in New York, chaperoned by agents. *Great, all I need, with god knows who listening in.*

She tore up that slip and shelved the rest, head swimming with queasy memories of the week she'd met both Cal and Larry, the summer before her junior year, at a house party with her Marymount gang.

☆

First came Cal, a tall blond "older man," visiting down the road with his uncle. She mainly recalled his clothes: madras cutoffs he even swam in. His weird, bright sarong on the night of the lobster roast, Hawaiian by way of Samoa, he said.

One look at that flowery skirt wrapped right down to his feet, and she thought, *How can I go out with a guy who dresses like that?* Mary Fran Feeney moaned ecstatically omigawd, look who Farragut brought—Mr. Gorgeous himself!

She cased the bronzy-gold guy clowning with Cal over a basket of lobsters and asked why, who was that? Senator Devlin's little brother Larry, the primo catch of the Catholic East Coast, that's who. But she wasn't at all interested in *him*, she wanted the guy in that ridiculous skirt.

When Cal barely talked to her all night, she drowned her hurt in five beers and turned on her "shimmer" for his friend Devlin. Her vamp act was a pale, no-guts Marilyn Monroe imitation, mostly jutting tits and corkscrew hips. When she practiced it in the dorm, they'd fall down shrieking with laughter, but some boys actually went for it, snapped to the bait. And so did Larry.

☆

So she really did owe the whole denouement, marriage et al., to Cal, for whatever that was worth. Except for Cal, Larry never would've noticed her at all. . . except for that shimmer. Now Cal was back, with a cargo of murdered children. Marveling at the kinks of fate, she put on Joni Mitchell and a lavender sweatsuit, and worked out her confusion with leg lifts and squats.

Years later, when she was still raw from Michaela's death, Michael had sent her and Larry to Cambodia to help them over it. On their first day there, parading past photographers at a reception, she heard, "You oughta see her shimmy like her sister Kate." And there was Cal behind a battered Leica, bony and mysterious as ever in Dr. Livingston khakis.

They lunched the next day. Cal had talked mostly in pearls of insight about "this miraculous country," his eyes like searchlights. Like surgical probes. Afterward Larry said, "Good case of jungle fever setting in there." She still thought he was the most exotic man she'd ever met.

That whole trip was magic, start to finish. Like the glorious blazing morning she woke up, rolled over, and told Larry she thought she was pregnant. He asked how many periods she'd missed; she said she wasn't due till the next week. He patted her head, said sure thing, Mom. But she knew what her body was telling her, and in his own sweet time Jason had proved her right. Some day she'd like to tell him about that, if she could get past the masked anger and wary standoff of his Joe Jock routines.

Now she felt almost pregnant with what Cal had brought to that table, so much more real than this White House fairy tale. Around ten she was grunting through sit-ups to Cat Stevens's wails when the door pushed open on one imperious rap.

An odd ripple ran through her, seeing Larry in shirtsleeves and black socks, cigar jauntily tilted, carrying a brandy snifter and Perrier bottle. "Rob, you still up?"

"Oh, sure." She pulled off her weight cuffs, demurely folded her legs. "Come on in, babe."

He peered around him, handing her the bottle. "So this is where you're hanging out. Sean's right, it's dinky."

"Thanks. Amazing dinner, by the way. I can hardly believe that was Beanpole Farragut. How'd the meeting go?"

So-so, he shrugged. "Cal ran up his balloon, and the rest shot it down. Mal Koenig's crapping in his pants at the idea Hanoi might be passing a signal through an oddball like Cal—'your eccentric young friend,' he calls him—but he'd kill for that kind of yank at the Soviet pecker. Lessard rolled out his fifty-six reasons why a Vietnam rapprochement wouldn't work. That goddam State Department's got more ass-kissing eunuchs than a Chinese court."

She sighed. "Well, don't listen too hard to them, babe. I know it's a real long shot, but you've gotta go for it if you can."

Wry, amused, he asked if she really thought for one minute that pipe-dreamer Cal Farragut could deliver Hanoi. She protested that it was *him* they were talking to, if they were talking at all, and what was so impossible about that?

Perching on a straight-backed chair, he said she'd find out soon enough. But that tight jaw said he wanted it already. He fired up a swirl of grey-blue cigar smoke. "Now, on the matter of this morning's hatchet job—goddam, Robin, I'd like to hear one good reason why you had to lay out all that stuff about the, ah, state of the union." Looking squarely into her face. "Domestic division."

All right. . . now!

She said she hadn't *intended* to get into anything like that. But when Stephanie asked point-blank, she decided not to lie. He might recall she'd been trying for months to talk to him, "get a few things clear between us before we get much deeper into. . . but every damn time I bring it up, there's always something—"

"Okay, okay. Sorry about that, I've had a few things on my mind. So what you're saying now is," voice rising in unpent anger, "you decided to talk to your pal Mayo instead?"

Stay cool. Say what you mean! "Larry, I just told her what I would've told you, if I'd had the chance—that as far as I'm concerned we're still separated, unofficially or not." In all the years they'd sawed at each other, she never broke their tacit compact: Risk no schism. But now she interrupted his retort with, "Hold on please, let me finish. God, after all the times I've rehearsed this, I never meant for it to happen like this. Especially not after that dinner tonight. But anyway. . . ." A ragged breath. "Larry, I want out. After this White House go-round, I want a divorce."

The word hit him like a slap. He ducked his head, fighting back a sting of tears. Fighting his own surprise.

That taboo word, unspoken between them. Sometimes, many times, he'd said it to himself like a promise of release. An insurance against more pain. Yet hearing it from her now, smack out of the blue, he felt a trapdoor swing open under his feet. An escape that wasn't what he wanted after all.

Low voice: "Just like that, hunh?"

"No, not 'just like that.' I can't tell you how much I wish it wasn't that—how hard I tried to make it work out some other way. But we're just no good for each other, Dev."

This was one hell of a day, full of weird vibes, one kick in the head after another. He still hadn't sorted out all the signals swirling around the dinner table. Now this—maybe not so out of the blue. Maybe he just hadn't wanted to see it coming, obvious as a truck careening down a road.

A word was still only a word, but this one tipped some kind of precarious balance between them. He hoped to god he hadn't let it slide too far already, remembering with grim clarity how much luck he'd had winning her over in earlier showdowns, like about her drinking.

She was running on about how she'd "finally come clear" one night last fall, September 17th, as a matter of fact, back from the trail bone-tired, catching a movie on TV. His baffled impatience must've shown on his face, because she cut it short. "Anyway, that's when I realized that for me this marriage is like the booze—something I've got to figure out some way to put behind me. Because I just can't live with it any-more, Dev."

He asked if he got any vote in this.

Wistful smile. "Not much, babe. Because nothing you say can change the sore truth. We just don't fit together, Dev. I suppose we never did, and just didn't have sense enough to recognize it."

"I suppose we never did. . . ." Now how in hell could you defend yourself against that?

She ticked off their differences: She was a dreamer, he pure doer. She was a recovering alcoholic who shouldn't be married to a heavy drinker—*that* got a wince from him. She was "a very private person, finally got that straight about myself, and you're public down to your socks. It's a bad match, Dev, and I can't spend what's left of my life trying to make it work, make me fit the box."

He argued that could be different, dammit. "Things change, people change. . . ."

Still thrown by that flash of tears from him, the one reaction she'd never expected, she groped for a way to make him understand that *she* had changed, into someone radically different from the wife who walked out on him. She'd had so many pleadings neatly, tidily rehearsed. But blurted instead the bottom line: "You're too dangerous for me, Dev. It's much harder for me to stay dry and straight around you, and I've decided not to die young."

He said in a pained voice: "Dammit, Robin, you make it sound like I want you dead. How'm I supposed to—"

She shushed him, feeling raw, unscabbed, saying that wasn't what she meant at all, but they needn't hash it out now, tonight. "I just— want you to know how things stand."

"Okay." He swirled his glass. "But I want *you* to know, Rob, that from my end the jury's still out on this."

"All right, fair enough." Avoiding his eyes, she said there was no other man in the picture, in case he was wondering. "I just don't want to be married anymore. Not to you, or anybody. I do love you, you know, Dev, in my way. Quite a lot, actually. But. . . I've got to go."

He grunted that she'd picked a hell of a way to make her point. She guiltily agreed, but she had "a pretty good idea of how much stress and pressure I can handle. And this First Lady drill doesn't help—a real shitload of work, let me tell you."

He said sure, he knew that.

"Not that I'm not proud to be here, babe. It's quite. . . amazing. Every piece of it."

Scowling at the wall, he said what really pissed him off about the chitchat with her buddy was "all anybody will remember from it is we're not. . . anh, you know."

Guarded: "We're not what?"

"Making love," he blurted loudly. "And in that case, I'd like to know what we were doing Tuesday night."

"Tuesday!" She sprang up from the rug, electrified with guilty indignation. "Listen, Larry, the main reason I talked to Stephanie was I can't handle this Cinderella marriage crap on top of everything else. Anyway, won't. You think I *like* going public over something like that? My god. But if you assume just because we jumped in bed a few times for auld lang syne that means this separation's over—"

"Okay, okay. Just simmer down, Rob."

But she paced, raking her hair, hissing that she had to stop living with other people's craziness. She'd been trying to handle this First Lady gig as well as she could, but if he wanted her to come through it in one piece, he had to at least let her do it her own way. "Understood?"

Curtly: "Yep. Loud and clear."

"Okay." The glare she turned on him dissolved into a testy smile. "Just so you've got it straight you're not married to no Cinderella, Prince. No offense meant, babe, I think you're a wise, honorable man and all that. But you know this fairy-tale crap wasn't part of the deal."

"Nope, sure enough." Chair tilted, cigar rolling in his grin. "That wasn't the deal." As she moved within reach he grabbed her hand, tugged her to him.

Startled by the detour, she smiled shyly, uncertainly, rubbing her thigh on his. Murmur: "Now there's a thought. . . ."

He was pouring a seductive, combative energy at her, as if she were another score, a game he didn't mean to lose. His grip pulled her awkwardly down toward his face. Realizing she was going to wind up either on his knees or her own, she chose to tumble into his lap, straddling his legs.

Ah, why not. He's claiming, but he deserves. . . . As his arms closed around her, she leaned into that urgent embrace. He whispered, "That's more like it," mouth closing on hers. Raw contact, as if each touched sore wounds in the other.

She tasted brandy and salt. And remembered pleasures. His hands roved knowingly on her body, under her shirt, teasing her nipples. She pressed her hips against his groin, sluiced in sensation. Through layers of cloth, her moist slit locked onto his swollen penis, hungry cunt swallowing him up. Sharp rush of pleasure, favorite flash flood, clinging to him, whimpering, kindling.

He cradled her till it ebbed, then carried her to the bed, spilling her on the turned-down sheets. She switched off the lamp and peeled off her sweats, in the dim john light watching his briskly efficient strip, swollen pecker a Johnny-jump-up. He rolled across the odd-sized bed, pulling her urgently against him. Soft chuckle as their bodies connected, skin kissing skin. "Ahhh good. You feel so good."

As he came into her in a stormy, healing spasm, one thought floated free: *Yes. Yes, babe. For you.*

CHAPTER NINETEEN /
January 24th
Prilla

Ginny thought the *Washington Post* soft soap on Robin Devlin showed her up "every bit as tarty as she looks. Did you catch that third-floor bedroom? Practically in the attic? My dear, talk about washing your dirty linen!"

Priscilla chuckled into the phone, feeling mildly cheered. She said she liked the part where Robin bragged about not considering herself married. Might as well announce she wasn't sleeping with her husband, although heaven knows that man had given her plenty of cause. This sort of trash you'd expect from the *National Enquirer*, but in an interview she gave the *Washington Post*, of all places. . . .

Ginny heaped on gabby indignation: Nobody had to stoop to discredit her, she was doing that all by herself. Priscilla sighed that it almost made her feel sorry for Larry Devlin, and she never thought she'd hear herself say *that*.

"Darling, don't waste your pity. Why the *Post* ran that mushy picture of them at the swearing in, I'll never know. They ought to show them going at it hammer and tongs, not all starry and gorgeous. . . ." Priscilla caught a faint whiff of admiring envy in Ginny's rant. Eventually she got around to "the nifty shot of you and Dan in today's *L.A. Times*. Getting presents somewhere down south."

Ginny always wanted to hear about the presents. "At the governors' conference? I thought I looked like I was picking my teeth." A timer on the Carlton dresser dinged a reminder. "Whoops! Got to go—take care, dear. We'll talk soon."

Taking a quick mirror check, Priscilla blotted a Kleenex to her face. These days she hated reading the papers anyway, so clogged with muckraking on the congressmen: one from Iowa mortgaging his D.C. house for five times what he'd paid for it, an Alabaman defending some $50,000 payments to his wife's decorating firm, and so on. Thank god the exposés didn't lend themselves to good TV, all Priscilla mainly cared about, though the decorator wife did have a brief run with her photogenic hats.

She strolled into the living room, where Dan was winding up a one-on-one with Congressman Lincoln Sheppard. ". . . high hopes we can find mutual interest in this situation, if you'll bear in mind I won 56 percent of the Indiana vote last November. Hi, Prilla, come on in."

The 3-by-5s said this round little 55-year-old baldie with raked grey strands owed his mediocre political career to his scrap-iron-heiress wife, who had a drinking problem and refused to live in Washington. But Priscilla wanted what Dan called her "skin test," direct contact with these faceless men holding Dan hostage. Then she'd trust her combative instincts better than the poop on those file cards.

Vanity—that's this bird's soft spot. She turned on her 100-watt smile.

"I hope you're listening to my husband's good ideas, Congressman Sheppard."

He mumbled about the pleasure of meeting them both.

Dan maneuvered him to the door, recalling the "fine times Prilla and I've had in your beautiful state. At the Indianapolis fair—by gosh, they had one pig weighed over 2600 pounds, wasn't it, Pril?"

"That's right, dear."

She noted the wattage ratio between the beaming fatso's arriving and departing smiles; Dan's awesome presence had done the trick one more time. She asked him how it had gone. Not bad: "He talks a tough line, but he might come around."

With a spurt of relief she decided stroking these pesky Democrats was a good investment of Dan's time, regardless of the risks. Next was Bill Pickett, the at-large Nevada congressman who Dave Elliott said would sooner come out against legalized gambling than jump the Democrat ship. Tall, rangy-handsome, Pickett wore a three-piece grey tweed like a British prime minister's. But the cards said he always called himself "just an old cowboy strayed from the ranch."

This one was a natural for Dan. He said Pickett looked like a man "more at home on a horse than riding those donkeys around the Hill. They tell me you've put in eight good terms down there representing a state that went 61 percent for the Sterling ticket, so I'd like to hear your wise thoughts on what we can do about that logjam you fellows have going."

When she left they were calling each other Bill and Dan, chatting happily about Pickett's steer-roping avocation—"mighty fine training for holding a House seat."

She set the timer for twelve minutes and took her worn Mark Cross case to the window chair. Her pen flew across thick ivory sheets: "Dear Mrs. Pancost, what a pleasure. . . ." Some day when they worked up final stats on this endless campaign she'd do some totals of her own. Like how many notes she'd dashed off in snatched moments—thousands, scrawled in look-alike hotels in two-bit towns. . . .

She realized she'd forgotten to tell Ginny about the Arkansas "presents." Most of their official gifts wouldn't get fifty cents at a yard sale—ghastly painted vases, engraved plaques, and tablecloths, good for nothing but the bins of their presidential museum. But yesterday she got a red-white-and-blue quilt with an appliquéd presidential seal bordered by cut-out squares depicting their life stories.

All the highlights were there: the Wyoming house where Dan was born, with the date—July 6, 1911. Bride and groom inside twined gold rings, "Daniel Sterling marries Priscilla Braxton, June 29, 1951." Their favorite movie roles—Sam Houston in *Home to the Alamo*, Lady Jane Grey in *Swords and Trumpets*. The WXY radio mike where Dan got started, their daughters' births, the Malibu ranch house. Bottom corner left blank—for the Inaugural panel they promised to send her "soon as we know the date."

She'd been moved almost to tears by that quilt—a crude piece of work, really, wobbly stitching and stick-figure appliqués, yet beautiful in its primitive way. Her pen slowed as she was reminded of Grandma Wickham's farm, and the crude tree house in the apple field. She'd spent days on that perch, curled up with Gran's patchwork quilt and the fairy-tale books her cousins scorned. Mostly she remembered that painful summer when Harry McAteer had disappeared from her life. Her last vivid memory of the man she wouldn't call her "real" father was one of him clapping before her eighth birthday party in Coral Gables, calling, "That's my girl! That's my pretty little Pris!"

When she'd mentioned that once to her daughters in a burst of reminiscing, Yvonne had said a good shrink could do something with that. Typical Yvonne—always so bitter, so quick to judge. Reading big things into incidental memories. But Priscilla knew she'd long ago come to terms with the nasty fact that her father had turned out to be a weak man unfit to shoulder his family responsibilities—"more in love with the bottle than he was with us," her mother had explained.

☆

All through her twenties, prime husband-hunting years, Priscilla was looking for someone plumb opposite to that man. No luck in a dead-end New York department store job, or back home working for a Grosse Pointe society rag. She wound up in L.A., dabbling in the movie business. Most of her prospects were older men, powerful enough to do her some good—which god knows Harry never had. Finally she was down to mainly seeing Joe Schatzberg, a good friend of Daddy Braxton who also happened to be an MGM VP. Joe landed her a small movie contract, and kept her in mind for parts.

She told Mummy and Daddy Braxton that she ran into Joe "from time to time." Not adding it was mainly Saturday mornings in his office, nine to noon. When Mummy remarked that Joe reminded her a bit of

Harry McAteer, "physically at least," Priscilla was appalled. So afraid she might finally have to fall back on persuading Joe to marry her, if she could, even though he was a Jew who'd had three wives already.

Then, finally, she met Dan, through strings she got Joe to pull. She thought it oddly generous of Joe not to mind her dating him and Dan at the same time. But Dan wasn't interested in "tying on the old ball and chain" either, and she was sure if she wasn't married by her looming thirtieth birthday she'd be an old maid forever.

When Mummy warily brought up Harry McAteer once, hoping he hadn't turned Priscilla against men in general, she flew into a rage: "How could you say that? How could you even *think* it?" But afterwards she wondered a bit why she always went for older men. Brooded on the eerie resemblance between Joe and Harry—not just the looks but the good-time-Charlie personality, so careless about the dangerous business of loving.

Finally her desperate patience paid off when she married Dan, a totally different sort of man. Any scars from that 8-year-old girl's hurt healed in her happy years with Dan. Yet it rankled that Yvonne—and Natalie—couldn't be more grateful she'd got them such a wonderful man for a father. They had no idea just how lucky they were. . . .

☆

The timer dinged off that reverie. The last pigeon was Kittyhawk, the Alaskan who could make it in the movies with his John Wayne jaw, sandy curls and chiseled face. Striding in, looking younger than 46, he headed straight for Dan, hand out: "Governor Sterling, sir, put 'er there."

Quick recovery in Dan's double take. "Well now, nice to meet you, Congressman Kittyhawk."

"And about time, too. Mrs. Sterling," green eyes bright with rudely calculated mischief, "pleasure to see you."

Strong, brisk grip. She tried on a wary smile. "Mr. Kittyhawk, I feel we've already met, I'm hearing so much about you." *And seeing your mug every night on the news.* . . .

He trusted all of it was good. She wagged her finger playfully. "Not quite, Mr. Kittyhawk. What I'd *like* to hear is that you put my husband in the White House by leading a drive on that House vote."

He laughed, flashing gold teeth. "Touché, Mrs. Sterling." Definite star quality to this one, like a young Robert Stack, only prettier and more unbuttoned. Self-made millionaire sass under his businessman gloss. From a dirt-poor start he'd made three million with a gravel monopoly on the Alaska pipeline and parlayed it through real estate into twenty or thirty more. He'd run for Congress as a Libertarian, but his staff were mostly bearded hippie leftists from some Ad Hoc Committee. And his wife showed no sign of moving to D.C.

Kittyhawk was odd-man-out among the congressmen—and she liked that. The rest talked more mumbo-jumbo than a convention of Masons, but she understood this grandstanding pretty boy who wasn't one of the club. A natural ally in his frustrations with the do-nothing wonders in the House, if they played him right. *Keep a close eye on this one.* . . .

The two men sat by the fireplace, Dan saying he appreciated this chance to "sit down and get acquainted, hear some of your valuable ideas. Especially since, like Prilla and me, you're kind of a newcomer to this dipsy-doodle town."

Kittyhawk called that a fair description of what he'd seen so far. Dan mentioned he'd heard Kittyhawk flew his own plane. "That's right, Governor. Look, to save us both time, I'll tell you what I told the press downstairs—whatever kind of deal you're offering, it better be good."

She stiffened, horrified. Chet leaped in: "Governor, I've assured Congressman Kittyhawk that nobody's here to talk any deals. We explained that you're only taking this opportunity to get some fresh input from—"

"Bull," said Kittyhawk. "Your friend Mort Hibbing already had a run at me, dangling a junk proposition for cutting me into an Aleutian fish plant." Cold fear in her gut, head clanging. "Maybe you could explain where your pal Hibbing got the notion he could buy up my vote with a gone-sour deal like that. But let's face it, sir, it's such a rank insult all around we'd best forget it was mentioned."

She choked on her fury as the men tripped over themselves to disavow any such deal. Mort, of all people! Jeopardizing everything with such a ridiculous ploy, when Talbott was dangling an eighty-billion-dollar pipeline! But if the press got onto this, the grotesque difference in the numbers wouldn't matter; for a two-bit piece of idiocy, Mort had made them hostage to Kittyhawk—as Talbott already was.

Dan recovered enough to test a cautious grin. "By gum, I sure don't know anything about fish plants. But I've heard about you Alaska fellows. They tell me you've got this unusual habit of just speaking your mind, laying your cards flat out. And that sure does seem to be the case."

Dead right, said Kittyhawk. "The days aren't long enough up there to truck around with the fancy pussyfooting I've seen in this dinosaur town."

She edged toward them, hands clasped under her chin. "Honey, I don't mean to butt in. But I can't believe Mr. Kittyhawk thinks for one minute you'd have any connection with such an unsavory arrangement."

Kittyhawk agreed with that.

"All right, just so we've got that out of the way. I wanted to ask Mr. Kittyhawk, if he's so all-fired independent, why he isn't supporting my independent-minded husband for president?"

He grinned. "Good question, Mrs. Sterling. To which I have this good answer: Because I'm not ready."

"Not ready *yet*?" she persisted.

"You can put it that way. If it sounds better to you. But it still translates as no deal."

That deliberate, slap-in-the-face word again. Who was this cocky pretty boy, what was he after?

She purred, "Oh, Mr. Kittyhawk, you *know* who won that election. You know Daniel Sterling will be president sooner or later. But the longer the Congress fiddles and faddles, the more this country will be just torn to pieces. You understand that as well as I do, Mr. Kittyhawk." He nodded. "Then can't you see your way clear to supporting him sooner rather than later? Can't you just show them all some responsible leadership and come out for Dan Sterling *now*?"

"Hear, hear!" from Dan.

Kittyhawk smiling, mocking: "Another good question, which deserves a candid answer: No, I can't."

She held his eyes, pressing the look she'd honed for years, her daddy's-lap melt: "But my goodness, why not?"

He zinged her with a one-upping smile. "Because I'm an old jock who can't pass up a good game. And like it or not, Mrs. Sterling, this happens to be the best game in town."

☆

Five hours later she huddled in the pool of light from the breakfast-nook lamp, pen scratching: "Dear Mrs. Peters, What a pleasure to see you yesterday in Hot Springs. . . ."

Footsteps thumped outside. An agent on the porch, stamping off snow. She cracked open the door. He mumbled, "Here you go, Mrs. Sterling," sliding a newspaper through.

"Thank you, Karl. I appreciate that very much."

She pulled out the Style section. Lavish layout. Second day, two-thirds of the page. . . . She read in quick gulps, then pushed it away, clutching her robe against the night chill.

That's it, then. They were hell-bent on making some kind of heroine out of that woman—or antiheroine. Everything that she stood for, that they were rushing to "discover" in her, was diametrically opposed to Priscilla's own image and values. Yet look how that flighty whimsy, that unrepentant disrespect, got flipped into some kind of political asset. First that Cinderella bit. Now this soap-opera joke.

She glared at the photo of Devlin with her sons. What kind of mother would abandon her family, run off to god knows what "life of her own" in New York? She was no more a responsible parent than she was a fit wife. But look at that, snuggling so wind-blown and photogenic with those boys. . . .

A sick joke, all right. But not one that could do her and Dan any good. Words leapt from the page: "Robin Devlin is a woman of my age and time who makes other women say of her, as a pediatrician did, 'So help me, I never thought I'd live long enough to see a First Lady like that in the White House. A real, believable, live-and-breathe woman.' "

She whiffed a faddish contagion here, a bonfire excitement. Playing that woman as big as. . . Princess Grace. Maybe she'd underestimated Devlin's knack for calculation. Look there, on defining "duty": "I suppose if your house was on fire or your brakes needed fixing, your first duty's to look after that. But I think the everyday duty's mainly to yourself—to become the best person you can, and find how to give something back to this curious adventure of life. Not just take."

They ask about duty, she answers adventure? Oh, nice touch, lady. Slick—but risky, so risky. What was she thinking of, even *her*, babbling like that? On the record, yet. "I think the duty's mainly to yourself. . . ."

Six times this past week, asked about her retirement from her stage career, Priscilla had given her push-button answer about happily trading that in for the more important and rewarding job of wife and mother. Amazing how rarely those press morons challenged that, even when they saw her day after day playing to a hundred million just on the nightly newscasts, the biggest role any actress could dream of.

She'd done it so long it was second nature. But still damned hard work—not counting the time and effort it took to keep looking good. She had to stick close by Dan, yet protect him from the schemers trying to get at him. Couldn't trust the staff not to overload his schedule, let alone fend off the hangers-on. It wasn't so much *who* they let in, as how many, and when. Sometimes it felt as if she were the only thing standing between Dan and that devouring mob out there.

All that plus her campaign-wife role took unrelenting vigilance, being constantly "on," so dangerously exposed. She froze every time they peppered Dan with questions walking to his car. It only took one chance remark. . . .

Now their fight was on two fronts. Talbott *and* Devlin. She used to feel she knew just where all this was leading them, in one straight line, but now they were jetting endlessly, pointlessly around the country, tensions clicking tighter every day. Yet that Devlin woman said herself, in cold print: "My husband has the job around here, not me. Which is just how I intend to keep it."

Priscilla rubbed her shivering arms. The media could be counted on to swarm all over that sort of flip crack. So crassly fickle, starved for novelty—and they'd found it in that insolent young woman. Playing her up like some kind of. . . superstar. First Lady superstar.

In the quiet, in the dim, the cold spot grew in her gut. That icy germ of her fear.

CHAPTER TWENTY /

January 25th
Robin

In the White House screening room Larry snapped impatiently, "Come on, let's get this rolling." Sean kicked at a seat; Jason asked how long it would take. After wheedling and maneuvering all day to get this launched, Robin was starting to regret the whole idea.

Cal warned them this was "an unfinished film about an unfinished country." Suddenly the screen filled with a temple gate carved into a giant face, ancient mossy stones alive with vines. Birds chittering, jungle rustling as two children in bright plaid sarongs ran under the godly face, the boy laughing, the girl scolding, trailed by a skittering monkey. Following those children off into the jungle, Robin tumbled down the rabbit hole of Cal's Cambodia.

She remembered that lush, bountiful land—gilded gingerbread temples, slow women with luminous smiles, children at play toting babies. And the playboy prince Oudong, plump and handsome at crusty royal ceremonies, playing his sax, making home movies, Princess Jeanne calm and stately by his side. Sean hissed, "Hey, neat!" as Robin recognized herself and Larry lined up with Oudong in his courtyard. *Lord, that miniskirt! And sappy hair. Barbie visits the palace. . . .*

Then, war metastasized on the screen: Kids playing in bomb craters, women keening over dead soldiers. Oudong pleaded for Cambodia's "sovereign neutrality," but was overthrown by his own ministers. Soldiers in make-do uniforms rode Pepsi trucks to war as cacaphonous tanks, planes and choppers swarmed in the joint invasion, Operation Rock Crusher—Nixon whining in black and white, "If, when the chips are down, the world's most powerful nation acts like a pitiful, helpless giant. . . ."

But the "pitiful" ones were the terrified refugees running from the bombs, the ragged soldiers camped with their families in wretched battlefield huts. Oudong and Jeanne popped up in peasant black at a Khmer Rouge hideout—Jeanne eerily unchanged, Oudong fatter but still smiling, embracing a guerrilla he'd once sentenced to death, plump, moon-faced Pol Pot. More children "played" in a dusty field, a flock of street orphans, wistful, broken birds—some scarred, some missing a leg or a foot. A beautiful girl twirled on a single crutch, long black hair fanning over the bandaged baby who rode her hip, smiling.

The Fall. Khmer Rouge victory. Phnom Penh, emptied of two million, got Oudong back as nominal chief of state—stricken, somber, head shaved in mourning, Jeanne by his side. Robin saw what he was mourning, what had become of his kingdom, in the crowded tents of the border camps, skeletal old women too weak to shoo flies, dying toddlers with Auschwitz eyes—the thousands who'd survived the death house Pol Pot had made of their land.

Then Cal took her back inside Cambodia, let the people tell her what had happened. The mayor of Kampot, thin, stooped, in granny glasses, toured the flattened wasteland that once was the town of Kep, known for the best bouillabaisse east of Marseilles. Squatting by a mound of skulls in a bone-littered Shell gas station, the mayor said the Khmer Rouge "made us take it down brick by brick, stone by stone. Like the French cathedral in Phnom Penh. I threw away my glasses because the cadres, who could not read, killed anyone who could. They let me live because they needed many hands to kill the town. But if you did not tear down the schools fast enough or destroy the Buddhas with sufficient enthusiasm, you were killed. If you grew too tired or too sick to work, you were killed. We learned to be deaf and dumb, trust nobody. . . ."

A bored, homesick young Vietnamese draftee said he didn't like the army, Kampuchea, or the Khmers: "But my country get attack so I got to fight." Another one, grinning, said back home they called the Russians "Americans with no dollars. We like you come back, bring plenty dollars."

A former army captain at a rock-guitar musicale had a message for his brothers "in Wyoming, U.S.A., and Arlington, Virginia. We cannot send mail or talk to Red Cross, so I like they know Chhay Sithan is okay in Takeo, Kampuchea." His wife and five of his seven children were dead. How had he survived? He said softly, "By eating every living thing."

A hotel waiter talked about life in a Khmer Rouge labor camp, sleeping in a 45-foot bed with many other men, making love on command to the woman he was forced to marry in a mass ceremony. "I do not love my wife. I love another girl. Even so, I was glad when I could feel like a man." So now there were three children. His brother had escaped to Thailand, but he stayed, "out of pity for them. The hard part about surviving is sometimes you are so very lonely."

Everywhere—in the crowded markets, on broken streets jammed with bicycles and rattletrap trucks bursting with human cargo—Robin felt life bursting out of death, life pouring from these unquenchable people like sunlight. And the children, beautiful babies, toddlers everywhere, ragged but so alive, faces ripping at your heart. Some with spindly legs and bulging ribs, chronically undernourished, were "likely to die from reduced resistance to disease. Two years after its deliverance from the Khmer Rouge nightmare, this wounded country is still sliding back into jungle. And no outside power sees fit to offer rescue from the century's second Holocaust, happening here still." *No, no, no.* . . .

In a crammed schoolroom, kids all ages learned to read and write, squeaking chalk over slateboards. An Australian relief worker said it would help if they had pencils or paper, but they managed well with their slates. "Give them brushes and paints and they make a mural. Give them chalk and they write stories. Or find a few musical instruments and suddenly there's an orchestra. I think there's no place on earth where human beings achieve so much with so little."

As if to prove it, Cal and his Land Rover stalled one day at the splintered remnants of a main highway bridge. Eighty-odd passengers poured off a bus and truck, digging out crude tools. Some chopped trees into timber, others made spikes from metal scraps. From the seething, they built their own River Quai bridge in less than three hours, with no blueprints, experts or money, with no one in charge.

On a hotel verandah Cal asked some Cambodians what they'd been saved from—who were the Khmer Rouge? One said the Khmer Rouge had fled to the mountains, or to the Thai refugee camps. But the hotel director, a tranquil, handsome woman, said, "I thought you knew, monsieur! The Khmer Rouge are everywhere. Only yesterday I saw the man who took my jewelry. The woman who made us work the fields now lives 10 kilometers from here. I see her in the market." No one would give them work, and the man's children had been very ill, so she gave him money for medicine, and cloth.

Cal said angrily that if he ever heard the Khmer Rouge had come back for more killing, he'd remind himself this was "a country of willing victims as well as mass murderers."

The woman fixed him with a gently reproachful gaze, hands lifted in a gesture of prayer. Softly: "I am sure I did not understand you correctly, monsieur. I imagined you were suggesting the solution for Cambodia is to kill more Cambodians." Eyes huge, glowing coals behind those steepled hands. "I apologize, monsieur."

☆

The house lights went up. Robin started, looking around in a daze. "My god, Larry. My god. What can we do to help?"

Sean said what those guys did was really gross. Jason couldn't see why Pol Pot got away with all that: "The rest of them, too." Cal, ghostly against the wall, said nothing.

Larry cleared his throat. "Good job, Cal. Powerful piece of work." He paused, watching that pale face. "I suggest you pass along a print to your friend in Paris."

That night in the family quarters Larry convened his braintrust, his top ten advisers including brothers-in-law Tim Brandt and Brian Rourke, to hash out the political ramifications of the Hanoi feeler. Robin had no idea what they'd come here, so abruptly summoned, expecting to hear. But when Larry tipped them, every one of them went straight into the fan.

Watching Larry's dark expression as their strenuous objections spouted, she realized he *wanted* somehow to pull this off. The others sensed it too, and fought to talk him out of it: "Kiss-of-death issue."

"Nothing but pitfalls." "No way you could count on those goddam treacherous Viets to come through."

Cal sat to the side, like a father listening to doctors argue over a dying child. She wondered how all this must sound to him, this wide-ranging ramble on great-power interests, Russian versus Chinese spheres of influences and so on, mostly homing back to the Vietnam War and its aftermath, "those running sores you'd be opening, Mr. President. . . ."

At one point, Cal quietly asked them to remember that one bargaining chip Hanoi might ante up was "the survival of Cambodia—the nation and the people."

Tim, her favorite brother-in-law, threw him a patronizing smile, saying quite frankly the President had many more pressing issues on his plate: the Mid-East, Central America, the Congress. Cambodia was "an unfortunate case, but. . . ." He shrugged, wigwagging his hand. She suddenly flashed Tim splayed and gutted, spouting blood like a Pol Pot victim. Faint voice like her own: *There, do you see it now?*

Bastards, blind sons of bitches! She decided right then that no matter what it took, she wouldn't let them walk away from that small corner of hell down Cal's rabbit hole. Brian said shouldn't Larry make a speech to the U.N., "pitch for world peace sort of thing." Cal's head snapped back. He got up and lurched out—to the john, she supposed.

Tim said how about some Oval Office TV, "address to the nation type thing. Rally the troops in this crisis period and so on." Brian said hell, yes, A-one priority on that: "Any reason you're holding it up, Mr. President?"

Robin wagged a wave to Larry and went to look for Cal.

She found him down the hall at the big arched window, head crooked up at the night sky as if to take his bearings in the sea of madness all around him. So sunk in himself he didn't see her till she touched his elbow. "Cal."

He looked down, piercing her with his unspeakable pain. Choking on his fury: "Robin, I can't sit there and take that shit. A U.N. speech, for god's sake. . . ."

Glancing around, she tugged his sleeve, pulled him into the fusty den at the end of the hall. She nudged the door almost shut. "Cal, don't you listen to those guys. I'll make them sit down and watch your film—that incredible film, Cal!" She turned to face him, gyros spinning, memory skimming on unfinished business long ago. "You did such a wonderful thing there, telling that story so it rips your heart out. . . ."

Hand raking his hair, he looked bewilderedly around. "What the hell am I doing here? Why'd I come at all? Those bastards in there, they're the same kind who did in Cambodia last time around with their venal, barbaric ignorance."

She tried to tell him it didn't matter what *they* said. Larry was the one who counted, and she was sure he wanted to make this work: "If there's any chance at all, Cal, he'll dig it out. Trust him, give him a chance."

He shook his head, heavy with despair. She moved closer, feeling each jerky step that tugged her to him like a wound-up doll, tock tock. "We won't let them forget, Cal. We'll make them see." She reached for his arm. "You can't quit now. We've just begun to fight."

As she touched him, her sea anchor reeled into his gut. Suddenly he spun around, crushed her to him with bruising force, surging touch. Her steel locked to his magnet, vibrating to his trembling rage. Fusing to his survivor pain, as if finishing something begun long ago.

The kiss tasted of despair and swirling, undammed need. His or hers—maybe both. They rolled locked together onto the couch. Distant, urgent voice: *Watch out watchout.* . . .

Too late. Wildfire all through her, sucking flame from his mouth, igniting her crotch. His hand slid up her leg to her wet burning slit. She whispered, "No, no," as he fumbled at clothes but her body with its own mind said yes yes, legs curling on his hips as his long thin penis snaked into her.

She came like an explosion. Again and then again, storms of feeling, fire flood.

When the brief, ferocious fuck was done, his impulse was to pull away. But he made himself hold her till her ragged breath subsided, till her quivering stilled.

He wasn't sure what that had proved, except maybe that he was still alive. He craned to see her face—plump, flushed, a little stunned. Feeling his eyes, she opened hers with a soft, nervous chuckle. "Damn, Cal. That was. . . nice."

"Mm-hmm." Her cunt still squeezing sporadically on his limp pecker. Better not be looking for another go, because it wasn't in him. When she moved to peel her skirt off her neck, he muttered, "Good show, lady," and pulled out of her.

They sat up on the couch, rearranged their clothes. Not that they'd gotten much off. He felt that something was expected of him, so he rubbed her back, squeezed her neck. She was talking, breathless, skittery, about how they certainly mustn't do this again, she wasn't quite sure how it happened, but oh, wasn't that just. . . nice.

He guessed he ought to feel something. Passion, maybe. Payback, at least. Truth was, he felt—nothing at all.

She stood up, fussing with her hair, saying please excuse her, this was a bit much to take, and she was going to her room. She asked about him. He guessed he'd go back to the meeting.

The brief pipe cleaning had done that much for him, at least. Cleared his head enough for another round with the bureaucratic dorks.

She slid between her odd-sized sheets, still lit up and reeking with sex. Feeling thoroughly, utterly fucked, afterglow saturating her ears to toenails.

Last thing she wanted to deal with now was why she'd done it. Or how she'd handle the fallout with Larry. . . or Cal. So she let her head skip and play, thinking how strange that a man would come into your life, into your body, and you found yourself forever printed with his strange dreams.

☆

She'd had another night of glorious fucking, a long time back—in Cambodia. Larry and she went out one night to a sort of nightclub with Cal, where they laughed and sang and did a slow, stately Cambodian dance, all joining hands in a kind of low-key conga line, the *ram vong*. Later, at the hotel, she and Larry made love all night under the ceiling fan and mosquito netting. . . and presto chango, there was Jason. At least she always believed that was his start.

It was Larry in her bed that night, so sweet, so wild, but Cal was all over the room.

CHAPTER TWENTY-ONE /

January 25th
Prilla

All that Sunday Priscilla tried to fine-tune Dan's mood for the meeting she'd talked him into, to hear Chet's ideas for "moving this off the dime." He was still grumpy, reluctant, but she couldn't let it wait.

Chet needed lead time for his plan, and every day slid them further from rescue.

At eight she let Chet in the kitchen door, warning, "I promised him short and sweet. So don't disappoint me, Chet."

Dan looked up from a Richard Widmark western, told Chet to come on in, fix himself a drink. Dan kept on watching the movie. She'd vetoed a video presentation by Chet, saying Dan got too much of that, yet here he was glued to the TV.

At the next ad he switched off, asked for yesterday's feedback. Running on about Dan's "exceptional impact" on the congressmen, Chet was short on specifics, except that Kittyhawk mentioned private parking for his plane at National.

Dan blinked his surprise. "Well, shoot. If that's all he wants. . . . Is that do-able?"

"We'll certainly check it out, sir. But the way Kittyhawk talks, I assume it's not a serious negotiating point."

"Of course it's not," she agreed. "Chet, what else. . . ?"

He said Morinski, the elusive Wisconsin Independent, would be at a Thursday bipartisan prayer breakfast: "Good opportunity for you to meet him. You're overnighting at the Carlton."

Dan grumped, "Gosh darn, I hate that crack-of-dawn stuff. What's wrong with a prayer lunch or dinner? Okay, but you make damn sure that fella shows up."

Chet said the Talbotts were moving from the Shoreham Hotel to a McLean estate, loan of a Democrat fat cat; Dan's fund-raising had beat theirs nine to one. Dan popped his first smile all night. "Good going, Chet. Keep the heat on."

"You bet, Governor."

She pointed out if the Talbotts were moving, they mustn't be counting on a win any time soon. Right, Dan agreed. "And what's Devlin up to?" he asked. "We haven't heard much from that fella. What's keeping him so quiet?"

Off on that old toot again, gnawed as a dog's bone: Just warming your chair, sir. Don't you bet on it. What's he doing for the top of his ticket? A few calls, but no Oval Office glad-handing, no rides in the family elevator. By gosh, he's out for himself, that's what he is. . . .

Chet unrolled his old line about Devlin being more acting than President, but Dan shook his head. "Nah, you keep a close eye on that fella, Chet. Watch what way he's blowing. And what's Charlie Whalen up to? In cahoots with his Philly buddy, selling Roy Bob short there too?"

She couldn't see why he was brooding so about them all "selling Roy Bob short." Unless he felt that way himself. . . .

Chet said Whalen was busting his zipper to hold wavering Democrats. Tomorrow he'd routinize the deadlock with "extraordinary," that is, ordinary, legislative business in the mornings, and four hours of presidential debate before a late-afternoon vote—one per day, for now.

Dan said gloomily well, shoot. With Devlin's polls up twelve points, they were routinizing that House mess? "Those fellas will be blowing smoke till the roof caves in, and where in hell does that leave us?"

Steadily advancing on our righteous goal, said Chet.

This kiss-ass routine was going nowhere. She spoke up: "Chet, I think the Governor would like to hear specific, concrete *new* suggestions for getting this thing moving."

"Yes, ma'am." He stiffened, feisty posture, as if he'd finally remembered why he was there. "Governor, in order to get us some live ammunition, I'd strongly recommend hiring sources to provide confidential information on our individualized targets, particularly regarding financial vulnerability—campaign debts, second, third mortgages and so on. With a better feel for those soft spots, we can mobilize more help in that direction."

Now that's more like it. . . .

Frown, perking interest. "You mean—private dicks?"

Chet's smile was so rare it looked like a tic. "Let's say researchers, sir. Discreet, fiscally oriented, to work the paper trails those guys cover their tracks with."

She shot him an encouraging nod, murmuring, "Now that's worth considering, don't you think, Danny?"

"Well, I don't know. That sounds like plumbers, dirty work, and I've said all along I won't tolerate any mudslinging. Darned if I want any job bad enough to stoop to that."

Two voices chimed together: "Sweetie, I don't think that's what he—" "No, no, Governor, if I might clarify—"

She waved him on. "Thanks, Mrs. Sterling. What I'm suggesting is straightforward and aboveboard, nothing unethical. Merely an informational process to guide our strategy—counterintelligence against the press, if you will." More doubletalk on ameliorative measures, letter of the law. . . .

Dan scowled as she got up and poured him a Sanka. She watched the struggle on his face. "Nah, I don't know, Chet. That kind of business has a way of backfiring on you. You know what Dave Elliott says about the brutal scrutiny those fellows are under right now. I haven't come this far to see it all chucked away by some ham-handed dick in the headlines."

Chet assured him these researchers would be "completely discreet and reliable," paid by private resources untraceable to the RNC or the campaign, "to emphasize the confidential nature of their assignment."

Lord knows it was little enough to work with anyway, and if Chet thought a few gumshoes might help pull off this win, she'd make sure he got them. Setting down Dan's cup, she said tartly, "Hon, we do have to consider that practically all the information we get on this *terribly* critical situation comes from the Hill Republicans and the RNC." Kneading the stiff spot over his collarbone. "Now wouldn't we all feel more confident with some independent pipelines into our own team?"

Chet talked smoothly, disarmingly about proposing "a legitimate means to help extricate certain congressmen from burdensome personal debt. Nothing more, nothing less, but some of those guys've been bleeding for years."

Dan wavered; she rubbed, pressed at his shoulder, purring, "Hon, isn't it worth at least a try?"

Dan finally told him to see what he could set up along those lines and report back: "But remember, Chet, I want this strictly aboveboard."

"Righto, Governor. Squeaky clean all the way."

She winked triumphantly at Chet, saying softly, "Of course, Danny. We know what you want."

She asked Chet what time frame he saw on all this. He said firmly they should see movement this week. "Overall, Mrs. Sterling, I'd project a wrap-up within thirty days."

Ah, that's more like it. . . .

CHAPTER TWENTY-TWO /
January 26th
Robin

Robin woke up feeling hung over, full of sluggish alarm. *Were you drunk. . . maybe you dreamed it?*

No such luck. She still reeked of his juices. Her sensitized crotch felt peeled open, demitumescent, ready for a replay as fragments of last night's impetuous tumble flicked in her groggy consciousness.

Groaning, pulling a pillow around her ears, she remembered she'd never actually got her panties off. Never knew you could even do it that way, but obviously they'd managed.

Panty hose, she thought gloomily. A nylon wall at least forced time out for second thoughts. But last night she had on her lacy black garter belt, Tish's joke Christmas present with about as much built-in braking power as a Chevy back seat.

In the family quarters, yet. With Larry down the hall. . . when she wasn't even plastered for an excuse. That sort of risky, hell-bent flyer she associated with Michael. Or Larry, on a toot. But not Mrs. Goody Two-Shoes. . . .

She wasn't sure why she'd done it at all. Her humming, aromatic crotch had no remorse, but the rest of her was riddled with reflex guilt, her congenital condition. Not so much toward Larry—his tomcat score was Everest to her anthill. But she felt she'd violated some part of the deal they made moving in here. Also trampled on his friendship with Cal.

Most of all she'd violated the fragile possibilities of the Indochina initiative. *That* was deadly serious—unlike the freaky, charged moment with Cal—and if her witless caper in any way jeopardized that. . . .

Reminding herself the best defense was a good offense, she tackled Larry over breakfast. "Dev, I hope your last word to Paris won't be that bilge they were feeding you last night." He remarked somewhat acidly, with a have-you-been-drinking squint, that she hadn't stuck around for much of what they said.

"That's right," she snapped. "I got the gist."

He lashed back, "For your information, I'm not talking just to them. Give me a little credit, will you?" She muttered an apology, saying she was probably a little strung out still from that movie.

"Well, I'd appreciate you not presuming to tell me who to talk to." Pause. Then, reluctantly: "Eric Lowenthal's coming by for lunch. If you want to sit in. . . ."

She heard herself ask casually if Cal would be there too. Larry said yep, he guessed. "I'd like Eric to take a run at him, see how he thinks this shapes up."

☆

She tendered a warm welcome when Eric Lowenthal came early to lunch, grand old lion of the Democratic establishment, involved in every major foreign-policy initiative over the last half century. A long-boned, high-minded Yankee like Cal, dapper as ever at age 84, Eric was one of those rare people who made Robin feel a little safer and saner every time she saw him.

She listened to his gabby reminiscence of "your remarkable brother-in-law," the late lamented Michael, one of Eric's favorite presidents, until Larry wheeled into the Oval Room, trailed by gaunt, familiar shadow. "Eric! Good of you to come. Sorry I'm late, I got held up downstairs. I'd like you to meet an old friend, Cal Farragut. . . ."

She looked timidly, warily at Cal—and this time all she saw were his wounds. A broken, bleeding man, veiled in pain. At dinner that first night she'd caught the burning light in him. But how amazing she hadn't seen the wounds!

He seemed calmly indifferent to her presence, except for a quiet "H'lo, Robin." Whiffing déjà vu, she echoed that indifference. *Sort this one out later. . . .*

Cal didn't expect any more from this go-round than from last night's, but at least it involved a tribal elder instead of ass-kissing in-laws. Robin too, who was maybe his only ace in the hole. His silent partner in this deal. She was coming at this from her gut, like she'd come at him last night.

That gut involvement was the only thing he trusted. He wondered how much sway she had over her slick know-it-all husband—not bloody much, he'd bet. The Devlin boys were all cut from the same cloth, macho bullshit overlaid on relentless self-promotion. But she might know ways to get to him on those grounds too.

Over a lunch described as Delia's "famous corned-beef stew," appetizing as cowpies, Larry crisply recapped events for the old guy. Cal watched the reactions: hiked brow; noncommittal grunts, nods; fiddling with his unlit pipe.

Asked to share his thoughts, Lowenthal whacked an ashtray and said among the range of Asian possibilities he'd always been "particularly intrigued by the natural symmetry of a U.S.-Vietnamese detente, minimizing the Soviet presence, and giving Hanoi some security against its overbearing northern neighbor. An umbrella of protection from the Chinese rains, if you will. Now it seems Mr. Farragut may have come calling with that umbrella in hand. An ancillary plus, of course, would be the potential rescue of Cambodia, that sorely beleaguered gem of southeast Asia. . . ."

Cal suddenly decided he was hungry after all. He picked up his fork and tucked into the Irish stew.

As she took in the broad discussion, leaping and focusing sweeps of history with Cal's two bits stuck in now and then, Robin felt her world turning sane again. Lowenthal reminisced about a Kremlin dinner in '45 when Stalin had told him the United States should put China back on its postwar feet, since Britain and Russia would be tied down with their own reconstruction. "Of course, Ho Chi Minh then looked to the U.S. to play essentially the same role for Vietnam."

She blinked her surprise. Ho Chi Minh?

"Ah yes!" Larry found it damned ironic that four decades later Stalin's Sino-American predictions had materialized. "But unfortunately we took the other route with Vietnam. Ho looked to us for protection against China and France—now China and the U.S.S.R. But the root motives for rapprochement may remain valid. . . ."

She'd forgotten how brilliantly his mind could work, crunching and dissecting vast networks of facts, where she knew only bits and pieces. Cal pointed out that China had more reasons than Vietnam for wanting the Russians off their backs. "So you could get a double play."

Two days ago he'd turned up like a hangover from a half-forgotten war, raving about how Larry could "save" Cambodia with a plan that seemed off-the-wall. But as she heard that canny pro Lowenthal dig into it now, playing out "the multiple potentialities in that arena," Cal's idea spun open like peacock feathers. *Then it's not so crazy after all!*

To Eric the towering figures of history were old friends, the stuff of good yarns. When Larry mentioned Vietnam's "young" foreign minister, Nguyen Co Thach, as a likely source for the overture since he'd shared several posts abroad with Cal's contact, Eric had a yarn on him too: "Ah, yes. Thach has an exceptional sense of humor for a Vietnamese. I recall one evening in Geneva. . . ."

The focus tightened on Eric's "intriguing array of possibilities, assuming Mr. Farragut's feeler has any substance to it—which may be a generous assumption at this point."

"To say the least," Larry agreed. They poked at it like jigsaw puzzlers: What might induce China, the area's major player, to trade support of the Khmer Rouge for a neutral Cambodia? How would the Soviets react to any deal jeopardizing their only Pacific warm-water port at Cam Ranh Bay?

Cal remarked that it was "way past communism" in Cambodia already. Except for the bargain-basement Russian aid, only the black-market economy kept them going, and if they tried to reverse that free-market drift, "the whole place would slide back into jungle."

On Pol Pot, Cal had the anecdotes: Pol raving in his speeches, "We are no Hitlers!" Slipping from his jungle lair for secret medical treatments in Bangkok, "in a white Toyota van with smoked-glass windows." Cal looked at Larry. "What I can't grasp is why your guys don't just. . . ."

Ripple of consternation. "Well, anyway. . . ." Cal had never seen the man, actually, but he knew the number two, Ieng Sary: "Same kind of moonish face behind heavy black glasses. Always zooming off first class to New York or Singapore in his little Mao cap, digging into the hostess baskets with both hands, stuffing his pockets."

Lowenthal said condescendingly it was a shame Cal hadn't observed him "in his natural habitat, so to speak." Cal said as a matter of fact, he got into the Khmer Rouge zone last year for *Stern* magazine: "There was Ieng to greet us at the end of the trail, holding out those hands with the blood of two million, all smiles and welcome. *'Bonjour, messieurs. Faites comme chez vous, faites comme chez vous.'*"

Larry swallowed a smile as Cal topped Eric with that rare trip inside the nightmare zone. Larry knew it from Cal's dossier, and didn't mind seeing the old pro one-upped.

Larry'd spent most of his life playing the easier odds, coasting on the advantages opened up by name and money. Got pretty far on them, too. Now here he was breaking bread with a certifiable flake itching to trip him into the biggest trouble of his life and a nostalgic old fart whose head was back on the Long March with Mao.

He felt like a nostalgic fart himself for calling in Eric to run on about the great old glory days of Michael's administration. What was he trying to prove by this anyway, except the questionable proposition that he could run this show as recklessly as Mike?

He stirred from his brooding to apply a little soft soap, praising Eric's "wise and comprehensive grasp of the Asian realities," asking for his views on the overture.

Patrician eyebrows twitching, Eric rumbled through the usual caveats: Cover all flanks, avoid undue optimism, and exercise "sharp vigilance in any dealings with the Vietnamese, as I hardly need remind you, Mr. President." He'd want to know if the Hanoi Politburo could be delivered, if the Soviet Union had wind of this. "But on balance,

weighing the inherent risks against the potential ramifications, I recommend that you pursue this opportunity, within the framework of
your April '79 statement, Mr. President."

Hearing that, Larry realized with surprise it was what he wanted,
after all. The boot-to-the-pants he'd counted on Eric to deliver. He
rambled into ass-covering, how he'd in any case act with "utmost prud-
ence and circumspection. . . ."

He'd never seen himself as courting danger, make-or-break political
danger anyway, except maybe in that primary run against Talbott—
which sprang more from pique and family momentum than sheer guts.
But now, by god, he'd need all the guts he could muster, edging up
to the cliff, leaning into the wind. *Go for it! Hold your nose and jump.* . . .

Over a rice-pudding dessert—damn strange food these people lived
on—Cal reacted with disgust to the five-syllable bureaucratic weaseling
going on at this table. Word concoctions with splendid structure and a
life of their own, but piss-all to do with the real, hurting world out
there.

He marveled now that he'd turned up here expecting anything *but*
ritual claptrap from Larry Devlin. Funny how it was all coming back
now: the fudged exams, the recycled term papers, the golf or croquet
balls that magically improved positions between strokes.

Well, more fool him, for nursing such a leaky memory. For wishing
—hoping—against all logical odds that Bad Boy Devlin might've acquired a few genuine balls along with the fancy office. Suddenly he
heard, ". . . can't reject out of hand any genuine opportunity to advance
the cause of peace. Accordingly, I'm instructing Mr. Farragut"—stern
gaze at Cal—"to convey my qualified interest in pursuing this discussion
with the appropriate parties."

What the hell. . . .

Larry laid out two nonnegotiable provisions: Vietnam must agree to
withdraw from Cambodia—and with no price tag "under any guise,
reparations or whatever. I don't hold out any great hope for this amount-
ing to much, but let's at least see where it goes."

Cal nodded. Softly, shaded with apology: "Thank you, Mr. President."

Good lord, he did it!

Feeling oddly deflated, itching for a little drink to celebrate, Robin
wandered down to her office. In front of the silk elephants and temple

dancers she murmured, "If you've got a dance for luck, do it now, little guys."

Minutes later Sally was droning on about the "*flood* of interview requests. I left a list on your desk. Did you. . . ?"

She nodded impassively.

"All right. Just so you've seen it." On to the "pressing matter" of the guest list for the Spanish royal dinner; Robin waved aside the nudge. "The press wants to know if the Talbotts are invited. If not, when they're expected back."

Robin said tartly, "That question belongs in my husband's office."

Her thoughts kept drifting to that lunch, spinning on the broad possibilities it had opened up. Suddenly she heard, ". . . urgent request from *Good Housekeeping* for your favorite Lenten fish recipes. They're already going to press, but willing to—"

"What's that?"

Sally blinked up from her notes. "But this won't involve a personal interview, Mrs. Devlin. And a major women's magazine feature seemed to me the kind of exposure President Devlin is anxious to have right now."

She snarled, "No fish, Sally. Do you think you can remember that? *No fish*." Then she bugged off to run thirty laps around the grounds, her mood tossing like the January wind.

She thought she was handling this roller-coaster day fairly well. But when Tish arrived and they settled over a tea tray in her sitting room, she realized she wasn't handling it at all. Tish cut off the chatty welcome, wanting to hear the "stupid thing" behind her SOS.

She winced. "Oh, lord. The stupidity was mainly calling you. Bad case of overreaction, I mean. You can see I'm fine. Haven't even thought much about a drink since your. . . ."

Stern glare: "Robin! Cut the crap."

No way to clue her in without breaching diplomatic secrecy. So Robin stressed the need for "utter, absolute confidentiality on this," telling it briskly and concisely, starting with "this old friend of his— ours—" turning up unexpectedly on Saturday night.

Tish took in the babble about how quickly that indiscreet moment with Cal had happened, like a storm, like something in war, people under fire. "It just sort of *happened*, Tish. But it didn't mean anything special. And Larry's already sent him back to Paris! So. . . ." Robin dwindled off with a timid glance. "Oh, say something, please. Don't just look like that."

It had been a long time since Tish had managed to be shocked by anyone's random screwing around. But she understood that for *this* woman, in *these* circumstances, the dip symbolized careening out of control, zooming smack into the danger zone. She sensed an anguish in Robin masquerading as heart, an unacknowledged rage veering into payback. And this time she decided not to pull her punches.

"Robin, I think you should get in touch right away with Dr. Traub. Or some other good shrink, if you'd prefer." Robin reacted like she'd been slapped. But Tish pressed on: "You're very manic now—too extreme for a dry drunk. That's outside my realm of experience, and I don't think any responsible layperson should take it on."

Cowed indignation in Robin's protest: "Come on, Tish, one lousy romp on a couch. *Now* who's overreacting?"

But Tish stuck to her guns. AA's root principles of truth and trust were "hard enough to hold onto living in a political zoo that functions exactly opposite to that. But damn near impossible if you're playing shell games like. . . . Are you sleeping with Larry too?"

Reluctantly, Robin said once in a while. On rare occasions. But they'd finally talked about where they stood. "I mean, I got a chance to tell him when this detour is over, I want a divorce."

A word so alien to Robin's tongue it came out sounding like Hungarian. Tish was genuinely frightened by the vibes she was picking up—scared out of her sponsorial wits. *And if she goes down, it's on my head.* . . .

Briskly, relentlessly, Tish pointed out all the stop signs Robin was going through. She hadn't just had an itch and scratched it—she was behaving in a way that intensified all her risks. At a *minimum* she should immerse herself in the program, go to a lot more meetings, get back to the steps. "Because if you keep on rolling like this, it's only a matter of time till you pick up a drink. And *you don't know* what'll happen then; it's absolutely unpredictable."

Robin felt like she was being knocked cold sober by a couple of wet towels. She slid into a self-defensive sulk, nursing the irritation she was too intimidated to vent.

She'd somehow expected Tish to poke her back into where it all started with Cal, on Block Island. But Tish wasn't the least bit interested in *that*; she was running on about how god knows she wasn't one to cast any stones about stepping out on a husband, but she was troubled by her sense that Robin was in free-fall, pitching out of control.

Robin flashed herself cartwheeling, tumbling end over end through a blood-red sky. She blurted, "But I fucked the wound in him, see. Florence Nightingale one more time. But why didn't I see that till after?"

Tish shook her head like a dog coming out of water and said please, please do herself a favor, quit fooling around with absolute TNT like that. "What's happened to your own work? Can't you hole up somewhere in this barn and get back to your painting? And/or go see Dr. Traub."

Robin said Traub was an idiot; she'd do better talking to herself. Tish said then at least take a week at Birch Woods.

"No, no, there's something much bigger going on now, Tish," she objected hotly. "If Cal's feeler works out, Larry might have the chance to end a fifty-year war and save Cambodia from being utterly—"

Biting interruption: "So now you're the queen of the country, out to save the world! Slow down and listen to yourself. You're on a *tearing* ego trip. Coming on—"

"See his movie, Tish."

"—like a manipulative little princess, playing some kind of head trip that's too dense for me." Tish said she was very sorry about the poor little Cambodians, but if Robin had sat down to *invent* a classic alcoholic contrivance, she couldn't've done any better than that. "All I can tell you is, if you CAN stop, *do it right now!*"

Robin sensed the gut truth in Tish's nag. Yet still she resisted, asking why not try to do something good and right for a change, dammit. "We're talking about the survival of a whole people, for god's sake, Tish."

Tish shook her head, heavy with gloom. "Hey, I'm busting my chops to help one individual to survive, period. And right now you're making that a very uphill fight."

CHAPTER TWENTY-THREE /

January 26th

Prilla

Knuckles still white from the rough flight down, Priscilla stood beside Dan on a platform outside a shut-down West Virginia steel mill. Eye cocked on the surrounding cameras, she listened to ". . . the bankrupt policies of big-spender Democrats created the economic ruin we see here in our great American heartland. . . ."

That gusty lead-grey sky was the kind she was most afraid to fly in. But even ordinary takeoffs and landings terrified her, always had and still did after thousands of flights—their best-kept campaign secret.

Beyond the mikes-and-cameras thicket, a crowd of laid-off workers pressed against barricades, booing, shouting something unmistakably hostile.

When Dan finished his riff he handed her down off the platform. Ezra said, "Very good, sir. Now we'd like some over here at the gate." She waved Dan away. Press-gang surging after him, he headed for the chain-link gate, CLOSED FOR BUSINESS scrawled above a huge padlock. Laurie Pendergast piped up, "Quite a turnout, wasn't it, Mrs. Sterling?"

The chanting louder, angrier. She asked what they were saying.

"I can't make it out. Mrs. Sterling, would you rather wait in the car? That crowd's getting a little rowdy. . . ."

Now she caught it: "Talk to the people, not the press! Talk to the people, not the press!"

Dan was only a short distance away, rattling the enormous padlock, talking to the mikes—inaudibly. "Laurie, where's the P.A. system? They can't hear him, that's the trouble." Laurie said she guessed somebody'd slipped up, but they'd all be out of here soon anyway.

Shrinking into her coat, Priscilla stared across at those faces—gaunt, anxious, pinched with pain. Bleak as that ugly factory, tombstone to their jobless future. Every few weeks now she and Dan turned up at another shuttered mill. Sometimes modern buildings, landscaped and manicured, not like this rusting hulk. But the faces of this political moonscape were always the same—so fearful, angry, steeped in ruin.

Her least favorite part of campaigning was this rubbing elbows with the wretched of the earth. Gorks, deadbeats, cripples, losers. Sometimes her nose stung from the sour smell coming off them. As Ginny put it, "Darling, we weren't made for unpleasant scenes like that." Ginny always said hats off to Prilla, she couldn't imagine how she stood it. You always knew that sort of thing existed, terrible shame too—but lord, how she dreaded having to see it close up, touch their hands, let them touch her. . . .

Usually Dan shook hands along the barricades going to the car, despite persistent Secret Service objections; getting close to the crowds produced good TV footage so that was one more gambit he was pressing to break him out of the House stalemate. But now she heard, "Move him right out. . . ." "Need more cops. . . ."

An agent snapped, "Mrs. Sterling, we're clearing you out," as she saw the first young man vault over the sawhorses. He glanced toward Dan, invisible behind rings of bodies—and headed straight for Priscilla.

Suddenly the crowd surged, swarmed at her. Agents grabbed her arms, rushed her to the car as she called out, "Dan? Where's Dan?" Hungry faces came at her, shouting, pushing. A man with a terrified kid on his shoulders raged, "We need jobs, not your goddam circus!" A wild woman in overalls clutched her wrist. "Just give us a chance! I've got six kids. . . ." An agent hurled her back.

Priscilla was screaming above the uproar, "Where's my husband?" as they pushed her into the back of the limo.

Dan liked an event like this where he got to show off some righteous indignation. The words weren't all that different, script 37 instead of script 53, say, unreeled from his lucky photographic memory. But against this backdrop he could ham it up a little, stoke the heat: "About time we got a leader at the top who can turn around this man-made Democrat disaster. . . ."

As he wound down to his punch lines, somebody asked would he talk to a delegation of furloughed workers? That threw him for a loop. He glanced over at Ezra, stalling for time. Ezra and Paul ducked heads, battlefield conference.

On second thought he figured okay, why not? If they gave him a rough time he'd say he couldn't do a damn thing for them till he got elected—he'd been looking for a spot to work in that line since Chet came up with it last week.

Paul threw him a nod, fingers circling O for okay. Dan said all right, he'd talk with a few. Right that minute, all hell broke loose. Pushing, shoving. The press swayed and lurched like cattle about to stampede. Agents locked around him, rushed him through the pack. Two guys by the car suddenly waving submachine guns, in the back seat Prilla screeching like a wet hen.

He tumbled in as if spewed out of the chaos, landing on the floor with two agents piled on his back, the car already streaking away, sirens wailing.

Prilla grabbed him by the lapels, pulled him up to the seat beside her. "Danny, Danny, are you okay?"

He said sure thing, you bet, Mommie, trying to catch his breath as he helped the mortified agents into the jump seats, everybody asking at the same time was he okay, was he all right. But it was Prilla hanging onto him for dear life, a world of panic in her eyes as she gasped, "Danny, for heaven's sake, what happened?"

Her heart was thumping so loudly she could hardly hear Dan. He guessed they had a little problem with crowd control back there. The agents guiltily confirmed that. Dan patted her hand, asked with reflex concern, "Are *you* okay, hon?"

"Of course," she lied, tom-tom boom in her chest. Obviously he didn't know they'd *come right at her*.

He brushed off the agents' apologies: "That's okay, you fellows did a fine job." He wanted to know if Paul and Ezra got out okay. The agents said they were in staff cars. Dan turned back to her, squeezing her hand, smiling reassurance, unfazed as ever. "You sure you're all right, Mommie?"

Her knees rattled like castanets. "Yes, fine. But I wouldn't care for a rerun of that, thanks very much." She babbled about the man with the terrified boy on his shoulders, hanging on by a handful of hair: "I was so afraid he'd fall and get trampled." Still shivering, she looked out at the desolate neighborhood whipping by. "Danny, isn't it awful how these poor people live. Look at those wretched hovels."

She touched her wrist, feeling those grasping fingers like a bruise. A tear in her paper-skin. *No no, don't say it. . . .* Yet it burst from her anyway: "Hon, if it's okay with you, I wouldn't mind if that's the last bombed-out factory we have to see for a while."

CHAPTER TWENTY-FOUR /
January 27th
Robin

Carmen was to the White House what Delia was to Greensleeves, Robin groggily decided over her wake-up coffee. At least in the gossip department: "Mr. Hamilton's grandbaby James popped his fourth tooth last night. That chile is growin' like a weed. . . ."

Delia used to vacuum up her crumbs from neighbors, paperboys, markets, god knows where. Amazingly accurate, if you followed her track record from the sunny Greensleeves kitchen. Now this cavernous house seemed to've somehow swallowed old Delia up, muted her sharp tongue. Pity, that.

". . . sez poinsettias was only for Christmas but Mr. Fletcher likes them as long as they last." Carmen opened the curtains, unkinked the strings. "Now Mizz Arnstein, she used to work for the President, now didn't she. That's prob'ly why she still be taking letters from him. . . or something."

Robin set down her cup, head cocked, blinking toward the window. "Taking letters?"

Carmen brushed at a dust speck on the curtain. "Well, I s'posed that's what she be doing when I see her Friday afternoon come from the Oval Room. With that notebook she always carry, you know? Then I see the President come from his office and go downstairs. So I guess maybe he be dictating something extra to her."

Head bursting with startled fury, Robin asked coolly what time Friday this was. About one-thirty, Carmen said. Neither one mentioning Larry's bedroom in between, with connecting doors. *Little lunchtime quickie, damn his hide!*

She thanked Carmen for that nugget, with a warmth meant to encourage more squealing from this new prime source. Her satellite spy. *Thank you god for Carmen, at least. . . .*

One week in this star-crossed house and of course he was off getting himself laid, like a dog peeing on lampposts. No surprise, why break the habits of a lifetime now?

Oh, the bastard! Soiling *her* nest, fucking around with that cold, humorless bitch he'd foisted on her as a goddam office watchdog. All the crap Sally'd put her through, all that supercilious business now explained itself only too well—while they'd been sneaking off for quickies on the side. God! It made her want to throw up, right in his lap. *Both* their laps.

It occurred to her that on that particular subject she was hardly one to cast stones, but she brushed aside the scruple. Whatever that crazy moment with Cal had been, it wasn't a deliberate, sustained, totally mocking betrayal.

Seething, stung by his inexcusably tacky behavior, she held off going downstairs until he'd left for work. *Have a go at the bitch first. . . .*

In her office she buzzed for Sally, who slithered in with an armload of work, smile wider than usual: "Morning, Mrs. Devlin. I trust you had a good night's sleep?"

"Yes, quite." Seeing that plastic-blonde hair and heart-of-an-accountant face, she was struck, not for the first time, by what lousy taste he had in women. Her ripping anger separated each word into icy compartments. "Sally, I'd like to hear where you were at lunchtime Friday."

"Lunch—Friday?" Pay dirt in that first reaction: jaw gaping, eyes rolling, looking for an out.

That little bombshell whistled in on Sally absolutely from left field. She clutched her papers, stammering, stalling for time to pull something together: "Let's see, Friday. Was that when I went to Maison Blanche, or—well, I might have to check my datebook, Mrs. Devlin."

"No, you don't, Sally." The Bird's voice was calm, level, as if she were ordering pizza. But the face was lit with a fierce intensity. "We both know where you were. Having tea and crumpets, shall we say, on the second floor."

Sally's first reaction was to stonewall, fish for how much else Robin knew. But that cold stare bored into her like a threat: *Don't try it, tootsie.*

In point of fact Sally'd never really thought much about the Bird in this whole business, except as one more logistical factor in the affair. At least she'd never thought of her in any conscience-stricken sort of way—they didn't even live together, after all! His *other* women always bothered Sally much more than the Bird.

A big part of his game was always layering the angles, compounding the secrecy. He liked to sneak around a little, even when he didn't really have to. Sally guessed maybe his wife was an element in that. Every so often a thought might flit across her mind: *Boy, what you don't know would fill a book, Wifey.* But she'd never considered herself responsible in any way for that woman's pain.

In point of fact, she'd always thought the Bird went out of her way to stir up trouble for herself. Sally never had a specially high regard for the woman—but seeing the stony anguish carved on that face now, she was wising up fast. Staring at her feet, Sally mumbled miserably, "I'm so sorry, Mrs. Devlin. I hope I didn't. . . ."

"All right, Sally," she said quietly, twirling around her chair. "I'd like you to go out there and spend the next ten minutes writing me a one-page description of how you see your functions in this office. I want that available as guidance for your successor. And as soon as you've finished that, pack up and clear out."

Christ, the sack! She gasped, "Oh my goodness, oh. . . ."

"I'm not ungrateful for your past services, for which I presume you've been adequately compensated. But I don't want to see you in this office again, is that understood?"

Still reeling from that kicker, Sally grabbed at a straw: She wasn't really fired until *he* said so. A wife on the warpath was always a big risk, but if Sally was very, very careful about how she played this, she might come out better off. At least she wouldn't be stuck baby-sitting the Bird any more. But the trick now was to disarm as much of that woman's fury as she could.

Meek as a mouse, she murmured penitently, "Yes, ma'am."

Robin's initial rush of satisfaction, her payoff for that minor payback, ebbed quickly after Arnstein skulked out. The kid was one of a long parade, after all. In effect, she was taking his rap.

At least Robin had gotten through the scene without breaking down. The unease that had churned in her for so many days like a hangover she couldn't shake off was suddenly gone. And to give the devil her due, Sally hadn't tried to stonewall her way out of it—which must've taken some guts. Robin could almost grudgingly admire that. . . .

A click of recognition so clear she seemed to hear it: Of course! The kid would try to get to Larry first!

She grabbed the phone and asked to be put through to her husband. He came on seconds later in a brisk, make-it-snappy voice: "Yes, Rob. What's up?" *Beat out Sally, at least.*

Her calls usually started out so sorry to bother, did he have a minute? But this time she went coldly, briskly to the point: "Larry, I think you ought to know about some personnel changes in this office. There's an assistant here, I believe you know her name, who I want out of here this morning. It's up to you where she goes from here, but I will not have her in my daily eyesight, have you got that straight?"

Stunned silence. "I gather you, um, want to get rid of Sally."

"Correctly put." Fury strained her voice. "Keep her on your end if you want to. I personally think she should be canned, but in fairness to her she's less responsible than. . . ." She choked back that "you." "Anyway, if I can't work with somebody I halfway trust, I won't do this damn job at all."

"Okay, fine, no problem." The syrupy Great Conciliator. "If you two aren't hitting it off. . . ." She bridled at his nimble reflex, trying to pass this off as a catfight between the girls. "So who'd you have in mind for a replacement?"

She snapped, "I don't know. When I decide, I'll let you know. Anyway, Arnstein is *out*."

He hung up stung with regret. *Somebody got to her.* . . .

He should've handled this thing better. When the situation with Rob was coming to boil, he ought to've been more circumspect about Sally. Maybe cooled it for a while. She wasn't the only handy piece of ass around, come to think of it.

An old line of Mike's rattled in his head: "Yeah, but she gives the best head." Damn if Sally didn't too. But that was no excuse for tipping over the applecart.

For some reason he was thinking of his Yale Law buddy, Gary Delevan, of the time they'd gone rock climbing from Gary's folks' house at Stratton, couple of months before they both got engaged. They kind of played around with the idea, rolling it between them, talking out the pros and cons.

Gary thought he and Pam would do it when she finished her M.A. in the spring. He aired fears about getting trapped, taken in. Said he had to do it right because in his family nobody got divorced. Larry said ah, tell him about it.

Gary brought up what it must be like to be "monogamous," stretching the word out slow and round, as if describing some amazing, marvelous thing. He was a cocky, good-looking jock who talked a line like Frank Sinatra; together they'd plowed a lot of prime meat up and down both coasts, and there he was talking about settling down to a one-on-one relationship. Laughing about how glad he was he'd gotten in plenty of running around, topped his tank off with that kind of shit before moving into a whole different connection.

Larry realized that he couldn't for the life of him imagine going to his grave fucking only that one woman, no matter who she was. The whole idea made him feel desolate, abandoned. Yet he remembered Gary's soft, unguarded expression, talking about that, as if he were discovering some strange new place in himself.

Larry knew he couldn't match that. But he didn't care; even way back then, he'd rather've had it that way, push come to shove.

Stephanie Mayo was cursing out the new computer for the third time that morning when the phone interrupted. White House calling. Robin Devlin, wanting to know if she'd like to drop by for a chat: "Off the record, by the way, Steph."

She dropped the phone into the wastebasket. Fishing it out, she said breathlessly, "Excuse me, slight mishap on this end. How's that for cool. Okay, I'm on my way."

She grabbed her purse and ran shrieking to her editor's cubicle. "Gus, Gus, she wants me over there again! Cross your toes on this one, Gus, it might just be a biggie."

With Stephanie's toothy smile beaming across the mounds of paperwork, Robin was stricken with second thoughts. *She's press, after all. And such a motormouth. . . .*

Stephanie chattered on about the family photos: "Lovely bunch of kids you produced." She remarked on the silk hanging. "Gorgeous piece. Cambodian, isn't it?"

She started. "Yes, right. How'd you know that?"

Stephanie'd seen one like it in a Phnom Penh market. Still kicked herself for not buying it: "The story of my life. I meant to come back and bargain them down, but next day I was off to the front."

Stephanie pressed for a reaction on the *Post* pieces. "You hated it, you loved it, somewhere in between?" Robin finally said they were reasonably accurate accounts, which was all she'd asked for. "Now, whether I should've talked that candidly, even indiscreetly, that's another question. Anyway, it's not your problem."

"God, I hope it didn't make trouble for you. We've had a tremendous response, nearly all of it positive."

She said dryly they'd had a few ripples here too.

Stephanie said at the risk of adding insult to injury, she'd run across an interesting quote, in terms of not reinventing the wheel. She read out, "If I wanted to be selfish, I could wish that he had not been elected. . . . I never wanted to be a president's wife, and I don't want it now. You don't quite believe me, do you? Very likely no one would—except possibly some woman who had had the job. Well, it's true, just the same. For him I am deeply and sincerely glad. I wouldn't have had it go otherwise. And now I shall start to work out my own salvation."

Stunned, Robin asked who'd said that. Urged to guess, she tried Martha Washington and Mary Lincoln.

"Nope. Eleanor Roosevelt, interviewed after FDR's first election. By AP reporter Lorena Hickok, by the way. The, um, 'special friend' who lived in what's now the kitchen, across the hall from Eleanor's room."

Robin took that as a bizarre signal for her own plunge. Voice like

Tish's singing in one ear, *Are you quite sure you've thought this through?* Too late, too late. She grabbed for her safety-line instincts and jumped.

All of a sudden Robin was asking her if she could get a leave of absence and take over here as majordomo and press secretary. The job probably wouldn't last long, but Robin would be so grateful to have somebody she could rely on to run the outfit even for just a few weeks.

Stephanie went blank, struck dumb. Robin added meekly, "See the method to my madness? I asked you up here so you'd have a harder time saying no dice right to my face."

No dice? Fat chance! Stephanie thawed into an incredulous squeal. "Oh lord. Wait a minute, wait a minute. How could you possibly think I'd turn down an offer like that?"

Her ecstasy was cut short when Robin mentioned a condition of the job: no writing about it *or* her, "now or ever, at least not without my specific permission. That means books, magazines, TV, movies—the works."

Stephanie muttered that was a lot to sign away in one swipe. But Robin insisted the deal had to cover her family too. "And any state secrets you stumble across. I'd like to have someone around to really talk to, bounce things off. But that only works if I know it's strictly entre nous."

The trade-off was clear: access for privacy. Seemed a reasonable price, considering Stephanie would've cheerfully killed for a slice of the fat pie she'd just been offered. She kissed off the aborted royalty bucks with a sigh. "Agreed. Do you want that in writing?"

Robin said no; if she was going to trust her, they might as well start now. "So that's set, then?"

"In concrete, from my end. If I have any trouble getting leave, I'll tell Gus McIvor to go piss up a rope."

Robin beamed, said that was a real load off her mind. Stephanie confessed, "For me it's the answer to a divorced maiden's prayer. I've been going to bed every night saying, 'Please, Lord, please. Just a little piece of it.' "

Robin was finally sensing some control back in her life. She tossed Sally's one-page parting shot across the desk, remarking that she and Arnstein didn't see eye-to-eye on what the job involved: "Like, for instance, whether my pet fish recipes belonged in *Good Housekeeping*." Stephanie would probably sniff out the real story of Sally's abrupt departure in two and a half minutes, but she might as well stop worrying about that *right now*.

Stephanie demonstrated her quirky single-brow-hike. "Ah, yes. Not tuned to the Big Picture, shall we say?"

"Something like that. Anyway, she'll do better out of here. And *I'd* like Santa to somehow get me free of all this paper, so I can stop pretending to be some bureaucrat."

"Righto. I get your drift."

Robin said she did want to do this job right, as well as she could. "The essential parts, anyway. But I need somebody I can rely on to sort out the claptrap, handle everything I don't have to. In other words, liberate me from this damn desk."

Stephanie said the paper flow was the least of the problems: "I assume you're aware you've become a hot media item?"

Robin slid three pages of interview bids across the desk. Stephanie scanned them rapidly: "Mm-hmm. Covers the ballpark, all right."

"Okay, so I'm telling you what I told Sally: I don't want to do *any* of it. Not now, anyway. And I don't want any guff on that, least of all from you."

But Stephanie, grinning exuberantly, said she was about to suggest exactly that. Right now Robin was like instant Redford or Fonda. About to bloom into superstar status—not just in D.C., but all over the map. Hearing this with a physical dread, Robin asked curtly what was so terrific about that. Stephanie hedged: "You don't find that a hell of an interesting possibility?"

"Interesting to you, maybe," she snapped. "Frankly, the whole idea makes me want to barf."

Cautious backtrack: "But a big enough player can write her own rules. That's the point, see. Look how Alexis built her mystique with deliberate inaccessibility."

She snarled that she didn't care a rap about "building mystique."

"No, no. But. . . ."

"And frankly, that kind of talk scares me half to death. It's just. . . damn depressing."

"Uh-oh." Dive for the cigarettes. "I hope I'm not about to hear, 'You just talked yourself out of a job, cookie.' "

"Not a chance. Quite the reverse." She pointed accusingly. "*You* helped get me into this mess, Steph. And I'm damn well counting on you now to see me through it."

"Woo!" Mocking thump on her chest. "You had me worried there."

"Glad to hear that. What I had in mind, actually, was for you to handle the worrying for us both."

She flashed crossed fingers and a crooked grin. "Scout's honor, that's one of the things I do best."

Against her will, Robin laughed. "Okay, big mouth, put that blarney to work." A half hour later, with Stephanie already immersed in schedules, Robin escaped the treacherous vibes of the office. If Stephanie could deliver on half of what she'd promised, it was time to stake out a hideaway, carve out rescue of her own space and time.

Prowling the third floor, she settled on the northeast corner, a dowdy room with a twin bed and matching imitation-French-provincial dressers. She summoned the chief usher to ask that it be set aside as her painting room.

Fletcher said they'd remove the furniture this afternoon. And what equipment would she require? She said he needn't bother, she wanted it all left in place. Already she saw those phony-French dressers littered with brushes, paint trays, her own creative mess. "But I'd appreciate your instructing the cleaning staff and so on to stay out."

At the end of her afternoon run she asked Jim Connerty, as a special favor, to put a good lock on her workroom door, so she'd have the only key. Then she went back up and scribbled a wish list of art supplies Stephanie could smuggle in.

They'd all do what they had to to survive in here. Larry had his Taking Letters; she'd have her boar-bristle brushes.

A bad match, all right, but she'd stick around for a while and see where it took them.

CHAPTER TWENTY-FIVE /

January 29th

Robin and Prilla

Tap, tap on her arm. "Pril, honey, time to get up."

Eyelids fighting not to come open. "Hi, pal," she managed.

"Shucks, if I had my way we'd both sleep till noon." Immobilized on the bed, she saw him yawning, finger-combing his hair. Talking about the damn caucus at 8:30; now why'd they always make those things so early?

Must've not heard the wake-up call. But how could she not hear a wake-up call?

He shrugged on his robe, saying Phil didn't have the vaguest idea where in heck Mort came up with that Aleutian thing he'd touted to Kittyhawk. Mort just had to toot off on his own hook every so often, that's how he operated.

She felt the frantic signals going out from her head but could. . . not. . . move. Couldn't even blink. Like she was dead, paralyzed. God help her, what was happening?

Drowsily, as he switched on the bathroom light: "Come on now, lazybones, don't you doze off again."

She heard his urine hit the bowl, voice raised above the splash: "Mort's had this bee in his buns about making that island they own up there pan out. I asked Phil what the heck it was all about—fish, he said. Can you beat that? The darnedest thing, right off-the-wall. . . ."

Her jaw moved but no sound came out. She felt her body frozen in a sleeping sprawl, but *she couldn't move.*

Louder splashing of cold water on his face, part of his morning ritual, saying by gosh, he hated to think what Mort would come up with next. At the john door he finally looked right at her. "Pril. . . are you back asleep? Hey!" He switched on the overhead light. Louder: "Mommie, are you okay?"

Now! Do it now!

Suddenly, miraculously, energy flowed back through her, surging like that snapped-on light. She pushed back the leaden blankets and sat up, wobbly legs dangling off the bed. Shaking off her dizziness as she touched her hair, smiling reassuringly at him, promising, "Be right with you, hon."

Cross-legged on her sitting-room floor, Robin watched Dan Rather prime the pump for Larry's first press conference ". . . in the crisis atmosphere that still pervades the nation's capital. Among topics likely to be raised, the role and limitations of an acting president will probably. . . ."

The phone rang. She snatched it up, half expecting Melissa, due home for the weekend tomorrow. The operator asked if she wanted to talk to Mr. Farragut. *Oh, lord. . . .* Even sitting, she felt her knees buckle. *Already. . . .*

She said put him through.

Flat, laconic voice: "Robin, that you?"

"Cal! Is it good news or bad?"

He guessed they'd find out soon enough. He was meeting Larry tonight, and thought she might want to be in on it.

"Lord, yes." Larry bounded down the aisle, jaunty, resolute. "Thanks for calling. Excuse me, I've got to catch his debut."

She pushed away the phone. On the screen he paused at the podium, tweaking at his tie, expression grave, forceful. Hugging her knees, rocking, beaming, she crooned loyally, "Go to it, babe. Give 'em hell."

Heart in his mouth, eyes straight ahead to the guns, Larry said, "Ladies and gentlemen, I have a brief statement before I take your questions." His voice came out slightly cracked but amazingly normal, all things considered.

A sea of faces swam in the glare. In his stage-fright buzz, he couldn't recognize a single one. Clearing his throat, he glanced at the cards slipped from his pocket. "Last week the American system of government once again demonstrated the extraordinary strength and stability that has characterized its two-century history. . . ."

His rah-rah statement was the best rendering they could muster on "the challenging events of recent days." The questions mainly hit the same theme. He fended off a tricky probe about the degree of authority an acting president could exercise: "The Constitution speaks directly to that matter, 'The Vice President shall act as President until a President shall have qualified.' " Tacking on, "In any case, I anticipate a prompt resolution of that matter with the reelection of my running mate, President Roy Bob Talbott."

More questions on "this paralyzing crisis." Hitting his stride, he fielded them with a slick statistical blizzard, citing the Cabinet role and so forth. Mary McGrory asked if he planned any Cabinet changes. "Not at the moment, Mary," he zinged back. "But if you want to send in your resumé. . . ."

His mood lifted on the warm, empathetic laughs, sailing, soaring. Like scudding in a hard blow under a huge blue sky, spirits racing like the wind, knowing if he lived a hundred years he might never get dealt a moment much better than this one right here, right now.

Asked "how enthusiastically" he'd campaign for his former running mate, especially in the Kentucky by-election, he sang a few obbligato choruses about his "vigorous and unqualified support" for Talbott and the Rumfels woman. Then, feeling sun on his face and stiff breeze on his back, he added a kicker: "However, I believe that my responsibilities as Acting President take precedence over any partisan concerns. Accordingly, I will not actively campaign. . . ."

In the Iowa hotel room, Dan Sterling said, "Damnation! Did you hear that? He turned tail on his own running mate."

Aides babbled, "Hear, hear!" "A plus for you, Governor." Someone said they'd like to hear Roy's reaction to that stab in the back. Yet Priscilla thought they all seemed a bit uneasy, watching Devlin's East Room matinee. And no wonder: From the minute he'd stalked out there, filling the screen, she was shocked by how *young* he seemed—and so vigorous, so commanding!

When the questions began she froze an unexpected perception. Not anything being *said*. Predictably, Devlin steered clear of controversy. But he'd done his homework. His staff had rehearsed him well.

What alarmed her was the subtler message. All through this mess Dan's men had kept focused on Talbott, insisting Devlin was only a stand-in, a traffic cop. She'd almost believed that. . . maybe because she so badly wanted to. But watching now, she was ripped with doubt. This handsome, animated young man handled himself with a glib, cocky grasp of detail. Even jokes. Each question started off, "Mr. President. . . ." And each time it sounded more natural.

In fact, he *looked* presidential. She knew how image was tied to power—Siamese twins, almost. Dan's whole career had been built on his genius for exploiting that simple truth. And in image terms, this Devlin performance was a whopping success.

Asked for his policy on Agent Orange, Devlin took off on the "justified grievances" of Vietnam veterans, the "urgent need to determine conclusively the effect of the toxins." Dan said if he didn't pry that foot from his mouth pretty quick he'd start enough lawsuits to break the bank.

Somebody asked when Roy Bob Talbott was expected back on a White House visit. No firm date, Devlin said, "but in any case, I anticipate he will soon be reelected by the House and resume his rightful residency here."

Dan muttered sourly, "In a pig's eye, you do."

Suddenly it was over. Devlin moved out, pausing for parting shots. Tom Brokaw said excitedly, "The President's talking to Judy Woodruff, we'll try to get a mike in there. . . no, there he goes."

Dan asked for reaction. Paul said smugly they'd gone easy on Devlin today, but his honeymoon was about over. Ezra thought Devlin's rubber-stamp backing of Talbott "reinforces the impression he's hog-tied to that caretaker role." They chortled over Devlin's bombshell about not campaigning for Talbott. On the screen Brokaw picked that up too: "In his tenth day on the job, President Devlin seems to have distanced himself from the top of his party's ticket. . . ."

She said, "Danny, see how CBS is playing it." He switched to Rather and Cronkite at a desk. Dan muttered in surprise, "By gosh, they got the old warhorse out of his pasture for this one."

". . . setting his own style as our first acting president. Today he demonstrated able command of our creaky ship of state, still sailing through a major constitutional storm. Devlin's freshly nonpartisan posture may indeed be warranted, since he could become the first Democratic vice president to serve under a Republican president. . . ."

Dan looked away, blank expression masking annoyance. He snapped fingers: "Okay, what's my comeback? Paul, do I make a statement or let 'em catch me on the run?"

Paul recommended the offhand approach: "Let him and Talbott slug this one out on their own." Ezra suggested that Dan let Talbott react first: "Nothing lost by your taking the high road here, Governor." Paul mentioned a coast-to-coast telethon the Southern Baptists might front for Talbott, "raiding our conservative base."

Priscilla thought scornfully, *Talbott, Talbott, they can't see past Talbott!* She patted Dan's knee. "Hon, maybe you all miss the point a little. Forget this 'caretaker' routine. Larry Devlin's coming on *like a real president.*"

Prickly silence. Dan said mildly, "Pril, he can come on like Tarzan for all I care. Once we get this vote out of the House, that fella's going to be yesterday's dead fish. But first we've got to whale the daylights out of—"

"Forget Talbott," she burst out. "Devlin's the one—just watch out for Devlin."

CHAPTER TWENTY-SIX /

January 29th

Robin

Cal asked Ben Boylan, "Who else is coming?"

At that moment the Treaty Room door flew open with a rattley snap-to of Marine guards. Larry strode in, shoulders hunched, shooting his cuffs, staring at the Vietnamese man next to Cal. Flanking Larry were three glowering chaperones. CYA reflex in full bloom: When in doubt, cover your ass with flunkies jousting for the presidential ear.

Cal still didn't see why Larry wanted the beaky National Security hawk and pin-striped Secretary of State dove sitting in on this session anyway, let alone the pouchy CIA chief. Yet as Larry crossed the rug, Cal realized some kind of circle was being closed. He'd come this far on brute luck and old-school boula-boula, but from now on the stuffed shirts would be calling the shots.

"Cal, good to see you."

"Same here, Mr. President." Ritual shake. Cal said he'd like to introduce "my friend and colleague, Le Anh."

Robin floated in behind the others. Her eyes glanced off Cal and peered at Le Anh like he had three heads. Even so, Cal found her presence vaguely reassuring. Except for her, a live soul in this gloomy dollar-green room, he wouldn't think any of this was real.

Feeling as if she were moving into a strange dream, Robin noted the wiry grey crew cut on the stocky prize pigeon. Young-looking, jaundice-colored, poker faced. Disarming—deceptive?—twinkle in his eyes. He said in a low, accented voice, "I am pleased to have this great honor of meeting you, President Devlin."

Larry's introductions were in protocol ranking, beginning with Secretary Lessard. Le's irrepressible smile when he shook hands with Hugh Pownell, the CIA chief, was echoed around the room. And at the bottom of the pecking order: "My wife, Robin—Mr. Le Anh."

He bowed over her hand. Soft palm, firm shake. She said softly, "Welcome to the White House, Mr. Le."

Savvy glint in those dark eyes. "It is my high honor to here make your acquaintance, Mrs. President."

While Larry asked about Le's flight from Paris, she smiled discreetly at Cal, standing like a bony ghost of conscience backlit by fireplace flames. *Thank god he called!* Worth anything just to see Mal Koenig glaring at that Viet like a butler guarding the family silver.

Larry took the red-leather wing chair by the fire, gesturing Le toward a smaller velvet armchair. The rest roosted around them in order of urgency—Koenig inching closer to Larry, Lessard disdainfully perched along the back wall. She tried not to gawk as Le murmured appreciation for this opportunity to speak with "the president of this great nation, whose time is so much demanded."

Gravely, Larry said he always welcomed an occasion to meet with foreign journalists: "But this conversation will, of course, be considered entirely confidential, Mr. Le."

"Understood, Mr. President."

Larry said Cal Farragut had "provoked my interest" by suggesting that an exchange of views might "bear on subjects of mutual concern and benefit to both our nations." He paused, waiting out the return serve.

Staring at his shoes, Le said he understood his government might be favorably disposed to bilateral talks on a senior ministerial level "for the purpose of better relations."

End of small talk. Larry made a graceful spiel about America's enduring commitment to advancing peace among nations, when avenues to that goal were "genuinely available." That cause could be well served by Vietnam's return to its rightful place in the world community, but this would require Hanoi's termination of its military occupation of Kampuchea, "as proposed in my statement of April 2, 1979. . . ."

That "pie in the sky" sounded oddly realistic as this Asian visitor took notes. Le said he understood his government might be prepared to review its fraternal relationship with Kampuchea, but under no circumstances would it tolerate a return to power of "the criminal lackey Pol Pot and his murdering henchmen."

Larry assured him the United States wouldn't either, and brought up the "urgent matter" of the 2500 Americans MIAs. Le said Hanoi would answer those legitimate concerns when normal diplomatic channels were available, but no records existed for "what passed in Kampuchea under the Pol Pot gang."

They spoke about the Khmer Rouge legacy, and on that mutual enemy Le seemed to talk from the heart. Robin sensed Cal's empathy—as if they, at least, understood that Le's quiet, matter-of-fact voice was describing an indescribable human disaster.

As Pownell had predicted, Le couldn't resist a riff on Lyndon Johnson's billion-dollar "pledge for reconstruction," sliding to Nixon and Kissinger's five billion. Larry barked, "Mr. Le, I hoped your government had learned from its abortive discussions with President Talbott's representatives that no era of rapprochement can begin between our nations as long as you persist in phantom reparations claims."

With a tweak of a smile, Le said he understood some in his government now recognized "an error was perhaps made in emphasizing such matters in 1977." Larry grimly assured him any further discussions would hinge on prior agreement that this issue not be revived. Le said he thought his government understood such a condition would "reflect the U.S. political realities. But Mr. President, please understand that a small country cannot easily lose two billion dollars a year in foreign aid."

Larry's brows went up. "Two billion?"

Shrug. "A billion from China, a billion from the U.S."

The idea of Hanoi complaining about "losing" U.S. aid to South Vietnam shot an amused ripple around the room. But when Larry asked what "degree of involvement" other countries had in this probe, Le swallowed his smile. Picking at his fingernails, he murmured about "utmost confidentiality. . . relying on the good faith and discretion of the U.S. . . ."

He rattled them with a claim that Hanoi had asked the Thai government to pass along a signal the previous fall. With shrugs and head-shaking, Pownell and Lessard indicated that was the first they'd heard of it.

Le said the present overture involved only "the private channel of Mr. Farragut." Mal Koenig asked what assurances he could give that the Soviets weren't a party to it. Le snapped, "Common sense, Mr. Koenig."

Relaxing a bit over coffee and cookies, Larry asked the Viet how his revolution had gotten so far off track. Le shrugged, said it "just didn't work out like we planned."

Larry unbuttoned his jacket, getting down to business. "Truth to tell, Mr. Le, your economy is a disaster, even with substantial Soviet aid. And your present economic trends are in a downward direction." Le winced, but didn't argue that.

Cal brought up the rampant bribery and graft he'd found on his recent trip: "They boasted in Ho Chi Minh City of how fast they corrupted new administrators sent down from the North." With everyone from farmers to professionals moonlighting on the black market to make a living, where did that leave bureaucrats on fixed salaries?

Le claimed the revolution must be "built on the sacrifices of the bureaucracy," his voice edged with apology for the knee-jerk rhetoric. He backed off when Cal snorted that was a hell of a way to sink a country.

The brief dip into party line made Larry appreciate the little guy's relative candor. He wished he had a better sense of what was going on behind those dark eyes, darting constantly around the room—not that it mattered; this guy was strictly the messenger, making disarmingly reasonable talk aimed at patches of common ground like Hanoi's "sincere desire" to cooperate on a solution for the Amerasian kids, the untouchables left over from the war.

In the mood of thawing cordiality, Koenig mentioned possible IMF or World Bank development funds, perhaps for the stalled billion-dollar Mekong River project. Pownell said the impressive technical skills of Vietnamese in this country "suggest your national potential might lie more in an industrial environment than in pursuit of a traditional rice-bowl economy."

Larry seconded that: "Particularly since your rice bowl of choice would appear to be Cambodia."

Le bristled—then lifted his cup in a wry salute: "Touché, Mr. President. Off the record, as you say."

Taking note of the twenty-five million enterprising capitalists Hanoi had inherited in South Vietnam, Larry said he'd be interested to see "what a remarkable country you might build for yourselves—if you could manage to stop your war making long enough to do it." The little guy perked to that like a politician sniffing a free lunch. That, at least, Larry understood only too well.

Robin tuned to the crackling vibes. Waspy Lessard was sulkily attentive. Koenig was triggered for a pounce; he hated the Soviets even more than he despised the cookie-pushers at State. Bland, lawyerish Hugh Pownell, the CIA chief, chewed on a cold pipe, looking cryptic but chipping in mellow, useful comments. She knew what was real to *them* were the flowcharts, "spheres of influence"—the chessboard, Ours versus Theirs. But Larry? Her radar fuzzed.

Yet Le, looking eerily like the driver in Cal's film who said he despised and feared the Vietnamese "but except for them we would all be dead," brought a powerful silent presence into the house. She felt its chill; maybe Larry did too. *A society of ghosts and psychotic children.* . . .

Cal said softly, "Anh, if you get sucked in by that old dream of swallowing Cambodia, it'll take you another thousand years to pacify the place. It'll be your cancer, your running sore—like you were for America."

Le argued that Vietnam had been forced in there by the "relentless attacks and incursions of China's criminal lackey, Pol Pot, after he turned his nation into a hell on earth." Larry interrupted the list of provocations, saying he saw no point in debating "the causes of your conquest of a neighboring country. The issue before us is the means and circumstances under which that occupation can be honorably terminated."

Abruptly, Le set down his cup and pulled out a snapshot of his son, a geology student "whose great dream is to some day attend your School of Mining in Colorado."

Larry pointed out that this commendable ambition could be better realized if the two countries resolved their present differences "in a process of fruitful negotiation." He spoke of his personal conviction that an enduring solution to long-standing conflicts "could take root from a reconciliation between us. We share enough mutual interests to forge a workable détente, if we approach the problems in a positive and mutually constructive spirit. But that will require some degree of accommodation on your side, Mr. Le—which hasn't heretofore been evident in our dealings with your nation."

He added that time was of the essence. "Your country has long proved its will and capacity for waging war, Mr. Le. But the business of building a viable, thriving peace requires similar courage and resolve, and it won't be achieved as long as you remain a pariah among nations—an isolation you bring down on yourselves by denying to Cambodia the same right of national self-determination you yourselves fought so long and hard to win."

Dryly, from Le: "If I may say so, Mr. President, it gratifies me to hear an American president speak so nobly of Vietnam's right of self-determination."

Combative reverberations from that crack. But Larry gracefully countered it by noting that "perhaps we've all gained some insight from our experience of recent years, Mr. Le. Our two countries have a shared heritage of blood between us, invested in a war which with hindsight we can see had tragic implications for both sides. The wounds of that war are not yet healed in either of our nations—but it's in the hope of advancing that process of healing that I agreed to meet with you tonight."

Yes! Go for it, babe, Robin thought.

Le started in again on his great honor bit, but Larry cut him off. "Let's get on with the job, Mr. Le. Because if this opportunity is lost, we may not get another."

CHAPTER TWENTY-SEVEN

January 30th
Robin

All day Robin heard a mounting hum, static from her Thirsty Voices. Around noon she called Tish, "just checking in. Hunky-dory on this end."

Tish said she doubted that. "I recognize your sound, you know. Right now it says you're not doing so hot. Did you call Dr. Traub? That's where I'd like you to check in."

At 3:15 Robin left for Chevy Chase, a black cloche covering her famous red hair. Jim beamed approval at the hat. "Ah, real good, Mrs. D."

"Only for you, Jim," she sighed.

At the meeting she spoke about trying to make amends to your kids for the sins of your boozing past. The women buttressed her: You have no control over people, places and things, but you *can* change yourself. You can't make them love you or undo what's happened, but the kids can share your healing. Don't dwell on the past, or project. . . .

On the way home she asked Jim to stop for a dozen candy bars, to block her vodka itch. At the house she discovered Larry had decided to brainstorm the Vietnam initiative that weekend at Camp David, a tighter lid for the talks. The boys wanted to go along—"In a chopper? You bet!" Stuffing down her pique at Larry for his unilateral disruption of the family plans, Robin polished off two Cadburys.

When Melissa turned up at 7:30, boyfriend Thad in tow, she balked on Camp David. Reeling with dismay, Robin offered to stay behind with her to "spend some time catching up."

She got an abrupt rejection: "Don't be ridiculous, Mum. I'd rather you go with them, I'm busy with Thad anyway." Of course, the boyfriend came first. *How soon we forget.* . . .

Yet that instant dismissal stung. She kissed her daughter goodby, wished her and Long-Nose a happy reunion, and bolted down another chocolate bar before the chopper roared off the back lawn like a furious night bird.

CHAPTER TWENTY-EIGHT

January 31st

Prilla

Priscilla's cold, hard spring wound tighter.

". . . any day now, darling, just you wait and see. Mort doesn't for the life of him know why it's taking this long, the way those congressmen have debts piled to their ears. . . ."

Naive little Ginny, of course, had no idea of the spot Mort had put them in with that asinine Aleutian deal for Kittyhawk. Priscilla wasn't about to clue her in, though she suspected Ginny cultivated her naiveté for times like this. Dan kept saying everyone was entitled to a few screwups now and then, even Mort. But Priscilla, still boiling, knew perfectly well why Mort had done it: His quick-buck cheapness out-weighed his smarts.

"Mort says some of those darn Democrats would be two skips ahead of the sheriff if they weren't perched in that catbird seat. So it can't take *much* longer, dear."

Hearing that, it was all Priscilla could do not to bust out laughing —or crying. She felt yanked, tugged every which-way. Sometimes she thought she should just lock the door, pull out the phone and figure out where they were going. And sometimes she knew if she stopped long enough to think she'd come apart like a plastic doll run over by a truck.

"Hon, Meyerson says we're holding right on target in the overnight polls." Dan made a point of passing along any good news. There wasn't much these days anyway, and she needed any perking up she could get—not that she'd let on to him. His gal was true-blue all the way, always looking for ways to cheer *him* up.

So they kept that little white lie between them. Momma used to tell him, in the years Poppa had them all on the roller coaster, that the good times would come a whole lot sooner if he just *believed* they would. But the stalemate had worn him down so, about all he *could* do was keep smiling and plow straight ahead. One foot in front of the other, and keep the faith. The one sockeroo he couldn't handle was if Prilla fell apart on him. But she never had yet in thirty years' sledding, not all of it smooth.

So he chose not to make too much out of her skittish moods, her short-fused temper. He just kept his eyes on the trail ahead and passed on any pick-me-ups he could: "And Smithers said the media spots are whistling up a darn good response too."

Whistling in the dark, more like it. Dan's Gibraltar optimism surprised even her. He just seemed to *believe* it was going to happen, as if he couldn't *not* win, Lucky Dan.

Yet she wondered if he might be picking up a few of her tricks, learning to hide his real feelings even from her. Increasingly often he slid into what she called his "grumps," actually fits of depression, and she just had no luck at all trying to jolly him out of it.

When she saw the mood coming back, she wanted to cry out, Danny, please don't. If she had to float them both, someday they might just sink without a trace into that terrible roaring sea out there.

CHAPTER TWENTY-NINE /
January 31st
Robin

Robin wandered in the Camp David woods, brooding on the unfinished business between her and Melissa, aching for the daughter she'd lost somewhere in her own nightmare. Digging past the bruise of the latest rebuff to memories of the bad old times: that junior-year cotillion when she'd "gone to bed sick" before Missy's date came; the three birthdays ruined, or was it four?

Voices crackling, crowding, *Too much, can't cope, you'll fall apart without.* . . . She struggled to sort out the birthdays, get them straight. *What could hurt, who's to know, just one little quickie.* . . . Tish's voice in the chorus, *Remember the insanity of the disease; it's the first drink that gets you drunk.* But fainter, fading, drowned by the tall whistling pines. *You earned it, you deserve it, just one treat.* . . .

She walked till her feet were numb, wishing heads froze that well. The demon voices trailed her back to the cabin where Larry and the rest were "attacking the issues." Gut session divided in warring groups. She caught snatches: "How in hell do you disarm an army of 30,000 kamikazes?" "Somewhere down the line, Mr. President, you might see one hell of a bargain in squeezing the Soviets out of Cam Ranh Bay for a few billion a year."

Not a whiff of optimism. Larry aimed a distracted scowl across the room. She smiled blankly in case it was meant for her. He turned back to Koenig and Lessard.

Waiters passed prelunch drinks. Eric Lowenthal called her over to see Cal's sketch of a strange, simple machine. A child's version of the homemade guillotine Khmer children had to use on each other, Eric said, his long fingerbones scissoring a demonstration, snip snap.

"Awful," she muttered. "That's really dreadful, Eric." She felt Cal's eyes boring, trying to make her look at him. She fought the tug like a riptide, deathtrap. *Watchout, watchout, he wants to suck you in, pull you down.* . . .

She smelled Cal's beer, strong as a skunk. Eric was halfway through a sherry, sweet as molasses. She whiffed a fragrant Pommard opened across the room. Siren song of popping corks mixed with the voices: *Come back, good times!*

She headed for her room, through the dining room set up for the buffet lunch. Bottles lined up on the bar, neat little soldiers. In a reflex flash she twinkled a Gordon's gin under her coat. *Magic fingers still! Nobody saw.* . . .

In her room she locked the door, set the bottle on the dresser. *Just in case. If I need it later.* . . .

She hung up her coat, then peed in the adjoining john. Rinsing her hands, she looked at the glass on the sink. *Call Tish. CallTish.* . . . Shaky dab of fresh lipstick, avoiding her eyes in the mirror.

Pacing the bedroom carpet. Kitschy log walls closing in. Bottle calling out: *Come back, let your old friend stop the pain.* . . .

She brought in the glass. Set it by the bottle. Seal already broken, level down two fingers. *Just you and me, kiddo, we don't need anybody else.* . . . Glass, hell. She could kill that bottle chugalug, into sweet oblivion. Nirvana. Blotto. *There but for the grace of god.* . . .

From the static suddenly came Tish's voice, loud, ringing: TRULY INSANE TO DRINK AGAIN. Shaking all over, she picked up the phone. "Get me Mrs. Varner, please."

"Yes ma'am, Mrs. Devlin." The phone line went dead; heartbeat like a jungle drum. "Then, ". . . sorry I'm out, be back shortly. . ." over the operator's, "Do you want to leave a message, Mrs. Devlin?"

"Yes. I'll do it." The operator clicked off. Forcing a breath through, ". . . after the beep, leave your pearl."

Beep-squawk. She gulped, choked, "Tish—please call."

Trying to remember Shirley's number. Or Ron's. Throat tight, warm, spit quivering for a bath. Bottle singing from the dresser, *Give me your grief, baby. Abracadabra! I'll take it away.*

She poured out an inch of gin. Looked like water, smelled like fresh flowers. As she lifted the glass, an almost physical force diverted it from her mouth. *Therebutforthegraceofgod, therebutforthegraceofgod.* . . .

She emptied the glass in the sink. Rinsed it and did yoga stretches on the floor, reaching desperately for the calming edge of the storm. Sacking her terrified turmoil for Bella's number. *Ask the operator.* . . .

A minute later she hugged the bottle to her chest, crooning a song. *Old lover back. Good as new.* . . . This time she poured a full glass. Inhaled the fragrance like wildflower musk. Teasing, humming, stretching out the exquisite stab of pleasure just ahead. . . . On her knees at the dresser, watching two red-tipped fingers dip into the glass, double-sized. Tentative mermaids swimming in the juice, teasing teeny bubbles up the glass. First sip always the best. She'd lick that off her fingers. Then sink, swim, float away—

The phone rang.

Tish's voice. Rough, real: "Robin, where are you?"

Lightning bolt to that rod, she crumpled in a sluicing purge of tears. "Oh god, Tish. Help me, help me."

"Robin, calm down and tell me what's happening."

Bent over ripped guts. Wailing, "Tiiiish, I can't stop. I can't. . . ."

"Yes, you can! Now listen to me, Robin, and do exactly what I—"

Strangled weeping. "Tish, I'm losing it, Tish."

"—what I say. Take whatever you've got there and dump it down the john. All of it, Robin."

She dropped the phone and flushed it all away, shaking out the drops. Flushed twice as she rinsed the glass and bottle clean, left them draining dry.

Still crying, she came back to the phone. Tish asked if she'd gotten rid of it all. "Yes. And I didn't drink any, Tish. But if you'd called two minutes later. . . ." She babbled about being stranded up at Camp David, way off in the woods, Larry "hunkered down in long talks with a bunch of guys. There's nobody I can talk to. . . ."

"Robin, you have to get out of there. *Right now.* Just pull yourself together and get the hell out."

Tiny voice. "All right. Where should I go?"

Tish asked if she could make it to New York.

"I think so. Could you meet me at the apartment? I don't know how soon. . . ."

"Never mind, I'll be there. Are you sure you can get here? Do you want me to call somebody down there?"

She felt a little of Tish's strength flowing into her. "No, I can make it. As long as I know you'll be there."

Tish said just put on her coat and *go*.

She doused her face in cold water, bracing to the shock. Patchy makeup hid some damage; the rest went behind dark glasses. Hesitating over the empty bottle, she finally zipped it into her suede sack-purse.

She found an agent in the hall and asked him please to tell her husband she'd like to speak with him.

When he heard the message, whispered over dessert, Larry's gut instantly knotted up.

He knew already it was trouble. He'd seen it written all over her when she came barging in from outdoors, eyes glazed, half-cocked. He'd seen it but didn't want to see it, so he'd turned aside and hoped it would go away.

She'd gone, anyway, when he looked for her about an hour ago. Not a long time, but god knows it never took her much time to get. . . . He excused himself from the table, irritation fighting dread as he headed for the hall.

She was limp against a wall, looking wobbly and beat, like she'd come from a street fight. She held up her hands as if to fend him off, mumbling, "Dev, I'm going up to New York to see Tish. I'd like to leave right now."

Bad news, all right. He took her arm and drew her down the hall, then turned her toward him, trying to sniff her breath and see through the dark glasses, trying to filter the alarm from his voice: "Robin, are you all right?"

"Yes. I think." She patted his shirt, hand like lead. Her words slow, thick. "At least I'll be okay when I see Tish."

Stabbing relief, *at least she's getting out*, quickly doused in. . . helplessness. He never did know what to do, what to say when she was teetering on the edge like this. Whatever he tried might make it worse. At least Varner knew what to do. . . .

He squeezed her arm, asked if he could do anything to help. She managed a smile. "No thanks. Well, maybe you could whistle me up a chopper."

He went to the phone, delivered a few orders and came back to her. He saw she was locked in some private kind of struggle, and he felt a surging protectiveness toward her. Wished he could hold her like a kid, kiss her hurt and make it right again. But he never had managed to make it right for her. Not this part, at least.

He settled for a parting hug. She leaned for a moment into that shelter; he rocked her soothingly, told her the chopper was all set, but if she'd changed her mind. . . .

She pushed against his chest, pushed him away. "No thanks. Don't worry, Dev, I'll be okay. You get back to your meeting, and I'm so sorry I. . . messed up."

He said she didn't mess up anything, wished her a safe flight. As she wobbled out of the cabin and took Jim Connerty's arm, it struck him that that fat Irish cop was more rescuer, Mr. Fixit for Robin than her husband ever had been.

Shivering from the chill she carried with her, Robin lit the logs in her Manhattan fireplace. Back in her living-room island of privacy, she was still feeling the soreness of her fight. The sight of the Chinese takeouts laid on the coffee table, Tish's auld lang syne brunch, nearly made her barf. Wincing at her twinges, she lay down on the soft white carpet, drinking in the healing familiarity, feeling her knots loosen like untangled string.

When Tish pried out the story, it came in a torrent. Tish pointed out stop signs she'd gone through, ways she might've headed off this attack. "When the noise in your head is so ferocious you stop listening to anybody or anything else, you can bet you're crazy as a waltzing mouse. That's when you've got to use some part of the program to pull yourself out. Holler for help. Grab for your mantra. Run to a meeting. . . ."

Hugging herself like she was nursing bruises, Robin whispered: "Oh, Tish. It was so bad."

Tish said picking up the drink was the last sign of a slip, and if you'd sailed past the warning flashes it took real luck not to empty every bottle in the house. Robin shuddered, saying she hadn't wanted a drink that badly in two years at least. Just the whiff had sent her through the roof.

Tish squinted suspiciously. "And what about the deadbeat roommate? Was he on the scene, by any chance?"

Robin did *want* to understand why, how Cal's sudden reappearance had tilted her gyros. So she dug for the part she'd been backing away from, that junior-summer house party, when her major obsession was how to unload her virginity. Tish moaned: "Don't tell me. The klutz did the honors. . . ."

Sheepish grin. "Yep."

The pickings hadn't been great anyway that week at Molly's, eight Marymounters fighting over a few summer-crowd boys and some hotel waiters. Robin found herself drawn to the tall, skinny guy camped at his uncle's down the road. He was older, and much more serious. On the beach he'd be buried in a book, talking about things like French existentialism or the different kinds of Buddhism, things she knew absolutely nothing about—"which was probably why he seemed so exotic and sexy to me."

They'd spent a lot of time together. She wasn't sure where she stood with him; after convent school, she was still fairly new to the flirting game. And all he did was *talk*. But near week's end, egged on by the romances swirling around her, she decided to make her big play for him one afternoon when they'd wandered off into the dunes.

Cal was rambling about Gandhi's nonviolence campaigns when they "fell into some heavy necking. And I just went past the stop signs. Forgot when to say 'no.' " She smiled softly, recalling that gritty tumble as "amazing. Not at all what I expected. I felt terribly grown-up. And proud. Delighted I'd finally done it."

But afterward, wriggling back into her sandy suit, she was "mostly wondering what on earth came next. Thinking idiotic things like wow, gosh, did this mean we were in love? Was this the big I It? All that knee-jerk conditioning, you know. But Cal just sort of zipped himself up and said gee thanks, that was real nice, and ambled home for supper."

Next night at the lobster roast, he "paid absolutely no attention to me. I realize *now* he probably didn't have the foggiest idea that was my first time—but of course I couldn't see that then."

So she'd turned her furious hurt into a shimmery assault on his Hotchkiss buddy, the handsome stranger. Larry called her Red and fetched her beers. Flirted with roughhousing, "inspecting" her tan, playing with her hair, dancing with her in the sand. She danced that night like Salome, feelers spread for the touch of Cal's eyes.

As it turned out, Cal was behind the dune all that while, plucking his guitar inside a circle of girls. But Larry rose to the bait meant for Cal. That scored big points with the other girls, who called him Mr. Gorgeous, Primo Stuff. Also with her mother, when Larry tracked her down that fall. "She said, you mean *those* Devlins? For heaven's sake, you could float to China on their money. She adored him before she met him. She thought he might make up for her great disappointment in life, that I hadn't come out at the Gotham Ball or the Junior Assembly."

Tish hoped that was meant as a joke.

Didn't she wish, but there were no laughs in that failed debut, her parents' long-planned assault on the Manhattan set. When she'd finally gotten engaged to Larry, her parents had swooned with delight, cracked out the Havanas and prewar champagne. Her father, three sheets to the wind, actually muttered something about "showing up that Gotham bunch." Later that night, alone in her bed, she wondered if she'd feel any different right then if Larry weren't the Rich and Famous Catholic Catch.

Tish sighed that none of us were responsible for picking our parents, thank god, but mainly she wanted to hear about the denouement with Cal.

What denouement? There were only crossed wires from the start. She'd thought back then she was suffering terribly, unforgettably, but when the incident crossed her mind in later years, she chose to recall it as the whole payoff with Larry springing from her spunky piss-off at Cal.

She only saw him a few times after that rite of passage, always with Larry. And never thought much about that star-crossed summer, "except when we ran into him in Cambodia. I remember thinking he still seemed awfully exotic. The way he was living, anyway. Maybe I wondered a bit what if Larry hadn't been along that night. But the answer is I'd probably be married to a Scarsdale proctologist."

She was pleasantly surprised to find herself spooning Hunam lamb onto a plate. "My god, I seem to be hungry. Is that a good sign, or what?"

"If you like." Scowling, Tish tossed back her peppery hair. "I have a peculiar hunch that Cal might feel he has some kind of claim on you."

Startled, nettled, Robin asked where that came from. Tish said who knows but it felt right and Robin might consider that. Meanwhile did Larry know about this? Robin shook her head. "Not either time?"

"I don't think so. God, I hope not."

Tish asked if she wanted some candid advice on this bad-news guy.

"Not much. Is that going to stop you?"

"Robin, if you know what's good for you, you'll run from him like the plague. Treat him like the booze. He's got the same kind of effect on you. And by the way, he strikes me as a manipulative son of a bitch, in his hangdog way."

Robin said well, weren't they all? Thinking, *But she doesn't see this time I could break him apart, he's so near the edge.* . . .

Tish knew Robin was barely taking in a word she said. She was relieved enough just to see Robin could walk and talk; with these emergency calls you never knew what kind of basket case you'd have on your hands. The torrential tale was pretty much the déjà vu Tish had been braced for since Robin had insisted on moving down there. This near-miss was a self-starter, an accident that had been waiting to happen.

It felt like trying to reason with a bleeder left waiting in an emergency-room lobby, but Tish had to keep trying, because this was the best shot she'd get. "You're quite a cunning manipulator yourself, please don't forget. It goes with your alcoholic package. Which is all the more reason to steer clear of that Typhoid Maxie."

Robin said she'd rather focus on the important thing about Cal, how he was trying to save that magical little country. Tish's hands went up. "Hold it! Stop right there!"

Glimpsing the automatic self-destruct Robin was heading straight into, Tish said urgently, "The reading I get is I'm dealing with a very arrogant, headstrong, grandiose woman—who's also very afraid. All this queen-bee stuff you're getting off on now, and Cambodia on top of that—a perfect Irresistible Diversion. Hey, don't tell me where you're coming from, queen of the country. Don't forget I've been listening to your bullshit for five years."

Robin grunted that Momma Varner was really dishing it out tonight. But Tish insisted she saw Cambodia almost as an alcoholic gambit which could push Robin in over her head. Any extraordinary dynamic like that had to be very suspect, since it could so easily become more important than her sobriety.

"Hey, come on!" Robin protested. "It doesn't make me a hopeless drunk to do something for a little country that's had every lousy break you could imagine, drunk *or* sober."

Like trying to polka with a snake. "Ah, sure. Great drama, isn't it? Just the kind of grandstand play we boozers love to get sucked into. But if you'd stop long enough to *see* how you're using this, letting your ego run riot. . . . Kid, it's the height of toxic arrogance to think your First Lady schtick can remake the world."

Robin said hotly that wasn't what she had in mind. Sometimes Tish's nagging crossed the line, sawed on raw nerves.

But the lecture wasn't over yet. Robin shouldn't need reminding, today of all days, that her alcoholic condition could take her right to the brink and kill her. If Cambodia was so important, leave it to Larry and his guys to fix it.

Wry glance. "You and the Tooth Fairy, boy."

Tish shrugged. "Well, they know more than you do, pal."

Contritely, obligingly, Robin totted up ways to alleviate her pressures: schedule more meditation; read the Big Book every day; maybe take a tea break with a chocolate fix, to scratch her cocktail-hour itch.

Tish went off like a rocket. "*Chocolate*, you think I'm talking about *chocolate*? Pry your head out of the clouds, Robin. I'm trying to tell you I think you need to seriously consider going under professional care."

Again that punch to the gut. And she wasn't finished yet: "Your current behavior is contrary to everything my experience tells me is in your best interests. I'm in way over my head already with this, but I do know I've got my own disease to deal with and right now yours is *overwhelming* mine. As your sponsor I'm responsible for your sobriety. Part of that responsibility is helping you get the help you need when you don't realize you need it. The point you're at now, if you insist on going back down there—which I devoutly hope you won't—I'd say as a *minimum* you should have a local sponsor and local doctor pretty much available on call."

Wincing at that threat of abandonment, she rocked on the rug, murmuring, "I'm listening. I hear you, Tish."

Tish couldn't believe she saw clearly what she was doing here. "I'm on your side in every way, but my job is to try to keep you from going down the tubes, and I can't accept the risks and pressures you're subjecting yourself to now." If they were on such different wavelengths, maybe she'd outlived her effectiveness and Robin needed a new sponsor.

Robin shook her head fiercely. "No no no." Reluctantly, she admitted she might be a little hooked on the adrenaline boost in this. Pointed glance from Tish. "All right, I'm mainlining adrenaline. So scared my teeth hurt."

Tish pressed: "If you're just running a train, tell me right now. *Tell me what you're doing.*"

Well, maybe she was acting "a bit like a spoiled brat." Manipulating, striking out. Angry at them all. Getting back at Cal for Block Island, getting back at Larry for Cal and a whole lot more.

The laundry list, Tish agreed. "One more reason you shouldn't go back there right now. If you can't be straight and truthful with Larry, you jeopardize your whole program."

Chanted like a "Dies Irae": She had to want to be sober more than anything else. It was her disease, her mess. She wasn't a victim; she was a cunning, self-centered manipulator, with a monstrous alcoholic ego that precipitated these events, wrecked her marriage. She was *attracted* to this stuff. "Alcoholics are as helpless as Hitler, you know."

Robin flashed coming back to the Birch Woods funny farm, Dr. God, old Silverlocks himself, dropping in for his ritual welcome back. Solemn as death or taxes, he'd say, "Today you take that big step, Robin, onto the road to good health."

Tish, unfortunately, never promised that much.

Easing down, they talked for hours as Robin roamed the room, grooming plants, straightening frames, poking at the fire—*her* fire, again. First one she'd really played with since—when was it? So long ago.

When the Devlin saga ran out they talked about Tish's two grown kids, the Roadie and the Carpenter. And her latest boyfriend, Maynard, a high-minded chemistry teacher who went abroad to watch birds. Tish was beginning to appreciate his saintly ex-wife but was still trying to more or less nest with him a few nights a week. Unfortunately, she was also seeing a good bit of Igor, the rascally undivorced father of five she didn't admire but loved to fuck. "And if the pot's about to call the kettle, bite your tongue, girl."

As the evening wore on, Robin got out her old quilts from the Maine yard sales. Tish wrapped herself on the couch and eventually drifted into sleep. Robin camped out on the rug, curled in her quilts, watching the guttering flames. In the White House she didn't let herself lie around on the floor, tracking the extraordinary beauty of a dying fire.

This one stirred echoes of the roast where she'd met Larry, raw and charged from that awakening with Cal. Remembering his hands, so sure and sly, so knowing. Not tentative like the boys she knew. He'd touched her like he was brushing the feel of Cal from her skin.

She rolled onto her side, watching the fire glow on the mirror wall. When she found this apartment five years ago, bursting with terrified hope, she'd built a pristine nest of white and old Maine pine, thinking if she just banned shoes it would stay her magical retreat. But already the couch was fraying, the carpet greying. Not her safe house any more, if it ever had been. Unmoot point, as Larry would say.

She recognized what she'd been skirting: a deep gut commitment to the strange truths unfolding. She floated a prayer from the heart, a cry of surrender. A choice. *They will, not mine. Lord, show me the way. Grant me the serenity.* . . .

A curious, healing peacefulness came over her. She felt the sickness leach out, leaving her whole. *Thy will, not mine, lord.* . . .

CHAPTER THIRTY /

February 1st

Prilla

Another working Sunday, marooned in Muncie, Indiana. "Next door to East Overshoe," Dan put it. While he went stag to the Christian Men's Fellowship convention, Priscilla squeezed in a visit to Fresh Start, an adolescent drug rehabilitation center founded by some desperate parents.

Rolling up to the Victorian gingerbread house on the outskirts of town, a press aide briefed her: "Good example of local privately funded initiative. . . opportunity to involve you in a broad issue with national appeal." She was mainly fixed on getting out of here to catch up with Dan—until she heard those wrenching kids.

"Then my mom found the stash in my room, so I moved it to the garage." Pale, flat voice, like the thin blond hair the boy kept pushing from his face. "I told her I was working on my Yamaha, that's why I spent so much time out there. I guess she wanted to believe me 'cause I didn't get caught again till I wrecked the car."

She said my goodness, was anyone hurt? He nodded, wan face so much older than 17. "Yeah. I broke my legs and my friend got a busted head."

Peter Franks, the tall, bearded housefather, said the first thing the kids put a stop to was "the b.s. factor": "They can smoke out all the lies and alibis they've used so often themselves."

Sitting in the patchy living room, listening to a dozen kids share their experiences, she lost all sense of time. Hard-luck pitches were a fact of campaign life she'd learned to guard against. But the casual way these kids told their awful stories—the boy who stole his grandmother's jewelry and wound up raped in a Chicago jail, the girl who turned her first trick on her thirteenth birthday—sabotaged her defenses. She kept thinking of those poor parents, the hell they'd been through. These kids looked like normal teenagers, but clearly they'd all broken their parents' hearts over and over.

She had no trouble identifying with that fear of your own children, that terror of winding up hostage to your own flesh and blood, undone by the family havoc they could wreak. She grimly recalled the day she'd let Natalie come back home once, when Dan was away. The Gnat was living then with some dreadful rock musician, even though Dan was about to run again for governor. After long, bloody battles on the phone, Priscilla thought she might be able to talk some sense into the child's head if they met face-to-face.

Natalie came in dressed like a zombie hobo. Hair a fright wig, raccoon eyes, ragged jeans and a virtually invisible top, cracking horrifying jokes about drugs, free love and abortions. At least Priscilla *assumed* they were meant as jokes. She didn't want to hear how appallingly her daughter was living; she only wanted to know how soon Natalie would stop "tormenting your father like this."

Her answer was to light up a marijuana cigarette and blow smoke in her mother's face. Priscilla slapped her and threw her out, told her not to come back till she was ready to live like a civilized human being. But that took months, years to happen, and how many nights did she lie awake imagining god knows what, always waiting for the bad-news call. She wasn't sure to this day if Natalie's rebellions were over and done with.

Mimi, a gangling 15-year-old with a Sissy Spacek face, sat at Priscilla's feet, talking about her fifth runaway when a "real smooth guy" she'd met in a New York bus station soon had her on the streets, "doing fifteen tricks on a good day. I used to get undressed in the john, if they'd let me, and then I'd try to think about something nice, like Christmas or riding my bike by the river, until they were done."

In a burst of feeling Priscilla leaned down and hugged the girl. "Mimi, I'm so sorry. But now you can start all over. You have the rest of your life to put that. . . nasty business behind you."

The girl laid her head on Priscilla's knee. "But it's real hard, you know," she said softly, dreamily. "All the kids think I'm some kind of freak. They know what I was, what I did—all that bad stuff."

"Never you mind, dear," Priscilla said firmly, stroking that flyaway blonde hair. "What matters is that you're going to be a fine, happy, successful young woman."

When the aide tapped his watch, she asked if the press could come in for a brief photo session. The kids had no objection—posed like old pros, in fact. Pretty Mimi still at her feet, Priscilla said how much she appreciated their talk: "I'm distressed to hear what you've been through—you and other young people all across the country. But you were fortunate to live in a community that organized its own treatment center. . . ." She hugged Mimi, patting that gold halo, promising to "do everything I can to see that your message of hope reaches other young people still struggling. . . ."

She caught up with Dan in their hotel room, going over the schedule with Paul. Dan asked how it had gone with the junior junkies. She said fine, better than she'd expected: "Honestly, it could tear your heart out to hear what those kids have been through. And we got some good footage, I think."

Sometimes—quite often—Paul wasn't sure when to speak up around the little lady. Risking it, he ventured a suggestion that she might want to get more actively involved in that antidrug issue, since so many of the families afflicted were middle-class, middle-income, from the Governor's natural constituency.

She looked away from him with a disdainful sniff. "Well, I don't know. Danny, what d'you think?" The boss said it sounded to him like a crackerjack idea, why didn't Paul work up a battle plan along those lines? She nodded emphatically, saying okay, she'd go along with that.

Paul realized she'd been pushing for that all along, maneuvering to give the old boy a chance to say it first. If anybody was boss of this outfit, it was the skinny little lady with the iron will and steel-trap head.

One tough cookie altogether, and she hadn't gotten any easier to live with lately. Sometimes Paul fell into bed at night praying it would just be over, never mind which way it went. But once when he had trouble getting to sleep, he realized he mainly felt burned out that way when he'd had to spend the whole day around Herself.

Priscilla poured herself a coffee from the thermos on the desk, agreeing that was one cause she wouldn't mind helping out. She still heard the echoes: I undressed in the bathroom, if they'd let me. . . .

"It's so sad, such a tragic waste. When I think how frantic those parents must be for an out. . . ."

Catching Dan's yawn, she hustled Paul out so Dan could grab a nap before they flew out. He offered no resistance, easing down with languid grunts of fatigue. Watching that instant slackening, she remembered when he wouldn't nap without her beside him—and sleep wasn't usually what he had in mind. Now he conked out as soon as he hit the mattress.

Looking so worn. So—old. Defenseless as those wretched kids. Sometimes she almost wanted to wake him and say let's just forget it, let's go back home. . . .

But never did, of course. Never would.

Back arching, stiffening to duty, she picked up the stack of phone messages.

CHAPTER THIRTY-ONE /

February 1st

Robin

Robin woke with a start. Green 5:06 glowing on the TV clock. Feeling as if a fever had passed—limp, relieved, revived—she tiptoed out to the hall.

Brian and some new agent were conked out in the second bedroom, light on, door ajar. She went to the john off her bedroom, turned on the radio dangling from the mirror, and reveled in a long, hot shower, serenaded by Van Morrison. "Feels like, seems like a braaand new day," she sang, slathering shampoo suds in her armpits and crotch. "Comes right in on time. Makes me feeeel so free, makes me feel like me."

Inside her closet she found a "from your Tooth Fairy" present Dennis had tucked away in case she made it back—buttery ankle-high fireman-red leather boots. She dressed with gluttonous pleasure from the remnants on her shelves: stretched undies, pressed jeans, Viyella shirt.

She roused the agents with marching orders. In the living room Tish was sleeping on her back, arm flung up, breath whiffling through her open mouth. Robin knelt beside the couch, laid a wake-up touch on her brow. "Tish, this is for absolution. Of any of *my* sins. You're not responsible, okay, Tish?"

Nose twitching, eyes closed, she mumbled, "I have to wake up to this?"

"You can't quit on me, Tish. This is one pigeon you can't ditch. Nobody else can talk me through this but you."

Squinting, Tish hauled up against the pillows. Flatly: "You're going back."

"Yes. I've got to do it, Tish, so I'd better leave here before I get caught. Or before the kids get all freaked out again." She lifted her hands, as if in blessing. "Tish, I made it to three years, five months and twelve days!"

Tish gloomily shook her head, saying it pained her to point this out, but the world *wouldn't* fall apart if Robin didn't go back. "You don't have to do it, you know."

"I know. But my gyros are set for it this time, Tish. I'll do whatever else you want, call five times a day if you say so, but I need one more shot at it. If I cave in again, I promise I'll leave, but please understand I have to give it another try."

Tish looked away, sighing, muttering she supposed it was too much to ask a sane person to walk away from all that. "All right then, Ms. Devlin. Two calls a day, please." Robin pulled on her coat. Tish added, "And call Dr. Traub."

She smiled. "I'll see. . . He's an idiot, you know."

Tish said no matter, he had the same credentials she did: "A track record with you."

"Have faith, Tish. It'll be okay, you'll see."

Tish rolled back down into the quilts, growling, "Anh, get out of here before my brains wake up."

☆

Checking back into Camp David, skipping bouyantly in the red boots, Robin found the boys racing golf carts, their greeting boisterously casual. *As if I'd never been gone. . . .*

The cabin gang was still going at it: ". . . must urge an aggressive U.S. stance, yielding no quarter on our geopolitical interests. . . ." When Larry saw her at the doorway he came out to the hall, a pouchy update of the golden boy by the lobster fire. With transparently wary relief, he said, "Hey, welcome back, Rob. Good trip?"

"Terrific." She pecked his cheek. "I'll tell you about it later, if you want. Right now I've got some sack time to catch up on."

In her bedroom the log walls were back where they belonged. A charmingly funky place, actually.

She rolled under the bedcovers and pitched into sleep.

CHAPTER THIRTY-TWO /

February 2nd

Robin

Outside Melissa's bedroom, Robin paused to pull together her scrambled wits and zigzag emotions, head ducked over the coffee tray. *Lord, let me get through to her this time. Let me find the words. . . .*

Pushing open the door, she called out cheerily, "Wakey, wakey, Missy. Rise and shine."

"Mmph, look at that." Sleepy drawl from the churned blankets. "Teaching the old dog new tricks, are they?"

She smiled to see the ratnesting, a crib-days habit oddly out of place in Cupid's rococo canopy bed. "This old dog wants you to know it isn't as easy as it looks. For starters, I had to fight off Hamilton to carry this up." She was still hearing that "Don't be ridiculous, Mum."

She'd been almost relieved last night, getting back from Camp David to find Melissa was out, up to god knows what. It was hard not to bring up the near-slip that loomed in her head, but any mention of her booze problem brought out the wounded fawn in Melissa—wary, fearful, hiding behind her silky curtain of hair. Last time they'd tackled it, Melissa said she knew Robin was trying hard and doing lots better: "But like you said, it doesn't ever go away, Mum, so I just don't want to start. . . counting on anything."

Missy'd heard it all before, too many times: the regrets, resolutions, fervent vows of never again. Anyway, despite Robin's best intentions, she'd learned the hard way that she couldn't honestly promise that— and couldn't deny that tensions with her daughter had contributed to the latest near-slip. *So just hope she doesn't find out. . . .*

Melissa kicked off the covers, knee socks and plaid panties under her voluminous Harvard sweatshirt. Robin asked if that was the latest in dorm pj's. Missy said sarcastically, zipping on jeans, "Sure, Mum. Come on, let's get breakfast."

As they walked to the solarium Robin reached over and patted her shoulder, stiffly, awkwardly. "So what's happening with *you*, hon?" The answer was polite enough, something about school, an econ exam. But Melissa made no reciprocal move—except in her clenched shoulder muscles, shrinking, flinching from that touch.

Robin dropped her hand.

Over muffins and bacon she asked if Melissa and Thad had gotten some time to themselves this weekend.

Edgy, moody face. "Oh, sure." Eyes averted, she blurted that Thad couldn't get enough of the place. "He ran around saying, 'Boy, this is the life, this is really the life.' "

Robin had sensed that boy's lust for the limelight when they first met, knew it was bound to collide with Melissa's craving for intimate reassurance. That fundamental mismatch was magnified now in the fishbowl glare, like the rest of their lives. But Missy had to learn that for herself.

She noted lightly that Thad had lots of company in that opinion. Melissa said, "Yeah. But sometimes that's. . . depressing, you know? Like at school, you wonder if your friends are really into you, or if it's that. . . whole other thing."

Robin's own lingering hurt dissolved in that blurted confession. She'd spent years sorting that one herself, and she was only a married-in, not a born-and-bred Devlin. She reminded Missy that despite the hassles of her father's job, she was still "a lovely, very lovable young woman, you know."

That dear, pained face gloomy as fog. "Yeah, sure."

"Missy, that happens to be true. One of these days you'll figure that out for yourself, Pudding."

Sudden gift of a sunshine grin. "Gosh, you haven't called me that in years."

"I guess. You wouldn't *let* me, I seem to recall."

"Mm-hmm. But I don't mind hearing it again now." Robin reminded her the name had come from her fights with Jason over who got first skin off the chocolate pudding. Melissa laughed. "Jason can be a pain in the butt sometimes, you know."

"Oh, sure. But aren't we all?" Robin steered the conversation back to Thad, asking if things were okay with him.

That grimace again. "Oh, sure. We're not breaking up anyway, if that's what you mean."

Perish the thought. Not when he can loll in the White House. . . . She said she didn't mean anything like that, she only wondered "how you feel about him—it—whatever."

Third degree, again!

The last thing Melissa wanted now was probing talk about Thad, maternal pokes into her queasy romance. She tossed the needle back. "What's with you and Daddy, by the way?"

Suddenly her mother was the one doing the fending: "Oh, we're both awfully busy, of course. But it's great to see him get his shot at this job."

"Come on, Mom. I'm not talking about the job."

Lame, uncomfortable chuckle. "Then I'm not sure what to tell you, hon." She rattled off a tinny speech about this time being awfully special for them all but she didn't consider it "real life," and when the dust settled she and Daddy would have to sort things out, see where they stood.

Melissa frowned. "That sounds like you're splitting up."

Her mother seemed to be groping for a workable evasion. "Mel, I don't *know* how things will work out. But it's nobody's fault, you know. Least of all you kids. And we're always a family, no matter what happens with me and your dad." Limp pause. She added, "He's an awfully nice man, Mel."

She knew her comeback line was supposed to be something like *fair enough, you're an awfully nice woman.* But her head had been haunted all weekend, playing house in this big old barn, by a memory she'd sworn years ago never, ever to mention to a living soul. A memory that had happened one morning when her father was away, that still slashed at her sometimes when she went home to Greensleeves. Or when she saw a blooming garden. Or when she was making love.

Now, suddenly, it burst from her: "You know my old playhouse?"

Her mother nodded, eyes wide with alarm.

Say it! Say it!

She blurted quickly, "One morning I got up early and went out there and I saw you. . . screwing some guy." Her mother just sat there like a block of ice, not budging. Melissa looked away, but the story poured out: "At least he was bouncing on top of you. Sort of grunting and. . . it took me years to realize you were probably passed out. Because your eyes were closed and you didn't move at all, even though he kept saying bitch, c'mon bitch, move."

Robin wished the earth could swallow her and never spit her out. She knew exactly which morning Melissa meant. When she'd awakened on the playroom floor in a heap of dirty clothes next to a young guy she didn't recognize. Feeling again the blind-panic discovery: *Where's he from? Get him out!*

He'd finally left, still complaining he needed a drink. She'd thought nobody knew about it. A merciful blackout had kept her ignorant of the sordid details, like who he was, or what bar she'd dug him out of.

Now she had to live with Melissa not only knowing, but having carried the ghastly secret for years. No wonder, no wonder. That explained so much. Wanting to hold her, not daring, she choked out, "Melissa, hon, I. . . wish I knew what to say. I'd give anything to've. . . spared you that."

Melissa pulled apart a slice of bacon, muttering that was okay, she guessed she knew what Robin would say for an alibi: "That the disease did it, not you. You wouldn't've if you hadn't been sick, but now you're better. Whoopee."

As Robin's shock wore off, she realized one part of this would always be tough to live with: knowing that brutal, wanton moment, branded into an 11-year-old head, would always share Melissa's beds, overshadow her own love life.

She said lord knows that was all true, but no excuse at all. There *wasn't* one, but she hoped eventually Melissa could understand enough to forgive her. "If only for your own sake, Mel." Awash in feeling for this dear, hurting child, she said softly, "You're a very special, loving person, Melissa, and you mustn't let your mother's craziness. . . put any dampers on your own life."

"Oh sure, I'm special. I'm the only porker at Michigan State who gets trailed by agents everywhere I go."

Robin snatched up her cup in shuddering recoil. "Honey, please don't put yourself down like that. You're a bright, perceptive, talented young woman with a—"

"Thin skin I inherited from you, I suppose. Boy, I'd've settled for the looks instead."

Bleakly, helplessly, she said she wished they could figure out some way to help each other heal instead of always dishing out more pain.

Melissa flipped off that she didn't need any help, thanks very much, except maybe in getting rid of 20 pounds and an overdue term paper. *Okay, back off. She's got to get there by herself. . . .*

She ached to hold her, but knew if they touched she'd break down. Maybe if they both let go, hugged and cried and mopped up each other's flood, they could bury it. . . .

Stephanie picked that moment to call in a reminder of Robin's *People* magazine interview about the kids. Bubble popped, Melissa said quickly she had to go anyway, she was lunching with Thad before the plane. "Just as well, I guess, if you'll be busy bragging about us kids."

"You got it, Pudding." Smiling uncertainly, she cupped her daughter's face. "Bless you, darling. Come home when you can, and don't run off so soon next time."

Unexpectedly yielding, Melissa embraced her, squishing the world of pain between them. "Thanks, Mum. It was great seeing you." So it ended better than it had begun. Yet still abrupt, unsatisfying, so much unsaid, undone. . . .

CHAPTER THIRTY-THREE /

February 3rd

Prilla

Chet wanted a brief meeting with Dan, so Priscilla squeezed him in that morning before she and Dan left for New York. As Chet came in, Dan looked at his watch: "Okay, you've got six minutes."

Chet zipped through preliminary results of his "fiscally oriented research." Lincoln Sheppard's heiress-wife "locked up her checkbook over his latest debts, apparently related to his reputation for womanizing, so. . . ."

"Dammit, Chet, stay off the hanky-panky. You told me your boys' job was zeroing in on the financial end."

"Right, Governor. But that leaves Sheppard vulnerable across the board. So as part of the general profile. . . ."

Dan snapped, "Keep your eye on the dollar sign. If there's a risk-free way to loosen up that end, let's hear it. But no smutty stuff. What else is so all-fired important?"

Off to a great start, Chet!

Chet stammered on: Morinski, the Wisconsin Independent, was pulling contributions from both sides of the fence, but he'd agreed to meet Dan after Thursday's prayer breakfast. Mosher, the Arkansas Democrat, had no obvious debt, but they were still digging. After a seven-figure reelection campaign, Nevada's Pickett could be in a hole: "He's covered his tracks well, but we've got our best man on that."

Dan asked about the House vote. Chet's gassy answer added up to little motion over the weekend, but they were geared up for "a strong drive this week." Leaving for the airport, Priscilla wondered why Chet had pressed for a meeting, if *that* was all he had to report. Dan's patience wasn't inexhaustible, and the less he knew about any backstage maneuvering, the better.

From LaGuardia Dan went to an Explorers Club stag lunch—her chance for a quick reunion with Billy Buntington, known to *Women's Wear Daily* as Baby Bunting. She needed to gorge on his gossip feast, his wicked spinnings of the magic prospects in what Billy called "the D.C. glory seat."

When her car swung by his Fifth Avenue apartment, he bounded into the back seat, spilling a tinkle of welcome. "Prilla darling, I swear I don't know how you do it! With all this nasty business, you still look lovely as a tulip."

Thawing in that combustive warmth, she sighed, "Billy, you're a charming old liar. I feel like I've been run over by tanks, and I probably look that way, too."

La Grenouille's headwaiter whisked them to Billy's regular table. In the dozen years since Ginny had introduced them, this round little bachelor-about-town had made himself Priscilla's indispensable New York escort, arranging entrée and discounts with top designers, squiring her to the latest restaurants and shows. Billy did that for quite a few star-class ladies, but she was the prize of his collection now.

She needed old friends like Billy, now more than ever. Even in her rare offstage moments so many strangers, climbers pecked at her. But with Billy she could relax her guard, joke, gossip—feel like her old self for one snatched hour.

His "bulletins" were served up like the veal cooling on her plate. "Oh, this is too delicious. You remember Sam Schwartzman, that hugely big TV producer. . . ." She bent attentively toward him, prodding her wandering thoughts, trying to shuck the grimy campaign for Billy's bubble-bath world.

"The spurned wife got into his Park Avenue co-op and slashed three closets of clothes. A dozen hand-stitched Armanis, sixty custom shirts. I mean to *ribbons*, my dear. . . ."

Peek-a-boo glances from the elegant, idle-rich women of the frog pond set. One called out, "Seeing you is my dessert, Prilla!" Yet she sensed a hint of stale news, flatter interest than, say, three months ago. Dan always said this country's attention span was forty-six hours. The looks today weren't so much excited as. . . curious. Ho-hum curious.

". . . Krazy-glued it to the elevator, written all over in fat Magic Marker, 'Property of Sam Schwartzman's whore.' They're still scraping bits of French silk at 855 Park."

She giggled that that was one way to get his attention.

"Oh, did I tell you the latest on Gloria Vanderbilt? *Huge* row with her young man of the moment, darling, at the launching of her new tight-buns line, no less. . . ."

The agents at the next table bolted to alert as a chic white-blonde woman barged up for an autograph, babbling, ". . . even prettier than your photos." As she signed "Best wishes from. . .," she wondered where a woman like that would keep it. In a scrapbook with dried prom corsages? No matter. She wrapped her best campaign smile around "Now you be sure to let those congressmen know who should be president!"

Profuse thanks. "I'll tell my husband to send off ten telegrams tonight!"

As agents nudged the woman away, Billy purred, "See how they all love you, darling. That adoring public of yours." She shot him a come-off-it look. Now his tone was hushed, confiding. "I swear, Prilla dear! Any day now you and Dan will roll right into that White House. The people just won't stand for much more Congress diddling, take my word for it, darling."

She launched an account of their visit to the Dartmouth Winter Carnival. "New Hampshire, Billy. Split state, one-and-one. Are you keeping up on those little numbers?"

"Yes, yes, of course. Following it tight as a tick."

She blabbed on about the snow sculptures. "There was me, like Olive Oyl with a nose a foot long. Icicles for earrings, if you can feature that."

"Poor darling!" he crooned. "I know how you *love* that polar-bear weather."

Shivering, pierced by chill even in this overheated room, she said the cowboy hat on Dan looked like "a teeny porkpie. And he had two double chins, and a belly like. . ."

Suddenly he clutched her arm, murmuring ecstatically, "Oh, no, this is too much. Did you see who just came in?"

A slight young man in a rust suede jacket followed two silky women to a table. "Why, who's that?"

Hissed: "Darling, that's Dennis Darien. That punky third-rate designer who's snug-a-bug with you-know-who. . . ."

"Goodness!" That wispy man chatting up his waiter had an inside track to Robin Devlin, of all people!

All the support-system men—the hairdressers, masseurs, designers —*did* get to know you in bizarrely intimate ways even your own husband didn't. It chilled her to think how much Bernardo could tell if he ratted. *Oh god. . . .*

Or Billy. Wicked old thing, Billy knew *all* the secrets. She knew he was quite a silly man, something of a fawner, coasting on his link to her. And that one over there, archly waving to someone, had the same tie to. . . .

As Darien's eyes finally brushed hers, he flashed a smirk of recognition. She looked quickly down at her plate, attacking the stone-cold veal.

Dennis Darien was gasping at his good luck. Mrs. Tacky in the very pink! Looking more anorexic than he'd expected, and old as Methuselah's mother. He had half a mind to barge right over there and ask her what diet kept her so divinely skeletal.

She obviously wasn't quite so delirious to see *him*. Kept trying to sneak in a few peeks without catching his eye. He hadn't had such a glorious hoot since Yves Saint Laurent turned up at a black-tie do with an open fly.

And Baby Bunting was floating on lavender clouds. That clown-about-town would be eating out on *this* little yarn for a month of Sundays. It was a sign of Mrs. Tacky's low-brow California tastes that she let herself be lugged around New York by that jaded old tart, a moocher par excellence.

But at least she'd showed up to let him parade her out for the frog-pond set. He'd love to do the same for Robin, now that she'd turned into the whole country's darling, hotter than Streep and Streisand rolled into one. But dear old Robin was too busy sitting on her throne. Even their once-in-a-while phone calls were all too short, usually ending with, "Got to go, Den, I've got a million things to do."

He must admit that made him a little miffed. She ought to make a bit more effort for dear old pals who were only trying to see her safely through the storm. But seeing Mrs. Tacky, and the fizzling stir her presence set off, made him a tad more sympathetic to Robin's fix. *She* was the top dog now, holding the Tackys and Frumps at bay, and when he saw close up what she was sparing all the rest of them from, he decided she had her priorities right after all.

Finally, he caught Mrs. Tacky's eye.

Glorious discombobulation! Wincing, blushing, she actually choked down a forkful of her lunch. If he'd died right that minute, Dennis would've gone straight to heaven.

Billy caught that mute exchange, of course. Delicious, too delicious, wait'll Ginny heard this! The run-in wasn't doing much for Prilla's mood, more's the pity. But the whole bit was a stunning poof, a tale to dine out on.

Shame that Prilla couldn't see the giggle in it. She needed more laughs, poor darling, to hold off the march of the wrinkle brigade. Of course he knew she and the hubby had been through terribly rough sailing lately—one look at Prilla's face told him that. He was so shocked it was all he could do to muster up the de rigueur white lies.

Well, never mind. If she just made it to the glory seat, some miracle-making plastic surgeon could make amends. If, if! Lately Billy'd begun to think the happy ending he always promised her might not materialize after all. The fickle winds of politics, don't you know, blowing hot and cold. Lately they were blowing mainly on Devlin.

Preening, playing to his alter ego who had Prilla hypnotized from across the room, he rattled on about the pair of thin, rich women lunching with Darien. She interrupted: "He doesn't look a bit like I expected."

"I should hope not, darling. That hairdo went out with Valentino. For that matter, so did his designs."

When Ginny first introduced them, years ago, he'd thought mm-hmm, less here than meets the eye. She'd seemed a pushy little thing, frantic to please. Thin enough to be one of the Really Rich, but not much else to recommend her.

Then when hubby got elected governor—a still-amazing tour de force, considering his IQ and general lack of smarts—Prilla began to pick up polish. Quick study, she turned out to be. Billy began to think there was some hope for her. So when all the talk started about hubby going "all the way," as Ginny put it—well, Billy found it fairly flabbergasting but didn't dismiss it out of hand. After all, if a dowdy, horsey dimwit like Elizabeth II could set the world on fire, think what he might yet make out of Prilla!

Whatever Priscilla had come here to get from Billy, she hadn't gotten yet. Now he switched to a mournful dirge on how much all her friends missed her. "Ginny says those gasbags in the House need a good high colonic, that's—"

"What on earth d'you suppose she sees in him? And those ridiculous clothes he comes up with?"

He chuckled reassuringly. "Well, darling, there's no accounting for taste. He seems to be quite her cup of tea, personally and otherwise, don't you know."

"Really?" She peeked dubiously at the offending object, prompting an ecstatic flurry of hands. "I would've thought he was more inclined. . . well, you know."

"Yes, yes, quite right. But then, those two were tight as ticks last fall, popping up everywhere, private jokes and so forth. Maybe a little AC-DC. . . ." He waggled his hand.

She slapped at his arm. "Billy Buntington, you are a very naughty man."

She'd scrambled this runaway lunch into the schedule because she ached for Billy to laugh away some of the tired gloom in her bones. But there were no laughs under Darien's prying eyes. She pushed aside her plate. "Billy, let's go have coffee at the suite."

Rolling toward the Waldorf Towers, his radar finally tuned to her need. Squeezing her hand, he purred, "Just you hang on a bit longer, Prilla dear, and you'll see the golden Sterling era ringing in." Crooned, almost. "Your Dan is going to make it, yes he will. And you'll be a fabulous First Lady—queen of the world, with kings and prime ministers at your feet, and the Pope twined around your pinky. . . ."

Their little game was like the one she played with Ginny—he painting glossy, fevered fantasies, she laughing, poking fun. Yet she fed on them now more than ever. Stored them up to warm cold days on the trail. She sighed, "Billy, it's so darn good to see you. Like going home for Christmas."

He beamed his pleasure, ever the optimist. "Now you listen to me, young lady. We'll all be waltzing soon at your Pennsylvania Avenue debut. Jimmy Galanos told me just last week what a stunning difference it will make. . . ."

As she drank it in, she caught a tone shift on the Secret Service radio. She hushed Billy. "George, what was that?"

The agent grinned. "Wire-service bulletin, Mrs. Sterling. Your husband's picking up another state."

"Congratulations, darling! Now look at that—the watched pot never boils, don't you know."

She shushed him impatiently. "What state, George?"

Wisconsin, he said. Fellow named Morinski. She asked if Dan was at the Waldorf. Cryptic shortwave reply: Yes.

As the car swung down Park, she furiously recalculated. She'd slipped off to lunch without staff chaperones—no time to mobilize now. "George, I don't want to talk to any press. Can you find out if they're in the garage?"

Brief consultation on the radio, Billy watching with saucer eyes. Then: "Okay, Mrs. Sterling, there's three crews plus about a dozen reporters. Shall we try another entrance?"

"No, no. Just get me in as fast as you can." As they turned onto 50th she said rapidly, "Billy dear, I have to run. If any press bother you, please don't talk to them."

"Of course, of course. But darling, I don't understand—it *is* good news, isn't it?"

"Oh sure, absolutely." She forced a quick smile. "I'll explain later. Right now I've got to get back to Dan." She stepped out, agents moving her rapidly toward the big brass doors. She ignored the shouted questions, smiling blankly.

Pandemonium in the suite. Aides scurrying while Dan held the phone, cheeks red, distractedly watching TV.

She rushed to his side. "Oh, Prilla. Hi." He bent absently to her kiss. "Dammit, Chet, here we are caught with our drawers down on this thing. Throwing away a good base hit. We should've been right on top of it, timed it to tip a few more rolls."

She thought bitterly of Chet's "update" a few hours earlier, the prayer breakfast with Morinski *next Thursday*. Chet would have some job talking his way out of this one!

From the TV, ". . . a 52-year-old Independent from Wisconsin's Third District, whose dramatic announcement was apparently a bombshell to both camps. . . ." Dan snapped angrily, "The hell you say. If our guys were on top of it, how come I got the news from AP?"

She tossed off her coat, choking on guilt. Look at this! The minute she slipped off to recharge her batteries by lunching with Billy, something like this had to happen. *All right, then. No more time off.* . . .

In a replay, Morinski peered owlishly from the House well, horn-rims sliding down his bony nose, droning about "the grave constitutional crisis confronting our great nation, which threatens the very roots of our system. . . ." Dan passed the phone to Paul, saying he wanted to catch Morinski. ". . . intolerable crisis of leadership must be rapidly resolved, in the best interests of the American people. . . ."

She watched Dan as he watched the screen, matching mirrors of intensity. She wanted for his sake to squeeze some relief from this vote, but sensed only brushfire anxiety. They'd let a big one through their gloves today. All right, a vote was a vote, and they'd take what they could get. But she knew this roll should've counted for more than one.

She moved to Dan's side, stroking his shoulder, murmuring, "Two down, sweetie."

He shrugged off that distracting touch. "Yeah. But if our guys had been on the stick. . . ." He trailed off as Morinski continued, ". . . after long and prayerful consideration, I have decided that the will expressed by the American voters on November 4th must be honored and upheld by this chamber. Accordingly, I will cast my ballot for the Republican, Daniel Sterling."

As loud applause rolled in, Morinski blinked. One aide muttered dryly, "You just saw a guy bust his media cherry."

Priscilla snapped, "That's not funny, Howard."

"Dammit, what's going on?" Dan asked. "Talbott's floor guys must be all over him. How soon is that vote?"

Very soon, Paul said. Delegations caucusing now. She trailed Dan to the bedroom, where his speech writers huddled. "Barney, let's see what you've got. And it better be good."

Peering past his shoulder at the rough typing, she said, "Play up the patriotic, Dan. Get those flags waving."

"Right. Punch up a good-of-the-nation pitch, Barney."

Paul popped in, "Live response from Talbott on NBC." Talbott pale, obviously shaken: ". . . remind you I am five votes closer than my opponent to election by the House. . . ."

She muttered, "Pasty-faced has-been."

". . . so while I endorse his conviction that this crisis must be rapidly resolved for the good of the nation. . . ."

Dan said, "Okay, strike that 'good of the nation.' Prilla's got it right, go with the 'patriotic.' " Her mood lurched into a passable calm. He was doing fine on his own.

". . . I believe with all my heart that my candidacy offers the best and fairest solution for all Americans."

Dan smiled grimly. "Listen to that—he's still trying to head off that vote. How're we doing on that, Paul?"

"Right on track, Governor. You'll want to milk it for all it's worth, but I'd hold off till the balloting's done."

"Hell, yes, I'm not putting my nose in that wringer. That gives us—what is it, ten, fifteen minutes to figure out some way to get out front of this thing."

At 4:07 they watched the House Republicans give a standing ovation to Wisconsin's vote for "the next President of the United States, Governor Daniel Morse Sterling."

At 4:15 Dan strode into an eighth-floor conference room, Priscilla beaming by his side. Eyes straight to the cameras, voice husky, solemn: "My fellow Americans, today we finally heard the true and authentic voice of the American people. We heard that voice eloquently raised in the House of Representatives debate by a courageous patriot who cared more for his country than any political party—Congressman Louis Morinski from the great state of Wisconsin."

CHAPTER THIRTY-FOUR /

February 5th

Robin

At breakfast Larry mentioned that Eric Lowenthal and Hale Wiley were coming for lunch. Robin asked if it would be more "blather à la Camp David."

Mild offense taken: "Robin, these things don't happen goddam overnight. I'd appreciate a little—"

"Right, babe. Excuse the rude RSVP. I assume you're inviting me?" He squinted, seeming to reconsider. She flipped a hand, Scout's-oath gesture. "Accept with pleasure, sir."

The main addition to today's menu was crusty Hale Wiley, who'd just lost his Senate seat—and his Foreign Relations chair—to the Sterling coattails. Looking more animated than he'd been since Cowboy Dan's trucks had run over him last November, Hale reminded them that as a cub reporter in World War II he'd once interviewed Ho Chi Minh.

Over the rat-a-tat table talk, Robin decided Cal looked like Eric's seedy nephew. About as sexy as a bent broom. Watching the brooding calculations on his drawn face, she wondered how she'd gotten it on with him even once. And Eric looked like he'd just had a B-12 shot. Thriving on the wrangling as Hale and Cal went at it over Prince Oudong, "China's faithful client since his overthrow, essential to patching together any sort of national reconciliation government. . . ."

Cal was trying to make these blowhards see it was all the same can of worms anyway—Phnom Penh's puppet government was loaded with Khmer Rouge rats like Oudong, who'd only turned on Pol Pot to save their own ass. Couldn't fathom why they had trouble grasping that, since Washington ran more or less the same way.

Larry harrumphed about Oudong once telling him his people were being "crushed and dismembered by the unbearable weight of an endless war which various foreign powers will keep alive—until the last Cambodian is dead." The golden boy loved to drop names: "So-and-so-told-me." But a knack for pretentious quotes didn't mean he understood squat about the dirt-real world out there.

Wiley reckoned Oudong had been proved "tragically correct." He seemed still in shock from his recent boot from the catbird seat.

Cal spoke up, begging to differ with them both. Oudong had also said the tragedy was created by only two men, Nixon and Kissinger. They'd set up their Lon Nol puppet, the mad, remote mystic who listened only to his astrologers. "Lon Nol was nothing without them, and the Khmer Rouge were nothing without Lon Nol and the four-billion-dollar bombing blitz Nixon called 'the best foreign policy investment the U.S. has made in my lifetime.' 'The Nixon Doctrine in its purest form.' My god, if he'd dropped even *two* billion on capital improvements, the place would be an Eden, a Utopia, instead of. . . ."

Antsy reactions to that. Dickie and Henry might be psychopathic war criminals who'd fortuitously beaten the rap, but they were also fellow members of the D.C. lodge. This bunch wasn't keen on bloodying the brothers.

The wordy, endless bull sessions had taken on a hallucinatory quality that reminded Cal of the weekly hashish dinners he and some press friends used to throw in Phnom Penh. All spiked from soup to dessert. One night they'd bagged the Russian ambassador, who by the second course was circling the table, muttering. Somebody in from a Moscow posting translated. The guy was saying over and over, "I don't believe this is happening to me."

That's how Cal felt about the present bit of business. Back on the chessboard: How would the Soviets react to a U.S.-Viet accord? If Hanoi cut a deal, could China be brought along? Wiley doubted that, but Lowenthal urged "appropriate inducement to participate in a negotiated resolution of their own dilemmas in that area."

He wondered if Robin spent her whole life inhaling toxic gibberish like this. What he'd prefer to do right now, given his druthers, would be pack up a pint of ganga soup and take that lady out for a picnic roll in the White House hay.

A few fresh nuggets startled Robin, like Eric's offhand remark that China had of course signaled approval of Talbott's abortive '77 negotiations with Vietnam, "in hopes of moderating Hanoi's pro-Soviet policies. But a bit later they were at war themselves—one more instance of untidy fact supplanting wiser policy." But mostly the talk went round and round what started to feel like familiar ground.

Cal interrupted Wiley's rant on the iron-clad guarantees required for any Vietnamese troop withdrawal to ask how he'd attack "the central sticking point: disarming Pol Pot and his Khmer Rouge? How do you yank their fangs if they're singled out as scapegoats?"

Larry noted that they had enough food and arms to fight on for several years, even if China and Thailand cut off their resupply. Lowenthal mumbled about a multilateral peacekeeping force to secure interim border camps: "But I'd like Mr. Farragut to answer his own question."

Cal shrugged. "Get China to unload him. Send in a plane and fly him and his top goons to exile. He might take over Oudong's palace in Peking, and his seven Chinese cooks."

"Funny, Cal," Larry said dryly. "Very funny. But—"

Cal burst out, "Listen, somebody's gotta go in there and throw a cage around that guy. It's no good talking about pulling out Hanoi's troops when those 40,000 homicidal maniacs could swarm back out of the hills. Somebody's gotta pull the plug, disarm those execution squads—"

"Well, it won't be us. That I can guarantee you."

"—because much as the Cambodians hate being occupied by a traditional enemy, nobody wants Pol Pot back instead."

Wiley wanted to know who'd bottle up the Khmer Rouge remnants, since no MLF force would take them on: "Pound for pound, those ferocious little bastards are probably the best guerrilla fighters in the world."

Like an endless maze. Round and round, no way out. . . .

Larry guessed he was listening for a watertight excuse to pack in the whole idea. Before the shit got much higher around his boots. Eric was doing a sonata on the awesome mutual antagonism between the Asian Marxist powers, Khmer versus Viets, Viets versus Chinese, and so on: "You're a brave man, Mr. President, to contemplate a dip in that pool of crocodiles."

He guessed he knew sooner or later somebody'd boil it down to a question of sheer guts. The one issue he couldn't walk away from. Smiling grimly, he said as a matter of fact he'd decided to invite Eric and Hale into the water—Hale and a secret negotiating team to Paris to hammer out an agreement with the Vietnamese, Eric to Beijing to "bring our Chinese friends aboard."

Robin gasped, clapped her hands: "Ah, Dev!" Eric beamed and grabbed his pipe. Hale lit up like the Fourth of July. Cal smiled his bent smile, touched his forehead in mock salute.

Talking fast to lock himself in, Larry laid out his two-track plan to expedite decisive action. As his special ambassadors they'd have backup teams discreetly recruited from State and National Security, but the major burden would fall on "your capable shoulders. I'm convinced no two men are more qualified to pull off this critical assignment—a tough, damn near impossible undertaking, as you well know." He paused, offer dangling like a dare. "Well, gentlemen?"

Eric rumbled a few reservations. But when Larry said he wouldn't trust the job to anyone else, the old guy said bashfully, "Mr. President, I guess you talked me into it."

Hale didn't need persuading. Bristling for battle, he warned he didn't hold out any great hope of "delivering the marbles here. But you'll get the best shot I can give it, Mr. President." Larry said that was good enough for him.

Robin raised her glass for a euphoric toast: "Godspeed and the greatest of luck to two *very* special ambassadors."

"Hear, hear!" Clink, clink.

Here goes nothing. . . .

Like a shaft of sunlight. *He's going for it!*

Yet Robin's glow dimmed when they got to specifics. Larry saw Eric's job as tougher than Hale's, since Hanoi had at least signaled a willingness to deal—which wasn't worth a spit in the creek unless China could be brought along. Wiley wished they had more to go on than Lowenthal's "legendary touch. Offhand, given present conditions, I'd estimate hell would be frozen over before China would agree to our normalizing with Vietnam. But on the credit side. . . ."

They totted up whatever pluses they could find—precious few, she thought. Mentioning the "glacial speed" of most diplomatic endeavors, Wiley reckoned that the unsettled circumstances of Larry's incumbency might "help move those ornery Vietnamese off the dime."

Jaw tightening at that thin-ice reminder, Larry barked out marching orders. "Hale, make it damn clear there's no Yankee dollar sign over the table this time. Eric, China should know we intend to review our position on Cambodia's U.N. seat, regardless of this outcome. It's about time this government got out of bed with Pol Pot."

She blurted, "And please don't forget Cambodia. Hale, I know you'll have a long agenda, but keep in mind the part about saving that little country if we possibly can."

Larry surprised her with, "Good point, Rob. We may find a mutual self-interest in circumventing Cambodia's slow murder. And every nation responsible for compounding that tragedy, however inadvertently, owes it that much, at least."

Eric said softly, "Amen to that, Mr. President."

Larry slapped the table. "Enough said, gentlemen. Let's get this show on the road."

In a flurry of handshakes and backslaps, they stepped into the hall, where Stephanie waited with a paper-stack. Robin hugged Lowenthal's arm, murmuring, "Use all your magic on this one, Eric." Beside her Cal said to Wiley, ". . . never cry uncle, that's for damn sure. Let's see which devious agenda the bastards operate on this time. Hello, Stephanie."

Stephanie stared open-mouthed at the men moving down the hall. *No ño, can't be. . . .*

Robin said absently, "Sorry I got held up." Double take. "Did he just call you Stephanie?"

She asked faintly, "Was that Cal Farragut?"

Robin broke into a fit of coughing, looking almost as astonished as Stephanie felt. "What, you know Cal?"

Grabbing for her scattered wits, she said she'd met him a few times, in Vietnam. "What on earth's he doing *here?*"

Robin said vaguely that he was an old friend of Larry's. "And an usher at our wedding." For some reason she seemed pissed off. "He dropped around for lunch."

"Well, my god. Small world, and so on." *Cal Farragut! Holy moley. . . .*

Robin stared at their backs. "You mean you haven't seen him since Vietnam, and he just says, 'Hi, Stephanie'?"

She laughed. "Oh, sure. That's why I knew it must be Cal. Who else would do that?" Cautious probe: "What's he doing here with Eric Lowenthal and Hale Wiley?"

Briskly: "Well, they have to eat too. So what's up?"

Stephanie reminded her of the Triple-A Life Saving Awards: "Your weekly offering to the rat pack. . . ."

"All right, dammit," Robin said crossly. "But let's make this short and sweet."

That collision left Robin in no shape to tackle the Red Room ceremony. Swamped with jeopardy, her numb stage fright was eased by a pair of black kids ecstatically acting out their rescue of a neighbor from a burning building: "I say, that lady still be up there. We gotta—" "So Jimmy and me, we run up them stairs. Couldn't see nuthin' but smoke. . . ."

Stephanie beamed in the background, totting up one more *succès fou.* This latest bombshell made Robin realize what a bad idea it was to've hired an old friend like that in the first place. Already she couldn't imagine coping without her—now welcome to the discovery that she'd slipped into that perilous dependency with *someone who knew Cal Farragut!*

As they headed back to the family quarters, Stephanie prattled,

"Excellent, A-one performance. I especially liked the way you let the kids do so much talking."

Bursting to ask about Cal, Robin wondered how much she could pump from Stephanie without giving anything away. Her itch was tempered by instinctive distrust of Mayo's reportorial nose. And there was vital secrecy to be protected here—not just the critical Vietnam initiative, but. . . .

Grim reminder: *Don't scratch the itch!*

Stephanie blurted, "Funny thing, I had no idea Farragut knew any Devlins." Robin felt Stephanie's eyes raking. "Typical Cal, I s'pose. He's a bit of a queer duck, don't you think?"

Robin offhandedly agreed. Leery of tipping her hand but obviously expected to say *something*, she settled for, "That's such a weird coincidence, you knowing Cal."

No weirder than the vibes Stephanie was picking up right now. She said well, not really so strange—a lot of press types were in and out of Vietnam in those days, and Cal just always seemed to be there.

Wary smile. "That sounds familiar, somehow."

Stephanie punctured the awkward silence by noting that she didn't know him all that well: "A nodding acquaintance. 'How's it going, let's go have a beer' when I bumped into him in Saigon or Phnom Penh."

She wasn't sure how much of this Robin wanted to hear. But once she'd started off down Reminiscence Road, tracking that crazy bastard Farragut, it was tough to stop. So she rambled on about Cal being one of the best war photographers in the business, and those guys took the brunt of the action—had to be right in it, not like the reporters filing from the back of the bar. He seemed in a crazy sort of way to be in love with war, she thought.

But that had changed when he was shot up in a firefight. "After that he'd help the wounded before he took his shots. So he wasn't doing the job. That's when my *New York Times* buddy switched to another photographer. But he still hired Cal as a field guide in Cambodia, because nobody knew how to get in and out of those combat zones better than Farragut."

Robin kept walking, saying nothing. So Stephanie babbled on about how Cal was "pretty hooked on Cambodia by then. A fairly lost cause, both of them. I used to think about him later when I heard about the grisly stuff going on there. I wondered what the hell happened to him. But the last place I'd've expected him to turn up was here. . . ."

Robin said abruptly, "He got back in last fall. To Cambodia. And filmed the trip. I hope some time you'll get a chance to see it."

A film that *Robin* had seen already? Somehow this didn't add up, fit together. Something was going on here. . . .

Stephanie tried the frontal assault: "If you don't mind my asking, what's he doing here?"

Robin would've given just about anything to be able to tell her. But she couldn't afford the luxury—not with everything riding on this. Stephanie was around every day, talking to god knows who. She might put together what Wiley and Lowenthal were doing at that lunch. Hell of a fix if *that* leaked. Or if she found old buddy Cal hanging around. . . . God! No way she wouldn't be whiffing after Cal.

So Robin rubbed her nose and smiled blandly. "Well, you know how it is. All your long-lost friends turn up when your jackpot comes in."

She knew she'd spill her guts in another minute, so she said if there was no urgent business she was off to her workroom. Stephanie asked if she thought she'd see Cal again.

She said lamely, "Can't swear to that. But if I do, I'll tell him you said hello."

CHAPTER THIRTY-FIVE /

February 5th

Prilla

Priscilla went into the Carlton john to dose her tummy-twinges with Maalox. She felt so bruised and sore these days it almost hurt to draw a full breath. But her job was to steer Dan clear of any wrong moves. Keep him fresh and rested, tight on target. And keep him from knowing how frantic she was—bone-tired herself, tasting panic like dry chalk.

God, she wished it could be over.

Back in the bedroom, Dan was still conked out. She lay on the bed, slid under his blanket, pressing against his warm, solid back, lighting her wick from his glow. Trying to bake out the pain, melt to his strength. *Let go. Let go. . . .*

She roused him with pats and nudges. "Hon, it's time." He flung out his arms, groaning protest. She snuggled, kissing him awake, cajoling, "Come on, tiger. Up and at 'em. . . ."

Flurry of glad-handing for the half-dozen House Republican leaders, sleek and hearty as door-to-door peddlers. Chet murmured introductions: Minority Leader, Minority Whip, Deputy Whip. Dan greeted them like old pals: "Frank, real good of you to come by. George, how's that golf game holding up?" She doled out more formal handshakes: "Always such a pleasure to see you, Congressman Whittaker. . . ."

Dan asked how things looked in the House. His floor manager Frank Whittaker, spitting image of a Marlboro man, started upbeat: ". . . every indication that your candidacy can prevail." But in his specifics, she heard brooding concern about the three votes Talbott needed versus Dan's seven: "That's a mighty small roll to make, Governor, if he gets any momentum." He mentioned the peculiar mood of the House, each member feeling heat, some quite intensely, "but right now they're damn reluctant to jump. In either direction."

They brought up various members both sides were courting—Iowa, Montana, Arkansas, West Virginia and so on. But the talk drifted obsessively back to Roy Bob, hot on their heels, making headway with South Dakota and Wyoming. Armbruster, the whip, stressed the vital Kentucky by-election, three weeks off. The Democrat widow was up in the polls, had the sympathy vote, the women vote. If Kentucky went, he wouldn't guarantee they could head off two more defections.

The longer they talked, the more she sensed their pervasive gloom. Yet Dan listened politely, smiling, responding to the more positive straws. She realized it was two mismatched conversations. Dan was talking about teamwork and touchdowns, all pulling together for the good of the party, "in this fight to win," urging them on like a locker-room coach. But the rest were trying to tell him this game's going sour, out of control. These men toying with Dan's fate were running scared, focused more on where Talbott was squeezing *his* votes than where Dan's rescue would come from.

Clear as a bell: *They don't know, either. . . .*

Seeing them out, she echoed Dan's rah-rah parting strokes, smiling through the blizzard of promises: "Hang in there, Mrs. Sterling, we're on the move." "Thumbs up, Prilla, he'll get this yet." All worth about one bent nickel.

Dan surprised her by saying he thought the session had gone pretty well. "Should help get those shoulders to the wheel." *Typical Danny. Always the silver lining.* . . .

Chet more or less agreed with that, when she slipped him in for a quick drink after they got home: "Close to target, all things considered, Governor. And a great morale booster to the troops, that chance to sit down with you."

As they batted around names and states like party balloons, she thought gloomily, *He's saying what he thinks Dan wants to hear. Or else he's denser than I figured.* . . .

She perked up when Chet mentioned his "special field operatives." That House seemed like a Byzantine puzzle palace, so infinitely complex yet so dull. She had no feel for it at all. But Chet's legmen—*that* she understood.

No good news on that score either, but plenty of red ink, a "generalized pattern of personal debt." Chet cited specific mortgages and partnership loans. Not a flicker of interest on Dan's tired, remote face. He wanted catchy little yarns like Dave Elliott's, not this droning recital that sounded like the federal budget.

Chet mentioned definite confirmation that Kittyhawk's wife would *not* move to Washington.

Priscilla snapped, "Oh, for heaven's sake, Chet, he's already told that on the David Brinkley show. His wife said one political nut per family was enough, so she'd see him down here when she lobbied for some Indian outfit. There's no way that ridiculous business is any use to the Governor."

"Darn right," Dan grunted. "I already told you, Chet—you steer clear of that hanky-panky stuff."

She headed off a good-scout lecture by asking if Chet knew how Kittyhawk was leaning. Halfway through his windy hedge, Dan turned him off by switching on the late news.

ABC caught the House brass leaving the Carlton, Whittaker pausing to talk up their "very productive meeting with Governor Sterling." Asked to assess Dan's prospects, he said lamely, "I think he still has an excellent chance of winning. Of course, this is a business where you learn pretty fast how to count, and unfortunately the numbers don't provide much encouragement at this point."

Dan went off like a firecracker. "Goddam! Did you hear that? Where the hell does Frank Whittaker get off, pussyfooting around like that?"

She tried to calm him down, tell him it didn't matter *what* Whittaker said, but he was still fuming about that "royal back-stab" when they caught the tail end on CBS, Whittaker adding, "But I'm fully confident that Dan Sterling will prevail, and the House will soon vote to affirm the results of the November election."

"There, you see, hon?" she purred anxiously. "He wasn't bugging out, he says he's 'fully confident.' "

Muttering that if this was Whittaker's idea of being a team player he'd sure like to know whose team the bastard thought he was playing on, Dan stalked into his den and slammed the door.

Fighting off that flutter she always got when he closed her out, she took their half-empty glasses to the kitchen. *He's phoning, probably. Leave him alone, let him cool down.* . . . Chet trailed with his glass, mumbling apologetically that Whittaker had "pulled a bit of a fast one."

"Par for the course, with that bunch," she snapped. "The way they've handled this whole thing, it's a wonder we haven't. . . ." She flipped on the tap to drown out the thought.

"Now that's going to turn around very soon, Mrs. Sterling." He picked up a dish towel as she furiously scrubbed.

She was fed up, *fed up* with these limp, lame-brained promises. Glaring into his cold grey eyes, she said, "And I'm not thrilled with what your bunch is coming up with either, Chet. We're fighting for our lives here, and we need better ammunition than what any Tom, Dick, or Harry can get from David Brinkley, for heaven's sake."

She angrily braced for more excuses. But he said quietly, edgily, "There's one other thing I might mention. . . ."

A big question for Chet was how much she really wanted to know. Her signals read both ways: "You know what the Governor wants" blah-blah versus a few broad winks she'd tossed him. But wired as she'd been lately, the winks could've been a nervous tic. Overdue for a Valium type thing.

He knew how essential it was not to misstep with Mrs. Boss. She'd had guys canned, shipped to Siberia for looking cross-eyed at her on the wrong day. In a way, the less she knew about any of this, the better for them both. But strung out as she was, he wasn't sure how much longer she'd hold up if she didn't see some kind of break coming from somewhere.

He stiffened up and took the flyer, saying certain rumors had come to his attention about videotapes "of an apparently compromising nature" involving Lincoln Sheppard, the Indiana Democrat, and "a certain female lobbyist." He held his breath, waiting for the trial balloon to crash.

She turned off the water. Staring at the glass in her hand, she asked what was on the tapes. He cleared his throat, said he couldn't be too specific, but he understood they might include "certain situations in a hot tub."

She looked up at him, and the cobwebbed eyes said it all. *She wanted to know, all right.*

She just didn't want to know too much.

Well, someone's got to do it, she thought.

She ripped off a paper towel and wiped her hands, picking her words. "Chet, you were certainly right not to bring up anything like that to the Governor. We both know how he stands on that sort of. . . unsavory thing."

Yes ma'am, he agreed.

"Under no circumstances could our campaign be associated with the sort of tactics that would involve—anything of the kind. That's rule number one, Chet, and I rely on you to make sure it doesn't get broken."

Solemn nod. "You can count on that, Mrs. Sterling."

She had to count on that and so much more, hoping and praying that Chet could do this right, with no slipups. It wasn't entirely clear just *what* she was supposed to count on, but maybe they were better off that way. She'd just have to screw up all her faith to believe Chet could *do it right*. . . if she had any faith left in her.

She still felt oddly cheered—lightened, somehow—when she saw him out the door and went back to her Dan.

CHAPTER THIRTY-SIX /

February 10th

Robin

Robin had rashly agreed to do the qualification, the "drunkalogue" at today's meeting. She tried to think of it as an AA bake-sale obligation, but her stage fright wasn't helped by Jim's sending her back up for "the hat." She was fed up to *here* with his antsiness.

As the cars rolled up to Bella's, Jim asked if Robin would please talk to the group about moving the meeting someplace where the security could be beefed up. The damn security was already tighter than she needed. What they wanted was to move this to the White House —"Let 'em come to you, Mrs. D," Jim put it. But she resisted. Hard enough to conjure up the healing routine of a normal meeting with this hand-picked, curry-combed bunch. She drew the line at transplanting the circus behind her prison gates.

First moments of the drunkalogues were always the worst. Like stripping in front of your ninth-grade gym class. But she loosened up on her father, how he hadn't been there much when she was growing up. Certainly not emotionally. But there'd be times she waited for, when he'd get fuzzy and affectionate. Call her his leading lady, his little princess. She was so hungry—grateful—for those times she hadn't minded that they only happened when he was plastered.

She touched on the jealousy that pushed her mother to punish her for that closeness. *Almost a sexual jealousy*, she didn't say aloud. Her mother also tried to control her father with rigid, unbending anger. The arguments leaked under closed doors, into cryptic sparring on the phone.

She grew up vaguely ashamed that her father obviously, at times, drank too much. She didn't know then that she'd been born into a typical alcoholic family, that even her light-drinking mother fit the classic profile of enabling partner—and she another, as the child-of-alcoholic who became one herself, although of course she had no inkling then of having the same permanent, disabling disease, like a kind of polio you could somehow inherit.

In fact, she'd grown up sure that would never happen to her. Especially after she and a 12-year-old girlfriend decided to get drunk. They'd killed a red wine and started on a pint of vodka when she got horribly sick all over the john, red vomit everywhere. She swore she'd never, *ever* drink again, and more or less didn't until she fell in with a college crowd of boozers. Then she discovered she could hold it as well as the guys (even guess who). She matched them pint for pint, finding out all the "fun" she'd been missing. A few belts dissolved her shyness, made her feel so much more confident, more attractive.

After she married, her drinking pattern shifted to cocktail-party routine and evenings "relaxing" with her husband. She decided not to mention that their best times in bed came when she'd drunk enough to numb the tip of her nose; she was still leery of leaks from this group, and she automatically edited out more here than she had in New York.

She'd managed not to drink during her pregnancies, though that got harder each time. Larry tried to be especially attentive, but she resented his rocking and rolling when she couldn't. In her last pregnancy she fought off an overwhelming urge to drink, but couldn't wait for that baby to be born. Larry brought champagne to the hospital to celebrate; she took off and didn't look back for ten years.

Pretty soon she was behaving "inappropriately" at parties. "People," in other words, Larry, suggested she'd better watch her drinking, but she got furious whenever they mentioned it.

After a minor car accident she let the housekeeper and the handyman take over the carpooling. That estranged her more from her family, but at least she knew the children would be safe. By now she was very careful of her public drinking, sticking to her two-a-night limit. But in private she was secretly tippling to get through lunch, to put on makeup, to write a shopping list—any excuse would do.

She made brief mention of her mother's visit the summer Sean was born, when she'd fussed over a Sunday dinner, trying to make it so perfect there'd be nothing for her mother to criticize. And then passed out on the back lawn where she'd gone to throw up.

She'd tried a few times to discuss this with her father, because she realized by then that they shared the problem, and she was finally looking for some way to handle it. But he died before she got through to him. She edited out the nightmare hospital scene when her mother hadn't let her in to see him: "You did this to him. You finally broke his heart. . . ."

Part of her mother's coded message seemed to be watch out or you'll wind up a sot like him. It took Robin years to realize that her rigid, punitive mother was only "trying to hang onto her own raft in the storm. As we all know, only too well, it's no treat to wind up married to a lush."

Eventually her rescue came from where she least expected: surrender to AA principles. "I admitted that I was powerless in the face of alcohol. That my disease could only be controlled by my reliance on a higher power. I've had three years and five months' sobriety now, knock wood. And that's all I have to say, except I'm very privileged to be part of this group, and grateful for your support."

Pit-a-pat applause didn't help her rocky gut. None of the relief she usually got from this confessional ordeal. Maybe because of all the gaping chunks she'd edited out?

She was still off kilter as they joined hands for the closing prayer. Escaping the usual easing-down chitchat, she made a quick exit. As Jim hustled her snappishly out the kitchen door, some kids perched along the fence popped flashbulbs at her. The three cars voomed down the driveway, tires squealing, Robin huddled low on the seat.

At the first red light, Jim cleared his throat. "Okay now, Mrs. D."

"I know, I know." Her voice flat, barely audible. "You want me to stay put."

"Or move the meeting someplace we can secure. The setup out here—hey, this is just one guy talking out of line. But I guarantee there'll be hell to pay over this."

Wearily, distantly: "Okay, okay." As they passed an appliance store filled with lit-up TVs, she thought suddenly, *If they won't let me out, I'll bring it in*. . . . She asked Jim to get her a remote-control TV, VCR, AM-FM, good stereo. ". . . the works. Biggest, best you can find."

☆

A hot shower helped ease her agitation. Downstairs she found Sean reading on a hall couch, head cushioned in his ski jacket. She asked where his father was. He thumbed toward the den. "In there, with Mr. Whalen and Cal."

"Thank you, dear," she said casually. *Walk, don't run*, as she headed for the closed door.

". . . goddamned harebrained idea. Good god, they're looking for jobs and mortgages, college loans for their kids—not another run at the Vietnam war!"

Charlie Whalen was glaring across the room, his looming bulk oddly balanced by Cal's lean intensity. *Porcupine takes on giraffe*. She murmured, "Sorry to interrupt, Larry, but we're late for a very important ball game."

"Right." Glancing at his watch, he said he had to cut this short and go watch his son imitate Larry Bird.

The lady sailed in like a gust of fresh air in a methane swamp. Cal said calmly, "How are you, Robin?"

She pinked up a little, mumbling fine thanks, Cal. "Charlie, always a treat to see you."

The old fatso rumbled distractedly top of the evening to her. Like a vaudeville hack whose best lines were leftovers from *Finian's*

Rainbow. Larry tossed her a warning cue, saying Cal had "mentioned his Indochina trip and the prospects for a foreign-policy shift from Hanoi."

She batted her eyes, said, "Oh, yes? Charlie, I gather you're not too interested."

"Damn right," the fatso growled. "No offense to your friend here, Mr. President,"—sarcastic stress on that "friend"—"but when this country's staggering through its gravest constitutional crisis since Watergate, I don't give a rap what those Viet Congs are up to. They can piss up a rope for all I care. It's got nothing to do with us."

Larry could chicken-shit this ignorant old gasbag all he wanted, but Cal wasn't bought off for hand jobs like that. He pressed: "Even if they showed signs of wanting to open up to the West, and loosen their ties to the Russians?"

"Damn right." Those eyes flicked warily between Larry and Cal. The old dog sniffed a live rat, right in this room. "Sonny, I've been around this town for thirty years. I went down that goddam war trail with Lyndon Johnson and almost lost an election because of some podunk country I never heard of. Did you fight in that war?"

Cal said calmly he'd like to stick to the point. "President Devlin may have a unique opportunity to exploit a significant split developing in the Communist—"

"I asked, where were you in that war? Dodging the draft in some goddam divinity school? Or picking up a Ph.D. in political science?" Scathing tone on those last two words.

"You lose, Charlie," Larry said with edgy amusement. "Cal was a combat photographer, in it all the way."

"Photographer, huh?" His dim view of that profession writ large on his flushed face. "Did you ever run for office, fella, or work on a campaign? Hey, do you even vote?"

Robin looked about to shit on the rug. But Cal had been raised around bullies like this and learned not to rise to their cheap bait. Larry jumped in, pointing out that Cal wasn't involved politically, he was just "an old friend who dropped by with some news from an area where we are significantly involved."

"*Were* involved, Mr. President." Shaking his wattles. "At what cost—in blood, shame and billions of dollars—I needn't remind you. Right now this country has only one piece of business on its plate: getting Roy Bob Talbott reelected as President of these United States."

Larry smiled grimly at that swipe. He'd been eating shit for half an hour, bitterly second-guessing his bright idea of throwing Charlie and Cal together. It didn't help that Robin barged in for the fireworks. Well, to hell with it, he'd see who was running what. Goddamn if Charlie Whalen and those nelly farts on the Hill would call the foreign-policy shots for this administration.

Charlie railed that's what his voters mainly wanted. "Bread-and-butter issues like jobs and inflation. You come up with ideas on those lines, Mr. President, and you'll have me with you all the way. But at this critical juncture, I won't stand for opening up the stinking grave of that Vietnam war."

Cal said, "Even if we win what's left of it? And in the deal save Cambodia from being wiped off the map?"

Uh oh. . . .

Beetle brows shot up like crows in flight. "What's this? What's this? I don't know what tree your friend here just climbed out of, Mr. President, but I wish you'd tell him a few facts of life about—"

"Right you are." Glaring at Cal, Larry slapped Whalen's back and maneuvered him out of the room, soaping all the way. "Always grateful for your wise input, Charlie."

Pouchy with suspicion, Whalen poked Larry's chest. "Mr. President, if you want to fool around with someone else's dirty war, try Poland or Belfast. I've got lots of Poles and Irish in my district—but sure as hell no Cambodians."

Larry swallowed a smile, wondering if Rob picked up on that one. But she was trailing behind, whispering with Cal.

What the hell was going on with those two?

Robin blinked into the glare as they stepped from the limo at the Kingston Academy gym. Shouted questions on Cabinet changes, the House vote, Talbott's chances. . . .

Larry turned on his business smile and did a riff. She waited beside him, deep-breathing, toasted by lights. ". . . only number I'm concerned about tonight is the Kingston versus East Riding score. If you'll excuse us, we'd better get in there before the game starts without us."

The crowd was dense, jostling. Tortured progress into the gym. The school band droned out "Hail to the Chief" as they reached their red-white-and-blue-cushioned seats on the front-row bleachers. *Take it where you can get it. . . .*

On the court the teams ran through practice shots. Sean pointed: "There's Jase. Number eleven." No trouble finding him; the TV lights got there first. Whistle for the ritual handshakes. *Like budding pols. Shake now, kill later. . . .*

Off-key "Star-Spangled Banner," and they were into the game, leggy waterbugs skittering across the glossy wood floor. She tried to lose herself in that raucous play, watching her kid play ball. Like any other mom. . . . Fat chance. They brought the zoo with them to this drafty gym. It *was* a treat to see Jason sweating and dodging, playing his guts out. But hard not to think of all the other games she'd missed—far too many.

It turned out a lively win—Kingston 88, East Riding 85, thanks to some zero-hour saves. Jason's team swarmed on the court. Larry asked her, "Want to congratulate the kids?"

"Sure, why not?"

A wedge of agents plowed their way onto the court. Two ecstatic mothers yelled past the cordon, "Thrilled to have you!"

"Thanks so much. Great game, wasn't it?"

Down on the floor she hugged her radiant, sweaty son. "Honey, that was terrific!"

Jason introduced his coach, who fell into instant replay with Larry. She turned to the kids, goggle-eyed and tongue-tied around her. "Hey, guys, that was quite a show. Do you make a habit of cliff-hangers?"

"Nah, sometimes we roll 'em flat." said a cocky blond.

She laughed. "I'll just bet. What's your name?"

"Pete Bracken, Mrs. Devlin. This is Mike Dean, and Joe Still-well. . . ." Nice kids, well-bred preppies. Grateful that Jason had this to belong to, she suggested they come over for burgers some night and work out in the White House gym.

Rapturous reaction. "That's a deal, Mrs. Devlin!"

A cadenced chant pounded from the bleachers. Fed up with the confusion, she turned to Larry—who was watching her, smiling broadly like the coach. Pricked with unease, she realized they were all edging backward, leaving her in a spill of light. Larry pointed to the crowd. "Hear that, Rob?"

Now she did. "Rah-bin! Rah-bin! Rah-bin!"

CHAPTER THIRTY-SEVEN /
February 10th
Prilla

"Natalie, how are you? Is something the matter?"

"Hi, Mother. No, everything's okay, I guess." Archly casual, slightly slurred. "I mean, the house hasn't blown up or anything, if that's what you're worried about."

Priscilla knew that voice as well as she knew Dan's, and she was hearing trouble dead ahead. Perched on a hotel john, juggling the phone and a half cup of coffee, she nudged the door shut. "Well, what *should* I think, Natalie, when I hear you've called three times in one day?"

Natalie was just "feeling kind of down. So I wanted to talk to you, find out how things are going." Pause. "I never know where you are. Where to get hold of you."

She said now don't be silly, they could always be reached through the answering service or campaign office.

"Yeah, sure." Sullen, verging on hostile. "But I'm fed up hanging around here. Why don't I help with the kid vote?"

Deliberately patient: "Darling, it's all such a mad rush." She vividly recalled Natalie's last bit of campaigning, the temperamental romp last fall. "And no fun at all. I guarantee you'd be bored out of your skull, as you put it."

But Natalie said she kept seeing the Talbott kids out campaigning. Like the Devlins did. They didn't get parked in the closet, treated as if they were invisible.

Priscilla snapped, "Now, Natalie, that's ridiculous. The Devlins are still going to school, which is an idea your father and I certainly wish you'd reconsider."

"Hey, please. I'm not *that* bored. . . yet."

She'd talked like this before her earlier runaways, off to god knows where with dreadful boys like that heavy-metal zombie. That time she'd stayed away two years and oh, the bloody scenes. . . .

God knows Priscilla did love this moody child, more than Natalie probably thought. Yet to think how she'd agonized years ago, running through beau after beau, fretting she might never land a husband to make a mother of her! All that guff about babies being your crowning joy—as soon as those girls were born, tearing her half to pieces, they'd stolen a piece of Dan away from her. Bad enough in their adorable stage—a nightmare in their teens. She loved the *wife* part about wife-and-mother, but she couldn't wish away those girls, the Other Women in Dan's life.

Now finally she had him to herself again, not counting all the aides and hangers-on, and she wasn't about to have Natalie cut into that. "All right then, Gnat darling." Straining for remote control, pitched between sympathy and brisk dispatch. "I hope we can at least count on you in this difficult time to just. . . get on with your life, do something constructive. How are the auditions going?"

Mother always asked her about the auditions when she wanted to get off some kind of hook. Unspoken little put-down in that: *She'd* managed to get parts when *she* was in the business. Why couldn't her klutzy daughter?

Yvonne joked once that maybe Mother did it on the casting couch. She had a way of coming out with things Natalie felt guilty for even thinking. Anyway, she couldn't imagine Mother would've had the guts for really putting out. She leaned more to sneaky, subtle stuff, like putting down her kids.

Natalie said she'd done two more auditions, but she thought they were "waiting to see how Daddy does. Before they take a chance on me."

Icy cold: "Well, I hope you don't blame your father for that. He's got a few problems of his own now, young lady."

She said sure, she knew that. She just wished she had something to do around here besides watch the soaps.

Mother reeled off her old song and dance about how she knew it wasn't easy, but Gnat should just be a little patient right now, "like your father and me." Natalie could tap-dance to that tune by now, but it didn't help. Didn't cut the loneliness, or her itchy need to just float out and escape. But if Mother wasn't so busy trying to push Daddy onto the throne, she'd probably be telling Gnat how to brush her teeth or when to come in out of the rain.

She asked, "How's Daddy holding up?"

Briskly: "Oh, beautifully. I'll tell you all about it when we get to L.A. And we'll sit down for a nice, long talk about everything that's bothering you. All right, darling?"

"Okay. But tell Daddy to give me a ring once in a while, will you?" Mother said sure thing, and they'd talk to her very soon.

One constant in her life was auditioning for her parents' ears. Mostly unsuccessfully. She said acidly, "Well, thanks for calling, I'll try not to bug you again."

"Please, dear." Stiff with reproach. "You know I'm always very *happy* to talk to you."

"Oh, yeah. Like you keep telling me."

The conversation ended, like so many before, with nagging grievance on both ends. As Priscilla irritatedly hung up, she spilled her cup of coffee onto her pale-blue skirt.

Incredulous at her clumsiness, she sponged and scoured the stain. Their luggage was miles away, sealed up in the plane's secured baggage compartment.

In the end she sent Laurie Pendergast out to buy a size six dress or suit, "as simple as you can find. And *not one word* to the press." When they got to the airport, forty-five minutes late, 2 inches of muck-brown polyester hung below her blue coat.

As they snapped on seat belts Dan tried for a joke. "Hon, you know I always liked you in brown."

Deep-freeze voice: "Don't!"

"Okay, okay." He peered at his schedule. "Hey, here's a treat. 'Reverend Sammy Joe Dallas and ninety-voice choir.'"

That sanctimonious toad. . . . "Ha, ha. Very funny," she snapped. "Natalie wants you to call, by the way."

"Oh yeah? How's the Gnat doing?"

"Not great. See if you can't talk her into taking some courses or getting a job. I don't like her hanging around at loose ends like this."

Drifting into a nap, Dan tried to think what that brown suit reminded him of. Maybe when he first met her, Dee-troit deb let loose in Tinseltown, as Stu Lamont put it. Stu also called her Mousie Braxton—at least until Dan straightened him out. But she *was* kind of brown-mouse with her white gloves and fussy little hats, a virgin-girl-next-door type.

At that point, after his knock-down-drag-out divorce from Debra, he and Stu were pretty much regulars on the nightclub circuit. He was mainly a tits-and-leg man, and as Stu didn't hesitate to point out, Pris Braxton had no tits to speak of, and "unfortunate" legs. Dan decided she was a sweet kid anyway, so he kept her on his list and told Stu to lay off the "Mousie."

They got pretty domestic, and he kinda liked the change. He'd woken up in enough strange beds with splitting headaches and lord knows who beside him. One leading lady he made quite a play for once left him cooling his heels while she screwed her chauffeur upstairs—which Stu called the laugh of the week.

He knew for sure Pris Braxton wouldn't pull that stuff. She was a sweet little gal with a steel underneath that reminded him of his mother. He told Stu he wasn't about to settle down, but she was a refreshing change from his other gals. Stu's answer kind of stuck in his head: "Watch out, my boyo, that one's aiming for the big brass nosering."

He knew from the start she wanted like hell to get married, but she never pushed it so hard he couldn't ease off the subject—otherwise he'd've called it quits. He caught a real desperation in her jokes about "making an honest woman" out of her. But he wasn't about to give up his other now-and-then women.

Over the years they dated he sure did feel a lot of love for Prilla, but never *in love* to the point where he couldn't live without her—and that's what he wanted this time around. Then she got in a family way. Feeling the bear trap closing on his leg, he suspected she'd done it deliberately—although when he tried to hint at that, she went into such hysterics that he backed off.

He guess he knew all along he'd wind up marrying her, but he dragged it out for a few weeks. Finally Stu, of all people, read him the riot act—said every day's stalling would only make it worse down the line. As Stu used to say round about 3 a.m., well, no turning back now. So they eloped down the coast the next day, but he thought just before the ceremony, *This feels like another rerun of Debra.*

Wrongest hunch of his life, miles off base, as it turned out. She'd been the kind of wife they wrote the old songs about, true-blue and pitching for him all the way. Sometimes she might pitch a little hard, like when she'd talked him into making this presidential run, which didn't look right now like such a swell idea after all. But at least he knew she was always right beside him, his biggest rooter—not upstairs screwing the chauffeur.

At Spartanburg, South Carolina, the swarming crowds materialized again—third time in four days. Priscilla tried not to panic as they drove through the jammed, howling streets. Four thousand, the police estimated. Paul mentioned other "spontaneous rallies" at malls around the country: 1500 in Flagstaff, 2000 in Raleigh. Dan said jauntily that sounded like good news. She still flinched from that bellowing mob, feeling like a target, trapped, under siege as the car moved through wildfire fanned almost out of control.

Reverend Sammy Joe Dallas waited with his choir on the steps of his Nation of Jesus Christ Temple, staring at his watch. Dan said, "Sorry we're running late, Reverend, but the gremlins sneaked into our schedule."

Puckered displeasure on that pale, fleshy face. Echoing Dan's apology, she watched Dallas shoot the cuffs of his thousand-dollar suit— navy three-piece, custom job, like a British prime minister's. *Come a long way up from overalls, haven't you just, Sammy Joe?*

When they'd groveled enough to suit him, Dallas said he was "honored to have you and your lovely wife visit our humble congregation, sir. Early or late." Snap-to for "Come to the Garden of Prayer."

Waiting in the wings of the ornate white-and-gold "meeting hall," Priscilla waved off the aide trying to take her coat. She took in little of Dallas's hellfire sermon, ritual swiping at "godless pornographers" and "licensed killers of our unborn." On the TV monitor, coal eyes glinted in that smirking white-dough face. *Like a stuffed, churchy peacock. . . .* She'd never liked this man or his smug, almost cruel righteousness, but that was irrelevant to the business at hand: Dallas fed political causes dear to his conservative heart from the million-a-week pulled in with his razzle-dazzle televangelism. Dan didn't need his money, but they needed to head off Roy Bob Talbott, who was after Dallas like a moose in heat, bleating "saved" and "born again."

And they needed the mobilizing clout of Dallas's evangelical network, those targeted letters, pressure points on vulnerable congressmen. If he had any pull with the mobs prowling his streets, they'd need that too. *So make nice*, she resolved, hearing, ". . . the good Christian man forty-two million Americans elected as our president last November, Governor Dan Sterling and his lovely wife Prilla."

They walked out onstage to organ thunder and applause. Dan held his own against Sammy Joe's scene-stealing, talking about "right-thinking Americans who want to see justice done in our sacred halls of Congress. . . ." Smooth slide to that day during the filming of *Home to the Alamo* when he'd had his "first personal experience of our blessed Lord and Savior."

Dallas wound into a wing-ding finale, bellowing, "Come to Jesus! Repent and be saved—the hour is late, but Jesus waits!" Cameras off, he staggered backward, aides rushing up with towels and ice water. *This went out with vaudeville*, she thought as she and Dan were whisked backstage "until the Reverend is recovered from the service."

The miserable man let them stew for ten minutes before they were ushered into his dressing room "office"—crystal chandeliers, wall-to-wall mirrors, gold plush. "Well now, Reverend, this is my idea of a swell place to work," Dan beamed, taking in the reclining barber chair at the makeup counter.

"Lovely," she agreed, wondering how soon they'd get out of here —hot as an incubator, reeking of pine deodorant. She finally gave up her coat, watching Dallas gape at the brown suit. Lord knows Reverend Sam hadn't felt the abrasive kiss of polyester since he got the word about satellite transmission.

In custom shirtsleeves, he waved them to brocade armchairs. After Dan praised his "inspirational sermon," Dallas ran him through a laundry list of pet issues: abortion, busing, school prayer and rearmament. No pay dirt there; Dan could top him in right-wing pieties any day. So he started on the evils of serving liquor in the White House, "which is, after all, the home and hearth of this great Christian nation."

Dan fobbed him off with the "crying need to reestablish right values at the head of our government." Danny was so good at this sort of stroking. If she had her way she'd scratch those beady eyes out and be done with it.

The preacher reminded her a bit of Billy Buntington—both thought they had a hot ticket to the Sterling White House. But Billy at least earned his privileges; Reverend Sam just wanted his ring kissed. Now he was off on "all our good Christian supporters who came out to greet you today."

She realized suddenly that those roaring street crowds had nothing to do with Dallas. They were trailing after Dan now like a comet's tail, dogging him around the country.

Dallas rambled off into traditional family values, premarital sex epidemics, outright promiscuity, and "Christian marriage attacked by the spreading cancer of"—beady eyes flicking over to Priscilla—"divorce."

She caught her breath. *No, no. He wouldn't dare!*

"Now as a divorced man yourself, Governor, I have to question what that says about your dedication to strict Christian thinking."

Her nails bit into Dan's hand, held on for dear life, rage surging like bile in her throat. That vicious Bible-thumping hypocrite was probably out dipping his wick every night but Sunday. How *dare* he. . . .

Caught off balance, Dan mumbled about "nigh onto thirty years. . . finest wife any man could be blessed with. . . ."

Hearing the howls outside, she said sweetly, "But Reverend Dallas, I've always felt our deeply spiritual marriage was what led us to Christ. And surely the good Lord himself would favor that—after all, He's the one who brought us together, didn't He?"

CHAPTER THIRTY-EIGHT /

February 10th

Robin

When she heard the light rap, Robin realized she'd been waiting. She kicked nervously at the sheets. "Yes, come."

Larry in socks and shirtsleeves, with two snifters—brandy for him, Perrier for her. "You still up, Rob?"

"Sure. Come on in, sport." She said he'd just missed a chance to say hello to Dennis Darien, who was "groveling abjectly about the Spanish dinner, by the way. He says he'll crash if he has to. I told him that's what those pretty Marines protect us from, thank god."

Fuzzy grin. "What the hell, invite him if you want to. Dennis can give the house a little fruity New York pizzazz."

She said they'd do fine without it, and lifted her glass: "Cheers. Here's mud in your eye, babe."

He echoed the gesture. "Hey, here's to you, Rob. The belle of the goddam ball tonight, that's for sure."

Nose wrinkled, she called it closer to a Queen of Hearts tea party: "Too close for my taste. Pretty gross."

"Come on, don't knock it. You're a big hit out there."

Her thready equilibrium still strained by that burst of mob love, she asked what was happening in Paris and Beijing.

Rump dropped on the straight chair, he said the talks were going "maybe better than I expected." Wiley'd had some trouble steering the Viets off the subject of money, but they were damn fed up with the Soviets. Lowenthal found the Chinese "reverted to their native inscrutability," but he saw hopeful straws in the wind.

"So. . . so far so good?"

He shrugged, eyes veiled. "Dunno. Too soon to tell." She asked how the rest was going for him. He grimaced wearily: "Okay, I guess. But I'll tell you, Rob, it's a tougher go than I bargained on. Even the goddam 'caretaking,' let alone making a dent somewhere."

She smiled. "You'll manage, Dev. I'd bet on that."

He talked about that "goddam barn dance" in the House, Sterling's guys screwing up as good as Roy's. They even had Dave Elliott pulling out their chestnuts for a while—that's one Republican who knew the House as well as Charlie did. But they'd already eased him out for an L.A. adman, another PR dropout, while Charlie was running the House "like an old-line Philly clubhouse, six tricks up every sleeve."

"But, Dev, Charlie's game is to get Roy Bob back in."

He looked away, face slammed shut. He didn't show up here to get put on the couch.

Robin had somehow gotten too goddam involved in his business already. Between her and Farragut he felt like he'd been letting the loonies run the bin. Somehow they were lumped in his head, like a Stan and Ollie pair. Now what in hell was behind that? Maybe that's what he'd come up here to find out. . . .

But he backpedaled from the thought. They'd had their fill of boat-rocking lately. Tonight he'd rather slide on the good vibes from that game. He'd been goddam proud of her standing ovation, thinking, *Attagirl, that's my gal Rob.* . . .

Maybe he was a little envious too. But mainly proud. He'd come up to share the glow, warm the sparks of the good times they used to have. The last damn thing he wanted to get into now was Charlie and that dogfight on the Hill.

He guessed maybe he'd come up to test the waters, see if he could undo any of that Arnstein mess. All he was really after was a little get-together with his wife.

Abruptly, he squeezed her foot through the sheet. "Hey lady, enough about me. How're things going with *you?*"

Startled by that move—and that question—she said warily, "Oh, pretty well. No complaints worth mentioning." She hestitated, weigh-ing the tiredness in his face, sensing Sally's presence between them, and so many others strewn across the bed, Cal's long bones somewhere in the pile. *If you can't be straight and truthful with him.* . . .

Timid plunge: "Well, one thing I'm trying to do is figure out where to draw the line." *Yes. Say it.* . . . Veering off: "And I hope you're doing that too, Dev. For whatever it's worth, I'm real proud of what you're trying to do with the job. Get done. But. . . please don't count on it to last."

He bristled. "Hey, this inning isn't over yet, Rob."

"Sure, but things could get awfully messy, babe, with the kind of money Sterling's sluicing around. So I hope you've got some idea of how far you'd go to hold onto the job." Lecturing like a schoolmarm, for lord's sake. "I mean, I'd like to see you come out of this looking like. . . ."

"A winner, Rob, dammit." His chair legs banged the floor. "At least I want them to know I was here."

"Ah, they'll know, Dev. For sure they'll know that." He hoped that was a promise, coming from the queen of the basketball court. She snapped, "Now why'd you have to bring that up?" before she realized, *My god, he's a little jealous.* . . .

Injured innocence now. The patient, aggrieved face he wore when he talked about AA. "Well, shit. What's wrong with that?"

She flipped her hand. "Never mind, Dev. But. . . easy come, easy go. Let's talk about something else."

Curtly: "Fine by me."

Groping uncertainly for the light mood so abruptly dissipated, she said how much she appreciated "moments like this, having a chance to yarn with you, hear what's going on in your fat presidential head."

Wary grin. "Jesus. I'm eating shit all day in the office, I hoped for a little respect back home at least."

Mocking smile. "Ah, come on. I see them kissing your buns all day, genuflecting when the Marines parade you by."

"Well, there's kissing and kissing." Slow, deliberate, he stretched out on the foot of the bed, rubbing her ankle.

Okay, here it comes. . . . Why else these furtive night visits? She welcomed his company—even craved it a little. But *this* wasn't necessarily part of the deal. . . any more than Sally had been. She twitched her foot. "Babe, I hope I'm not presuming, but—is that sort of a pass?"

Uneasy laugh. "Well, maybe. Sort of."

She said if he didn't mind she'd like to get a few things straight between them: "God, I feel like I'm saying 'No, no, not above my knee.' But if this is kind of an affair we have now, not just conjugal duty, married stuff. . . ."

Grin more tentative, he said call it whatever you want.

"Well, the point is—I always thought affairs were different. And you could say, 'Thanks very much, I'm not really in the mood right now.' Instead of having headaches."

His hand sprang away. "Okay, I get the message."

She said she wasn't sure he did. "Thing is, babe, I really like these—visits. Private visits. They're very special for me, and I'm glad to have you here. I just don't want your dropping by to mean we're always expected to fuck."

That word he rarely heard her use sent him spinning up from the bed. He said okay, he'd let her get some sleep. She asked meekly if she could have a goodnight kiss, at least.

"Sure." He leaned cautiously over her, arms straddling, not touching. She lifted into that cold embrace, cradling his head. Brusque peck became hard kiss. They played it out, nibbling, tasting, stroking. When he pulled away, she murmured, "God. I'd almost forgotten what a good kisser you are."

"Yeah, well." He edged off, not risking another turndown. "It isn't every night I get to kiss the queen of the gym." That again. As if he were impressed by it.

She said thanks for coming, babe, remember the door was open, any time. His face sad, pain-etched in the soft light, he said, "Okay. Take care, Rob."

She was already furious at herself—confused, dismayed over what she'd done. Her old boozehead talking up, pushing him away. *Dope. Why'd you make such a big deal of it?*

It was good to have him here. Have him close, whatever way. All her idiotic babbling about "the point of an affair"—in *his* affairs the women were instantly on tap in his brief schedule breaks, more available than a wife. But she could hardly whine about that, when she wasn't sure how much Beanpole Farragut had to do with the bleak scene tonight.

This was the first "no" she'd said to him, in so many words. At least since they'd gotten so awkwardly, tentatively together again. If he just hadn't kept up that "queen of the gym" stuff. . . . *Tit for tat*, she thought wryly. Payback for Arnstein, she supposed.

Even so, it felt cold and alone in that odd-sized bed.

CHAPTER THIRTY-NINE

February 13th
Robin

Alexis's throaty boarding-school voice confided that Mr. Fletcher's birthday was Sunday, in case Robin hadn't heard. His sixty-first, if she was counting them right.

Birthdays were another item the Devlin clan always did up royally, a knack Robin had just never picked up. She asked what on earth to give him. Alexis said he did have a secret passion, actually: collecting old needlework, samplers, especially with an early American motif. "Doesn't have to be by Betsy Ross's niece if you could just find a few stars and bars. An eagle would be fantastic, of course."

She wondered glumly if Stephanie's magic was up to antique patriotic needlework on two days' notice.

From the sighs and moans coming over the phone, Alexis gathered the honeymoon was just about over. *Tant pis* for that; in fact, Robin was having a much easier run of it than Alexis had expected. The sympathetic buck-up offered in these calls was partly masquerade for her grisly curiosity. She didn't for a minute expect little Miss Swann would have the guts or stamina to stay the rough course down there. Question was, how soon would she fall on her photogenic face?

Asked if she was looking forward to the Spanish royal visit, Robin said not much, to be perfectly frank. Gloomy tones suggesting, *about as much as a dose of clap.*

Alexis thought she might change her mind once they got there, since these royals were really rather fun. Sophia was a much tougher cookie than first impressions suggested, but a vast improvement on her ghastly mother. Talk about queen bees—that one was pure wasp. Hornet. Vain as Hugh Hefner, and she'd had more face-lifts than all the Gabors put together.

Robin mentioned that she'd been bagged into a Ladies of the Senate luncheon next week. Alexis said instantly, "Gad, I hope they don't expect you to wear the rig."

Another groan: Oh lord, she'd forgotten to find out. Probably because she was afraid to hear the answer. She really didn't think she could handle showing up at one of those ghastly lunches in the candy stripes and starched apron.

Alexis was amazed they still actually wore the bandage-rolling outfits. A cross between Mary Poppins and Florence Nightingale, she'd always thought. Civil War leftovers. "Well, just tell them *you're* not going to wear the idiotic thing, at least."

Robin sighed that she made that sound so easy. But that Senate bunch were such sticklers for tradition. . . .

Lily-liver all the way.

She pointed out that Robin could set a few traditions of her own right now, and a good place to start would be that silly uniform. The next crop of Senate wives, at least, would be eternally grateful to her. "By all means don't encourage the old bats, my dear. It's high time they came into the twentieth century, ready or not."

Robin said she'd think about it, see what she could do. From the sound of it, Alexis didn't expect she'd find enough moxie in her to just say *no*. And if she couldn't say it even to those Senate harpies, how on earth would she stand up to the rest of the piranhas in the fishbowl?

As she hung up the phone, Alexis gave it two weeks, more or less, till Robin threw in the towel.

The call left Robin laughing at Alex's tart gift for gossip. Amazing to hear what she'd kept the lid on all these years. But it also stirred up questions on the subject of loyalty. Alexis seemed so cosy, confiding on the phone, but that crisp, acid tongue must also be doing a job on Robin, etching ripe vignettes to pass along to. . . god knows who.

At least Alex had proved for twenty-three years she could keep a secret. The ones Robin really worried about were her AA contacts. Sooner or later they wouldn't *all* resist the big bucks they could get for ratting on her. Sooner or later somebody'd talk.

When she'd petulantly thrown that up to Tish once, Tish had reacted like she'd been gored. Said never, never, never, she'd go off the roof herself before she'd betray that trust. And Robin believed her, hugged her contritely, murmured into her long stork neck that it got so damn hard sometimes to know who you could count on to never let you down.

Larry she didn't trust that way. Couldn't. The kids—sort of, in some ways. But nobody had the inventory of her scabrous parts like Tish. Nobody knew her, loved her anyway like Tish. Tish she trusted flat out, nothing held back, because she had to. Tish was her raft in the storm, her lifeline. She had to believe Tish at least wouldn't ever sell her out, peddle the sweat of her soul. . . .

But the nine strange ladies invading here today for the first "in-House" AA meeting were another matter. She felt like the prize in the freak show, chafed and confined by the weird isolation of this situation, convinced that one of those nine at least would blab the whole business sooner or later. They'd become targets themselves by showing up twice a week at the pearly gates.

She'd talked out the procedures a few times with Bella, so they'd know what to expect from the new routine. But it took three calls to Tish that afternoon to get *her* ready for it. Trying to defuse her own paranoid fantasies, Robin muttered that it would probably be one of the raunchy New York gang who did her in first anyway, come to think of it. Tish laughed and said easy does it, keep it simple, and read the Big Book before you go downstairs.

CHAPTER FORTY /

February 13th
Prilla

Coral and Ralph Marsden, a Sun Oil VP Dan called his "main line-backer," waited at their apartment door behind a knot of agents. "Prilla, darling!" Coral flung her arms out, showing off her beaded orange-and-pearl dress. "And Dan! We're just thrilled to bits to see you."

Typical Coral! "Oh, dress down, darling, it's only a few dowdy backbenchers," while she decked out like a banana split. *Wait'll Ginny heard this.* "Coral dear," Priscilla cooed, offering her cheek, ruefully aware of her own beigey-blah silk. "If you aren't the sweetest thing to invite us."

Sweeping entrance into the spectacular Watergate living room, guests shiny with expectation. She raked the crowd, noting that Kittyhawk, the Alaska pretty boy, was missing.

You could see something was terribly wrong with this whole deadlock just by a glance around Coral's living room. Her usual guests were men with real power, sleek, confident. You couldn't tell Senators or House chairs from the big-business CEOs. But tonight there was Ken Mosher in a funeral-director suit. And Preacher Morinski in brown-turkey plaid.

These weren't the sort of politicians the Marsdens hobnobbed with, these oddballs nobody'd heard of before this ridiculous vote. *And they shouldn't have that power over Dan!*

She was talking houseplants with Coral and Mrs. Morinski when a ripple crossed the room. Skin prickling alarm at the magnetic shift, she spun around: *What. . . ?*

Wayne Kittyhawk stood in the door, reeking cocky charisma, on his arm a strikingly pretty girl in a tweedy, inappropriate dress. Now *this* was the pigeon she wished would roll next; him they could really do something with.

Coral barreled up to greet "our latecomer." Kittyhawk introduced the girl as Carla Florian, "my right hand and general factotum around my office." Priscilla goggled. His *secretary?* Crashing this elegant sit-down dinner?

He walked past her with a wink: "How's it going, Mrs. Sterling?" Walked straight up to Dan: "Sorry to get here after the guest of honor, Governor. I was tied up on House business, which god knows isn't much of an excuse."

He was rude at best, and probably a liar. Office-couch quickie sounded more likely. Florian's lush eyes were taking in every wrinkle of the room. From a look rolled at Kittyhawk's back, Priscilla *knew* she was sleeping with him.

She purred to the crasher, "How nice to meet you, Miss Florian. It is Miss?"

Thin smile on that magazine-cover face. "Or Ms. Whichever you prefer, Mrs. Sterling." Ah sure, one of those. . . .

She told Kittyhawk she was sorry his wife couldn't be with them tonight. *Instead of your office bimbo.* . . .

"Matter of fact, I talked to her this afternoon. She figures she isn't missing much." Devilish, teasing smile: "But she said to tell you hello."

Priscilla slipped away to ask an agent who Florian was. His administrative assistant, she ran his House office. *Aha.* . . .

She did more listening than talking over the four-course dinner. Dan held the floor as usual, running out old-chestnut movie yarns for this star-struck bunch. "By gosh, that chimp learned our business so well sometimes the director told him, 'Bingo, in this scene you should. . . .' "

She'd heard them so often she sometimes felt she'd been there. But she'd missed his peak Hollywood years, and most of his famous carousing with Bill Holden et al. She hated being reminded of all that time they hadn't shared. She especially hated hearing about his female costars like Stanwyck, Colbert, Angie Dickinson—worst of all, the ones she knew he'd slept with.

"Came the moment in that sneak preview when I said to Shirley Temple, 'I love you,' and the entire audience cried, en masse, 'Oh, no!' You couldn't've gotten me to face those people for a million bucks. . . ."

Working, working, she searched out cracks in the deadlock wall. Lincoln Sheppard was the Greaseball Pol: slick talker, shallow thinker, crooked as his pinky. Ken Mosher was Mr. Clean: dull, solid as old pewter. Good match for his potato-faced wife. Morinski was Preacher on the Move, dazzled by it all—unlike his wife Rose, a Protestant nun.

And Kittyhawk the Wild Card, brash, smug as a lapdog. Yet she caught his hesitation about which fork to use for the salad, glancing at Florian for cues.

Kittyhawk's lady mostly smiled, but Priscilla overheard her talking to Ralph Marsden about the House evolving from pork barrel to PACs, special-interest constituencies as much as geographical districts. Later Florian mentioned Speaker Whalen's clever casting of the presidential vote in terms of party loyalty: "Going against the party means losing money, since half the campaign funds come from the national committees and PACs they control. And money means reelection. . . ."

After dinner Dan cornered Mosher and Morinski in the living room. She caught a whiff of Bible talk as she drifted to the glass wall overlooking the river. Kittyhawk and his "friend" leaned on the balcony rail. Too good to pass up. She slid open the door: "Mind if I join you for a minute?"

"Sure, come on out," Kittyhawk said, resisting the added dig, *right on time*. He'd just told Carla give the old gal two minutes and she'll be after our ass.

Carla hadn't been keen on crashing this party, said she wasn't dressed right. He told her piss on that, come anyway, so she had. That's what he liked about Carla, always dead-game sport to kick over an applecart or two—cart-kicking being the main reason he'd come to this stuffed-monkey town in the first place.

"Brrrr!" The grande dame rubbed her arms, shivering. "I can sure tell you're from Alaska, Mr. Kittyhawk."

"Well, look at the show." He waved at the twinkling Potomac lights. "That'll get your mind off your goose bumps."

She plunged to the point: "Miss Florian, I was struck by some sound things you said about the House. Can't you help the congressman understand how vital it is for the country to get this presidential vote resolved *soon?*"

Carla smiled. "I think he knows that, Mrs. Sterling."

He protested: "Hold on a minute, Carla. You could make a fair case that things run pretty well just as they are."

"Oh, Mr. Kittyhawk." The old bitch slapped his arm, like swatting horseflies. Skinny little bird she was, probably 90 pounds soaking wet, but he didn't wonder for one minute who wore the pants in that family. "Don't you even joke about that when the Congress is paralyzed and the whole country's staggering through this appalling crisis."

"No, I'll tell you quite frankly, Mrs. Sterling—since I've joined that banana factory on the Hill, I'm coming to the view that the country's probably better off with a nonfunctioning Congress. If we padlocked the place, the people might find out how well they'd manage without it."

That smile looked like it might break her lips. "Well, if you're hellbent on doing away with Congress, you'd better get a real president in the job first. Because *somebody's* got to run the country, don't they, Mr. Kittyhawk?"

He said he wasn't sure we needed an effective president either. Seemed to him most of the things they did just tended to compound the screwups.

"My goodness." She turned to Carla. "Does he talk this way all the time? Or just to rag me?"

Carla turned on her Mona Lisa smile. Guaranteed to curl the toes of a professional wife like this one. "All the time, Mrs. Sterling. You're just no exception."

"Well, I wish you could talk some sense into his head. Because I *know* you, Mr. Kittyhawk." She wagged her finger, admonishing schoolmarm. "I know a successful, imaginative businessman like you will come out for Dan Sterling sooner or later. What I can't for the life of me understand is why you don't do it *now*, when you could take some real leadership—when it would do you some good."

That last crack could be read as promise or threat. He hoped it was meant as promise, because the other might just tip him over and he had no intention of bugging out of the game early as this. Brow hiked in counterthreat, he said the truth was he hadn't decided who he wanted for president.

She teased, fighting down the shivers: "Oh, come on now, Mr. Kittyhawk. You don't expect me to believe that."

He looked out over the river, as if he were searching his thoughts. Actually weighing whether the view was worth moving in for. "Well, maybe you're right. I guess I do know who I'm going for."

Blurted too soon: "And it's Dan Sterling?"

Grinning, jaunty with pleasure, he turned back to her. "Not necessarily, Mrs. Sterling. I'm going with the winner."

"He was smirking, that cheeky pup," she told Dan indignantly. "He might as well've said, 'That's not you, yet.' Honestly, I could've dumped him off the balcony."

He chuckled. "Well, he was probably trying to score points with his lady friend. I won't be surprised to hear they're shacking up. Quite a looker, that one is."

She didn't care for that last crack, not one bit. He asked if she wanted to join him in the shower. She said coolly no thanks, she didn't need one tonight. *Sure, it's Friday. His night for being 'in the mood'. . . .*

Her women friends mostly seemed to hope the husbands would just get old enough to lose interest. As Ginny put it, "Darling, enough is enough." She insisted it didn't bother her one bit that Mort seemed to've finally "outgrown the whole business." Priscilla wouldn't dream of contradicting that white lie. Or passing along rumors about Mort's pretty young "friends." What Ginny didn't know wouldn't hurt her. . . .

Ginny said of course it was different for her and Dan, with their "one-in-a-million marriage, you lucky girl." And Priscilla worked hard to protect that image, even with Ginny. Not just out of pride: Their "perfect," "storybook" marriage was a priceless political asset. Also the taproot of her life, the one constant spring from which all the rest flowed. She thought—believed—Dan had never "wandered" in their twenty-nine years together—and never would. He got all he wanted right at home.

True, she'd never been as interested as he was in that whole business. Once, when the girls were young, that almost turned into a problem. He wasn't working much in those days, and wanted a lot of "napping." What began as snatched, romantic love-in-the-afternoon turned into aggravating routine. She couldn't crank up a sexy mood when she was worrying where the kids were, when the shopping would get done. But just as her patience finally frayed, he was hired as a

Lockheed spokesman, and began to travel constantly. She hated having him gone so much, but she got her afternoons back. And the reunions were almost worth the separation.

So what might've been a problem was set right. She kept it that way, never rejecting him. She'd seen too many marriages come apart when the wives slacked off on that part of the job. If she felt less enthusiastic sometimes, he never knew it: she made sure of that.

He emerged from the tub and flicked his towel at her. "Good shower you missed, Pril." *Definitely in the mood. . . .*

She smiled, "Well, that'll teach me." He said by the way, Chet mentioned some guy apparently working on a special project for Devlin, coming and going from the White House family quarters. She perked up. "What's that?"

Nothing much, Dan figured. Chet said the fellow was an old roommate of Devlin's, a Paris-based photographer, so he might be doing a feature on the family.

Wondering why Chet hadn't mentioned that to *her*, she snapped, "Oh, please! Spare us *that*." Dan said by gosh, you'd think they got enough of that business as it was.

She said Chet better keep an eye on that. "We don't need media-outflanking by Devlins, thanks very much."

He patted her hip on his way out. She'd need a shower in the morning anyway, the way things looked. She stripped and stroked a layer of lotion over her body, listening to him ramble about his conversation with Mosher: ". . . would've made a great undertaker. He kept saying, 'These are grave times, Governor, very grave times. . . .' " Shivering as her skin soaked, she brushed her teeth, rinsed with mouthwash.

". . . can't believe those Democrats aren't strong-arming Devlin to cash in every IOU he has in the House. . . ." She slipped on a long-sleeved gown, sprayed on perfume and bent to the mirror, checking her face, touching her hair. She'd "fix" the set under her turban when he was asleep.

Grousing, impatient: "Hey, when're you coming?"

"Right away, sweetie. In two jiffs." She marveled at how differently it had turned out from what she'd expected: to be this old and still looking good, still making passionate love to her 70-year-old husband. Somehow she'd never imagined them so old and still so much the same. Well, almost the same. She passed up the estrogen cream for a dollop of K-Y jelly spread into her vagina. Didn't do much for the pain, but it eased the penetration. Extra squirt of lotion into her palms as she called out, "There now, I'm on my way."

He lifted the covers in welcome. "Hi, stranger," she beamed co-quettishly as she slipped beside him.

"Hi yourself, Mommie." She cuddled against him as he kissed her, tongue pushing into her mouth. *Ten. . . nine. . . .*

She lapped at his tongue, rubbed her wrist over his chest. Felt her nipple stiffen under his probing fingers. He rolled back into his pillow, moaning lightly as she nibbled and sucked at his tiny ear hole. *Seven. . . six. . . .*

She untied his pajama string. His penis lay along his thigh, barely stirring. She opened her hand and wrapped warm lotion around that shaft, stroking it back to life. Time was when his "best friend Peter" was up in a wink—a little too ready, if anything. Her job then was mainly to lie back and let him take her.

Now it was more work. She rubbed expertly at that half-limp shaft, fingering the tip, the undervein. The sigh whispering from him seemed to come from thoughts—memories—but she chose to hear it as passion, murmuring, "Oh yes, yes. I want you too, my darling man."

It scared her half to death to think that someday her touch might not do the trick. That he might still want what she couldn't coax from him. Please god he'd lose interest before that terrible night.

Flooding relief, feeling the swelling under her fingers, she realized that wasn't tonight. "Mmmm, delicious," she whispered, squeezing, stroking. As he lifted her nightgown she rolled onto her back to take in one more reprieve.

CHAPTER FORTY-ONE /

February 16th

Robin

Hamilton said icily to Robin, "Mr. Farragut would like to see you at your convenience, Ma'am. In the. . ." his glower pointing down the hall, ". . . Treaty Room."

Tiny voice: *Call Tish?* Deep, armoring breath. *There but for. . .*

Robin found him at the big table in the gloomy green cave, frowning at a paper litter. "Cal! What's going on?"

"Oh, Robin!" He waved her in, saying god, was he glad to see her. Larry'd said he could use this room to pull some background stuff together, he hoped that was okay with her. She said of course, no problem, was that all he wanted?

"No, no." Raving with distress, he said Koenig had let slip a plan to push Prince Oudong and his rag-ass refugee army into a coalition with Pol Pot's Khmer Rouge. Koenig actually seemed pleased with the idea, calling it "the realistic military solution," to consolidate the anti-Viet forces. But militarily it made no sense; Oudong's guys would be run over by Hanoi's tanks, eaten alive. Politically it was pure suicide —if they tossed the bastard back to the Khmer Rouge they'd destroy his last shred of credibility. . . .

Staying edgily distant, she told him take it up with Larry: "I'm sure he won't let that happen, if there's any hope for the Hanoi feeler. What's going on with that?"

Cal said the bastards were still talking, at least. But they were "a lot more interested in bailing out their own ass than in saving Cambodia." He paced, railing at those "Hanoi cocksuckers who've been after Cambodia for a thousand years—Thailand too, that's next in their gunsights. . . ."

She felt his despair ripping at her gut, tugging her into deep, dangerous water. *Back off, leave it alone.* . . . She said abruptly, "Cal, I hope you're not kidding yourself about how long the odds are against this."

Startled, blazing glance. "Piss on the odds. This is no horse race, Robin."

She saw now that this fragile man was crazed with hope, blinded by his consuming light. *Don't let him fly too far out.* . . . "Just don't be too devastated if it doesn't work. Because. . . it's probably won't."

He spun away. "No, no. Don't say that, Robin."

"Oh, it *might.* Maybe as a long shot it still could, but please just don't count on it, Cal."

Talking like them. . . .

Whatever grip he had on her was evaporating, slipping away. If she quit on him now, the Koenig types would have free run and any feeble chance for a bailout would be shot. As the whole enterprise slid into mush, he realized how much was riding on the stuffed shirts he'd been mocking since he got here. He had only one real ally, and if she couldn't head off the looming disaster. . . .

Down to the hole card in his deck, he made himself ask her, "Did Larry tell you about the children?"

"What children?"

"The ones I tried to get out." Words carved from grief. "It's in the files. I thought he might've told you."

He let her pull the story from him, starting at the end of '74, when he was with NBC in New Delhi, living with some wounded Khmer children he'd brought out for medical treatment. But he knew the end was coming for Cambodia and couldn't stay away. So he quit and went back on his own.

In the doom and resignation swirling through Phnom Penh he found an old friend, Keo Svay. Former teacher and damn good chess player, wife and seven kids. Yet he'd opened a home for orphans salvaged from the streets, hundreds crammed into one house. Cal helped out with the fingers-in-the-dike operation. One night he and Svay got very drunk and decided to "get the kids out, at least."

In dogged calls to Hong Kong, Washington, anyplace that might send a plane, he got thin leads, vague promises. Australia was possible for a while but wanted names, birth dates and photos for travel documents. He said that wasn't feasible but they said regulations, you know. . . .

So he shot and printed the 500 photos. But every day the chances stretched a little thinner. On April 12th a helicopter fleet swarmed in to evacuate the U.S. embassy staff—"big grown men. But nothing for those children, throwaways from that vile war."

She burst out, "Cal, why didn't you call Larry? Or me? I'm sure he'd've done something, if he'd known. . . ."

He got through once to Larry's office: "They said he was having surgery, they'd get back to me. That's the last I heard." Pause. "And I never thought to call you, Robin. That's one more thing I'll have to live with."

She grabbed her throat, muttered something about being into a quart a day when Larry had his gallbladder out.

With the dam of memory broken, he talked on compulsively in a dead-flat voice, not so much to her as to himself. Two days after the embassy evacuation, he and the few newsmen left behind talked by army radio to a DC-47 at 3000 feet, chartered by colleagues who'd flown in to rescue them. "After a while I realized they mainly came to do interviews. One guy kept saying, 'Tell Farragut no orphans, repeat, no orphans.' But in the end they didn't try to land anyway."

She winced. "Ah, Cal."

Softly: "Oh, it was such an awful time. The Khmer Rouge came closer and closer, and the spirit in Phnom Penh began to die, the lifeblood choked off. People became resigned in that strange Khmer way to what lay ahead. They saw no way out. So, wrapped in Buddhist fatalism, they waited to die."

But Cal's children were not resigned. One boy brought home a rumor that Khmer Rouge troops had infiltrated through the Monivong Bridge, which "sparked an absolute panic. Shrieking with terror, the kids scrambled out through windows and doors, running hysterically through the streets."

When Svay turned up from his daily scrounge for rice, he and Cal went looking for the kids. At the market by the stadium, where most had lived before Svay had taken them in, they found a few huddled under an empty stall. Like a Pied Piper, Svay led them around and around the market. With each lap more terrified children crept from hiding until they headed back to the house. "Such a strange, sad parade we made, with the last stragglers hurrying to catch up."

He only cried twice in Cambodia—once when he "said goodbye to those kids for the last time. I just put my head on the wheel of the car and completely broke down. I remember trying to understand how anyone could just throw away a battalion of children, a kind of small army—teenagers, babies, one-legged girls, 3-year-olds without pants. . . ."

She gasped. "Not the kids in your film?" He nodded, tears finally wrung from the stone of his ravaged memory.

Those broken birds. . . .
Shivering with dread, she saw them in her mind, vivid as his tormented Yankee face. She understood now that those terrorized children were the root of his madness. It took every self-preservative instinct in her not to cross the room and embrace that suffering man's pain. Feeling his breaking heart, she asked what had happened to them. He turned away, head down. "Oh no, Cal. Not all of them, surely!"

He said he'd looked for them when he went back. But couldn't pick up even a cold trail—not Svay or his family, or any of the kids. Curtly: "So I assume they're in the boneyard with the three million others."

She protested that *some* must've made it through. "Out of 500, Cal, surely. . . ."

Eyes glittering, he said with no adult to protect them, they had almost no chance. "Some were already sick or crippled, or too small to survive on their own in that hell."

His anguish searing into her, she made him talk about the nightmare of his own rescue from Pol Pot's inferno, as one of the seven Americans taking refuge with 1200 other foreigners in the French Embassy. The French had locked their high-risk Yankee guests in a room where Cal lay on the floor "in a manic-depressive state. I'd reached the point where I wasn't frightened—I just didn't care." He heard the loudspeakers, the appalling atrocity stories drifting around the compound. Three different squads of Khmer Rouge came demanding the seven Americans, and each time the French chargé d'affaires talked them out of it.

Cal left in the last convoy to evacuate the foreigners. All he remembered from that final trip through the city were wrecked cars with tires slashed for Ho Chi Minh sandals, a red flag flying over the smashed, deserted airport, and an empty magnum of Moet et Chandon '68 on the hotel sidewalk.

As the trucks thrashed along a trail to the Thai border, a three-day trek that used to take four hours, he "knew instinctively what was happening. Not the scale of the horror—only a monumental madman like Pol Pot could've conceived that—but I didn't need to see the bodies. In one peasant hut we found half-eaten food on the floor. The poorest of the poor had been moved out as brutally as the capital had been emptied. I didn't need convincing after I saw that."

Prodded by her questions, he talked vaguely about "drifting through Europe for a while after that." He'd lost his eye for photography—"my taste for it, anyway"—so he'd taken any other kind of job that came along. Hearing about those broken years, she realized where his ghostly quality came from: In some ways he'd died in Phnom Penh after all. When the woman he was living with left him, Cal "took that pretty hard, although god knows she had cause. A friend dragged me to a psychiatrist, who told me later, 'You hardly mentioned that woman. All you talked about was Cambodia.'"

Wrapped in brooding silence, he stared at the rug. Then he pierced her with those haunted eyes: "I can't forget that battalion of children, see. They trusted me to save them. I was their commander-in-chief and I let them down and that's why I can't forget."

She babbled denial: He couldn't blame himself, he'd done all he could. Those children were engulfed in a firestorm—"at least you tried, Cal." He shook his head; he'd heard that before. "But nobody can live like that, Cal. Just carrying around that ton of grief."

He made a slight shrug of denial. He said sometimes he'd go two or three days without thinking about it, "but then somebody mentions something and it all comes back. And if I forgot those things I'd be as bad as the coldhearted bastards who let those children die." Jolting from his funk, he said that wasn't meant to include her or Larry, by the way.

Too late. She was already hooked, a guilty accomplice drowning in his unbearable grief.

So last year he'd gone back to Cambodia for Oxfam, thinking he might be able to find a few of the kids. After three weeks that "ripped open my guts and what was left of my heart, I thought maybe if I put together that film, that record of what happened, I might lay those kids to rest."

But he already knew that wasn't going to work when Le Anh turned up and invited him to lunch. "And the next thing I know, here I am"—bemused glance around the green cave—"where it all began. So this is the last shot I'm giving it, Robin. And if this doesn't work, nothing will."

Ah god, back to that, she thought, sick with dread.

He talked with jaunty irony about "the kinds of things that run through your head, working in a room like this, where the reality of history reeks out of the walls. I used to think I'd never be able to live in this country again, after the loathsome betrayals of so many Americans—mainly press and government, not so much the military. . . ."

But now he saw another perspective. Smiling softly, he recalled a Cambodian friend who was a U.S. history buff: "Narah loved making long-winded toasts to the Four Freedoms and the 'great revolutionary concepts of your U.S.A. Founding Fathers.' He was shocked I hadn't read Jefferson or Tom Paine. He'd say, 'Cal, you must understand these great, true ideas were not heard in the world until your American fathers gave them voice.' He loved to quote FDR on 'nothing to fear but fear itself.' Of course, that was before Pol Pot set us all straight on *that* bit of horseshit."

He liked to imagine what Narah or Svay would say if they knew where he was now, talking about them. "And I think of Narah when moral shitheads like Mal Koenig say the 'best solution' for Cambodia is to handcuff the playboy prince to the psychotic mass murderer and turn them loose to kill Viets. That's the crazy, murderous politics that made this happen in the first place. My god, can't those fools see that?"

She said softly, "Well, unfortunately your friend had a better grasp of us than we ever did of him."

He turned back to his papers, frowning with concentration, tidying the stacks. "Well, maybe what we need is one guy with enough guts and imagination to get a handle on it. And look past that malevolent bullshit and moral blindness we've been palming off as our 'geopolitical interests.' "

"Oh, god. I hope you don't mean Larry."

"Hey, don't sell him short. He's got a first-class head—and he listens. There's two surprises that put him light-years ahead of guys like Koenig and Lessard."

She agreed that Larry was doing his damnedest. "But I can't bear for you to count too much on him—or on it."

Scratching ruefully at his neck, he mentioned a song he'd heard somewhere that ran, "Please don't tell me how the story ends." "I know what you're trying to tell me, Robin. But I don't want to hear it. Sometimes I feel like I'm back on the phones, trying to scare up a plane somewhere."

She thought she'd done such a risky thing, letting him into her pants—pinscratch jeopardy compared with this goring. Yet no way to undo it now. She choked out a smile. "Okay. Who knows, stranger things've happened, I suppose."

Fiercely: "It's *got* to work, Robin. And maybe that will exorcise my battalion of children. Because otherwise they'll pull me into the grave with them."

She recognized that crack for the emotional blackmail it was no doubt meant to be, but that didn't pry her off his hook. *Just make damn sure you're not dragged there too. . . .*

CHAPTER FORTY-TWO /

February 16th
Prilla

Priscilla was watching a man in the audience with a coonskin cap and a chestful of campaign buttons sprinkled among military medals. Every time Dan punched a point home, Fur Hat jumped to his feet, waving a Confederate flag, honking a gooseneck horn.

"And I say it's about time to light a few fires under those fat old easy chairs in Washington, D.C., paid for with *your* hard-earned tax dollars!" Roars of applause. Fur Hat jigging in spastic leaps, hairy coon tail jerking around his swollen red face, shouting "Get 'em! Get 'em! Get 'em!" flag whipping above the raucous horn.

Colors suddenly so intense. Deep blues, shimmering greens. Reds lit like fire. Ah! Sound system out. Dan tweeting, very far away. Fix the glitch!

But no one reacted. Faces rapt, lit, like before. She knew that was Dan at the mikes, making noises like a bird. "Feewit tweee ssimittt. . . ." She couldn't make out words. What did those sounds mean? Why didn't anyone care what was happening? *Please god, not again! Heaven help me. . . .*

Fur Hat jumping up and down like the jack-in-the-box years ago at Grandma's. Making no sound but squeak squeak like the wooden lid. That funny hat like the Daniel Boone cap Cousin Joey played soldier in.

She realized she couldn't move, was even afraid to try. Mouth dry, palms sweaty, heart baroom baroom in her chest. She knew she was in a Legion Hall in Des Moines and Dan was talking, but suddenly everything felt so different, whole room twinkley, strangely transformed. . . .

Yet it seemed to be happening to someone else. Like her mind had tripped off, run away. As if she weren't sitting here frozen to this chair, seeing all these *feelings* dancing at her somehow, vivid as the colors. . . .

Bodies leaping from the seats. Hands beating pat-pat. Good god, that meant Dan was done. Fat man sitting next to her leaned over, beaming, hands clapping. Mouth opened.

Blessed words: "Great speech, wasn't it, Mrs. Sterling!"

CHAPTER FORTY-THREE /

February 18th

Robin

In the bedroom Robin picked up the lavender wool suit windowpaned in fine red lines that Carmen had laid out. Stephanie said she'd just come from the State Dining Room, which Mary Moriarty, an assistant social secretary with hitherto unsuspected talents, was busily transforming with cymbidium sprays on emerald tablecloths: "It looked good enough to eat. Feels like a good party brewing."

Robin said if this came off tonight, Mary could rescue as many parties as she wanted. "Now, tell me quick. Everything I never wanted to know about the Spanish royals."

Scanning her clipboard, Stephanie said they'd just done two days in New York, opening a "Treasures of Spain" show at the Met. "You can see it when it comes to D.C. Royal kids left home are Elena, 17, Christina, 15, and Felipe, 13. . . ."

Robin zipped up and moved to the bathroom to repair her makeup. "Want to bet the queen's getting her own goose feed right now? '. . . Two kids living at home, 15-year-old Sean and 17-year-old Jason.' " Her eyes crossed Mayo's in the mirror. "Don't mind me, I'm a little punchy."

Stephanie forged on. "Since they're big on sailboat racing—he is, anyway—your main gift is a spiffy new radar-navigation thing. They're addressed as either Majesties or Highnesses. She also answers to So-phie. . . ."

Twenty minutes later Robin stood nervously at the Diplomatic Entrance as Larry and entourage swept in—Gil muttering in one ear, Ben the other, Larry listening distractedly as they slid him into position by her side. He looked up, startled. "Hey, Robin." Cocky grin. "How's it going?"

Background hum of agents muttering into radios. Tuning riffs from the Marine Band. She asked in a low voice, lips barely moving, "What're you looking so tickled about?"

"China rolled. Lowenthal's on his way to Bangkok, and Wiley may go to Hanoi."

"My god. What does that mean?"

He chuckled, shooting his cuffs. "Means we're still in the game."

"Fantastic." The snap-to by the door meant the motorcade was through the gate. Last twitch to her skirt, steadying breaths. "Don't forget the king's big on sailing."

"Yep." The band struck up "Ruffles and Flourishes" as they stepped forward for the royal welcome. The easy part was the bowing and scraping, handshakes and speeches and on-cue smiles for the arsenal of cameras. The hard part was sitting down over tea and cakes in the Red Room. Robin hungrily eyed the dainty cucumber sandwiches, realizing she'd forgotten to stop for lunch.

Larry ripped off her opening line, asking if the royals had a good trip from New York. Blah-blah from both sides, dragging that out. The men switched to fencing about NATO. Yellow light to the wifey contingent. Clearing her throat, juggling her cup, Robin squeaked nervously, "It's a treat to have this chance to welcome you to America, Your Majesty."

She heard little of the woman's shy, murmured response, but recognized the rabbity flutter in those eyes. The stage fright she knew so well. She said warmly, empathetically, "It's a shame we missed your New York opening, but I look forward to seeing the show when it comes to Washington."

☆

Four hours later, back in her bedroom, she swished her velvet skirt as Dennis scolded, "Hold still, hold still. I'll never get this right with you twitchy as a mouse."

"Dennis, it looks fine just the way it is."

"Shame on you, lazy girl. Two minutes it will take, hardly worth bitching and moaning. Stand up straight, for pity's sake. Posture, posture. Like a little queen, please."

She tried not to laugh as he scampered on hands and knees around her, jabbing pins into the flowing skirt. "Dennis, come on. Nobody's going to notice that tiny droop."

"Carmen, you tell her how wrong she is. That army of zoom lenses down there will be shooting you from top to toe, and then some." He stood up, sighing as he brushed off his hands. "All right, unzip and let Carmen get after that hem."

As the maid helped her out of the dress, Robin groused, "All this fuss over nothing."

"Oh, no, ma'am, Mr. Darien's right—that's a big dip on the left side," Carmen said gravely, still smarting over Dennis's having spotted that hemline wobble before she did.

She slipped on a bathrobe. "Well, I can't fight you both. Please, Carmen, if you wouldn't mind basting that up while Mr. Darien fixes my hair, and then it'll be perfect."

"Perfect?" He threw up his hands. "Oh, hardly, thank you—a making-do rag from the back of the closet isn't even *suitable* for an occasion like this."

Frowning, she watched Carmen stalk out. "Dennis, be a little more tactful around Carmen," she snapped. "At least tell her she did a nice job on that damn dress."

Hushed contrition: "Oh yes, yes. Sorry, dear, no offense—she's a jewel, an absolute treasure. The perfect lady's maid. Now come sit at this dressing table while I do something with that rat's nest on your head."

Dennis was gagging with excitement, prostrate to think he'd see his shy little darling up there holding her own with kings and queens and whatever else the cat dragged in for this tip-top-of-the-line party. He'd read coming down that all of Washington was so hot to get to this first Devlin winging that local hostesses not invited were claiming to be out of town. He'd see movie stars. And Benny Goodman!

He'd thought the poor dear might be swooning with nerves, but here she was, calm as a cuke, thank goodness. Maybe a little *too* calm. A bit of pit-a-pat seemed in order when you were about to have la crème de la crème kissing your hand. He clucked reprovingly as he drove the brush through her long hair. "A perfectly gorgeous event and here you are, queen of America, wearing prom-night retreads. . . ."

"Just can it, Dennis," she said angrily. "Leave it alone, I don't want any crap about new clothes. And for heaven's sake knock off that 'queen of America' business. I've got enough to handle around here without *that*."

"Rude girl," he purred happily. "Speaking of queens! You've got me so *bouleversé* I forgot to say who I ran into at the frog pond." Hiss in her ear: "Three guesses, ducks."

"Charles de Gaulle, Charlie Chaplin and the Pope."

He smacked the brush against her scalp. "Wicked thing, you didn't even try. Well, it was, lo and behold, Mrs. Tacky in the very pink, lunching with one of the more precious queens of New York, her great and good friend Baby Bunting."

She groaned. "Oh, Dennis. Cut that out."

Wide eyes reproaching, hand up, Scout's-oath gesture: "Dear one, I swear. There they were, large as life, chatting it up. Him a good deal larger than her, of course."

"Well, I hope you were terribly polite. Did you shake hands, or what?"

"Mmm, wouldn't dare get that close." His flying fingers braided a skinny rope of hair. "We just played snake-eyes across the room. If looks could kill, darling. . ."

She said poor Prilla, he was such an evil old dog. "She doesn't need more grief from you right now, Den."

Mock astonishment. "What have we here? Bleeding heart for Mrs. Tacky, is it?"

"No, not much. Actually I'm more concerned now with that other one, your old friend. . . ."

"Mrs. Frump!" His tasseled black pumps drummed a tattoo on the carpet. "Norleeeen herself, back at the scene of the crime," he hissed ecstatically. "Dear one, I'm thrilled out of my wits. Wouldn't've missed it for the world. I'm going to dance with her tonight if it kills me."

Stern glare from the mirror. "Listen, don't you go anywhere near her. You hear me, Dennis? Promise, now. Or you don't come to the party."

He swore to behave like an angel. "You'll see, dear."

"And I hope you don't think I'm wearing"—she pointed to the ivory shawl laid out on her bed—"that piano tarp?"

"Piano tarp, is it! Rude, rude. That exquisite silk shawl belonged to your Great-Aunt Marie. It's not only *not* that apparently horrid thing, new—it's a Spanishy family heirloom I sacked your apartment to find. It's bad enough you making me root for found objects, but we must do a *few* things, darling, to remind them of what a stunning, original beauty they've got here in their reigning you-know-what. So we'll hear no more about it, thank you very much."

When Carmen brought back the dress, Robin asked for an opinion of the shawl. Carmen rolled her eyes dubiously. "I can't say, ma'am. It's sure—a nice piece of silk."

"An *exquisite* piece of silk," Dennis crooned. "You'll see, Carmen, it's going to look perfect. Just like that splendid job you did on this dress. Such fine, tiny stitching, where ever did you learn to sew so beautifully?"

Robin stood in the center of the rug, sapphire velvet rippling like cascading water, long-fringed ivory shawl spilled from one shoulder, miniature gardenias peeking from her shoulder and her artfully up-tumbled hair. Dennis cocked his head, sternly appraising his work. Then clapped, screeched, "Bravissima! Bellissima! Perfecto! You look like a crown jewel, old rags or no."

Hand pressed demurely to her bosom, she dropped a deep curtsy. "Thank you kindly, sir."

Carmen beamed, turf wars forgiven. "Mrs. Devlin, you sure do look pretty as all get-out."

Wafted by their enthusiasm, she paraded down to the second-floor hall where Larry, in penguin rig, huddled with Ben Boylan and two other aides. Ben scrambled to his feet: "Whups! Mrs. Devlin, you look like a million bucks."

Larry grinned. "Yep, sure enough. Looking good, Rob."

Good lord. He noticed. . . . She plucked at her white suede gloves, murmuring shyly, "Well, thanks. But I didn't have much to do with it. Dennis, take a bow."

He did it with musketeer flourishes. Larry said dryly, "You've earned your dinner, Dennis."

"Thank you kindly, Mr. President." Dennis always threw nitwit fits around Larry. "But of course, with such lovely material to work with, I mean, of course, your wife, sir. . . ."

She rescued him with, "Enough of that." She told the kids to be nice to the Talbotts, and enjoy the king and queen. "They're what you call boss."

The VIP guests were loose in the Oval Room when Robin and Larry elevatored down to greet the Talbotts. Seizing on the privacy, she said, "That's fantastic news about China. So does that mean the deal's out of the woods?"

"Not by a long shot. There's a hell of a way to go."

"But at least they decided. . . ."

"To 'neutralize' Pol Pot. And go for a national coalition alternative."

"My god." She blinked. "They're dumping Pol Pot? That's incredible."

Broad grin. "You might say. Good old Eric pulled the rabbit out one more time. After the word got out, Wiley was invited to Hanoi. I think we'll take them up on it."

She asked when Roy Bob would hear about it.

"Tonight, if I get the chance."

"Oh, lord. Lots of luck, Dev." The door clattered open on a squad of agents.

Media buzzed like picnic flies as the Talbott car rolled up the drive. Norleen stepped out with military snap, drawn up like an aimed crossbow, icy dignity laced with pure pain. Robin's calm dissolved under those steely eyes, peering with thinly veiled outrage around "her" house. *Count the spoons if you want,* Robin thought as she complimented Norleen's "charming" yellow satin dress.

"Thank you," Norleen said stiffly, declining to return the favor. "I must say I'm surprised not to see those lovely palm trees by the door." *Ah, boy. Long, hard night. . . .*

The two couples were briefly entombed in the elevator. Larry broke the silence: "Kentucky looks good in that Harris poll, I see. A five-point lead, that's closing nicely." Roy Bob pointed out the undecideds were hanging at 19 percent.

Robin tried a smile: "I've watched your campaigning on the news, Norleen. Very effective."

She sniffed, "Well, one does one's best."

In the Oval Room the limping conversation was helped along by the assorted VIPs, who mostly owed their jobs to Talbott. Norleen had no time to tour the family quarters before the Devlins went down to greet the royals, North Portico. Watching the queen maneuver her peach gown out of the limo, Robin felt as if she were greeting a long-lost friend.

Back up for champagne, chitchat and exchange of gifts. Robin had barely thanked the royals for the "lovely and most unusual" reclining bronze mare when Norleen drew her aside to hiss concern for "our family furniture."

"Oh, yes," Robin said pleasantly, thoughts of root-canal work on her mind. "Any time you want it back, Norleen, that can be rapidly arranged."

Like a diamond-dusted fairy godmother with great timing, bless her, the queen came over to remark that Jason was apparently "as much a basketball fan as our Felipe."

Onward march down the ceremonial staircase, in ranked order—Devlins paired with royals, Talbotts trailing. On through the receiving line, twinkle twinkle, to the dinner. Tonight the booze smell, the gurgling wine bottles, didn't bother Robin as much as usual. The king told jolly stories about ocean racing, and Roy Bob did a touching reminiscence of his first trip to Washington, as a spelling-bee winner.

After the last flowery toasts, Larry stood up and offered his arm to the queen. With Robin and Juan Carlos alongside, they marched to the East Room where Benny Goodman's orchestra tootled "And the Angels Sing." Larry bowed to the queen. "Your Majesty, would you care to join me in a dance?"

Juan Carlos smiled gravely at Robin. "Mrs. Devlin, would you do me the honor?"

She bobbed her head. "With pleasure, sir." The ivory shawl dropped away with one yank on the gold stickpin. She handed it to the nearest Marine and stepped, floating as if in a brightly lit dream, onto the polished wood floor, into the stiffly presented arms of the king. After several trial steps he took a firm lead, turning her in sure, graceful circles. Leaning back against his arm, smiling shyly up to his face, she murmured, "You dance beautifully, sir."

He swept her into another spin, velvet swirling around his legs. "If this is true, Madame, it must be that I am particularly inspired by such a beautiful partner."

She smiled acknowledgment of that bald royal flattery. Other couples drifted onto the floor, bobbing to the catchy "Running Wild." She tossed a smile to Charlie Whalen, who waggled a wave over Gertie's back.

Quite a crowd on the floor, Cliff Robertson and Dina Merrill right next to Dennis—grinning like a Cheshire cat, prancing with a Spanish countess twice his size. Robin's glance swept on to a dashing, magnetically handsome man dancing with a woman in a peach dress.

Shiver of surprise when she realized as he twirled past that the man was Larry.

CHAPTER FORTY-FOUR /

February 18th
Prilla

Today of all days, it had to happen. While Dan was doing a quick stand-upper in the Lexington, Kentucky, airport, Norleen Talbott and her entourage swirled in. Priscilla instantly connected on the White House dinner, which guaranteed this run-in would get big play. But too late to dodge a confrontation, so she and Dan crossed the floor for a brief "chat" while cameras furiously clacked and rolled.

Back in the plane, Paul tried to explain away that "unfortunate collision" by saying the Sterlings were running a half hour late, and Talbott was "pushing ahead of her schedule, heading back to Washington for that, ah. . . ."

She snapped, "I *know* where she's going. What I don't know is why you let us run into her. Sloppy, sloppy work!" Dan shrugged it off as "a goofy coincidence," but she knew the media would lap up "exile factions meet on the trail." Then en route to L.A. Paul gave them the latest Harris poll on Kentucky, the Democrat widow pulling five points ahead—their worst showing so far, six days before the election. She fought off a jolt of panic as she reassured Dan.

Not a great start to a "home" visit already fraught with emotional baggage. Yet approaching their Brentwood house, Dan grunted happily, "By gosh, it feels like years since we've been back."

"Silly. It's only two months." Two months and six days, to be precise. Her mind worked that way, always squirreling away odd details and figures. But she never rubbed in what Dan couldn't remember—he called that "showing off."

Natalie waited at the door, in a thoroughly inappropriate yellow halter dress. The reunion turned into an audition for the cameras: "Daddy dear, welcome back to your California hearth. Mother, it seems like you've never been away."

Priscilla felt her eternal ambivalence. Part of her wanted to sweep up her baby; part steamed at the shameless two-bit mugging. She always told Gnat work on your presence, work on your aplomb; she might as well save her breath.

Determined to make the brief visit as happy as possible, she promised herself not to mention that ridiculous dress—slip was more like it. Inside the house Natalie hovered by the window, peering out at the press. Dan roamed the big living room, drinking it in. "By gosh, I'd forgot how good the air smells around here."

"Natalie dear," she said brightly, patting the glazed-chintz couch cushion. "Come over here and let me have a good look at you. We've got so much catching up to do."

"Sure, Mother." Natalie moved away from the window, feet dragging with reluctance, feeling like a 5-year-old about to get chewed out. She wanted this overnight pounce to go okay, but Mother just never let up on the brakes. Somehow always managed to make her feel fat, unlucky and dumb.

Natalie asked if they wanted coffee or a drink. "Consuelo's here to do dinner, so whatever you'd like. . . ."

Daddy suggested a rum collins all around. Mother agreed, so Natalie did too. She'd gotten a pretty good buzz on before they came—preventive medicine, an old boyfriend used to call it—but a drink wouldn't do it any harm. Daddy headed for the kitchen, calling out, "Hey, Consuelo, where are you hiding, you bad girl?"

"Now, darling." Mother beckoned for the command performance. "Sit down and tell me everything I've missed."

She perched awkwardly on the edge of the red chair, saying there really wasn't all that much to tell. When Yvonne came for dinner maybe she'd have more news.

A sharp question shot out. "She's coming alone, I hope?"

"Well, I guess. She knows how you feel about. . . ." Awkward pause. Yvonne should be here to take her own heat, but as usual she'd made herself busy. "So how are things with you and Daddy?"

Her mother's face screwed up. "Ah, don't ask. Not today, at least. I'd rather forget it." Suddenly noticing how beat she looked, really done in, Natalie felt a burst of compassion and decided to try very hard this time around. Mother sagged into the cushions: "So tell me how you're keeping busy, how things are going with your agent and all that—you know."

She said she was mostly playing tennis, going to Jane Fonda's Workout. A slight smirk, watching the reaction to that name. "But Derek says something's coming up I might have a good shot at."

"Really, dear! Wouldn't that be marvelous!"

Daddy brought in the drinks. "Consuelo's too shy to come say hi. She says she's got a big pimple on her chin."

"Thanks, sweetie." Mother picked up a glass, saying brightly, "Danny, Gnat's agent has her lined up for a part."

"Hey, terrific!" Beaming enthusiasm. "In a movie?"

"Uh-huh. But it's only a made-for-TV."

"Well, shoot, that's where the good stuff turns up these days." Daddy always put the best face on anything she came up with. Thank god *one* of them was usually in her corner, at least. "What's the plot? Studio or independent?"

She said she didn't know, and didn't want to talk about it—rapping the table—"till I get it. Right, Daddy?"

Chuckling, he headed for the fireplace, a predictable part of his fuddy homecoming ritual. "Well, we'll all cross our fingers and say a few prayers that you get it, Gnat."

She beamed at him, trying to put across how much she'd missed having him around. "Thanks a lot, Daddy."

Touching a match to the kindling, he said absently, "Consuelo's brother-in-law just got diagnosed with liver cancer. Damn, that's bad luck. Only 39, too."

Her mother asked, "So what else is happening with you, darling? Any interesting suitors on the scene?"

She said dryly, "Gee, I haven't heard that in years."

Tartly: "Well, you know what I mean. Are you dating anyone, or whatever you call it these days?"

"Oh, once in a while." Laughing edgily, she gulped her drink. If the third degree went on much longer she'd have to slip away to get herself high enough to make it through dinner. "Nothing to write home about. So don't start on the hope chest, Mother."

Priscilla went to the powder room, tucking away a mental note of Natalie's reticence on that movie. Also how deftly Dan's loyalties could be adjusted where his darling daughters were concerned. He never used to give the time of day to TV movies. Called them "two-penny soaps," or worse.

Coming back to awkward silence in the living room, she assumed she'd interrupted talk on "the boys," Natalie's twin half-brothers, a matched pair of no-goodniks. She picked up her drink and walked over to Dan, by the hearth. "Gorgeous fire, hon." She hugged him, murmuring, "Glad to be home?"

"You bet, Mommie." He kissed her upturned face.

When they broke apart she said brightly, "So Gnat, darling, aren't you proud of your father?"

Natalie said uncertainly, "Well, sure. Except. . . Daddy, I'm really sorry those Washington guys are giving you such a hard time. It's so unfair, when you'd won it and all."

"Don't worry your pretty head, Gnat," he said, forcing cheer. "We're whipping that situation into shape, and you'll be visiting that White House before you know it."

For the nightly news Priscilla put NBC on the TV, CBS on the VCR. Dan watched in brooding silence as Brokaw led off with Polish concessions to Solidarity. Switch to ABC: Reynolds on the Harris poll on Kentucky. Dan said dryly, "Well, at least we're not headlining tonight."

". . . day for close encounters of the political kind. In Lexington, Kentucky, where a hotly contested congressional by-election campaign is in its final week, the Republican presidential candidate, Daniel Sterling, and his wife, Prilla, crossed paths with former First Lady Norleen Talbott."

Watching that run-in—Dan smiling while the women glared—Priscilla said hotly, "There's no excuse for Paul letting that happen, Danny. No excuse at all." He grunted. She sensed his anger steaming, but as usual tightly contained. Dan tended to let her talk out unpleasant emotions for him—until finally he'd explode in a tantrum of rage. Then back to make-nice, until the next time.

". . . and this evening President and Mrs. Talbott came back to the White House for a state dinner honoring the King and Queen of Spain. On this visit to their former, and perhaps future, home, the Talbotts were greeted by Acting President Laurence Devlin and his wife Robin. . . ."

She stiffened, staring at the screen. Natalie said, "My god. What's that thing she's wearing?"

Priscilla said with brittle sarcasm, "A piano cover, I believe." *Look at her, little princess in that outrageous outfit, waltzing so blithely down those steps. . . .*

ABC ran a humorous montage of "a day in the life of a former First Lady still campaigning for her old job," with Norleen's airport and White House encounters reduced to brief walk-ons. "Short and sweet," Dan remarked.

"Short, anyway," she snapped. He wandered out to the patio. She called after him, "You don't want to watch CBS?"

"Nah. You'll tell me if there's any good news."

Eye cocked on the screen, she chatted with Natalie until the "royal welcome at the White House as President and Mrs. Devlin rolled out the red carpet for King Juan Carlos and Queen Sophia. . . ." Eyes glued to that flighty redhead chatting with the Queen. *That runaway, usurper. . . .*

Natalie murmured sympathetically that some nights she just hated watching the news. Startled, touched by her concern, Priscilla patted her knee. "Don't you worry, dear," she said briskly, determinedly, as much for herself as her child. "We'll win this thing yet, just you wait and see."

Close-up of Robin and Sophia as the front door banged open. "Well, there's a sight for sore eyes," a loud voice called out. "Two queens in the big house tonight, is it?"

Feeling that presence like an icy blast, Priscilla switched off the TV and turned, a neutral smile frozen on. "Well, hello, Yvonne. How nice of you to drop by."

"Think nothing of it, Mother." She delivered a breezy peck, brassy Clairol curls bouncing to her honeydew breasts. "I happened to be in the neighborhood. Where's Pop?"

"In the garden, I think," murmured Natalie.

"Sure. Where else?" Swishing the red suede skirt that didn't match her spike heels, Yvonne stalked outside, calling, "Hey, Popsy! Where the hell are you hiding out?"

Dan never understood her bitter complaints about their willful older child. *And no wonder*, she thought at dinner as he leaped on Yvonne's teasing, flirty jokes, trout to fly. She felt uncomfortable, almost excluded, watching those two carry on like vaudeville partners.

After his favorite dessert, Consuelo's bread pudding, Dan went to his study, presumably to phone "the boys." Priscilla asked Yvonne if she was still seeing "that man."

"His name is Jock. And I'm still living with him, if that's what you mean."

She stiffened, guarding her tongue. "And what does his wife think of that?"

"I couldn't give less of a damn, Mother dear."

She poured another Sanka. "And what about his children? Do you ever stop for one moment to think about them?"

"Quite often, in fact. I think they're rather neat kids, given that witch they have for a mother."

She sipped her coffee, asking, "So you think this man is doing right by his children, his family, to lark off with you, absconding on his responsibilities?"

"Some 'lark,' Mother. He pays for their keep—as do I, when he's short. Which I think is pretty decent of him, considering she got herself knocked up in the first place, and had three more when he didn't want any to begin with."

"Ah, very nice. So you both think you can buy your way out of his responsibilities to his children?"

Dry mimicry: " 'Pay,' 'buy.' What is this, a life or a white sale? Jock shouldn't go on 'paying' with his misery for one mistake." Pointed, insolent stare. "After all, Mother, I guess he wasn't the first man to get railroaded into a marriage he hadn't planned on by a timely little pregnancy."

Breath froze in her throat. "Just what do you mean by that remark, young lady?"

"Well, Daddy sure must've been damn surprised to hear about little me."

Hard slap too quick to see. But not the bruised astonishment on Yvonne's face, the red finger marks on that brazen cheek, as Priscilla hissed between clenched teeth, *Don't you dare. Don't you dare ever speak to me like that again.*

CHAPTER FORTY-FIVE

February 24th

Robin

As she dressed for breakfast, Robin got the news from Tom Brokaw: the Prince of Wales was engaged to 19-year-old Lady Diana Spencer. She yanked a sweater over her head for a glimpse of the beaming couple, Diana as glowing as her neon-blue suit. "My god," she muttered. "That poor kid."

She followed up her breakfast greetings with, "Larry, I'm not going to that wedding."

Fat grin. "What, you're not up for a dance at the royal do?" She shook her head, saying no sir, absolutely not.

Dryly, he explained to the boys. Jason popped off, "Hey, good for Lady Di. She bagged the big score, boy."

Sean said placidly, "Yeah, but that's 'cause she's practically the only virgin left in England."

She stared indignantly. "Sean Devlin! What a thing to say! Where'd you get a barbaric idea like that, anyway?"

Looking faintly injured, Sean said, "Hey, Mom, that's what all the papers said. He had to marry a virgin 'cause he was gonna be King of England." Larry, straight-faced, thought he might've heard a rumor to that effect too.

"Oh, for heaven's sake. Listen, the point is she's practically a child herself. A kid like you guys. Nineteen's just. . . too young to have any idea what she's getting into."

Derisive hoot from Jason. "Hey, Mom, she's old enough for what he wants. And bam"—fist slapped to palm—"she's got him. Gonna be queen of England, hot damn."

Sean said, "Yeah. She'll be real rich now, won't she?"

She rolled her eyes. "I don't *believe* this conversation. Larry, will you civilize the tone a little, please."

Mock grave, he stage-whispered, "Your mom objects to child brides 'cause she likes to think she was one herself."

They chortled as she threw her napkin at Larry. "Actually, that's almost true. For all practical purposes, anyway."

"Come on, Mom," Sean said. "You were 21!"

"That's right. Barely out of my teens, in other words."

Jason lashed out, "They're not all like you, you know, Mom," his voice so hostile, so cutting that Larry snapped back, "Hey, watch your mouth, Mister."

A few minutes later they clattered off. Jason's outburst unsettling her thoughts, she went downstairs for her morning briefing, moved from the family quarters to keep Stephanie off the trail of Cal. Stephanie's update ended, ". . . and it's raining in Kentucky. Conventional wisdom calls that bad news, but maybe the widow's voters have better umbrellas. Anyway, I trust you've heard the *big* news?"

"You refer to the wedding of the century, I presume?"

"Ah, yes. Capital W, capital C, please." Stephanie pulled out a Telex, read a highlight of the royal press conference. "Question: 'Are you in love?' The prince said, 'Yes, whatever that may mean.' Lady Diana said, 'Of course.' "

She sighed, "Now *that*, pal, is Cinderella for real."

Stephanie said yep, and the fashion craze after old silk shawls would no doubt be French-blue suits.

"Right!" She slapped the arm of her chair, mildly cheered. "Nice to have that straightened out. What else is up?"

Not much. "Except—I could've sworn I saw Cal Farragut lope across the lawn last night. Is he back in town?"

Robin froze, bolted by fear.

Mayo pressed: "The grapevine said he might be involved in some kind of West Wing project. That sounded pretty off-the-wall, but I thought I'd check it out with you."

Oh lord, here it comes. "Where'd you hear that?"

Hedging, seductive smile wrapped around, "Jungle drums. Here and there. . . ."

Enough! Tell her!

Still she hung back, sensing the jeopardy around her fragile roost, shrinking from it, toes curled on the perch. Hawk eyes boring, Stephanie said she'd definitely track him down this time, she had her hounds on where he was staying.

She made herself cough out, "Yes, he's back. Actually he never—listen, there's something I'd like to tell you. But you've got to promise me to keep it absolutely confidential, I mean not one word to anyone. Understood?"

Stephanie flipped up her hand, eyes like dinner plates. "Scout's oath, guaranteed."

It dawned on her, as she watched Stephanie's astonishment, that this was indeed a remarkable story. Also that hiring Stephanie Mayo was probably one of her worst ideas ever. Pouring it out finally, she felt the treacherous undertow, like a dam bursting. She got relief in the letting go—but sharks all through the water now.

Stephanie always liked to pride herself on being immune to real surprise, but this one knocked her socks off. She listened in stark, utter amazement to what sounded like a raving barstool fantasy, muttering, "My god. Fantastic."

One amazing part was that Robin seemed to've been right in the thick of it all along. And Stephanie hadn't twigged! Not peep one! Boy, only Cal could get away with that, in this fishbowl. He had an eerie knack for walking through walls without anyone noticing. But Robin had pulled it off too!

Awash in fresh, grudging respect, Stephanie asked what the odds were this might actually pan out. Robin thought it would take "the earth plates moving. For everything that's gone right, like China coming around, there are fifty more time bombs fizzling. And nothing could sink it faster than a leak. That's why I'm so concerned about this rumor you heard. Any chance of squashing it?"

Stephanie said that might've been easier to manage if she'd gotten on it earlier. Meekly acknowledging the swipe, Robin swore she'd been planning to tell her soon anyway. Before the proverbial hit the fan. "I promise you'd've found out before Larry announced it, which is maybe pretty soon. *I* don't even know when."

Nose working furiously, Stephanie wanted to know who else knew. When she heard that Talbott had been sitting on it for six days, and, though "less than thrilled," hadn't leaked it yet, she sniffed, "Now there's a one-line explanation of why the guy's not still president."

Cal Farragut, of all people for Hanoi to use to pass its signal! Yet the more she mulled that shocker, the more bizarre sense it made.

Head swimming with visions of his wild weekly hashish dinners, she babbled about Cal, how of all the old Indochina hands he was the one they cut the mold from. "Cal *belonged* there, couldn't even be pried away for R and R's. I heard he cracked up after he left Cambodia, had a nervous breakdown, whatever that means. Which struck me as a bit redundant—I'd always thought he was about as crazy as he could get."

For the rest of the day Robin had luminous clarity in her head—and queasiness in her gut. Her purgative relief in finally tipping Stephanie yielded instantly to doubt. As payoff against the risk of breaking silence—what? Now Stephanie would hotfoot after Cal. Lord knows what else she'd hear from that mournful crazy.

On her run Robin flashed an odd vision of the interlocking relationships that balanced and sustained her here, twined like the branches overhead: Tish and Stephanie. Carmen and Mr. Fletcher. Bella and the CC Ladies, Larry and the boys. Even Cal and—Alexis? No, Alex was always better as a solo act. For that matter, so was the Protestant saint.

She was gripped by a sense of her utter dependence on these different souls to see her safely through this perilous bubble of time. Tish always nagged her about where was she coming from in this. But her flash today was pure perspective, God working through the skein of people clothing her life.

On quirky impulse she slipped upstairs to tape the Buckingham Palace fairy tale on the evening news, skipping through Kentucky updates—heavy voting, flash floods, roads and phones washed out. Whatever she was after had to do with that gangling, coltish blonde. The exultant glow. Soft schoolgirl voice. Smug rapture hinting utter innocence of what lay beyond Diana Spencer's debut into the lights.

She flashed the night she brought Larry home to Greenwich like a Crackerjack prize, after he'd proposed over a Plaza Hotel dinner. Diana's parents couldn't've been more thrilled than Harry and Babs Swann had been; sometimes she felt the only thing she'd ever done completely right for them was bagging Larry. Mummy practically fainted when she heard that he'd popped the question overlooking the fountain where Zelda Fitzgerald used to romp because he once heard Robin call it the most romantic place in the world to get engaged.

That was, by the way, the first and last truly romantic gesture she'd ever gotten from him. Yet look at Diana lit up with having it *won*, the roller-coaster ride just begun. She muttered, "Lots of luck, kid. You'll need all you can get."

☆

Later that night Robin heard Charlie Whelan's angry voice through the Lincoln Bedroom door. ". . . absolutely no authority to strike out on a dangerous, half-cocked business like that, when the country's going through a constitutional crisis and half the civilized world is questioning whether the government's in collapse." Soothing murmur from Larry.

She turned, looked back down the hall. From the dining room door

Sean and Cal flapped napkins at her, go-ahead signals. Cal back to his cagey old tricks, baiting her into his game. Now Sean was in on it too, both egging her on. . . .

A muffled roar snapped her eyes back to the door. "Goddammit, man! There's only one issue on our plate right now—electing a legitimate president. We've got 200 million Americans clamoring for leadership and a government in total disarray, and here you are with some harebrained scheme that could provoke god knows what kind of Soviet retaliation. I repeat: You have no legal authority to bring those risks on the heads of the American people."

She hesitated. *Steer clear. Leave it to Larry.* . . .

Inaudible comeback from Larry. Then: "Bullshit! Are you telling me you're ready to stick the American tit in the wringer for a cockeyed pie-in-the-sky shot like that?"

There but for, there but for. . . . Even as she fought the tug, her hand came up, rapped on the door, pushed it open.

When he saw who barged in, Charlie's first reaction was what the hell is this. But as she apologized for butting in, saying she heard he'd come by and wanted to say hello, he grabbed at the straw. "Hello there, girl. Come talk some sense to this husband of yours. Tell him what a damn fool he's making of himself—not to mention the rest of us."

He swept aside his cigar smoke as she planted a light kiss on his cheek, saying no good, Charlie, she was all for it and he would be too, if he'd just simmer down and listen.

A goddam pair of them. And Larry must've put her up to it. First time he'd seen a Devlin hiding behind a woman's skirts—for a pernicious piece of nonsense like this! He'd never thought much of this fella, but he sure as hell never expected to see him sell this country down the river either.

"Don't bet on that, girl," he growled. "I'm not about to see our national interest jeopardized by a no-win proposition like this one."

"That depends on what we're trying to win, Charlie," Larry said calmly. "If we can negotiate an end to that war, reestablish Cambodia's national integrity, and open Vietnam to the West while pushing the Soviets out of southeast Asia, that would constitute one hell of a win for our side."

"Would constitute a Nobel Peace Prize for you, you mean," he snarled. "All this comes down to is you're promoting your political ass with no legitimate grounds to do it."

Stunned by the assault, Robin perched warily on the settee, fixing on one jarring detail: "Larry," he'd said. Not "Mr. President."

While Larry did his Buddha-with-cigar number in the room's biggest chair, anger showing only in his bright-red ears, Whalen spouted invective: "The way I see it, right now you have one constitutional mandate. Only one. That's ending this crisis by getting the head of your ticket elected—not waltzing off on some half-baked overseas gamble. . . ."

My god. It's a cockfight, for real. . . .

Larry smiled grimly as he flicked his cigar, saying come on, Charlie, what was he smoking besides that Corona? But the old grouse stuck to his guns, saying there weren't many rules in this game not made to be broken, but that sure as hell was the big one: The man who won the nomination got the party support. What would it be worth if a leader who owed his job to the party just walked away from it?

He pointed out that Larry had run in the primaries, "and you lost, fella. So your job is get out the vote for Talbott. If you do right by the party now, you'll get my support for top of the ticket next time around. But while this country's paralyzed and goddam torn apart, it's not your turn. Or your time. Especially not to drag this hurting country over the brink of god knows what."

She caught her breath, afraid to look at Larry. Wishing she'd never barged in, hating to see him on the rack like this. Yet a tiny voice out of reach of Cal's contagious madness was murmuring, *and what if Charlie's right. . . ?*

Larry recognized that some of this invective came from the built-in rivalry between them, salty old Speaker promoting himself as the number-one elected Democrat. Charlie was bleeding badly, scrambling to hang onto his job as the crisis eroded his grip. He'd come here tonight to wangle more support for Talbott—i.e., bail out his own butt.

So his reaction to the cold shower on Vietnam was no surprise. But that didn't make it any easier to take. Larry's big brothers used to goad him when they were kids, rag him to where he'd lash back—so they could punch out his lights. It was all he could do to sit still in the chair, absorbing abuse, tasting shit in his mouth. And goddam Robin horning in again—Cal's stand-in, he supposed. Funny how that weirdo could get her to do things *he* never could.

Aggressively stabbing the air, Larry wanted to "get a few things straight here. *Your* job as Speaker is to get that vote out of the House. I'm well aware your ass is on the line there, Charlie, and you're looking for a speedy resolution. But *my* job is to be vice president of this country for the next four years, and until your House gets off its duff and brings in that vote, to act as president."

He prowled the room, his bearing grave and purposeful. "And as long as I have that constitutional authority to preserve, protect and defend the nation, I'll pursue a major opportunity to advance world peace and American interests. I'd like your support in doing that, Charlie, but I'll move with or without you." Bit of a poker bluff there: He couldn't get off the dime without Whalen and Talbott behind him. Chin jutting, cigar pointing the Speaker to a chair: "I've been acting on a unique opportunity that opened up last month, and if you give me five minutes, Charlie, I'll tell you about it."

With Charlie's bulk finally roosted, Larry apologized for not bringing him into the picture before now. "We've had extra-tight security to prevent any leaks, after Hanoi passed us a signal on January 24th. . . ."

He kept it tight but dramatic, focused on Cambodia's role in the overall picture—assuming Whalen's total ignorance, stressing a gut-level schools-and-churches pitch any Philly pol could grasp. "They leveled the French cathedral stone by stone, Charlie. Destroyed all the temples and schools, burned every book, every historic record. . . ."

Charlie listened in gloomy silence, wetting down a fresh cigar. He perked up slightly hearing that Hale Wiley had opened secret negotiations with the Vietnamese in Paris on February 6th, when Eric Lowenthal went to Beijing. Charlie asked if he could get independent verification of that.

Pay dirt, finally! Trying not to show the one-upping glow radiating through his gut, Larry slipped two letters from his pocket: "Personal communications from Wiley and Lowenthal, detailing the negotiations for you, Charlie."

Score one for you, babe! Amazed by the sight of those letters, Robin was awed by the complex orchestration he was pulling off, to have had them in hand as "credentials" for Charlie. But she was also tipped to how thin the ice was under his skates.

Charlie ripped them open, scanning, grunting with satisfaction. She reminded herself that Charlie'd once been surprised to discover that

China was still "touchy" about Taiwan. Phnom Penh could've been Ouagadougou for all he knew—or cared—but those Democratic totem names worked on him like Alka-Seltzer.

Larry said, "There's some urgency about the timing of this announcement, in order to keep the jump on the Soviets. I've held off several days to get the Kentucky election out of the way, but Joe Kraft has been on my ass to verify a leak about this since Friday, so we can't sit on it much—"

"Are you going on the air when those results come in?"

Larry said he'd certainly call Helen Rumfels. If she won, he'd get cameras in to cover the call. "But my hunch is the widow may go down, Charlie."

Irate burst: "And a shitload of responsibility on your head that'll be. If you'd made even one appearance there. . . ."

Larry brought up "the grave crisis you're always telling me about, Charlie. In response to which I see my duty as providing leadership at the helm. Consonant with that, in order to prevent any leaks from sabotaging this initiative, I'm asking for air time Thursday to go public with it."

Already! Butterflies leaped.

This time Charlie took it in. "Go public with what? What the hell have you got to announce?"

Larry said he'd outline the background and progress of the initiative, and the areas of mutual agreement that laid the basis for an international conference convened on—

"In other words you haven't got shit to announce, except you're holding buddy-buddy talks with the country responsible for the death of sixty thousand American boys."

Larry tried to slide into strategic advantages like overall stabilization of the peninsula, but Charlie hung on. "Dammit, Larry, who knows if those Viet Congs aren't just jerking your cord at this critical time, looking to take us to the cleaners one more time. . . ."

Larry asked him to consider how much the Viets were risking with this move *they* had initiated. "Chinese too, for that matter. It's one hell of a lot more than we are." Back on the Paris talks, he accidentally slipped in Cal's name.

Off like a rocket: "Jesus Christ, man! Don't tell me that photographer flake has anything to do with this!" He pleaded for Larry to hold off till he could announce something concrete—"even a partial troop withdrawal. You gotta have at least that much to go on, Mr. President."

Larry shook his head. "It's too complex, too delicately balanced. Say the Viets did withdraw. What's to stop those Khmer Rouge goons from swarming back out of the hills?"

He started on the multilateral peacekeeping force, but Charlie roared, "Hold it right there! This cockeyed pipe dream has got no place on the American agenda, Mr. President. At least till we solve our own problems back home. I tell you right now, I won't go along with any part of it."

Push come to shove. . . . She shivered with dread, feeling the thing killed before her eyes.

But Larry said coolly, "Of course that's your right and privilege, Charlie. But I think you should know the mountains have been moving these past weeks. Thailand and the ASEAN countries have signed onto our tentative accord with Vietnam and China." He looked at his watch, ticking off the governments already informed by our ambassadors: Britain, France, Japan, Canada, Australia. . . . She gagged on a queasy thrill. *My god. It's really happening.* . . . Charlie felt it too. She watched that beefy old face pale as Larry wound up, "And our Moscow ambassador has instructions to inform the Soviets two hours before my Thursday speech."

Hoarse rasp: "My god, man. What have you got us into?"

"Peace, maybe. Absence of war. That mean anything to you, Charlie?"

Charlie argued passionately that he should let this ride until the country had a legitimate president. "If the deal's as good as you say it is, Roy Bob can go after it, and I guarantee you'll get the lion's share of the credit."

"You still don't get it, Charlie. Why the hell d'you think this feeler came along *now*?" He flipped his hand. "Because Hanoi knows our next president may well be Dan Sterling. They've got a pretty good idea how far they'd get with an old Commie-buster like him—that's why they decided to hold their nose and jump now." She jolted on a painful flash: Larry jigging to Cowboy Dan's strings.

Charlie slapped his head. "Sterling! Christ, he'll jump on this like a bandwagon. Ride it right to a win."

As Charlie finally focused on the only enemy that registered clearly on his radarscope, she caught a whiff of shared Philly-pol blood. She knew he wanted—needed—to be convinced Larry's "thing" was legitimate. And Larry talked now in the tribal language Charlie understood. "My pecker's on the line here, Charlie, and I'm ready to take the fall alone if it comes to that. . . ."

Then, on Vietnam's incursion into Cambodia: "They took another guy's land, Charlie. That's all it comes down to." *Click!* She heard from across the room that snap that translated as *roll with the dice.* . . .

Sigh like a whisper of air from a shrinking balloon as Whalen bowed to the inevitable. "Well, Mr. President, at a minimum you'll need Roy Bob aboard. Have you talked to him?"

Faint smile as Larry said yes, briefly, last Wednesday night. She read Charlie's flick of reaction, instantly suppressed, to mean Talbott had lost a few points by not getting to him first. Larry said Roy Bob wasn't favorably disposed, but he "agreed not to oppose. We discussed priorities and so forth. Quid pro quo."

"Damn right," Charlie growled. "He'll want a lot more from you than he's been getting. But I'll talk to him, help nudge him into line. And you'll need the solid Democratic leadership—which won't be easy, Mr. President."

Brittle relief in Larry's chuckle. "Right again, Charlie. And that's where I count on you. Now, I realize you'll report to the caucus before tomorrow's meeting. And I trust that will be a positive report."

Back on familiar turf, Charlie's mind leapt nimbly. "You'll need broad congressional support too. There's no ground for an acting president to pull off this kind of deal on his own hook. You might address a special session. . . ."

They chewed on that, decided against it. Charlie didn't want the damn thing tied up in committee. "But if your speech goes over big. . . what the hell, world peace, that's a motherhood issue. Maybe I can push through a general resolution, use that to blast loose the Talbott vote."

Larry heard out this burst of strategizing with a faint, ironic smile. "Good thinking, Charlie. That vote's gone damn stale. Why not toss a wild card into the game?"

Charlie peered warily. "Quid pro quo, after all. . . ."

"Right again, Charlie. If you can use this to loosen your logjam, slide Roy Bob in, that's okay with me. But I'm going all the way with this thing, Charlie. And I want you to know I'm not doing it to wipe Roy Bob's ass." Charlie said gloomily he was asking one hell of a lot with this Vietnam foray, so it better be tied to "substantive matters."

Larry threw her a gracious-winner grin. "No argument, Charlie. Any way you can use it. But do me one favor—try to crank up a little enthusiasm when you come aboard."

CHAPTER FORTY-SIX

February 24th
Prilla

Priscilla's morning was so rushed she only heard about the royal engagement from an agent, down at the barn. "Dan, what marvelous news! I must call Raine and Johnny—imagine! They'll have a queen of England right in the family."

He asked her to hold off till after their ride. Cantering off, she savored that bombshell. Almost a good omen, since it happened Ginny was the "dearest friend in America" to Countess Spencer, married to Diana's father.

Ginny'd made sure the Sterlings met them, years ago, after Dan had retired as governor. Priscilla really got to know them one day when all the Hibbing cars were out of commission and Ginny asked her to take the Spencers out to the Getty Museum in Malibu. She jumped at the chance and spent six delightful hours "playing chauffeur," as Ginny put it. Lord Spencer seemed a bit fuddy and eccentric, but awfully sweet. Typical English lord. Raine's relentless charm had reminded her of Ginny. Same impeccable grooming, same unslakeable appetite for collecting "little treasures" like art, jewels, antiques. . . .

Everything she'd learned that afternoon about furnishing and running a stately home she planned to put to good use when. . . . Now, in an amazing quirk of fate, Raine would be mother-in-law to the future king of England. Imagine that!

Back from the ride, she flew to her bedroom phone. A gofer had an "urgent message from Mrs. Hibbing." She tried for ten minutes to reach the Spencers, then asked the operator to try again in a few minutes. "This very important call *must* get through." The rude snip said she'd have to do it herself. If they were in the White House now, that call would go through like greased lightning. Or if she'd called before their ride. . . .

But a golden rule of her militantly disciplined life was don't blame Dan if you can pin it on anybody else.

Ginny hadn't got the Spencers either, but was "utterly gaga," planning what to wear to "the Wedding of the Century. Darling, can you *imagine* the parties? Ooh la la. . . ."

Feeling chest pains as Ginny babbled on, she said she had to run.

"If you talk to Raine before I do, darling, tell her how absolutely thrilled Dan and I are with her news."

Of course Ginny would be invited. And they might be, too. Certainly if Dan was president—which he *would* be, by then. Inconceivable that wretched vote wouldn't be. . . .

Sweating a little, fighting off an upset tummy, she took more Maalox. For the rest of the day she veered between worry over those stabbing pains and dreamy ruminations on the engagement. Imagining Diana as a moody teenager suddenly stepping from her make-believe world into the real thing—claiming her prince. Almost like her and Dan. . . .

Dan was already a star when she'd met him—like Charles. Not as big as now, of course. She hadn't thought of herself as a consort then, but she realized later that's what she'd planned all along. Picking a husband was like betting on a horse—you wanted one who'd go all the way, come in on the money. And Danny had been a great choice for the long haul.

Of course, the most important part was that she really, truly loved him, so in the end she had a fabulous storybook romance like Diana's. All Diana's schoolgirl friends must be saying, god, I knew her when, already treasuring every memory scrap of that suddenly Very Famous Person. . . . A summer wedding, she guessed. But the well of strength she'd been drawing on these past months would be drained long before that. Odd thumping in her chest as she realized no way could she keep up this killing pace until then.

Finally she dashed off a note to Raine: "Daniel and I are so *thrilled* to hear your glorious news. Please do convey our warmest congratulations to Diana. . . ." She took it with them to be mailed at the main D.C. post office when they drove in for Frank Whittaker's fundraiser—a gambit to get them to the Carlton, to sit out the Kentucky results.

☆

The Carlton suite was transformed into an election command post, cluttered with machines, phone lines and aides. She shooed them all out of the bedroom and made Dan come watch the evening newscasts, perched beside her on the bed. CBS led with the lucky couple. She beamed, clapped. "Oh, Danny, look at that darling girl. Just look at her."

He grunted. "Mmph. Pretty cute."

"Oh, she's absolutely lovely, and so much in love—she'll make a *perfect* queen." She gorged on this exquisite fairy tale, a classic Cinderella story, not even make-believe—as true and real as her own. But this one was magic from the start, not an image built brick by brick over years. . . .

On ABC she caught the Earl Spencer talking to a swarm outside the Buckingham Palace gates. ". . .in fact he asked my permission, which sure was sweet of him I thought." Asked why he wasn't inside, Spencer waved his camera like a dotty old P. G. Wodehouse character. "I'd prefer to be with the photographers, heh heh. . . hope for a very fine, sunny day. But I expect it'll be raining though. Usually does, doesn't it?"

Dan said shortly, "That's Johnny, all right. They'd better fix those teeth of his before the wedding." Those Spencers were too foreign and formal, too la-di-da for his taste. But Pril bristled at the crack, said he might show a little more enthusiasm for their first pipeline into the royal family, after all.

"For all the good that'll do us. Switch back to CBS, I want to see what Rather says about Kentucky."

He'd been on edge all day about this, vibes reminding him of election night last November. Closest he'd come to losing in twenty years. The whole thing went so much against his grain, he'd finally gone down and claimed "what looks like a victory here" before late returns yanked it away. The damn nets were still playing tapes of *that* fiasco.

God knows he hoped they weren't in for a rerun tonight. He wouldn't mind a little bucking up, but Pril was out in left field, binging on that royal flap like the mother of the bride. He'd slipped a few clues that their rosy scenario didn't look so rosy right now—went right over her head.

He supposed he should be glad her mind was off the countdown, but that didn't help get him over this hump. He'd been promising her for so long things would work out okay. . . . He just wished she'd feed him back a few of those lines.

Barney brought in a draft of the victory-party speech. Dan skimmed the pages. As he told Barney to punch up the unity theme, Rather got to Kentucky: "Heavy rains and flash floods have hampered the count in a by-election still too close to call. A must-win situation for both President Talbott and Governor Sterling. . . ."

Dead silence in the room. He heard Barney swallowing.

"Three votes shy of the needed twenty-six House votes, Talbott needs Kentucky to generate momentum. And Sterling, seven votes short, needs this victory just to stay alive. Bill Plante in Lexington, how does it look to you down there?"

More aides crowded in while Plante spoke of "contagious gloom in the Republican camp. The rain that knocked out a third of the rural precincts' phones may have also dampened the prospects of attorney Jonas Pryor, who despite a record two-million-dollar campaign failed to generate much grass-roots enthusiasm. . . ."

Shaping up like a rerun, all right. But this time they might not get a runoff. The guy said Talbott had campaigned eleven days there, his wife Norleen twelve, "a total of twenty-one, compared to eight trips by Governor and Mrs. Sterling."

A spark of anger lit his edgy gloom. By god, if they *did* go down tonight, he didn't want to hear one more damn crack about "only eight trips."

She somehow hadn't let herself realize Dan had to win this to stay in the game, but now that thunderclap, impossible thought: *Maybe he'll lose!* Suddenly she was shaking, sweating, too weak to move. Heart bounding, stomach burning.

She huddled on the bed, trying to catch her breath. Choking, dizzy, shaking like a leaf. ". . . record $800,000 spent on television advertising by nine independent PACs. . . ." Acid taste in her mouth. Barely able to breathe.

Paul called Dan out. The rest swirled after him, only Chet noticing her distress: "Mrs. Sterling, are you okay?"

She made herself say, "Yes, sure." Made herself pick up her purse and walk into the bathroom, where she sat on the toilet seat and quietly fell apart.

Like that nightmare election night when she'd almost found out what it was like to lose. She was too exhausted then to feel much. But now she was burning with pain, choking, trembling uncontrollably. So weak she hung onto a rack to keep from toppling off the john. *Like a heart attack.* . . .

In her terror she pushed down the urge to call for help. *Get hold of yourself. Pull it together.* . . .

She'd learned in these last terrible months how unbearable losing could be. And she couldn't handle it now, couldn't face those cameras without breaking down if Danny lost. Not feeling raw as a scab, rattled, utterly undone. . . .

She opened her purse and took out two blue Valiums. Crazed,

jumbled thoughts: Could she plead sick, just go to bed? No, no—Dan would flip out, call a doctor.

She toughed it out for a half hour, alone in that john, talking herself through. By the time the pills began to work she'd convinced herself this was just a bad case of nerves. And the only way out was on her feet and smiling.

In the living room, milling confusion, piecing results from phones, TV and radio. In the noisy debate about when—if—Dan should leave for the victory party, no one noticed her wobbly state. Chet argued that Dan couldn't afford to jump the gun. But at 10:05 Paul convinced him if he left it any longer he'd miss the 10:30 NBC Election Special. *Oh god, don't make us leave here without knowing. . . .*

In the kitchen she grabbed a quick belt of brandy. Going down in the elevator, Dan looked at her. "Mommie, are you feeling okay?"

"Sure, of course." Onward sweep past the cameras, dodging the mikes, into the motorcade. More debate in the car going over, Chet flipping channels on a portable TV. She drummed in her head, like a magic spell to ward off the abyss, *He can't lose, he can't lose. . . .* Then, as they rolled up to the Four Seasons, ABC projected the winner: "Jonas Pryor, the 48-year-old Republican lawyer. . . ."

Celebration in the car. Limp with relief, she clung to him, whispering, "Oh, thank god, Danny. Thank god."

The press were kept away as she and Dan were hustled backstage. Raucous blue-grass in the background. She stopped at a mirror to fix her face. *God, like 100 years old. . . .*

Peering over her head, Dan fussed with his hair, muttered, "Okay, hon, one more down."

"And only six to go. Work up that idea of momentum in your speech, rolling the snowball. . . ."

They moved onstage in an explosion of fiddling; triumphant waves; red, white and blue balloons cascading as the audience roared with delight, shouting, screaming as if they'd won the whole game. Instead of just one more step back from the brink.

CHAPTER FORTY-SEVEN

February 25th
Robin

The 3-by-4-foot work on her easel was a breakthrough for Robin, a bold-stroke, free-form impression of the airport mob that had trapped her a day before the Inaugural. Looking for a big moment to capture for that larger canvas, she'd hit on the instant when Kevin flailed in to rescue her. Swirling movement captured in broad slaps of color and light, broken into a fractured harmony, gave off a claustrophobic sense of being trapped in that mob.

The Woman, the target, she'd got about right. So to Stravinsky on the FM she pulled up background detail, painting Kevin's head in the crowd, his long arm reaching toward her.

The phone rang. She debated not answering, but folded on the third ring. The operator asked if she wanted an urgent call from Calvin Farragut. She winced. "Yes, all right." Eleven-twenty on her watch. Crisply: "Cal? What's up?"

"Ah, Robin, good. Listen, Larry's been meeting for an hour with the Democratic brass." Voice lulling, beguiling. "Could you just pop down and find out what's happening?"

She told him firmly, "Not a chance, Cal." And beat off his soft, level insistence with a dozen variations of that: "No, no." "Ridiculous." "No way."

☆

". . . potential for indefensible risk here, Mr. President, a risk I frankly don't believe you're justified in taking," Roger Tillman was saying. Robin caught the mood from the gloomy faces mirrored on the long, polished table.

Larry glanced up, made no reaction as she slipped into a back seat. No one else seemed to notice her except Mal Koenig, who scowled. She whispered to Ben, "How's it going?"

He scrawled on a pad, "Plenty flak. Keep yr head down."

Charlie and Roger seemed to've lashed the party brass into line, but the quid pro quo was venting rabid objections: "Totally unsaleable." "Dangerous adventurism." "A Molotov cocktail out of Hanoi, in this time of national emergency and escalating concern. . . ."

Larry sat, calm and patient, as they heaped abuse. She realized they were using "Vietnam" as a code word for "defeat"—and still gagging on it, after six years. All except Harley Richmond, the House Foreign Affairs chair, grand old silver bear she always wanted to hug. She'd had a special thing for him since one night at a party when he'd brought an extra jacket out to the porch and sat with her, reminiscing about riding his mule to a one-room schoolhouse, until she sobered up enough to go back in and face the music.

Harley tweaked his purple tie. "If I might be permitted to dissent from my learned colleagues, Mr. President." Harrumphing on his "deep and abiding respect for their wise opinions." She smiled at that graceful gavotte. *Good old boy! Now stick it to them, Harley. . . .*

He said he was with the President all the way on this initiative. He realized there were no firm guarantees of success despite favorable signals from Hanoi and Beijing. "But I say godspeed and go to it. This opportunity could heal many wounds in our battered nation, and significantly contribute to the prospects for peace in the world, which is surely the overriding aim of our foreign policy."

"How about some peace at home for a change, Harley?" cracked Charlie Whelan.

"That too, Charlie. That too. I think we may be a tad shortsighted on the implications of what the President proposes—which, by the way, I find refreshingly bold and original in scope. Even brilliant, if it should work out along the lines he suggests."

Tillman said that was a hell of a lot of "ifs." Harley agreed. "But I say let's take a chance. No doubt we can anticipate a long, uphill struggle. But the President has the mighty sword of right and justice on his side."

Biting off a fresh cigar, Charlie drawled, "Well, Mr. President, you'll need that mighty sword and then some if you're taking on that Pol Pot bunch."

He'd never held a particularly high opinion of Larry Devlin, but at least he'd never thought of him as pussy-whipped. Yet, by god, there was the little lady horning in again. You'd almost wonder if this whole Pearl Harbor might've been cooked up between her and that photographer flake.

Harley was taking exception as usual, the old Southern windbag, claiming that the President had "reminded me to my considerable chagrin of our morally groundless policy of tacit support for that murderous claque." Harley could give off enough gas in one sitting to lift the Goodyear blimp.

Harley said as an old mountain boy who'd seen too many wars he was sick to his heart with seeing old men send young ones off to die in godforsaken corners. "And if President Devlin has the courage to make a few bold moves in search of a lasting peace, I say more power to him. You'll have me with you all the way, Mr. President."

So the Cisco Kid had one recruit. Gnawing sourly on his cigar, Charlie waited to see how many more he could rope in.

Seizing that opening, Larry said he was "always gratified to hear your wise and reasoned advice, gentlemen. Although today I find Harley a little wiser and more reasonable than the rest of you." That drew edgy chuckles but no goddam applause. He'd hoped for a better shot, but. . . .

Go!

He crisply reminded them that the initiative had originated with an unanticipated overture from Hanoi. "We have a unique window of opportunity here, which could open to a major victory for our long-term geopolitical interests if the implications of the agreement are realized." Roger leapt on that, asking hotly what agreement, what the hell did they know about what was going on? Larry tossed that potato to the NSC staff, "available for further briefing. . . ."

Branch Foley wailed about the live ammunition Dan Sterling would get from this. Larry stared him down. "*We* still control this government, gentlemen. *We* lead the nation, and will continue to with the reelection of President Talbott."

Jake Kenzer said passionately that he was anxious as the next guy to get the presidential vote resolved, "but the American public don't want to hear about Vietnam. Much less Cambodia, sir."

Larry said he didn't wish to minimize the gravity or complexity of that vote. "But at certain historic junctures we've been challenged to look beyond momentary concerns to a greater good achievable by bold, unswerving American leadership. I believe we confront one of those times."

He nailed his own ass to the line, assuming "total personal responsibility," urging unified support for "a pivotal opening to strategic advantage that may not come our way again. It's essential we be out front as a party on this. Your courage and vision light the way for others, and fortify us on the difficult but navigable road to peace. I ask for your loyalty, your help and your prayers." Then he was off, aides swirling behind him like trail dust.

Robin beckoned Cal out of the Treaty Room, catching what-have-we-here glances from the speech writers holed up there with him. In the hallway he asked, "So?"

She led him to the big arched windows, away from lurking maids. "Cal, if that's any sampling of what you're up against, all I can say is lots of luck." He asked if they'd go along with it. "Yes, I guess. But I don't know how long they'll stick. That was a *very* unhappy bunch."

"Unanimous?"

"Close. Harley Richmond was the only one for it." He said calmly that was one more than he'd banked on, reaching toward her. She jumped back like she'd been stung. "And they weren't any too happy to see me there, either," she hissed, edging away from his snakish touch. "Anymore than I was to elbow in. Don't try to use me for your spying any more, Cal. If you want to know what's going on, ask Larry."

"Aha!" Aggrieved by the accusation, head tilted huffily away but eyes still on her like a hawk. "Sorry about that. I guess I just assumed you wouldn't mind helping out."

Wouldn't mind helping out. . . . As if she hadn't had her tit in the wringer for him since that first night. As if she hadn't already taken risk after risk for him and his crazy cause. But she saw now that none of it would ever be enough, hearing, *Get out get out get out!* like a drumroll in her head.

"Cal, I've tried my damnedest to help. I'm sick with worry about how this will turn out, and all I hear is more sky-is-falling. Listen, I just can't get pushed into the middle of it anymore—I can't and I won't."

He nodded. Stiff, curt: "Right. I won't trouble you again."

She couldn't save him, mustn't let him beguile her into trying. Or she'd lose herself too. . . . Softly: "Cal, I hope you know how much I want it to work. It's just—I can't make it happen. I would if I could, but I can't. So please don't make me try."

This time he seemed to hear what she was saying. He threw her a sad, lopsided smile. "Yeah, sure. Well, okay. Cross fingers and spit in the wind, Robin."

She wheeled around, turned her back on him and his ghosts and walked briskly back upstairs to her workroom. For the rest of the day she furiously painted the bug-eyes of the cameras swarming around The Woman—fractured, glinting lenses like the compound eyes of some giant horror-movie bug, trapping her inside that circle of hell.

CHAPTER FORTY-EIGHT /
February 25th
Prilla

After Dan's brief appearance at the Veterans of Foreign Wars' L.A. convention, the Secret Service twinkled him and Priscilla off in a Century Plaza freight elevator for a secret meeting with his kitchen cabinet in a twentieth-floor suite. She was kiting on anxiety, leery especially of Phil. Except for Kentucky, the timing on this couldn't be worse.

In the welcoming stir she counted seven of the ten kitchen boys. Trading hugs and compliments, she eased as she saw the bluff enthusiasm—almost awe—they still had for what Mort called "our formidable Number-One Communicator."

Yet a hint of chill, too, especially from Phil.

Chet and Paul bartended. She sat by Dan on the sofa, chiming into the congratulations on Kentucky. Phil said dryly, "Three down, six to go, Dan." She and Phil were alike that way—always counting.

Hard to believe: five weeks' bloody battle for three miserable votes. She kept reminding Dan that Talbott hadn't gotten even one, but it took more than that to satisfy Phil. . . .

Dan lifted his glass. "If Prilla and I could propose a toast: To our good friends and loyal companions of the trail who are making this happen. Gentlemen, our warm thanks. Your good health and success. In all our mutual ventures."

Ah, nice. Good preemptive touch. . . .

The rest rumbled, "Hear, hear!" Phil said blandly, "Behind you all the way, Dan."

Sure enough. Just a whisper of cool. . . .

Dan made a light joke on the Talbott exposé all over the *Washington Post*, Roy Bob's vote-dealing with the Iowa, Alaska and New Hampshire delegations. Kittyhawk was obviously a prime source for that, and all Priscilla could think was if he'd blabbed on Talbott's Alaska pipeline deal, why not Mort's fish-plant fiasco? Fine mess *that* could be. . . .

Yet Mort was the first to laugh at Dan's feeble joke. Didn't even have the good grace to look embarrassed. If anybody gave Dan any grief over still being six votes short after thirty-seven days, she'd say, Blame Mort!

Phil wasn't in a laughing mood: "That's strictly a Washington story, Dan. Won't play worth a plugged nickel outside the Beltway. But I understand our new vice president, Mr. Devlin, has something he's fixing to say to the great unwashed tomorrow night." His gaze chill, almost mocking. "Now what d'you suppose that would be, Dan?"

Her heart sank. Dan glanced at Chet, passing the question. But he'd already roasted Chet in the elevator coming up: "Don't give me tight security lid, I want a full report from your fellas within the hour!"

Chet fished dutifully for an answer. "Our sources are firming that up. . . some speculation he's going after the economy, or unemployment." Maybe Devlin had been pressured into an all-out pitch for Talbott on the House vote? Phil said he wouldn't bet on it. "That's one fella who flies on his own agenda."

Chet rattled off Democrat-agenda items Devlin might tackle: Social Security. Jobs programs. "Maybe a grain deal. There's an outside possibility it might involve Vietnam." She bristled again, hearing that kicker: Vietnam!

Phil took the pipe from his mouth, saying dryly, "You're joking, of course."

"No sir, Mr. Laubert." Chet shook his head, dogged, defensive, insisting they'd had indications to that effect from four different White House sources.

"Vietnam?" Phil's scowl dissolved into a wolfish grin. "Good god, man. Why, we'd rip him apart."

Crossing her legs, she managed to give Dan a private poke in the ankle. He said with an edgy chuckle, "Like I always tell Prilla, I won't bank on that kind of luck. But that Devlin's a great one for surprises."

Phil pressed for specifics. Chet mentioned a flurry of position papers, status reports, high activity level on the CIA's southeast Asia desk: "And some photographer friend of Devlin's been hanging around the White House. We're not sure where he fits in, but it may be with this Vietnam business."

Dan thought Devlin might be aiming to grab some headlines by announcing new MIA recoveries, something like that.

"What, he's got more boxes of bones to ship home?" Phil was smiling as if he'd won a jackpot. "He better have a bigger rabbit than that to yank out of his hat if he's going prime time. Well, shoot, Dan—if they're handing you *that* kind of ammunition, you might as well use it on 'em."

Softly, from Dan: "And here's the windup, here's the pitch, floating high and inside—*chock!*" Wrists flexing as if swinging a bat. "Out of the ballpark with that one, boy."

The men ate up that baseball outburst. Except Phil, who was scowling again, cautioning against any underestimating of Devlin. "We don't need to get bushwhacked by any 'February surprise,' now do we, Dan?"

Dan figured if Devlin was pushing himself into the picture, he'd probably go after "a real flag-waver. Some apple-pie thing."

"Whatever it is, you'll need a quick-on-the-trigger response," Phil drawled. "What's chances of our getting equal time to shoot back?" Not good, according to Chet. Phil said if Dan had to put out the fires in instant rebuttal, "you'd best find out what the sam hill Devlin's up to, Mister."

There—another opening for Dan to whip off a take-charge, flag-wavey little speech he did so well. Instead, he prodded Chet for "a full report in my hands by tonight."

Sometimes she almost thought he might be more cowed by Phil than she was.

Phil stabbed the air. "Now get this straight, Chet. We don't want that also-ran Devlin poaching on the Governor's turf out there."

"Right, sir. Absolutely right."

"So what in hell are you planning to do about that?" He fixed Chet in a baleful glare. "And it better be an improvement on what you fellows have come up with on that damned shameful mess in the House."

Ah! Fat into fire. . . . Phil was reminding them this hired hand he'd brought aboard to begin with could be tossed off the sled any time. *But if Chet goes.* . . . Hard enough keeping her head above water *with* his help—impossible without him. She counted on him to rescue them from other people's idiocy. Like Mort's. And sometimes Phil's. . . .

The meeting didn't improve. Even Mort's report on the 130-million-dollar war chest had scathing references to "our overpaid lawyers" and the "goddam pussyfooting FEC." At one point Dan tried to joke about no more Holiday Inns—"Shucks, just when I'd gotten used to calling those places home."

Phil said he didn't expect Prilla'd go along with that.

"Oh, Phil, now you're putting me on the spot." She said as long as she was with Dan, that was all that counted.

Mort proposed a toast to "putting the bankroll to work for our worthy cause. Here's to votes four through nine, and may they arrive in jig-tight order."

"Hear, hear," from Phil, rattling the ice in his empty glass. Chet leaped up to refill it. When he brought back the drink, Phil left him standing there, cooling his heels, balancing the glass on a tray like a Marx Brothers waiter.

Feeling the slap of that calculated slight, Priscilla was about to speak up when Mort burst out, "By golly, there oughta be some loyal old sharpshooters out there we could throw a few bucks at, to get Larry Devlin out of our way."

Her chin dropped to her chest. *Done it again, Mort!* Good lord, what if the room was bugged. . . .

In the prickly silence Dan looked at the opposite wall, in his wish-I-was-somewhere-else face. Phil cleared his throat, whacked his pipe on the ashtray. "Now, Mort, I don't find that a particularly helpful—"

"Mr. Hibbing, sir," Chet interrupted, "in point of fact, all that would get you is Speaker Whalen installed in the job of acting president." *That* set them all off, but Dan said yep, sure enough, Charlie Whalen was next in line to the throne till they got that vote out of the House.

Phil glared balefully up at Chet; he had a way of detesting people for being right. Lifting his glass from the tray, he drawled, chairman-of-the-board, "Vietnam, you say? Well, we'll just see about that, now, won't we, Chet."

CHAPTER FORTY-NINE /

February 26th

Robin and Prilla

Jitters peaking, Robin and the boys hustled down the hall to the Oval Office an hour before air time. Inside the Big Egg she found a few TV technicians and aides. She asked, "Where. . .?"

Someone pointed to the Cabinet Room next door. She barged in and found Larry tight-faced at the foot of the table, caught in a dogfight between Koenig and Cal.

". . . gotta go with the original draft," Cal urged hotly, Larry drumming on the pages. "If you let the Viets snooker you on this, you're inviting trouble all down the line."

Koenig said "trouble" in this context could be defined as zero-hour monkeying with specifics tediously agreed to. Crossing Hanoi on the open siting could jeopardize the whole deal. "And need I remind you, Mr. President, of the untenability of your position if they pull the rug out *now?*"

Robin shot a questioning look at Ben. He shrugged, murmured, "Slight difference of opinion on the conference site."

Like a drowning man thrashing toward air, Cal was trying to make them comprehend enough of the devious workings of the Vietnamese mind to give this frail effort a chance at life. Trying to make Larry understand that they'd go along with a fait accompli, but if he knuckled under, accommodated, they'd walk off with the barn. Koenig snapped, "Yank the plug in Hanoi, more likely."

Cal spun away, turned his sharp stare on the man at the end of the table. He remembered years back, swimming in a quarry, Larry frozen with fear on the 30-foot ledge till he'd goaded, shamed him off it with jump, you damn fool, jump.

"Go for it, Larry," he urged passionately. "Give it a chance." Larry's eyes like back then on the ledge, begging for an out. "You've gotta get them in there, man—that's the only way this'll work. If they get in there and see for themselves."

Larry peered at the two drafts. Then shoved one aside. Flushed, puffy with stress, he said, "End of discussion, we'll go with Phnom Penh. Ben, make sure that rolls on the idiot box. I don't want any ad-libbing on this one."

As he got up from the table he glared at Cal, muttering quietly, "Damn your ass, Farragut, you better be right."

Back in the Egg she took a sideline seat as Larry settled behind the carved desk, snapping off orders: Check the line to Wiley, and the satellite hookup. No snafus please. . . .

Ben ordered everybody out. Cal tossed her a wink from the door. Suddenly the swarming room seemed empty as a depot at midnight.

Larry went into the adjoining john. She saw him at the mirror, his stress reflected, before he pushed the door shut. She felt oddly tuned to his wavelength, resonating to what he was going through. *Lord, let it go right. Help him, be with him, let him pull it off. . . .*

When he came back, he seemed eased and fortified—controlled again, like his fresh-slicked hair. He shrugged on his jacket and sat at the desk, counting off a sound level: "One, two, cha-cha-cha. All aboard for the Hanoi Express."

Ben cracked, "Is that a nonstop, Mr. President?"

"You bet your bootie, fella. Just don't ask where it's going."

Chet burst into the Carlton living room with a tip that this speech was going "worldwide, live, through the USIA."

Priscilla blinked up from the scene on the floodlit White House lawn. *Around the world! That's insane.* . . . Dan grunted, "What the hell is that?"

Paul said that confirmed a foreign-policy angle. Chet spoke of a fresh trail on the photographer friend: The White House had been screening some movie he made about Cambodia, which could fit with their earlier leads on Vietnam. Dan bitterly reamed him out for leaving them "still fishing in the dark while Devlin's set to go worldwide." He stalked back to the speech writers.

She tried to sort out the rumors floating over the three TVs— Brokaw touting a Middle East peace offensive, Chancellor possible Vietnam POW-MIA accords. Rather said despite "rampant speculation in the past twenty-nine hours, White House sources say only that President Devlin will 'deal with a subject of major concern to all Americans. . . .' "

Judy Woodruff in a hallway: ". . . just informed by a reliable source that President Devlin's address will be beamed via the U.S. Information Agency to seventy-eight countries, with simultaneous translation into forty-two languages. . . ."

Priscilla called out, "Danny, did you hear that? NBC's got the word on that overseas feed."

"Damnation!" Dan exploded. "Why don't we have a bead on this? He's damn near on the air, and we don't know what he's saying?"

She hadn't seen him so angry since election night. Aides scurried in and out, clutching papers like charms to ward off Devlin's "surprise." She got up and touched Dan's shoulder. "Simmer down, hon. It's all right, it's. . . ."

In the babble of tinny reassurance—"ready response for any scenario," "no way he'll catch us off base"—she was only aware that he'd moved irritably out of her reach.

———

Hushed tension in the Oval Office. Larry cleared his throat, fiddled with his buttons, deep in concentration. Flashing on Mike before a sailboat race—Mike slapping his back, saying you can do it, kid, I'm betting on you.

A technician counted: "Five. . . four. . . ."

God, grease my wheels. Put silver on my tongue. . . .

"Two. . . one." Pointing at him as the red eye lit.

"Good evening, ladies and gentlemen. I want to inform you tonight about a major development in our efforts to construct a lasting peace in the world. I speak not only of an absence of hostilities between nations, but of a climate of mutual respect in which human endeavor and humane ideals can flourish. . . ."

". . . over recent weeks representatives of the United States government, led by the distinguished former senator Hale Wiley, have conferred with their counterparts from the Socialist Republic of Vietnam. . . ."

Dan looked at Chet, stunned. "By god, it's Vietnam!"

Chet smiled, grim I-told-you-so. Paul babbled, "Governor, he's playing right into your hands." Prilla snapped, "Listen!"

". . . team led by Ambassador Eric Lowenthal, whose fifty-year record of service to his country has no equal, conferred with the People's Republic of China and our Asian allies. . . ."

Dan couldn't see how in hell Paul figured this for playing into his hands. It felt like being bombed and strafed, his whole operation shot to hell. The House fight might be aggravating and tedious, but at least he knew just what they were after there. Not this open-ended nest of snakes. . . . "Red China too," he muttered. "Next one'll be the Kremlin." Prilla was grabbing at his arm, asking what did that mean, Dan, what was Devlin saying?

No point telling her he didn't have the foggiest goddam idea. He said grimly, "It's war, that's what. And if that sucker Devlin wants another Vietnam war, by god, that's what he's going to get."

". . . concerning the fate of the small nation of Kampuchea, formerly known as Cambodia. According to ancient prophecy, the Cambodian people would one day be forced to choose between being eaten by tigers or swallowed by crocodiles. In recent times we have seen that prophecy tragically fulfilled. . . ." Cal heard the words from the set, and told himself this was what he'd come here and fought to get: someone to bear witness, someone to tell the world.

Larry tried to describe the Khmer Rouge record—in brief phrases barely hinting at the monumental madness. He spoke in resonant, reassuring tones of the genocide of "perhaps as many as two million people," the cultural and religious annihilation, the ethnic massacres.

"The Vietnamese invasion of Kampuchea in 1979 rescued the Cambodian population from the Khmer Rouge devastations. But no lasting solution to the agonies of this suffering nation could be achieved through military occupation by their traditional enemies. . . ." All words. Easy, empty words.

Okay, so that was what he'd fought for. He just hadn't realized how short they'd fall. What a damn puny difference they'd make.

"In some respects the world may owe a debt of gratitude to Vietnam for terminating the Khmer Rouge massacres. . . ."

"Gratitude!" Dan echoed that incredulously, staring at the screen, hawk tracking his prey. "Listen to that—from where *he's* sitting, sucking up to the Vietnam Commies!"

Priscilla felt like they'd been torpedoed. Paul was muttering unbelievable, Devlin must've taken leave of his senses. She wished he'd shut up so she could fathom what was going on.

"After extensive negotiations, the government of Vietnam has agreed to the principles of phased withdrawal from Cambodia and establishment of an interim national reconciliation government in Phnom Penh, with guarantees of free elections. America would then take a lead in welcoming Vietnam back to its rightful place in the community of nations, a position forfeited by its continuing occupation of a neighbor state. . . . with establishment of diplomatic and trade relations, Vietnam will fully disclose all available information on the 2500 Americans still missing in action. . . ."

She sighed, "Well, there's your MIA bones."

"To achieve the promise of enduring peace implicit in these developments, I join with the government of Vietnam in proposing to reconvene the Geneva Convention on Indochina of 1954. I further propose that the site of this convention be moved from Switzerland, which has no direct interest in these matters, to Phnom Penh, the capital of Cambodia."

Robin sensed his grave, measured words like birds of flight winging from this room to the circling metal moons, bouncing speed-of-light back to earth.

"Let the parties to these talks assemble on the scene of the enormous tragedies that have prompted their coming together. Let the nations of the world witness for themselves one of the major crimes of this century—the virtual destruction of this proud, ancient civilization. . . ."

His voice was strong and sure laying out the rationale for Cal's "crazy little idea." No hint of the earlier blood on the walls. In her turmoil, Robin magnetized to overwhelming pride. *You're doing it, Dev, you're making it come real. . . .*

"We have an opportunity to make amends for the holocaust that occurred in Cambodia after the American departure, and to redeem the future of that suffering nation. We have the means, if only we can find the will. . . ."

"Some balls he's got," Dan muttered. "Stick to your own wars, boy."

Priscilla whispered, "Danny, I don't like this. I don't like this at all."

"Let Pol Pot come from his jungle retreat to defend himself before the assembled nations, including his own, at the Phnom Penh conference. Or let him and his Khmer Rouge leadership accept exile in another country. But above all, let the citizens of Cambodia and its neighbor states be assured that no future government will be led by a man who by any standards ranks among the great mass murders of world history."

Chet said, "God, he's trying to run against Pol Pot."

Robin was swept along by his firm command, sure, ringing cadences—the best speech she'd heard from him. "History's choices are too often between the lesser of two evils, and too often resolved by military force. But in this instance, the world community can seize a rare opportunity to build a stabilized peace—an opportunity made possible by the wise decision of the government of the Socialist Republic of Vietnam to respect the sovereignty of its neighbors, and seek peaceful redress for its reasonable grievances and legitimate security concerns. I applaud that decision, and urge international cooperation to ensure that the seeds of this extraordinary effort will bear fruit in an enduring peace."

He paused. She thought he was finished. He glanced at a technician, then added, "In the spirit of this mutual enterprise, I now invite the

Foreign Minister of the Socialist Republic of Vietnam, Mr. Nguyen Co Thach, to respond by satellite from Hanoi."

The red light blinked off. Instant of silence, then scattered applause. Jason called out, "Way to go, Dad!"

"Hear, hear," she murmured.

Larry sprang from his chair, staring at the empty monitor screen. "Hey, what's going on? Where's the Hanoi feed?" He clutched his hair. "Come on, you bastards! Hold your nose and jump."

The three screens went blank. Dan said, "What the hell. . . ."

ABC flashed the floodlit White House exterior. Babble of voices— "Danny, my god!" "It'll never wash, Governor"—as Dan Rather said excitedly, "President Laurence Devlin has capped a potentially historic speech with the surprise announcement of an immediate response from Hanoi. We're standing by for clarification—ah, here it comes."

Long shot of a handsome Oriental man, grey temples, oddly young face, sitting behind a plain desk. The focus tightened on his face as he said in fluent, accented English, "On behalf of the government of the Socialist Republic of Vietnam, I wish to express sincere appreciation to President Laurence Devlin for this opportunity to extend fraternal greetings."

Dan blew up. "Look who he gives free air time to! By god, this is one show I never thought I'd live to see."

She shriveled against the burning in her chest, watching that slick Hanoi operator, so cool and controlled. "If the United States can make a war here, it can make a peace. When relations are restored through the great effort of these negotiations, a new page will be turned in the history of our peoples, from hostility to a concord of friendship, not only for the immediate period, but for the long term. . . ."

She blurted, "Danny, he makes it sound like Devlin's already made this happen."

"Not by a long shot. Paul, where's our workup on this guy? And how soon can we get a transcript?"

"Coming right up, sir," Paul sang out.

She couldn't concentrate on what the slant-eye was saying—mostly propaganda about the long and heroic struggle of the noble Vietnamese people and so on. Dan was charging around the room, punching his hand, seething. "If that crackpot Devlin thinks he can waltz away with this, he's got another think coming. Paul, I want the heavy ammunition on this one. Let's give it everything we've got. . . ."

Robin goggled as Thach talked on. And on, words winging from the run-down palace in picturesque postcolonial Hanoi out across the earth—into the Oval Office where they tensely waited to see if Larry had blown the ball game. After five minutes Ben muttered, "So what's he say, yes or no?"

Larry shrugged. "Damned if I know."

"Vietnam is the only country engaged in the recent hostilities on its soil which is still at war. We wish to make peace. The restoration of peace is the aspiration of the Vietnamese people, the American people, the Kampuchean people, and also the peoples of the world. The Vietnamese came to Kampuchea to liberate that suffering people from the terror and massacres of Pol Pot, the evidence of which is plentifully available for objective evaluation by representatives of the international community. . . ."

Larry said, "Jesus Christ, I think it's yes."

"Accordingly my government welcomes convening this conference on the site of these tragic crimes against humanity and the Kampuchean people in Phnom Penh." Unrestrained whooping in the Oval Office. The kids jumped up and down, thumping their father's back. A skinny young woman from Larry's office threw her arms around Robin.

In the general exuberance Robin hugged her back, thinking dazedly, *My god, they did it. . . .*

Even in her shock, Priscilla knew they mustn't jump the gun on this utterly weird development before they sensed how it would go down. Paul hurried in with more of the draft. "Dammit, I want this short and sweet," Dan said testily. "I want this joker put away with a one-two punch."

"Right, sir. And you've got the ammo now to do it."

Revising the draft, Dan couldn't keep his eyes off the TVs. The Hanoi man finally signed off, "We extend the hand of friendship to Kampuchea, to the United States, and to all nations dedicated to the noble goal of a just peace."

Instant-comment babble: "Astounding, controversial." "Dramatic historic bombshell." "Bold, stunning initiative."

Dan huffed, "They want hardball, they'll get hardball." He penciled chicken tracks across the pages. "So this is his idea of warming the throne. He thinks he can pull a goddam Commie sellout just like that? We'll teach him a thing or two. . . ."

Roy Bob's pudgy face popped up on two screens: ". . . heartily endorse this important step toward our great goal of world peace, which will have my full and unqualified support when I am reelected president. . . ."

Her fog coming clear. Dan should be ultrawary of this line Devlin was pushing. "World peace"—awfully catchy ring, bound to have a big market. "Danny, be careful," she fretted. "Don't let them set you up for anything here. Maybe you should sleep on it, make your statement tomorrow."

"Hah! Not a chance." Raring to go, like a racehorse at the starting gate. "Come on, let's get this over with."

They marched into the banquet room, hand in hand, smiling confidently for the hundred-odd cameras. She stood solemnly beside him as he said, "My fellow Americans, no man in this great free country of ours is more foursquare for peace than I am. But the peace dearly bought in Vietnam with 60,000 young American lives can't be squandered and betrayed for the benefit of a godless Communist power that refuses to account for nearly 2500 missing American servicemen. . . ."

Robin hung around the office, like a party she didn't want to leave, till the shock troops of the press corps invaded. She shrank against the wall as they scrambled for position, Leslie Stahl interrupting Sam Donaldson on Soviet reaction to ask if there was "any significance to the Phnom Penh conference site not being mentioned in the advance text?"

Overwhelmed by a need to escape, Robin slipped out the nearest door. In the hallway commotion, Jim and Brian waited. Jim's stolid Irish-potato face was like a lightning rod, grounding her zigzag volts. She smiled. "Hey, I thought you two had packed it in."

"No way, Mrs. D."

As they strode beside her down the hall she asked what they thought of the big news. Jim said, "Big is right." Dead serious, disapproving. "It's that for sure, Mrs. D."

Her first raw sample of reaction "out there." She poked his arm. "You'll see, Jim. It'll be a good, terrific thing, if we just let it happen. For us, too, not just Cambodia."

He grunted suspiciously. She let it pass.

As they neared the passageway to the mansion she heard Larry's voice from an office. "The bottom line here is survival of a unique nation and a brave, extraordinary people. We have an opportunity now to bind up our wounds from that bitterly divisive war, and in the process save the life and future of a sorely afflicted country. . . ."

Hushing Jim with a gesture, she stopped at the office door, nudged it open. Desktop TV for an audience of one. On the screen Larry was somber but confident, saying, ". . . discover how to reverse this second Holocaust. . . ."

The solitary man watching the screen straddled a wooden chair, his hunched back to the door. "And in winning this peace, we can rediscover the true greatness of America. . . ."

Cal.

CHAPTER FIFTY /

February 27th

Robin

Robin found Larry over by the dining-room window, staring out at the lawn. She winked at Sean. "Skip the Pope imitation, Dev, nobody's there to cheer. Alexis called, by the way, crack of dawn, thrilled by your speech."

Larry said oddly, "Rob, come here. See what you think."

The sidewalk beyond the fence was crowded with people, dark, vaguely menacing shapes shuffling along in the early-morning light. "Good heavens. What's that?"

He said he wasn't sure. They'd started gathering along the fence some time last night—several hundred by 6 a.m., the cops said. Jason looked up from his math book. "They were singing in the middle of the night. With guitars and a trumpet. I figured they were drunk as skunks."

She asked Larry who they were. He said nobody had a handle on that yet, but a few looked like Vietnam vets. She watched them gliding by, patient, mysterious trudgers, some toting signs, a few stopping to stare in through the fence railing, mirror image of her staring out.

Larry sat down for his usual two-minute demolition of breakfast. She asked if that crowd was good news or bad. He said wryly he couldn't swear either way. "But I'll tell you this much, I think they're the least of my problems today."

CHAPTER FIFTY-ONE

February 28th

Prilla

Over the weekend the Sterling operation snapped into high gear. With all five circus rings suddenly going at once, they needed to keep the media spotlight on *Dan*. In breaks from what he called "the real work," plying the phones, he did a blitz of interviews from the Carlton.

Priscilla also squeezed in a few, in a sitting room down the hall from the suite. For years she'd wished she could tell one of those blood-sucking reporters how many hundreds, thousands of times she'd already fielded their sly, pointy little questions. Now suddenly this whole new barrage she'd never heard before, with new answers that somehow had to be woven, invisibly mended, into the old script.

Asked by the fat little *Houston Chronicle* boot-kisser what she thought of Devlin's Indochina initiative, she said the only initiative *she* supported right now would be to put her husband in the office he was elected to. "Let's be sure that the foreign policy of this great country is run by the right hands. The right, safe, sure hands. Not someone who's supposedly just a caretaker. . . ."

Looping back to home ground: "In our travels around the country it's always such a pleasure to get out and meet the people, MaryBeth. Dan said to me just the other day, 'Honey, I really wouldn't mind campaigning forever—except there's more important things for us to do right now, like straightening out this mess in the Congress.' Of course that includes defending the peace already so dearly won in a noble cause, as Dan said about Vietnam. And I feel the same way."

Ghastly mishmash till she got saddle-broke to the new lines. Between interviews she dashed back to the suite to check on Dan, feeling the water rising all around them.

In the bedroom Frank Whittaker was tipping Dan and Paul to a unanimous-consent resolution that Whalen and his Democratic whips would try to railroad through the House on Monday. They had plenty of mechanisms to head it off—only took one member's objection. But the trick would be to avoid riling the peaceniks, triggering any adverse public reaction. Dan's side should be careful not to stampede any Talbott votes. "That's an area of utmost concern, Governor."

She hadn't entirely trusted Whittaker since she heard he often golfed with Whalen. What kind of double-dealing was that, from Dan's floor manager? Now his "best guess" was that Whalen would use this motherhood issue of peace as a gambit to squeeze out three more Talbott votes.

Dan had expected Whittaker to lead his "zone defense." But Whittaker suggested Tony Curreri, ranking minority member of the Foreign Affairs Committee, who was "personally hell-bent on resisting this on a nonpartisan basis."

Dan didn't know Curreri, and Curreri refused a meeting, saying he "respectfully considered the matter best resolved outside the divisive context of the presidential vote."

That had sent Dan straight up the wall. "Dammit, doesn't that bird know we could get wiped out in what Whalen's trying to trigger? That House has diddled for three months with a vote that should've taken one day to get through, and now those Democrats are getting set to march down the aisle and crown Devlin the king of peace."

But Whittaker said Curreri was highly regarded for his fairness, stature and bipartisanship—which was "traditional to that committee." The mood of the chamber right now was very touchy, very volatile. A bit like that odd business at the White House fence; nobody quite knew what to make of it.

So Dan reluctantly agreed, but said have the heavy guns ready, "in case this guy falls on his bipartisan face."

She went back down the hall, praying they wouldn't slip into the sea of trouble roiling all around them. A few minutes later she told the *L.A. Times* witch, "Deanna, no one's stronger for the cause of peace than Daniel Morse Sterling. But let's get my husband into the job he was elected to do before we squander a hard-won victory with another Vietnam giveaway. . . ."

CHAPTER FIFTY-TWO /

March 2nd

Robin

Through her bedroom window Robin could barely make out the slow-moving chain of bodies along the back fence, like a living necklace flung around the House. Carmen said the ones back there were mostly antiwar

Vietnam vets, while the Missing-in-Action families and the "groups that lean more to anti-Comm'nist," gravitated to the front sidewalk. "And in between you got every different kind of pea in the patch out there. All just talkin' and walkin', talkin' and walkin'."

Robin hadn't decided what to make of that dogged, persistent crowd. Vibes so far were. . . elusive. The marchers weren't hostile. But perturbing, vaguely threatening. One more Great Unknown.

"Twenty-four years in this House and I seen lots of different things out there, yes, Ma'am. But never a bunch like that. You ask me, most of 'em don't know what they be doin' out there. But they go day and night, marchin' up and down, back and forth. Now you know the police don't like that. . . ."

Right on that score. Jim had talked her out of running since "those nuts" had descended. She already feared so many intangibles; she hoped to god her generalized panic needn't be stretched to include the constant trudgers so tangible at the fence.

But Larry's approach was more upbeat; he saw them as evidence that "maybe somebody's listening to me out there, dammit." If those guys wanted to demonstrate legally, exercise a few First Amendment rights with their feet, he wouldn't have them driven off. She noted his tight smile as he added, "Meanwhile, I'm trying to figure out whose side they're on."

At the Monday roundup, Stephanie produced a fat stack of clippings. "At least you can't say nobody's heard about Cambodia." Robin asked how the score came out. "Some raves, versus George Will's wet-hen routine." U.S. reaction was mixed, lots of noise, not much consensus except from the ultranoisy right. But internationally, it was glowingly positive. Kudos from Europe, Japan, Australia, et al. The hotly debated conference siting now seemed "a brilliant stroke, the nets in hand-to-hand combat for visas and so on. The cumulative effect's about the best reinforcement your husband could ask for, at this point."

At least from her office window Robin couldn't see the fence. Peering at the lowering sky above the alley wall, she said she felt as if they should nail up the storm shutters, they were in for a hell of a blow.

Stephanie said by the way, she was finally seeing Cal's movie tonight, at the loft where he'd been working on it.

Robin gulped, "Oh, nice," and fled for a quick run, piss on the Secret Service. Jim made a last stab at talking her out of it. "Hey, how about you get a Nautilus, Mrs. D? Nice little rowing machine." She told him he worried much too much, she wanted to be free enough at least to fly around her cage. He said okay but please keep it in the woods.

Crunching out double-eights in the trees, she heard the crowd at the fence like a cicada hum, felt it like a magnet, but couldn't see beyond the protective shrubs. Finally, poked by curiosity, she sprinted out across the lawn, heels kicking high. Along the fence, guys in raggedy jungle-war outfits leapt in salute, fists punching the cold air: "RAH-BIN! RAH-BIN!" She laughed and waved, running fast. Crowd friendly but dense. One guy was imitating Jim chuffing indignantly behind her. A deep voice roared out, "Robin baby, go get 'em!"

Back at the house she thanked Jim contritely for "a lovely run" and escaped to her workroom, shucking the mood outside like her street clothes. Cross-legged on the bed, she sketched White House impressions: her breakfast tray; penguin-photographers at a state-dinner parade; her easel by the phony-French dresser, last resort of bone-dry inspiration. Gutless crap, so orderly. Dull as a stone knife. She found herself roughing in Stephanie and Cal, nose to nose. . . .

Cut that out!

She thought of checking out Charlie's grandstand play on the C-SPAN cable, decided against it. She doubted it would work, and more cliff-hanging she didn't need today. Besides, if Charlie got what he wanted with his support resolution, Larry's number was up. They'd be packing, moving out. *No no, not yet, please, lord, not yet.* . . .

She tried out a new First Lady perk, news tapes culled by her office. Half-watching as she doodled, she caught Dan Sterling's ritual demand for equal-time rebuttal. But mostly a flood of Vietnam, glimpses back at a war so poorly understood and so well forgotten that a recent poll found half of the American high school kids questioned didn't know which side we'd fought on.

Now, like an old bear rolled from his winter cave, that war came alive again in half-astonishing, half-familiar scenes. Vietnam's swords-to-ploughshares industry, smashed plane and tank carcasses melted into tools, helmets fired into cookpots. A peasant woman paddled her boat on a canal in a timeless vignette of ancient life—except for the wrecked jet jutting from the bank. Personal, animated interviews—kids, women, vets unrolling their old war stories. But the biggest shock was simply seeing the world that had been there all along—so amazingly primitive. To think *this* beat the mighty Yankee war machine!

Then she got back to Cambodia through Tim Crispen, a mussy young NBC stringer who interviewed Heng Samrin, head of Cambodia's "puppet" government. From Phnom Penh, Crispen translated his French: "Kampuchea invites the world to come and bear witness to the historic crimes committed against its people by the regime of Pol Pot and his criminal henchmen. The evidence is clear, we have nothing to hide. . . ."

He toured the "true monuments to the Khmer Rouge regime," like the skeletal ruin of the once-majestic National Library, where pigs were farmed in the ash of ancient treasures. Or the field of neatly stacked skulls, gleaming white against the lush-green vegetation: "Silent testimony to this extraordinary experiment in 'national purification'. . . ."

Or Tuol Sleng, the schoolhouse that became the Khmer Rouge torture headquarters, classrooms converted into "laboratories for crude experiments on human pain, done with blunt knives and wire garrotes. . . ." A wall papered with photos taken moments before the victims' deaths. Neat rows of anonymous faces, "many showing evidence of their torture. Some, bizarrely, are smiling. In a land where human images were systematically destroyed, this was the visual record Pol Pot chose to leave behind."

Tuol Sleng was now preserved as a museum, "like Auschwitz, like Dachau. But will the outside world's renewed interest change the outcome of this holocaust still in the making?"

Crying a little, shivering from those brutal images, Robin went to the john to splash cold water on her face. She came back to a Sterling ad—minidocumentary, actually. One of their three-minute promos saturating the tube: Dan and Prilla riding horses, chatting up senior citizens, posing with kindergartners. Christmas-card glimpse of home with the kids. Snatches from the trail—miles of bunting and balloons: "It's time to make America Number One again!"

Her eyes stayed glued on Prilla. God, she was good at this. Amazing old trouper, never missing a beat, Barbie smile nailed under the cast-iron hairdo. Yet you sensed a fragile trembling, like a dry leaf set to fly. She seemed rubbed raw, trapped inside that smothering madness. . . .

Robin was limp with empathy. Under banners of PRILLA IS AMERICA'S FIRST LADY, the old gal took airport bouquets from two small girls in colonial costumes, one white, one black. As Prilla bent awkwardly to hug the little black girl, knocking her bonnet askew, Robin suddenly saw a stylized Madonna and Child, backed by massed cameras and mikes.

She reversed the tape, ran it slow-motion, eyeing the swoops of that embrace, awkward intimacy juxtaposed to cameras. Again, backward, forward, tracking the moves.

She froze one slice on the screen and pulled a blank canvas from her stack. Humming, energized, she set to work transplanting that fragile moment onto a blank white field.

CHAPTER FIFTY-THREE /

March 2nd

Prilla

When Priscilla sat down with the men to watch the ghastly House show, Chet mentioned that it turned out they *had* had a tip on some unusual USIA activity, which wasn't passed up the line.

Dan glowered at him. "A couple more fumbles like that, Chet, and we could be out of this ball game for good. If we'd had a whack before Devlin went public, we could've chopped him up good. Headed him off at the pass." Every time he talked so grimly, Priscilla felt tummy twinges. Since Thursday he'd been charged up—black, determined, hell-bent as she'd seen him in years. . . .

Now she was steeling for hours of watching what Dan called his trial-by-House. At least it wasn't the jungle boneyards suddenly all over the nets. Who cared if Chet didn't catch that blasted satellite thing? Sometimes she thought Dan was veering further and further off the point.

Chet offered "a bit of major news": Arkansas' Mosher was all set to roll. Devlin's hanky-panky with the Asian Reds was the last nudge they'd needed to get him aboard.

She beamed at Dan. *There! That should lift his mood a little.* . . . Dan grunted well, that's more like it. How many others would roll along with Mosher? Chet babbled about progress with South Dakota, Iowa, New Hampshire. . . an itchy Pennsylvania eight-termer named McGrath. . . .

Dan snapped, "If we're picking 'em off one by one, we could still be hip-deep in this Shinola by Christmas."

"Christmas!" She shuddered. "Hon, don't even joke about that."

Chet said he had definite confirmation that Kittyhawk was "pretty much living with his AA, Carla Florian. Sleeping at her place three, four nights a week and so on."

Dan said sarcastically, "Now there's a real big surprise, Chet. You got any more?" No, sir. "Okay, here's one for you—Whalen told Frank Whittaker yesterday this Vietnam sellout was 'bigger than politics.' "

On the TV some Democrat ranted about "the dire need for this chamber to go on record supporting President Devlin's bold initiative in the cause of enduring peace." She'd never last through hours of this. A Texas Republican spoke of "a fit time to rededicate ourselves to pursuit of America's preeminent goals, peace and prosperity, at home and abroad. . . ."

"Dammit!" Dan barked. "Don't our boys know how the vote has to fall on this one?" Oh yes, sir, Chet said, but those Congressmen never wanted to get left off a bandwagon—not that this one was going anywhere. . . .

She wished she'd taken more Maalox.

Suddenly "the gentleman from Missouri," slight, crusty-looking Tony Curreri, stepped up to the mike. She said with as much reassurance as she could muster, "All right now, hon. Let's see what he can do to turn this mess around."

In a quiet, raspy voice he said we could all agree we want peace on earth and a better world for our children and grandchildren, but he was still answering to his own for the vote he'd cast on the 1965 Tonkin Gulf resolution. He wanted no more tragic national legacies from any vote cast today, in haste or heat of emotion. "Never again will I give another president—or acting president—a blank check in crucial matters of war and peace. Never again will I vote on another resolution like Tonkin Gulf before I know what we're giving away—and what we can expect to get. . . ."

Yes, yes! Dan hissed, "Good stuff. Right on the nose."

Curreri said as ranking minority member of the Foreign Affairs Committee he was regularly briefed by the CIA and other agencies on matters of national security. Yet he'd learned about this monumental initiative "at the same time you, the American public, did, watching the President's speech."

Building to thunder: "I have no wish to make this a partisan issue. I urgently desire peace, and would support any prudent moves that could bring it about. But this bombshell was put together in secret, and no president can make decisions in a vacuum. Just what is this 'overture,' Mr. President? If it's such a good deal for America, why haven't you fully informed and consulted with the appropriate members of Congress, by closed-door session if necessary?"

Did the Speaker know all the details of this secret plan? Could he assure them he'd studied it in depth, explored all its implications? Curreri and his fellow committee members assumed there were negotiations in cutting this deal, but didn't know what was in the package, financially or otherwise. "Where's the great sense of urgency here? No Americans have been killed in Vietnam or Cambodia since 1975. Yet how much will peace cost us this time around?"

He wanted it "clearly understood, Mr. Speaker, that if you ask for a unanimous-consent resolution, I will object. If you move to bypass committee hearings, I will resist with all my fiber. Mr. Speaker, you would abuse the processes of this House if you sought their circumvention on such a critical issue. Let the Foreign Affairs Committee thoroughly investigate this plan and report back to this House, in accordance with our regular rules. And let the chips fall where they may."

Standing ovation as Curreri stepped away. Dan grinned—the first really happy look on him since Thursday. "Well, good show! I couldn't've done it better myself."

She purred, "See, sweetie, didn't I tell you?"

Chet said, by god, they'd shown Whalen they had a few aces of their own. "Excellent, sir! Very effective—and a genuinely bipartisan pitch."

Amid warmonger talk from some Democrat, she picked up a sense of off-camera rippling, scurrying. On a long shot, changing speakers, the Philly fatso leaned down from his perch to confer with a silver-haired man in a purple bow tie. Chet said, "That's Harley Richmond, the Foreign Affairs chairman. We may see motion here before we'd anticipated."

Whalen broke off to recognize the next speaker, a New Mexican who raised "the basic issue here: This great deliberative body has been whistling in the wind since last November, resisting its holy duty to recognize the fact that one man has already won this election, by an overwhelming majority. . . ."

She waited impatiently for another glimpse of Whalen. There—still bending heads with Richmond. Chet said after the partisan bloodbath Curreri just promised him, Whalen might have no choice but to go the committee route. Dan wouldn't bet on that. "Whalen's a pragmatic old dog, all right, but I don't see him folding his tents easy as that."

She tugged at her fingers, nerves shredding. . . . Whalen suddenly handed his gavel to someone, stepped down to the floor and asked permission to address the House.

To her amazement, Whalen begged to "assure my colleagues—in particular my good friend, the distinguished gentleman from Missouri —that I have no intention of circumventing the processes of this House. A rare opportunity for advancing the cause of world peace has been presented, and will most certainly be acted upon by this body. But I respect the gentleman from Missouri too much to eschew the involvement of the Foreign Affairs Committee, of which he is the ranking minority member. Accordingly, I have asked the chairman of that Committee, the honorable gentleman from West Virginia, to expedite this bill and get a resolution to the Rules Committee as soon as possible, for action on this floor at the earliest feasible date. . . ."

"Danny, he's folding!"

". . .at which time I am confident I will welcome the gentlemen from Missouri as a cosponsor and strong supporter of a bill to affirm a leading American role in this great international peace initiative."

Burst of celebration. Chet checked his watch: "Half hour from the opening prayer! That must be some kind of record." Paul crowed about their fella knocking out the Speaker "with a one-two punch. By taking the high road—and we didn't have to vote down any resolution."

"Okay, that's more like it," Dan said cheerily. "Now, Chet, I want our guys to get this thing good and buried in that committee. Up to its neck. Work on those Dixiecrat conservatives if you have to, but *hold that line right there.* I want this strung out for as long as we need it. . . ."

She thought dazedly, *All over? Just like that?* Relief flooded through her, carrying a soft, unfamiliar sensation—absence of pain.

CHAPTER FIFTY-FOUR /
March 13th
Robin

Melissa was three days into her spring break before she made time to sit down and talk to her mother. Robin didn't push it, didn't dare to. She could barely look at Mel now without flashing the grisly playhouse scene—through her own eyes, waking on the floor, and now through dear, broken Melissa's peep in the nightmare window. Dam of memory opened, what other horror stories might spill out? Terrified to find out, not sure she could handle any more right now, she was sneakily, cravenly grateful for Missy's dodges.

When the kid finally showed for a late breakfast à deux in the solarium, it helped to have the scenic view along the fence for distraction—pup tents pitched like dandelions on the Ellipse, backside of a 800,000 VETERANS ARE STILL FIGHTING THE VIETNAM WAR banner marching on the walk. Robin said this was her favorite angle on "what your Dad hopes is a good-luck omen to counteract the Sterling ruckus. Anyway, they sort of keep me company out there."

Melissa said gosh, she ought to get across the front yard to Lafayette Square. A self-policing squad of veterans with red-bandanna armbands had set up soapboxes under each of the five statues, and anyone wanting to talk could sound off. "Some still want to nuke Hanoi and others are real pacifist, but they work it out somehow."

Robin kept hearing about the eerily protective aura of the Fence. "Self-elected sanctuary," one ex-Marine medic put it. But Melissa called it livelier than that, "sort of a rock-'em sock'-em street fair," mixed-bag crowd mainly rather jolly and open to whatever came along. Her biggest surprise was the kids, 12, 14 years old, who were drifting in there like the vets. Street kids who'd been living in little wolf packs, in cars, abandoned piers, warehouses. "You should talk to some of them, Mom—I didn't know anybody lived like that in this country! Let alone 12-year-olds on their own."

Robin asked what they were doing there. Missy thought they mostly came to find out something about their fathers who were in the war. "Those kids are *our* Amerasians, Mum. You oughta get over there and sound them out."

It wouldn't help their edgy truce to point out that Melissa could manage that more easily than she could. Ransacking her head for neutral ground, Robin hit on the economics course Missy'd said she was probably flunking. Curt response: "Please, let's not get into that."

The silence seemed long, spun with the memory of the days they used to take bubble baths together, that chattery little voice spilling questions like water from the pipe.

Melissa knew she was being bitchy and she really didn't want to but she also didn't want to. . . make-nice. Pretend everything was hunky-dory, A-OK. They dipped into prickly sparring about her visit up to now. Thad's name kept popping up, but every time it did, Melissa chilled a little more, sending out don't-tread-on-me vibes.

They lurched on to the neutral zone of whether the White House was beginning to feel like home. Her mother supposed that was more true for Daddy and the boys, "but it's surprising how the old place can grow on you, don't you think?"

She said no, it still felt like a fuddy old hotel. Mom said don't tell Hamilton that. "You'd break his heart."

Groping for some unobjectionable topic, Melissa remarked that her brothers seemed very "put together lately. Sean especially's in pig heaven. But I think that's maybe partly because of you and Daddy being back together."

Mom launched into her wary old string of caveats. Of course she was delighted the boys were so happy and productive, but Melissa should remember her parents weren't necessarily "back together." "We're always the same family anyway, however it sorts out. The thing I want most is that whatever happens won't be hurtful to you kids."

She said don't worry that they'd get bent out of shape, they were "pretty used to rolling with the punches, you know." Her mother agreed with that, but still didn't want their hopes cranked up for something that maybe wouldn't happen.

Dubious sniff. "But it already has, hasn't it? I mean, you've come back, and you're getting along pretty good."

As her mother rolled out her usual bit about how you couldn't call these freaky circumstances "real life," Melissa felt an unexpected yearning. A pang like a freshly discovered sore tooth, that made her realize Sean wasn't alone in wanting that. She asked abruptly, "Are you and Daddy making it?"

Blankly: "What?"

"Are you, you know, having sex or something?"

"Oh, my gosh." Hand covering her mouth, Mom murmured, "I don't believe this conversation."

Melissa said curtly, "Okay, forget it. Sorry I asked."

"No, no, hon, you just took me by surprise." She patted her chest. "Shoot. I don't want to lie about something like that, least of all to you."

Sly, satisfied grin. "That means you are."

"Well, once in a while. But don't make too much out of that." Blushing, even! "Good lord, I feel like I'm trying to explain this to my mother or something."

Melissa chuckled. "Hey, welcome to the club."

"Well, I guess it's kind of like. . . an old habit we took up again." Stumbling, nervous, as if she were feeling a little guilty or something. Which was weird, after all the years they'd been married. "You know, he's really one of my best friends."

"That's okay, Mum. I'm not fishing for alibis."

She said well, thanks, but she wanted Melissa to understand their occasional getting together didn't necessarily change how things would turn out—one reason she didn't want this discussed with anyone else. Especially Sean.

Indignantly: "Come on, Mom! Of course I wouldn't."

Fiddling with her locket, groping for words, she said she guessed Daddy and she were "kind of like old buddies tossed together in this thing. But I'm not sure that means anything more than—just that."

Melissa spilled her hair through her fingers, sighing, "That sounds sort of like me and Thad, almost."

There—the crack in the door. The first time Melissa had brought up Thad in that delicate context. For so long she hadn't felt close enough to this dear child to broach that subject. But since the shoe was on the other foot now. . . .

Melissa said she couldn't imagine her parents being "as dumb and crazy about that as I feel, sometimes. I mean, I'm pretty sure I really love him. But I didn't expect it to be so—mixed up, sometimes."

Carefully masking her relief, Robin said gently, "Mel, I guess you *are* growing up. If you're finding that out."

That drew a shy glance, lush lashes fluttering. "Finding what out?"

She shrugged. "Just that this whole man-woman thing can be 'dumb and crazy' a lot. But terrific too, sometimes. And maybe that's just the way it is, darling."

The kid thumped her head, mock dramatic. "God, I hope not! I don't know if I'm up for sixty more years of *that*."

Slouched in her chair, fingers knitted over her belly, Robin watched her daughter with a grin of unrestrained pleasure. "You know what? You're terrific."

Shy giggle. "Thanks. You're not so bad yourself."

As she beamed, basking in Melissa's kindling smile, Hamilton shattered that perfect moment by asking if Ms. Mayo should come up. Back to business-as-usual. . . .

She reached out to stroke that long hair. "Know what, Mel? I just realized how much I miss not having you around."

"Same here." Picking up her coffee, Missy said bashfully, "I'm kind of—glad for this talk, anyway."

"Good heavens, I thought that was *my* line," Robin purred happily. For the first time in such a long while she wasn't feeling that old gnaw of concern for Melissa. *The kid's okay, she'll get there on her own. . . .* "Well, I'm glad too, honey. You're a very special lady, Missy. And I think you can learn a lot from this relationship with Thad, Like how to build your happiness, from the inside out."

Catching a wry glance, Robin pinched her nose. "Oh, lord. Did that sound as preachy-pontifical as I think it did?"

"I guess. But that's okay." Melissa said with startling vehemence, "That's one thing I love about you, Mum—you always level with me, no bullshit."

On that golden, vulgar note Stephanie appeared with her paperload, including a New York *Daily News* layout of four of her "original art works." Robin winced at the classroom studies, murky, cadaverous fruit-and-bowl still lifes. "Yuk, *awful* stuff. What garbage can were these dug out of?"

Melissa loyally decided they were "pretty nice. Maybe not your best stuff, but still. . . ."

Stephanie said she'd been fielding inquiries about "having a peek at your latest. . . ."

"Absolutely not," Robin snapped.

Melissa cackled. "She won't even let *us* in there."

"That's right. Leave me at least a *few* shreds of privacy, please."

Stephanie said that seemed little enough to ask of life. She inquired if Melissa was coming to the lunch. Robin said firmly, "Yes, she is. As a special favor to her mum."

Melissa wrinkled her nose. "Sounds corny, but okay. See you later, then." Off she went, Devlin-on-the-go again. Her dragonflies, Robin had called them when they were small, always darting in and out. But this time, at least, they'd had that good talk. She tucked it into her head like a fresh flower as she reached for the day's folder. "So what's up?"

Mainly Cal's film, tonight's hottest-ticket-in-town for the first of a series of White House screenings—Mayo's idea, which Robin kicked herself for not coming up with first. The guest list included "most of the Hill committee poohbahs sitting on that resolution, plus, for an authentic touch, three Vietnam Veterans of America honchos who happened to be in Hanoi at the same time as Senator Wiley."

Stephanie thought Cal's movie should help blast the resolution loose. Odd echo as Robin heard her own ravings from Mayo: "When they see the devastation in that beautiful little country, and get to know those crucified people. . . ."

Peering at her lap, Robin said abruptly could she ask her something rather personal. Stephanie guessed warily she'd have to hear it first.

"I just wondered if you and Cal were ever. . . an item?"

Dive for her cigarettes. "You mean. . . ?" Her hand waggled.

Brusquely: "Yes, but come to think of it, that's none of my damn business. Forget I asked."

"No, that's okay." Blushing as she fired up a butt, Stephanie said, "I'm flattered you'd want to know. But I'm not sure what to say, except. . . would a one-night stand eight years ago count for an 'item'?"

Gagging on alarm, Robin managed to say, in what she hoped was a casual, unembarrassed tone, "Sounds like a 'well, sort of.' " *Talk about lousy sick-joke coincidence!*

"Right. After a fashion, so to speak. . . ."

Stephanie thought Robin seemed a little shocked by that casual reference to a one-night stand, so she probably wasn't gonna like the rest of this either. But now that Stephanie's tongue was finally loosened, it all poured out—the loony weekly hashish dinners, the all-night press parties, the long string of Cal's Khmer and Vietnamese whores. He'd make a point of taking them out to dinner before they got down to business. Apparently his modus operandi in that vein. He found it quite a "decent arrangement" on all sides, he'd said.

Near as she could tell, he was cut to fit mainly disposable women, often the for-hire kind, though god knows not exclusively. He seemed to consider them rather like. . . Kleenex. Useful momentarily, easily chucked. She assumed he was too nuts, too obsessed for any other kind of connection.

Robin was sitting there still as a stone, looking as if she wished very much she were someplace else.

But now Stephanie had started, it wouldn't stop. So she babbled on about the night they'd charged back to Phnom Penh from the front in his Land Rover, dodging patrols all the way, high as kites on war. And she'd weakened and wound up under his mosquito netting, even though she knew his druthers were really those perfect, exquisite little Khmer whores. "So I don't know if that counts for an item. Maybe more a one-liner. I just remember at the time it seemed like a damn good idea. Eye of the beholder, you know."

Robin sat stunned, paralyzed with jeopardy. Yet fascinated to realize she was hearing one of her own mysteries unraveled. "Disposable women"—of course, that explained so much! She'd been that for him back on Block Island, before she came to understand that a man's strange sexual dreams could leave tracks on your soul, on your life.

She also realized that old-pal Stephanie was becoming a potentially lethal Trojan horse. Rue the day she'd hired her! But too late now to change *that*. So she ransacked her head for the cautious points of mine-field etiquette covering two friends who'd screwed the same guy.

Tone softening, Stephanie guessed Cal Farragut was actually "quite a special guy. Pretty screwed up but still a good, caring man." Peering shyly at Robin, she recalled that night with him as "not an *awfully* lousy time. So I've been thinking maybe I should tuck old Cal under my elbow and bundle him home for supper. . . or something."

Not what Robin wanted to hear, and no good wishing she'd never asked. Stephanie seemed to be somehow asking for her approval, so she choked out, "Sure, that's worth considering. As long as you don't. . . expect too much."

Nodding stiffly, self-consciously, Stephanie switched the topic to the backed-up mail. Robin fled with the excuse she had to dress for lunch.

☆

Thank god Melissa'd come along to break the ice. In the little old P Street row house, Robin was trying to fit in comfortably with Polly Hannaway's half-dozen guests, all vets of the sandbox gang called the Montrose Park Moms in their diapering days.

Robin hadn't set foot in this house since Larry'd sold it nineteen years ago to her Marymount friend Polly. Out the window she saw cops, agents, Robin-Watchers and sidewalk gawkers behind ropes, all straining to peek inside—where this tongue-tied bunch goggled at her nonchalant comments like pronouncements from on high.

Choking on the thin, ordinary air, straining to fit in as "one of the girls" again, she babbled about the wonders Polly'd done with the dear old house, pointing out the fireplace where Melissa'd cut her eyebrow learning to walk. "When I ran to pick you up you were covered with blood. I thought for one horrible moment I'd be raising a one-eyed kid."

Melissa discovered the patio where Robin had photographed her and her father squeezed on a favorite rocking horse. Georgie and Sharon jumped in with anecdotes of Melissa's sandbox adventures. Over the chicken-and-endive lunch, Stephanie and Polly got onto Mother Coogan, scourge of their '57 class.

The whole visit chafed on Robin. One more tricky Mayo event, blurring the boss/worker lines even more. Why'd she let herself get roped into this old-timey bath on babies and nuns?

She felt like a hostage to Mayo, helpless to manage now without her—or to shuck their past entanglements. Remembering her first official date with Larry, his red convertible wheeling her home bang on the 11:30 curfew, Stephanie one of the pack hanging out the Marymount dorm windows, whistling, hooting catcalls. Rushing around her when she came upstairs, squealing, "Oh lord was it marvelous, where'd he take you, did he kiss you, was he terrific, did he ask you out again, that car, I'd kill just for that car, never mind Mr. Gorgeous. . . ."

And now Stephanie was going after Cal.

Maybe Robin had come back here to catch echoes, elusive whispers of her earlier self. But in this antic prattle. . . .

She excused herself and walked upstairs to the john, memories flying at her like bats from the crawl-space attic.

The back bedroom was done up now in bold olive-and-brown geometrics. Hardly looked like the same room where she'd struggled to paste up dainty wildflower wallpaper, crooked and badly matched. Memento of her bridey days, before she'd learned not to tackle jobs like that herself.

She touched the doorframe, flooded with memory of that summer day she'd flown in early from their Maine cottage for some senatorial do. The odd noise when she slipped in the front door, like curtains flapping in an open window. . . .

Without stopping to think she'd come upstairs—dumb, stupid thing to do. In the dim light she hadn't really seen *them*, just a strange heaving motion. Then the girl screamed. Like a fuzzy slow-motion film in her head, she saw the man's head turning toward her, red-faced, eyes glazed, unfocused. . . .

Larry! Raspy breathing in that utter stillness. Footsteps clattering down the stairs, door slamming. . . .

Shrinking from that bit of déjà vu, old bad dream never quite exorcised, she went into the flower-tiled john and perched on the toilet, noting the nick on the sink, souvenir of the morning he'd dropped a bottle of after-shave. Room like a little time capsule, rocketing out of control through that brutal memory she'd run from for years.

She never found out who the girl was. She'd only seen a leg flung over his back, spill of dark hair on the pillow. Her gut instinct even then was that it hardly mattered—Ms. X was interchangeable with the swarms of brainy, terrific-looking young women that came with the politics game.

It was herself she faced up to now, how she'd handled that awful day—wrong, all wrong. Running off to the Dunbarton Gardens. Crouching under weeping willows, too frozen to cry. Wandering in and out of bars. Flying back to Maine, dodging Larry's frantic calls.

When they finally talked two days later, she was cool and remote. No confrontation, no anger or tears. Playing the game she thought he wanted, that she was too afraid not to, in case she lost it all: the it-never-really-happened merry-go-round. If she could pin down any one turning point in the accumulated disaster of their marriage, that was probably it. Why hadn't she fought him, stood her ground, hammered out some kind of fresh start?

They never did talk about that day. He sold the house to Polly and bought Greensleeves as a "surprise" for her—his alibi for doing it without having to deal with her. Her comeback was to leave the moving up to him, so after that it was strictly his game they were playing, not hers at all. After that she'd somehow acquiesced to his status quo.

Of course, she'd wondered earlier about the girls. Especially before Michael's election, when Larry was gone for weeks on end, flying high on twenty-hour days, juiced up by the wild, never-better war of that rough campaign. But she'd been pregnant with Melissa then, full of bridey bliss, somehow persuaded his tomcat ways were laid to husbandly rest.

After that afternoon she knew better. Eventually it got so she hardly cared about the women, as long as she didn't have to confront them. By then she understood this was *his* disease, like the booze was for her.

She used to wonder why he'd married her in the first place. She always thought it was that Montauk weekend when Pete Wadham and Giles Brubaker had brought along townie girls they were obviously sleeping with, boozy gum-chewers in tight pants and too much lipstick.

Stricken with contrition for that breach of class, he took her for long, tender walks on the beach and chastely shared her bed, sheet wrapped between them like a bundling board. By then she'd screwed a few boys, mostly from pique or curiosity, but had managed for two years to stave Larry off because she thought he'd never marry her if she capitulated —and then next time she saw him, two weeks after Montauk, he proposed.

It occurred to her now that Montauk might've had very little to do with it. He'd probably married her for her pliant budding-alcoholic reflex of escape, which played to his instinctive need for the it-never-really-happened game. This was their fundamental yin/yang: collusion on Let's Pretend. And he'd have her at it again if she gave him half a chance.

In the end that girl in his bed was just one more straw in the stack, one more notch in the smoking gun. Later her own "escapades" tended to even out the score. But sorting the blame for their cumulative disaster—a Catholic habit she'd tried hard to break—she saw now it fell almost as much on her as on him.

All right, fifty-fifty. Even match. If *she* hadn't been willing to stand up and fight, to work through that crisis in their painful yoking, why expect it of him?

☆

At the buffet dinner before the Cal's screening, Robin suddenly connected Kittyhawk's lady to the Carla Florian who used to work in the Speaker's office. So she was Charlie's plant on the Alaska cherry— well, so be it. *Somebody* had to get a leash on that cocky, self-invented young spoiler.

In the buzz of pressing the presidential flesh and palming White House matchbooks, her old Pennsylvania buddy Peggy McGrath broke past the wifey-talk to say she was "real glad you invited Joe tonight, Robin. I think he's been feeling left out lately, a bit taken for granted. Maybe I'm imagining things, but if the President could call him some-time. . . ."

Pass that on to Larry! He didn't need his own state bolting from the barn at this point. Squeezing Peggy's arm, she said how glad she was to see them both. "You and I are vets of the Pennsy trenches, Peg. And we don't forget that."

She chuckled, "That's right, Robin. We don't forget."

Robin picked up her Perrier from a table behind her. Her nose blanked out the warning whiff, but a sip fired her tongue, lit her mouth.

Yes yes! Swallow-reflex slid half that mouthful of vodka and tonic down her throat, to a howling chorus: *Quick quick, have another, nobody knows! THERE BUT FOR.* . . .

With a wrenching spasm of will she spat the rest back, slapped the glass down and staggered away. She gulped a Tab to drown the taste with a caffeine jolt. Mouth still burning, seared, taste buds screaming for more, she helped herself to a dark, gooey chocolate dessert, shoveling it in, praying that would block the thirst, hold her on the cliff.

CHAPTER FIFTY-FIVE /

March 13th

Prilla

"Now that was a fine speech Mosher delivered, Governor, no doubt about it. But the fact is, right now school prayer and the abortion amendment aren't front-burner issues. . . ." Chet doing his darnedest to explain why only Arkansas had rolled on this "Big Thursday" he'd promised for so long.

The pitch seemed to mollify Dan, but Priscilla, foot tapping, waited to see if Chet would lay it on the Vietnam business. Sure enough: "With that resolution hanging fire, the solidified party lines make it extra tough for any Democrats to cross over while the ball's still in play. . . ."

Somehow she'd assumed that Dave Elliott's promised "avalanche" would materialize with the Arkansas roll. She'd just expected Chet to make it happen better and quicker, but now, bitterly, she heard, ". . . sure no sign of momentum for Talbott. Look at it this way, sir: four down, only five to go—you're almost halfway there."

Too much! She snapped, "I thought the grand plan you sold us on weeks ago had *all nine votes* in by now."

"Right you are, Mrs. Sterling." Chet groped miserably for the silver lining Dan always wanted. "Mind you, we're into a new ball game now. Party ranks have to hold on this Vietnam resolution business."

Dan said damn right, he didn't want any Republicans straying off the reservation on this. Whalen was counting on that. Chet said similar considerations had made the Democrats "more leery about jumping the fence. As far as the Independents go, in effect we're down to Kitty-hawk."

Dan asked sourly what that pup was up to. Chet said the latest was he might want to run Public Broadcasting.

"Never mind that," she snapped. "We've got better ways to get to Kittyhawk than jumping at his ridiculous bait."

Dan groused that they'd given Devlin too much lead time, and now he was running with the ball. Sometimes she wondered how men had talked politics before they invented sports. "And dammit, we've got to get it back in our court—*right now*, Chet." He pounded his armchair. "We've got no more time to fool around with this thing."

"Right, Governor. Absolutely right."

"So now you say we have to pick those votes off one by one?" She winced at how he put that: *One by one by one. . . .*

Claiming "significant progress," Chet rattled through updates on Pennsylvania's McGrath, Nevada's Pickett, Indiana's Sheppard, South Dakota's Spaetz. . . . Her head reeled into stupor. She never *could* get any feel for those miserable men. *Almost two months. . . and we're not even halfway!*

She slipped away to take a call on the private line in the bedroom. Natalie, breathless with excitement. "Mother, I'm so glad I caught you in. Is Daddy there?"

"Yes, dear, but he's tied up in a meeting. What's up?"

She said she had great news. "Guess what, I just—"

"You got that TV movie?"

Disappointed hiss. "Damn! Where'd you hear that? I wanted to tell you myself."

"Oh, darling, it was just a lucky guess. But that's true? It really happened?"

"Yep, I guess." For once, a sigh of satisfaction. "Ten days filming, starting April 6th. And it's a lead part."

She raved about that "splendid, wonderful news. Your father will be proud as punch." But asking what this marvelous movie was about, she got instant evasion. "Oh, I'm not really up on that. I haven't even seen the whole script."

Warily upbeat: "Well, you must know *something*, Gnat. Who directs, who produces, who stars, what's the plot?" She took notes on the few names Natalie provided, with a vague description of "some kind of show-biz story line, I think."

"Well, we'll have a champagne toast to that great news when we see you—soon, I hope. How's everything else?"

Deflated, subdued now: "Oh, fine, I guess. Nothing much happening. Do you think maybe Daddy could call me later?"

Back in the study Dan was reaming Chet out for "another big fumble," not having their PACs retire every campaign debt in the House months ago, before the press made a federal case out of it. She didn't bother to point out that couldn't in all fairness be blamed on Chet. Part of his job was to take the lumps when Dan was in the mood to hand them out.

When Dan went off to the bathroom, she quietly asked Chet to find out anything he could—"on a strictly confidential basis, you understand"—about an ABC movie produced by Ron Magdoff, scheduled for filming on April 6th.

They set off for dinner with "our farmer friends next door"—Dan's worn-out joke that never got a laugh from her. As the cars sped up the long driveway, she fretted one more time, "Danny, couldn't you just have put him off? At least till things calm down a little?"

"Listen, I told you it seemed like a good idea when I ran into him. Warner may help us chip loose a few of those Virginia Democrats, don't forget."

Fat chance. But what's done was done, and she was grimly determined to make the best of what already looked like a bad night.

He might've known she'd have her dander up for this one. Prilla never would come right out and admit it, but he'd noticed over the years she didn't cotton to spending much time with any female star who was bigger than she was. And Elizabeth was bigger than all the rest of them put together.

Had been, anyway, in the days that counted. As this darn presidential thing dragged on, he found his thoughts drifting more and more to those great old glory days in Hollywood. Seemed like the best years of his life, looking back. He'd shot from nowhere to become a star, and it seemed then like his luck would hold and his roles would fatten and the good times would roll on forever.

Didn't turn out quite so lucky in the end. He made a few bad choices, maybe, and all of a sudden the well ran dry. By the time he met Pril, the best was over. He'd thought for a long time it might still turn around—shoot, that town was full of comeback stories. He hadn't realized till the lights had gone down on him how much he wanted that party never to end.

He guessed if given the choice he'd rather've had an all-star movie career like Cary Grant or John Wayne than be president. But he'd missed out on one, and the other looked a bit iffier every day. At least he'd gotten Arkansas today, but it didn't feel as good as the first roll did, maybe because he realized by now that none of them was going to bust open the dam.

While he was out dragging his butt through the monotonous rig-marole that went with this fight, he kept his spirits up by daydreaming about the good old Hollywood days, remembering the great carousing he'd done with Bill and Hank and Jimmy in their bachelor prime. Or he'd riffle through memories of all his on-camera kissing scenes, comparing which gals did it best—which ones better yet off the set. He'd had a whack at quite a few, but a lot more he'd had his eye on got away—like Elizabeth. Shoot, for a while it seemed like she'd run through just about every fella in town *except* him.

He still always looked forward to a get-together with old Liz, because nobody had a better string of yarns about the good old days. Just talking with her made that time more real in his head. Took some of the sting out of the bullshit he was wading through these days. He could pass it off as good politics too, thanks to the latest gent she was nesting with. And if that didn't set so right with Prilla—well, he guessed that was how the cookie crumbled.

No surprise to find only Warner waiting with the agents at the door. Warner slipped into his hearty greeting, "I'm afraid Elizabeth's running a little late, but she'll be down any minute." If she made it down inside the hour, Dan would be mighty surprised. But rank had its privileges, and Liz was always a gal worth waiting for.

When Warner congratulated him on the Arkansas vote, Dan said he wished he could find five more Democrats in that House with as much guts as Ken Mosher. Warner said maybe Devlin's Vietnam campaign was "clouding the political air." Dan argued that was all the more reason to get a duly elected president into the job. Warner agreed with that, but rambled off into how party mechanisms tended to "work against expeditious solutions in instances like this, unfortunately. . . ."

He'd always thought for a movie part Warner would get cast as the wolf-next-door. Prilla's nickname for their handsome neighbor was the Dilettante—no more a real farmer than he was a real senator, in her book. But by gosh, he was a genuine political junkie who could happily swap shop talk with Dan till the last of his cows came home.

They settled down over drinks. Just as they were getting warmed up, he heard a rattle of jewelry coming down the stairs. "John, sweetie, was that the doorbell I heard?"

And in she floated, in something violet that matched her eyes. He jumped to his feet for the grand entrance. A long way from *National Velvet*, but by gosh, she was still one in a million. He said in a nostalgic burst of chivalry, "Liz, great to see you again, looking gorgeous as ever."

Looking like a dime-store clerk in a purple chiffon tent, you mean. Priscilla said sweetly, "Hello, Elizabeth. How nice of you to ask us over."

"Well, Prilla honey, we do like to keep in touch with the neighbors," she drawled, embracing Dan, leaving a bloody scar of lipstick on his cheek.

From that point, Priscilla's evening rapidly deteriorated. Warner kept trying to talk politics, the only thing that interested him. But Dan was in his old-timey mood, bent on recounting the hoary Hollywood yarns he told so well. And every one of his stories, by Priscilla's grim count, was interrupted by Elizabeth, who was into her cups coming downstairs and had three more drinks before dinner.

Now she ragged him over slapping Angie Dickinson in *The Assassins*, the only time he'd played a low-down villain. Dan squirmed and said he still regretted letting them talk him into taking that part, by gosh. "A nice guy like me."

"That's your trouble, Danny, you never did learn to put tarts in their place," Elizabeth purred, glancing obliquely at Priscilla.

She held her breath, waiting for the next swipe. A favorite trick of Elizabeth's was to drop the names of actresses he might've slept with before Priscilla's time—a fairly long list. And Elizabeth played it for all it was worth: "Danny, you must remember so-and-so, that adorable blonde who played such-and-such. . . ." Dickinson certainly wasn't one of *them*—he was happily married when he made that awful turkey. But Priscilla felt those flexing claws.

More of same over the warmed-up dinner. Dan slogged on with his MGM war stories, while Warner concentrated on keeping the wine bottle out of his wife's reach. Elizabeth, as usual, held center stage, periodically pawing at her husband when he wasn't paying enough attention. But for all her self-absorption, she was tuned to every nuance of Priscilla's carefully guarded reactions.

Onto your game, Elizabeth. Your tiresome old sport. There were even moments in Dan's reminiscences when she felt a flick of pity for this blowzy, age-frayed woman who'd been such a major star, a so-called immortal. A bigger star even than Dan—in her time.

She still remembered the awe Elizabeth's name evoked when she herself was one of the army of struggling starlets, wheedling and scheming for two-bit parts. She'd always treasure the photo taken last year of her and Elizabeth in the VIP box at the Convention, on the night Warner addressed the delegates. The agelessly glamorous star in that photo was clearly Priscilla—while Elizabeth, at least ten years younger, looked like one more fat, unhappy pol-wife.

Elizabeth hadn't forgotten that photo either—and the old empress wouldn't like playing second fiddle in D.C. to someone she'd once described as "a retired starlet." Priscilla felt a cutting edge in Elizabeth's solicitude for Dan over "that ridiculous dogfight they're giving you in the House." Now a sly dig about the Warners going to the White House to see "that film on Cambodia everyone's talking about."

Warner blanched. But she wasn't done yet: "I'm afraid that's where you and I don't see eye-to-eye, Dan. I'm always a strong supporter of anything that leads to peace."

Warner snapped of course they were *all* strong supporters of peace. "None more so than Dan, Elizabeth." He and Dan fell into mutual reassurance about Devlin's "dangerously adventurist" moves actually threatening peace prospects.

Priscilla stayed out of the game. She knew the mischief Elizabeth was up to—she'd seen her on TV cozying up to Robin Devlin at some Senate wives' event, looking like a blue Ultrasuede whale in 3-pound eyelashes. . . .

Elizabeth feigned polite attention. "Oh, yes? Well, I suppose you could make a case for that." Swishing the sleeve of that purple getup as she reached for the breadbasket. "Well, Dan, you can bet they'll all be hopping to a different tune if you make it to the Oval Office."

Priscilla felt that slurred "if" like a knife in her chest. Warner said anxiously, "*When* he makes it, you meant to say, Elizabeth dear. Which will be very soon, Dan, I can confidently predict from my soundings on the Hill."

"Oh, sure." Staring insolently at Priscilla, brazen in her boozy bravado. "*When* you make it, Danny boy, this town should be a hell of a lot livelier place. Which isn't saying much, god knows." Yet Dan let it go right past him. Rambled off into some story about Monty Clift and David Niven.

On the drive home, still tamping her anger at Elizabeth's swipes, she snapped, "Well, one thing about this House mess—it shows you who your real friends are."

"You mean Liz?" He chuckled. "She was in pretty good form, all things considered. . . like 40 or 50 extra pounds."

That didn't help. But she was determined not to spoil his mood, after all the day's disappointments, so she turned off her tongue through their bedtime rituals of face creams and exercise wheel. Dan ran on about the first time he'd met Elizabeth, in the MGM commissary. Thirty, forty times she'd heard that one.

In bed his probing goodnight kiss cued her that he had something besides sleep on his mind. *No, no. Not now, not tonight.* Shrinking from his hand on her breast, she murmured, "Honey, do you mind? I've such a throbbing head. . . ."

He said curtly, "Okay then, sleep tight," and rolled away from her.

Lying in the dark, she knew from his breathing that he wasn't asleep. God knows what was going through his head, after that run-in next door. . . .

Sometimes when they were making love, she could call back the risky rapture of their first furtive embraces, when she was still stunned that he'd chosen *her* from all the women he could've had. Sneaking past the concierge in the Claiborne Arms to come together on her skinny spinster bed. Once he'd rolled right off. Easier at his apartment, when those snot-nosed twins weren't around at least. God, how grateful she was for him then.

In some ways she'd never lost that gratefulness. She needed his need for her, more than anything in her life. She rubbed at his shoulder, murmuring, "Danny, hon, are you still awake?" He grunted, thrashing his legs in cold response. "I was wondering. . . can a girl change her mind?"

"Mmmph. . . want to sleep."

Quick-freeze through her body. She must never, *never* let this happen again. "No" was a younger woman's luxury.

Whispered: "Okay, sweets, get your sleep. Maybe in the morning. . . ."

She lay very still beside him, listening to that rhythmic breathing that finally signaled his escape into sleep. Thinking of Elizabeth, of Arkansas, of Devlin, of so many things as she waited out the night.

CHAPTER FIFTY-SIX

March 26th

Prilla

"This great country of ours. . . ."

From the audience: "Greatest country in the world!"

"That's right, friend," Dan said. "And we deserve *the president we elected last November 4th*. Now you and I know that. But how about those tin ears in the Congress?"

On the Alabama Christian College stage, Priscilla was thinking about White House toilets. When Dan was still governor, she'd had a good look at the old plumbing and cracked tile in the ladies' room.

"Let's elect a real president before we cut secret deals with godless Communist countries. Don't sign any blank checks, or squander the peace we've already won in a noble cause. . . ." She'd do those bathrooms over in white marble, to match the halls. . . and the lovely Washington monuments. Marble was much more suitable for the nation's showcase, after all.

He rolled into "the prayer Prilla and I say every night, that almighty God will lead us through this dark valley of crisis to a brighter, stronger tomorrow," the latest run-for-the-bus cue. She led the standing ovation. *Maybe pink marble. . . .*

The campaign crew swept Dan to a nearby office to phone local contributors. She paced the hall outside. His presence worked on her like a tuning fork, holding her at true pitch, but when he was off doing one-man chores she felt the chafing, monotonous routine like fingernails on a blackboard.

She wandered backstage. Two kids were clearing chairs, three more clumped around a TV. She strolled up, ready to joke about a soap— and saw Robin Devlin in a circle of Asian kids wearing sarongs, making slow, strange moves. Devlin said, "Now Mathi will dance the part of the tiger."

Behind them a small audience sipped coffee in an elegant room. *Good god. Must be her press conference. . . .*

Priscilla asked what network this was. ABC, a girl said. Incredible! Even Roone Arledge couldn't concoct a news special from this folksy little coffee klatch—yet the screen flashed, LIVE FROM THE WHITE HOUSE.

She felt them goggling at her, but her eyes were rooted to the astonishing scene. Devlin asked, "Phala, the lovely way you bend your hands and fingers—does it take long to learn?" A tiny ballerina demonstrated that extraordinary angling, saying softly, "Not long if you practice every day."

With icy urgency she calculated what this meant, soaps bumped coast to coast. LIVE FROM THE WHITE HOUSE, yet. . . .

Dance lesson over, Devlin snuggled into an armchair with the lead ballerina, telling how she and her husband had once seen a hundred dancers from this 1200-year-old Royal Cambodian Ballet performing in the palace. Years later a few survivors escaped to Khao-I-Dang refugee camp and rebuilt the troupe of thirty-five dancers now living in America.

Devlin touched her fat, elaborately tooled silver bracelets, "given to me by Princess Jeanne, the wife of your country's former leader, Prince Oudong. They're very special to me, because almost all the traditional Cambodian art—like these lovely bracelets—was destroyed by the Khmer Rouge. . . ."

Now she dangled a gold medal around her neck, "a gift from Prince Oudong. You see that statue stamped on the gold, Phala? That's your Independence Monument, built in honor of your country's birthday, when it stopped being a colony of France. Now I hope we'll see the day when you can carry your dance back to where it began, many hundred years ago. . . ."

Coup de théâtre. Priscilla's rocky tummy knew that. Snapping her face to attention, she grappled for a comeback. "Well, that was quite a show."

Silence. A boy said, "We're a thousand percent behind your husband, Mrs. Sterling."

"Well, thank you. *He's* just as much for peace, you know, as. . . ." Platter eyes stared back at her. She burst out, "I'm sure the Governor wants to see those children dance in their palace as much as anyone. But for heaven's sake, let's stop and look at what's happening in our own country, the way they're trying to steal that election. . . ."

Dan finished up his calls feeling mildly down—not a man jack of them had said the check was in the mail. He came out looking around for Prilla. She always knew how to tune him up, point out a silver lining he might've missed.

But she wasn't anywhere in sight. Someone checked the Ladies'— not there either. The Secret Service started to stir and mutter into their

Dick Tracy radios, while he stood in the hall like a bump on a log, trying to figure out where she might've gone.

Just having her up and disappear like that put a jolt right through him. He never thought much about how he counted on her, leaned on her a hundred ways a day, till she suddenly wasn't there. And what if sometime she got sick, or some crazy went after her. . . ?

The idea clobbered him with anguish, left him swamped and utterly alone. Impossible to imagine going on without her. She'd become the motor of his life, the one thing that made all the rest work. He wouldn't last three days without her—wouldn't know how to start.

He felt like a damm fool just standing here, so he set off down the hall. Fighting off a weird impulse to bust out crying, he called out, "Where's Prilla? Where'd she go?"

She heard that mournful foghorn bellow right through the walls, like an SOS, and fled back to him. In the crowded hallway she sang out cheerily, "I'm right here, hon," running to Dan's side, to his embrace.

"Well, Mommie! Where the heck've you been?" She could tell how tickled he was to see her by his fuming and fussing. "We've been looking all over for you."

She purred contritely, "So sorry, darling, I got waylaid backstage."

He peered at her. "You sure you're okay, Mommie?"

"Of course, hon." And she *was*, she would be. Quick on the uptake, tough as he needed her to be. On the plane to Washington someone mentioned the ABC news special to Dan. He reacted with mild surprise, not much interest. *Sure, of course. The wifey stuff never counts, to them. . . .*

But it did to her.

Chet waited at the house with bleak news: Pennsylvania's McGrath was scratched from the possibles, since Devlin had just named him to the blue-ribbon pro-initiative commission he'd cooked up. "But we're getting favorable signals from Colorado and Iowa. . . ."

For heaven's sake, more dry-bones talk! She'd counted on Chet to be different from that congressional lot, but every day he talked more like them. That wasn't why she'd stuck her neck out to get him in this slot. He'd better start remembering why he got it: *to pull off Dan's win. . . .*

Whatever it took.

Paul rushed in with news of a Talbott switch on South Dakota's hung two-man delegation—Ray Nimroy.

They caught the end of Nimroy's floor speech: ". . . no wish to be a kingmaker, or to forget where I came from. I don't want to abandon the Republican Party whose banner I've proudly carried for nineteen years." Voice wavering, emotional. "But I've never seen a national agony to equal what we're going through in trying to resolve this presidential vote. With a sorrowing heart I have decided that a mandate for leadership must be given, so this country can go forward again. Accordingly, I will vote today for the man who carried my state last November, President Roy Bob Talbott."

Dan snapped, "Get that. The Dakota Judas. By god, that fella's going to answer for this." Frozen in dismay, she watched them spring into action to head off that vote. Phones rang off the hook, aides dashed in and out. Dan said loudly, "Okay, I want the bottom line here. . . ."

The bottom line was Talbott 24, Sterling 21, Balch 1, tied 5. Paul pointed out that the shift had come from a tie state, not from Dan's column. Chet insisted it wouldn't necessarily stick "once you get a chance to make your case directly to Nimroy, sir. So you'd best leave him some elbow room." Ezra even said they'd anticipated a move like this.

No one put into words what she well knew: This was a disaster. A body blow to whatever slim chances Dan had left.

She stood by him at the mikes, face gravely composed, tummy twinging, as he unloaded "sincere regret that a member of my party has misread the national mandate," but he remained "fully confident of my ultimate vindication. . . ." The questions came like bullets. He ducked most of them, reaching for her hand, leading her numbly back to the precarious refuge of the house.

The living room still swarmed with aides. She needed to be alone with Dan, have him tell her it wasn't going to matter. Or she'd tell him—

Couldn't pry him away. She escaped to the john and doused her face with cold water, her tummy with Maalox. *Hang on, hang on, it's not over yet. . . .*

Paul and Chet watched the news with Dan. She quietly stiffened her drink as the bad tidings rolled, South Dakota leading on all three nets. Tonight's word was "momentum." CBS said Talbott clearly had it. NBC said two votes short of victory, could Talbott's momentum carry him over the top?

They ran Dan's reaction. But Talbott's Bugs Bunny grin got more time as he congratulated Nimroy's "courage and statesmanship," predicting "a prompt resolution of the crisis. . . ."

Dan's mood was amazingly high. He even joked about a "necktie party" for Nimroy. She chuckled dutifully and swigged her drink.

NBC and ABC gave several minutes to a press swarm around some Khmer Rouge biggie coming through the Bangkok airport. And Robin Devlin's press conference got big play on all three. Wincing again as that artless glow came off the screen, Priscilla picked up an awkward tentativeness she hadn't noticed first time around. But Dan muttered, surprised, "By gosh, she's better at this than I thought."

"Oh, I don't know. Leave out the cute little props. . . ."

"Nah, she's pretty good. So Arledge threw that on live? He's playing politics with this, all right."

"Oh, isn't he just!" She shivered, hugging her ribs.

He said watch out they themselves didn't take any potshots at Robin—"We don't want any hornets' nests stirred up, Pril." She snapped, of course, she was well aware of that. After the news she shooed Chet and Paul out, trying to rescue the quiet night at home she'd managed to schedule for a change, just the two of them.

Eating on TV trays in the living room, they caught the tail end of his favorite show, *Little House on the Prairie.* In the breaks he skimmed the daily polling printouts, peering through the glasses he was careful not to wear in public. She soothed her raw nerves by dashing off notes, stray alarms still ringing in her head: *Two votes. Only two votes. . . . That woman, that damned, wanton woman. . . .*

After *Little House* Dan tuned in a *From Here to Eternity* rerun. He loved to check back on the work of old pals, and this one not only had Burt Lancaster and Deborah Kerr, but Sinatra's breakthrough role as Private Maggio. "Hey, sweetie, get a gander at this," he chuckled. "Frank looked pretty good when he still had his hair."

"Yep, he sure did." Watching, a notion sprang to mind, so good, so obvious—"Danny, I have a marvelous idea!"

Her bitter confusion shriveled in its glow, as if she was coming home, finally, to sure, familiar ground. "Hon, what this campaign needs is a big rally. Someplace like the Hollywood Bowl. And all your good pals like Frank and Bob—maybe Jimmy and Charlton too, you've got dozens to pick from—could do an all-star show to get your message across."

He beamed. "By gosh, Pril, that's a first-class idea!"

Warming enthusiasm as she tugged at the thread. They'd need singers, like Donny and Marie, or Debby Boone. Maybe a few comedy routines. But mainly it would be "just a marvelous showcase for what you're trying so hard to put across."

His radiant face said he could see it all already. He chuckled, "Darn, that could be one terrific show."

"And a big boost for our campaign. You might even get Rich Little. I'd love to see him do Bugs Bunny Talbott. . . ."

Before those two votes turn.

CHAPTER FIFTY-SEVEN /
March 26th
Robin

Robin huddled by the firelit hearth like an abandoned child, knees to her chin, head bent in anguish. Tish had learned to beware this Little Match Girl routine, which as a rule led fairly directly to a Josephine outburst. Yet a stone gut would be moved by that quiet, desperate musing. "It can't be over yet, Tish. We need a *chance*, at least, to make it happen. Lord, please don't let it be over. . . ."

No sooner did Robin lurch through one dip on the fun-house ride down here than the next loomed ahead. When Tish looked back on the last few months—as rarely as she could—she was amazed Robin had come through as well as she did. So far so good for "one day at a time," but those buzzwords could also be taken to mean the roof might cave in tomorrow.

Tish reminded her dryly she'd sung a different tune not long ago. "What was it? 'A few days, a few weeks at most'?"

She said that didn't help, to rub her nose in it.

"Robin, where's your damn perspective? What you can't change, accept. It might even save your ass in the long run, if it comes to that, to be out of this pressure cooker."

Robin glared as if Tish had said burn the house down. Stretching out her legs, bending over them, she said she just wasn't ready for that. She'd "sort of written Roy Bob off in my head, when he couldn't—but now he only needs two votes. He could get that in ten minutes if those goats decide he's got a bandwagon." Soft, broken croon: "Tish, I can't bear for it to just. . . end like this, so soon."

Tish urged horse sense: From the start she'd known this wasn't going to last. They'd had a longer run than anybody'd bargained for. Whatever happened wasn't the end of the world.

"But it might be the end of Cambodia, Tish, it really could. Talbott *hates* what Larry's done, how he's been upstaged. He'll wipe out every trace Larry was ever here, and the Cambodia deal will be the first to go."

Tish supposed it was asking too much to get through an entire conversation without hearing that place mentioned. In the beginning she'd fought this Cambodian obsession like the plague, convinced Robin was only dabbling with a gimmick tied to her automatic self-destruct. But by now Cambodia seemed almost like a bubble in the black sea roaring all around—a relatively harmless diversion. Tish even found herself rooting for the cause.

Robin brooded about the reactions to Cambodia she picked up from so many people—"sort of an 'annhh, so what' attitude. Guys like Koenig who kiss it off as 'not germane to our interests' and so on." Each crack triggered a bizarre violence in her head: "I see them gutted and slashed like Pol Pot's victims. I know now what people mean by the urge to kill. I feel it every time I hear them flick off Cambodia without the faintest awareness they're doing just what the Khmer Rouge did, dishing out horrendous deaths. . . ."

Tish still couldn't get a fix on the roots of this obsession. Guilt-ridden Catholic childhood? Or some kinky urge to prove she could save the world like a *real* Devlin?

Tish commented mildly that the fixation wasn't doing Robin *or* Cambodia much good. They talked it out until she felt Robin's anxieties venting, leeching out. Acknowledging that, Robin smiled shyly, said thanks a lot, she felt more human now. "Calm enough to try for that Buddhist fatalism Cal always talks about. Qué será, será, Asian version."

Tish grunted suspiciously, asked what was happening with that oddball. Robin said she was the wrong one to ask, she'd hardly seen him lately, but heard he was peddling his hit movie for the refugee fund he'd set up. "He's sold it to twenty countries already, Larry says, with more signing up every day."

She asked if Robin missed him.

"Yeah, I guess I do." Blinking into the flames. "I miss. . . his goofiness. And his way of keeping you tuned to what really matters. Like —well, you know."

She asked again did Robin *miss* him.

A shy glance shot in her direction. "You mean, do I miss him personally?" Tish said that was closer, anyway.

Robin hugged her knees. "I better not, because I think Stephanie's taken over in that department too. I'm too terrified to ask for the gory details, but my nose says they're making it, all right."

And out poured a stream of lubricious fantasy—how she'd catch herself looking speculatively at Stephanie, imagining her sprawled back on a mussy bed, legs splayed to accommodate Cal's long, skinny pecker. Or that pecker poking down into Stephanie's throat, nuzzling her tonsils, pressing on her voice box. Or the pair of them screaming and heaving and straining the bed slats, coming at the same time. . . .

Rigid with new-found dismay, Tish switched the subject back to Cambodia.

Robin sighed and said she thought that's what she was really in love with, "crazy as it sounds. I see it as a sick child, a dying child, and I want so much to 'save' it. I can't remember ever wanting anything as bad as this, except maybe to stop drinking. And Cal's the one who brought that to me, see. But Larry's the one who could make it happen. So it's all—terribly mixed up in my head. But it won't get unmixed by us getting booted out by Talbott, so soon. . . ."

Tish said wryly, "Count your blessings, kiddo."

CHAPTER FIFTY-EIGHT /

March 28th

Robin

Latest news from Stephanie's grapevine: Two letter bombs addressed to Larry were sniffed out by the dogs working the mailroom. Distressed, dismayed, Robin thought, *That must explain his foul mood at breakfast.* . . .

Stephanie joked cheerfully that the mailroom pooches at least earned their keep better than Kilkenny. Robin didn't care much for that crack, didn't like having those hawk eyes boring in when she got news like that. She said curtly that she'd come downstairs to sign the outgoing mail, but after that she wanted free time to "go do a few personal things."

Stephanie smiled at her sweatsuit, chuckled, "Can't imagine what. Maybe a dogtrot through Wonderland?"

She couldn't even take a run without Mayo a few steps ahead of her. She snapped, "Steph, don't try to make a living at stand-up comedy. You're excused, thanks very much."

Lotus-tucked on her office chair, Robin signed the stack of letters, wondering if whoever sent those bombs had any idea how long ago Larry'd stopped opening his mail. But maybe they'd settle for a clerk's eyeballs, a secretary's hands. . . .

Jim knocked and stuck his head in, saying this wasn't such a good day for a run if she didn't mind putting it off. She peered at the cloudless sky. "Sure it is. They don't come any better. Get the lead out, Jim, we've—"

He meant *would* she please shelve it for today, there was a bit of a dust-up out there. Seeing the worry on his face, she flashed Larry, bloody, shattered. "Oh god, did something happen to my husband?"

He said no no, the President was fine and dandy, just an incident at the gate he wanted her kept clear of it. Butterflies leaping, she asked what he meant by "dust-up." He said nothing she had to worry about. She waved him angrily out, got Stephanie on the horn and asked her to please find out what the hell was going on at the gate.

Scribbling on, thoughts jumpy as her pen. *So what, extra workroom time. . . he said Larry's okay. . . Therebutforthegraceofgod. . . not the kids or they'd tell me. . . .*

Stephanie brought in a VCR cartridge, "raw footage from a Channel 7 crew out prowling for local color." On-screen the front sidewalk of the White House, pickets in scraggly lines, signs like NO GO, HANOI LARRY; WE WON THAT WAR ONCE, DON'T START IT AGAIN; and scrawled in day-glo across a 6-foot plywood crucifix: JESUS LOVES THE PEACEMAKERS!

A yellow cab lurched onto the sidewalk by a gate. A young Oriental man jumped out and kissed the fence, kneeling, shrieking something. Two women, one young, one old, and four kids piled out to kiss the gate, guards shouting that they couldn't park there. The young guy said excitedly, "Hello, America. Hello, United States. This is Choun Sem from Kampuchea, come with my family to say hello at the White House of U.S. President. I am very happy to thank you America for bring us to this great country."

Somebody asked what he was doing here. He said after his first week on his first American job, driving a cab in Kansas City, the boss lent him the taxi to drive to D.C., to "say hello and thank you, from my heart to America, for save my family from life like hell, give us chance to start again and be soon Americans too."

A marcher boomed out, "Brother, welcome to freedom and the Capital of the Free World!" and hugged him. The lady with the day-glo cross chirped, "Lord be praised, seven more lambs are saved. Welcome and god bless!" Suddenly a human chain passed the family along the fence, most hugging, some weeping. Even the old mother cried and embraced total strangers.

When the tape ran out, Robin realized the hairs on her arm were standing on end. She looked blankly at Stephanie. "Good lord. Would you care to translate that?"

"Probably Chapter One of something-or-other. Just don't ask me what. But for your information, it's got two names already—the Fence and the DMZ. Care to vote your pick?"

CHAPTER FIFTY-NINE /

April 10th

Robin

Passing a hall mirror, Robin muttered, "Oh god, I look like Howdy Doody. And she'll look like two million bucks. Have I got time to run up and change?" Stephanie said no, and anyway she looked smashing, as usual.

"Ah, sure. 'Smashing' as in wrecked," she whined. "Who got the bright idea for this hoedown, anyway?"

Stephanie shut her up with, "You, and I must say it was one of the better ones you've come up with lately."

A few minutes later she strolled down the Diplomatic Entrance steps, smiling for the thousand cameras: "Hello, Alexis. Welcome back to the old homestead."

Alexis offered her cheek, looking like a *Vogue* cover in a red twill coat. Ignoring the shouts, they chatted for a few archly self-conscious moments: "Big treat for the whole house. . . ." "Quite thrilled to be back. . . ." She always felt like a bumpkin next to her swanlike in-law, who managed to look gracefully relaxed even in a buzz of paparazzi.

Finally they headed up the steps, ignoring "One more! Just one more!"

The upstairs staff lined up like an honor guard to welcome "Mrs. Alexis," Hamilton swooning with excitement, even unflappable Carmen somewhat agog. Alexis greeted them warmly, remembering names, even some of the children's names. She asked if Hamilton's son still ran that Christmas-tree nursery, if Ginette still collected stamps for her nephew. Complimented Portman on "that handsome mustache, so much like your father's." All told, an impressive performance—after almost twenty years, frosty Alexis still knew more about the servants' personal lives than Robin did.

Hamilton ushered them to the Oval Room. "Chablis for Mrs. Alexis, Perrier for Mrs. Robin?" Finally they were left alone, on facing couches by the fire. Alexis's eyes flicked around the room, dusting off every detail. She sighed, a rueful smile. "Oh, it's good to be back at the dear old barn."

Brief dip into kids, in-laws and so on. Alexis said Robin seemed to've adjusted rather well to "the gilded fishbowl life, all things considered. You're quite a hit at it, too."

She was shaking her head in reflex denial when she realized with a jolt, *but that's true. . . .*

Alexis hadn't been too thrilled about this whole visit. She came out of morbid curiosity, to revisit the scene of her happiest times with Michael. But that also meant reviving the nightmare of those final days. And confronting the reality of Little Miss Swann perched in the catbird seat Alexis used to consider her exclusive property.

Lord knows she wished her well. Alexis hadn't forgotten what the poor girl was up against. But seeing her smugly ensconced in the lovely old "round room," as Shelley used to call it, Alexis felt a bite of begrudging envy.

You could scarcely say Robin belonged here at all. She'd run out on Laurence for that hippie nest in Manhattan, and only came back to piggyback his freak success for a free White House ride. Yet now she'd become quite a *succès fou* in her own right, for reasons that somewhat escaped Alexis. Must have something to do with a fickle public lapping up the old phoenix myth, fallen woman rising from the ashes. . . .

Whatever it was, you could hardly turn around these days without running into Robin this or Robin that. What a gargle Michael would've had about that. . . or Willie, the randy old patriarch. First time he met her, Michael had described her as "a flame-head sexpot," and he probably went on thinking of her that way too. Not that Michael ever objected to sexpots, of course. One tricky aspect of this return to the scene was how it stirred up memories of Michael's various romps under this roof. At the time, she'd managed to avoid or deny most of the clues, for want of a better way to handle them. But years later, she discovered she'd only been ignoring the tip of the iceberg.

She was still pissed off with him for that. But so many other problems they had seemed to've melted away after they moved in here. He'd somehow had more time for family. It seemed as if they were building a real marriage, a real partnership. Bowled over by the happiness that had sprung up between them, she'd gloried in that time when they "had it all."

Now Robin was squatting on the golden roost—with a what-am-I-doing-here sort of glaze to her expression. Alexis realized this little tête-à-tête was probably a bit sticky from her end too. She'd caught Robin's green-eyed glances over the servants' effusive welcome.

Groping for safe middle ground, they fell into talk about the bizarre phenomenon going on out there at the Fence. That gesture of kissing the White House gate seemed to've become the new rite of passage for newcomers to the States, especially from southeast Asia. They came four and five a day now, always raw with emotion, welcomed by the marchers—and reporters—in that ongoing carnival.

Alexis said she was particularly struck by the stories the refugees told. "They're repetitive, certainly, but so powerful and distinct. I find myself hanging on every word. Somehow having all this unroll in front of the old house. . . ."

Robin agreed it helped to bring the message home. She'd heard that remarkably diverse crowd in Lafayette Square now included conscientious objectors back from Canada and Sweden, former black marketeers, ex-bar girls from Saigon. . . .

Alexis wondered if that didn't make her a bit nervous, so much constant to-do right at the gates. Robin said no, the crowd was organizing and policing itself very well. She never felt safer than when she was jogging past the rabidly hospitable Vietvets along the back fence.

Alexis noted with a sigh that in *her* time a variety of old characters hung around out there too, mostly anti-Bombers. "But I must say your bunch puts on a much better show." In a generous burst she added, "And I give you some of the credit for that. That charming bit you did with the little ballet dancers in the Red Room brought a fresh breath to the whole Cambodia issue. I personally think that had a lot to do with the Fence story taking off like it did."

Robin was stunned, tongue-tied by that verbal bouquet—the first real compliment she could remember from Alexis. She mumbled about "mainly the luck of the timing. I mean, having something going on that I really wanted to get into. . . ."

Timing impeccable, Hamilton interrupted with the drinks. When he left, Robin got up to retrieve the gift on the mantlepiece. "Speaking of Cambodia and the initiative, here's a small token to remind you of this nostalgia trip."

Alexis lit up. Always a great one for presents, she unpeeled the scrapbook filled with 8-by-10s of her trip to the Angkor Wat temples, four years after Michael had died.

Robin cut into her exclamations. "It turns out our old friend Cal Farragut covered that trip for *Life*. He found these in his files when he was digging out material on Cambodia." Alexis seemed deaf, absorbed in the pics. "If it's okay with you, we'd like to release some through the East Wing office. We're pulling out every stop we can think of to help plug the initiative."

Alexis said of course, she'd be delighted to help out. Glowing, chuckling over herself with Prince Oudong: "Will you *look* at that skirt! I can't believe I ever wore anything that short." She said solemnly how sad it was to think what had happened there. "Just look at those incredible temples. The magnificent carvings—and I suppose they're all in ruins now, like everything else."

Robin said Angkor Wat was fairly undamaged, "compared to the rest. That's not saying much, of course."

Alexis closed the book, stroked it, said how terribly proud she was of Laurence to've taken on this peace plan. "Sure, you can release the pics. Anything else I can do, please let me know." She was especially thrilled to have these photos taken by the man who made "that unforgettable film. I happened to see it last week on Paris TV, and it was a *huge* hit over there."

Thawed by that bolt, Robin in a burst of empathy thanked her for "all the help you've been since I landed here. The calls were such a boost. All that good advice."

Fingering her pleats, Alexis thought she probably hadn't been much help at all, "but I certainly do have some idea of what you've been going through."

Sour smile: "Ah, yes. I guess nobody knows it better than you, Alex." Remembering when she married Larry, floundering through her cold-turkey initiation into the ferocious Devlin clan. Never did like swimming in rough surf, and in that family it was high water around the clock. She'd ached then for a helping hand, but the last place she'd've looked for it was from Alexis the Ice Queen.

Now she surprised herself by wishing out loud they'd started talking years ago. "You probably understood better than anybody else what was going on with me. After all, you're the family's other female interloper." She paused. "I don't count Cecily, she's so much like one of them."

A smile twitched the rosebud mouth. "Ah, yes. I always considered Cecily an honorary Devlin, too."

Anyway, she did kick herself now for "not trying harder to get through to you. You knew what a lunatic family we'd married into, and some of that stuff got me sidetracked for years. Looking back, I think you're the one who might've helped me sort out some of the family stuff, pressures, whatever I was making such a mess of."

"Robin, are you suggesting the family was why you drank?"

Blink of surprise. "Lord, no. It's just part of the package I wish I'd handled a whole lot better." She plunged nervously on. "I've just realized lately how little you were in the picture for me then. And in retrospect, I was awfully gutless not to've made more effort to break through."

Looking distinctly uncomfortable with this conversational drift, Alexis murmured, "Well, you're certainly making up for lost time. I must say you're doing frightfully well at this job. I've been so pleased to see that."

She blurted, "Thanks, but I wish you didn't sound quite so. . . surprised." Alexis popped an indignant frown. "Oh, excuse that last crack, Alex. The fact is everything happened with so little warning, I was overwhelmed and paralyzed for the first few weeks. But once I got the hang of it—well, you know. It isn't such an awful job, after all."

Alexis crossed her legs, tiny smile tugging at her mouth. "Mm-hmm. You've discovered that, have you?"

"Alex, I'm beginning to appreciate what you've put up with all these years! Since we inherited the same ridiculous job—look, it helps to be able to touch down with someone who really knows the ropes. And thanks for being there."

Quiet protest that no thanks were in order. "But I'm glad we've gotten past ancient history, at least, Robin." Alexis set down her glass, glancing at the marble mantlepiece. "Oh, I see you're still using those lovely Princess Elizabeth candelabra. She gave them to the Trumans in '51, you know, on a state visit the year before she became queen. . . ."

Translation: *Case closed, off my back, tootsie.*

Smarting from that rebuff, Robin felt her ugly-duckling bloom. *So much for kicking open locked doors. . . .*

☆

Over lunch in the family dining room, Alexis relaxed into diverting yarns about how she acquired "that rather militant wallpaper," and tidbits on Fletcher and the downstairs staff. As Hamilton urged a second serving of veal cutlets, clucking like a mother hen, Larry suddenly burst in, booming, "Who's this I hear came by for chow?"

"Laurence, dear!" Alexis floated gracefully up from the table, into his open arms. Robin watched the flirty body language of the greeting, so much warmer than the ritual words: "So dear of you to pop by. . . ." "Looking good as ever, Alex."

When she and Larry had gotten engaged, part of his argument to talk her into bed was family tradition: Michael and Alexis had done it. Even Stephen and Cecily, both more Catholic than the Pope. Robin told him she had trouble imagining Alexis doing it anywhichway, even married. Larry just laughed.

From a distance, she'd always found Alexis about as sexy as an ironing board, but that was before she saw how Alex could turn on the juice for a male fitting her need of the moment. Obviously her sort of chilly class could be catnip to men. Especially one with a bent for getting down and dirty himself—one like Larry.

It used to send Robin straight into tailspins, seeing them together like this. Their special closeness, so transparent, came from all they'd been through together, so many painful times she didn't—couldn't—share. She saw now that it had mainly troubled her because it defined one more part of this man she couldn't touch.

Even so, just a little, she felt the knife. Yet in her good-Scout mood, she called cheerily across the room, "For lord's sake, where's Bing when we really need him? This one's a must for the family album."

Larry said he'd do better than that if they'd "come put a match to some dry tinder downstairs," Eric Lowenthal briefing the blue-ribbon commission on the Vietnam initiative.

Alexis purred, "Laurence, I'm thrilled to be asked."

So they trotted down to the Roosevelt Room, where Robin noted

Congressman Joe McGrath, pop-eyed as the rest at this interruption. *Score one for Peggy and the Pennsy vets.* . . . She and Alexis each spoke a brief piece, rah rah for the initiative. Then Bing photographed the commissioners with the reigning Devlin stars.

As Bing went on clacking off more candid shots, Robin shrank away, yielding center stage to the family's paramount show-stealer. But Alexis came up and slipped an arm around her, murmuring, "I really do think you're spunky and terrific, you know. Even if I don't often show it. Now come on, let's do one we can autograph for each other."

She laughed and said okay, that was a deal. "Let's do one for the Fence." Hugging, heads bent together, they turned on their two-million-dollar smiles for Bing's lens.

CHAPTER SIXTY /

April 14th

Prilla

"Things We're Forgetting" was a long list in Priscilla's head right now. Mostly golden rules Dan had used in his rocket climb to the top, that were getting trampled under in the panic over this vote.

Right at the top, number one, was *control the media agenda!* Yet ever since Devlin had launched his Vietnam diversion, the media ball was mostly in his court. First that maudlin gush out of Asia, country-of-the-month on TV. Now this ludicrous flap at the White House fence, night after night of refugees with the same sob story—all told in bad English.

Chet said some who turned up for their spin in the lights were actually former prostitutes or black-market kingpins, not that anyone seemed to care. A few of the scruffy peacenik vets were even getting themselves deliberately arrested. And they all got big play on the nightly news.

She finally convinced Dan it was time they got back on the offensive. Along with a new blitz on the House, he ordered up a rush-job half-hour TV special on Priscilla's antidrug campaign, to be financed by foundation contributions to "get around the FEC fine print."

Her initial forays on that campaign had played well in the media, except for one vicious syndicated column that asked if her qualifications as a spokesperson for the cause mainly sprang from the fact that her daughter Natalie had recently lived with a heavy-metal rock musician targeted in several drug investigations.

The concept of the show was to pull together various locations in Houston, Atlanta and New York for a national flavor. But Priscilla suggested a central focus on Fresh Start, the local treatment center she'd visited in Muncie, Indiana. That photogenic old Victorian house symbolized the traditional values they wanted to put across, and the kids wouldn't clutch up around the cameras.

As her motorcade arrived at the old house, she was boisterously cheered by the several dozen parents and children waiting on the lawn. Peter Franks, the bearded young housefather, said they were "so grateful for this recognition, and for the great honor you're doing us, Mrs. Sterling. . . ."

Cameras fired as she doled out handshakes. "Thanks so much for this fine welcome. Grand to be back!" The 15-year-old ex-hooker got a special hug. "Mimi dear, I'm so pleased to see you again!"

Inside the house Jon Hodgson, director of the ten-man L.A.-based production crew, sketched the action for her. "Fifteen minutes shooting with you and the children, and fifteen more with the parents upstairs. . . gives you plenty of leeway, since we'll edit that down to a few minutes each. . . ."

He asked if she'd gone over the script. She snapped, "Yes, of course." They weren't *all* amateurs he was dealing with here, after all.

Any ad-libbing would "generate a sense of authenticity if you can just roll with the punches, Mrs. Sterling," he said. "And we'll roll your closing spot on the telepromp—"

"Fine. Let's get on with it."

Waiting for her cue, she heard a lighting man crack, "Ready, set for 'All-Out Total War Against the Weed.' " She silenced him with a glare, making a mental note to have that wise guy fired.

The kids seemed a bit overrehearsed, rattling on about pot stashes, pills and poppers bought on the school bus with riflings from their mother's purse. Somehow the horror stories didn't move her quite so much this time around.

Upstairs, ten parents poured out profuse thanks for her support. Priscilla said, "I'm only here to listen and learn. But I'm so impressed with your children's progress against this dreadful epidemic crippling so many of our youth."

"Epidemic, yes," said a fat woman introduced as Mimi's mother, Thelma Semple. "Progress? I'm not so sure."

Her radar flashed red alert: *Watch out for that one!* She said she was especially anxious to learn from the parents who'd "been through it," to help mobilize the family—the heart of our society—against that tragic scourge.

"I dunno about that," the Semple woman retorted. "But I do know those kids can break your heart, bust your bankroll and peace of mind till you wish they weren't ever born."

In what one father called "our regrettably expert testimony," intense vignettes of anguish and resolve, Priscilla was moved by their bewilderment. " 'Cause there's just nobody there to help you with a kid hell-bent on this kind of trouble," said one man.

"Which was why we finally got together this group, support system, whatever you call it," Mrs. Semple added. "So we could throw a rope to other families in the same fix."

When the fifteen-minute taping was over, the press aide alerted her to a call from Dan. She rushed to a private phone. "Danny? What's up, is anything wrong?"

Not hardly, he said cheerily. "Just wanted to let you know we're getting another roll. This afternoon, I guess."

She beamed. "Oh my gosh. Who is it?"

"Somebody pretty close to your neighborhood right now."

She flipped possibilities like Rolodex cards. Did he mean Indiana? "Lincoln Sheppard?"

"Mm-hmm. Good guess."

"Well, for heaven's sake." Why hadn't she heard about *that* one from Chet? "Is he making a speech?"

"Yep. Around three, D.C. time. You'll still be out there, so batten your hatches and hurry on home, Mommie."

For her closing remarks, Hodgson wanted her sitting under the unusual archway, with the children positioned in the room behind her. Settling into the chair, she realized what was wrong with this setup: The parents were lined up on the stair railing, gawking right down at her. She thought of having them moved out. Instead, she pushed aside her irritation, twiddling a wave to them as Hodgson cued the cameras.

Indiana! That's five down, four to go. . . .

For once the teleprompter worked right. She reeled off the chilling statistics, the anecdotes to point up "the gravity of this critical threat to our generation of tomorrow. But help *is* available, right in your own community."

Her skim of the programs emphasized parent-sponsored local initiatives "like this remarkable volunteer group you've just seen here. So please remember, if you need help yourself, or if you want to help others who are fighting so valiantly to wipe out this critical threat to the young Americans who represent our country's future, just write to me, Mrs. Daniel Sterling, Box 2000, Washington, D.C., 20050. And I promise each letter will be personally answered. Thank you, and God bless you all."

Hodgson asked for another take, since she'd transposed two figures. She nodded grimly, determined to get it perfect. And this time she did, adding a kiss blown spontaneously from her fingertips. "Cut! That's a wrap. Beautiful job, Mrs. Sterling," Hodgson said happily.

In the congratulatory stir, the Semple woman said loudly from the stairs, "I thought it was *us* she was supposed to be helping. Not herself."

The original game plan had scheduled a ten-minute photo session for the waiting media, but she ordered that scratched. Last thing she needed now was the press getting wind of that woman, especially with Indiana due to roll any minute.

As she left the house, she knew from the shouted questions the word wasn't out yet. *Thank goodness for that.* . . .

☆

En route to the plane, an agent relayed the wire-service flash on Sheppard's roll. As her aide babbled, "Now there's a coincidence! Great news for the Governor," she frowned over her notepad, jotting down the points to hit in her airport statement. This time around she'd get to play Dan's part.

They swarmed all over her as she stepped from the car. She said she was "especially pleased to be visiting the great state of Indiana on the day when Congressman Lincoln Sheppard made his courageous move to restore leadership and constitutional government to this country. . . ."

The flight home took forever. When the cars got to the house she ran inside. Someone pointed her to Dan's den.

"Pril, there you are!" He jumped up from behind his desk. "Didn't hear you come in."

Chet was in there too, looking. . . like he'd just had a trip to the woodshed. Dan gave her a welcoming hug. She kissed him and asked, "So what's up?"

Dan said Sheppard had rolled right on schedule. "But when I saw him later, I thought, by gosh, that fellow sure looks nervous. Pretty unhappy for a man who's just seen the light and voted to 'put this country back on the track.' " Scathing sarcasm in his tone. "So I asked our House vote coordinator what was going on. You want to tell her, Chet?"

Picking his words with miserable caution, Chet talked about "some misguided, overly zealous parties" who'd apparently "taken it upon themselves to help bring about the Governor's election, which they sincerely believed to be in—"

Harshly: "Can it, Chet. Just get down to the tapes."

Ah, sure. Of course. . . .

Chet said Dan was referring to videotapes of Sheppard involved in "compromising situations with a young lady lobbyist for the milk industry." She avoided Chet's eyes, watching Dan's steamy reaction. "Now, anyone working on the Governor's campaign is well acquainted with his strong, uncompromising stand on matters like this. But apparently—"

"In other words, Chet's trying to lay this on the milk fellows. He says *they* got the tapes to Sheppard, and let him know what it would take to keep 'em from going public. Or going to his wife."

Well, good for them. . . . Dan raved and ranted, said he'd nail Chet's hide to the barn door if this happened again. "I told you, Chet, I don't want any job bad enough to stoop to guttersnipe shenanigans. . . ."

Trying to cool him off, she said those milk people probably meant well and good. "Sheppard should've thought ahead before he played his dirty games with—didn't you say there was a hot tub involved, Chet?"

No he didn't! Heart bounding. . . .

But Dan didn't catch her slip. He stewed away, in a mood to lecture for half the night. Finally she said, "Sweetie, I know how important this is to you. But I've just come home from a long, hard trip, and I'd like to spend a little time alone with my husband."

He wound down with a last warning. "One more stunt like this and you're off the team. You hear me, Chet?"

"Yes, sir. Loud and clear, Governor." The ringing phone finally got Chet off the hook. As he left the den, he threw her an odd, pointed look. Dan was chuckling, "Well, don't rest on your laurels, Frank. Keep those votes coming. . . ."

She saw Chet waiting in the hall, looking back inquiringly at her. While Dan was tied up on that call she reluctantly slipped out, dreading what Chet might say. But his terse message had nothing to do with the damn videotape. She thought at first she must've heard wrong, so he repeated it.

Dan came to find her in their bedroom, still muttering about "that look on Lincoln Sheppard's face. By gosh, I'm as shamed as he is by this whole business."

She said briskly, "Well, never mind that. Let's just make sure his vote stays put, Danny—because now it's five down, only four to go. Honey, we're finally over the hump!"

She coaxed him into a nap before dinner, then slipped back to the den and phoned the Brentwood house. With chill fury: "Male strippers? You actually signed your name to a filthy, pornographic movie about male strippers?"

Natalie said it wasn't porno, it was prime-time TV. "Anyway I play a nice girl, kind of a talent scout."

"I don't want your feeble excuses, young lady. What I want to hear is that you're resigning from this horrendous project *right now*."

She couldn't pull out, the contracts were signed. "Besides, this could be a big chance for me. I'm practically 28 years old, I have a right to my own career. You're not going to run my life, Mother, much as you'd like to."

"Oh, so now you plan to make a 'career' out of this? Disgracing your family, mortifying your poor father, feeding ammunition to his enemies?"

They argued bitterly for a few minutes, pangs searing Priscilla's tummy. Finally she said curtly, "We'll talk about this later, Natalie, when you've had a chance to think it over. And realize how much harm you could do to your father with this kind of filthy, pornographic blackmail, dragging his name in the dirt like a common guttersnipe. . . ."

"Hey, wait a minute! It's got nothing to do with blackmail—or with him. It's just my first shot at a movie that's actually going to be made. That's the way you and Daddy got started, after all—taking what you could get."

Hissed: "It seems to me, young lady, you could at least have the decency to wait until this election is over before you go jeopardizing everything with your tawdry schemes." Suddenly she heard the rage choking her voice, felt it burning her chest. Shaken, abrupt: "All right, Natalie, you take some time to reconsider this foolish, destructive, self-centered behavior. And I won't say anything about it to your father until you've thought out what you're doing to him."

She hung up with a sense of smothering dread. *Oh god, will it ever be over. . .*

CHAPTER SIXTY-ONE /
April 24th and 25th
Robin

When the President decided his initiative was "buried in gas" and invited Prince Oudong for an "unofficial" lobbying visit, Stephanie atoned for her *lése-majesté* opinions of the royal couple by working up a backgrounder memo on them that read like an Asian version of *War and Peace*.

From her war-reporter days she remembered Princess Jeanne's reputation among the foreign correspondents for owning half of Phnom Penh, plus a healthy chunk of the war blackmarket which she shared with Oudong's ministers and generals. Her Western-style good looks came from her French-Corsican father and mostly Vietnamese mother. At Cal's weekly dinners, she and her mother had once been coelected War Profiteer of the Year. Then after the prince's overthrow she'd been propagandized as 'Oudong's Vietnamese whore,' her face superimposed on photos of a naked Western woman.

At that time Cal had predicted Jeanne would soon dump the royal has-been and have a long, happy life screwing movie stars on the French Riviera. But the White House files detailed what had come instead: exile, house arrest and constant jeopardy, shared with her husband. Oudong lost four children and fifteen grandchildren in "the terror"; Jeanne lost much of her family too, but stuck by him, then and since.

Stephanie was contritely struck by the bond between them, so different from the tenuous connection between herself and Cal. Since the night she'd taken him home to dinner and bed, where he put in a brisk if detached performance, he was turning up three or four times a week. "Kind of a steady date," her daughter Becky put it. But their talk was mostly political, including shouting matches on "that rat Oudong"; it rarely verged on anything she'd consider personal. He wouldn't talk about those kids in his film, or the nightmares that sometimes left him moaning and weeping in his sleep.

Oddly enough, they never talked about the Devlins either. She who'd always leaped feet first with any nosy question found herself reluctant to ask Cal about Larry and Robin, as if she might dissolve any fragile link between them by exposing it to glaring limelight. What she *really* wanted to know now was whether she and Cal could weave together any sort of bond from the strong, ragged strands of what they'd shared over there.

If she'd wanted only wham-bam sex, there were other men whose bedroom style she actually preferred. But she wanted his head to be there too. Maybe a bit of his heart, if he had any left. She couldn't tell yet.

Ten or fifteen years ago she'd've given up on him by now, moved on to the next body in line. But she had more patience now. . . or maybe just less zip. Anyway she was still hanging in, trying to muddle through. Laying the standoff to his trauma over Cambodia, hoping one night the dam might break and she might touch something live in him.

It helped now, when she was most impatient with him, to think of Jeanne, who'd stuck by her guy through horrors inconceivable to Stephanie. She wondered if, in their rootless wanderings through three continents, Oudong ever had those screaming dreams. If he'd sealed up huge chunks of *his* memory like a stinking crypt. . . .

But of course Jeanne was there with him, through the worst of it. Stephanie'd never in her life come through like that for a man, even her ex-husband. She doubted she was about to start now. But thoughts of Jeanne, so loyal and gutsy in remarkable travails, gave her pause.

When the royals turned up for their low-key greeting ceremony—indoors with Bing's cameras, no press horde—Stephanie's first impression was how eerily unchanged Jeanne was from photos of her whirlwind decades by his side.

The aging little ex-king was still round as Humpty Dumpty, warmly effusive, high-pitched voice somehow matching his darting, talkative hands. But the Mona Lisa wife shadowing him with regal silence was serene, majestic. . . thoroughly intimidating. Robin might find this a rather rough go.

Agog with curiosity, Stephanie managed to stick around for the Blue Room tea pouring. Robin was armored in the jewelry they'd given her. Tickled to see her wearing his gold medal, Oudong said so at eloquent length. Jeanne peered at the silver bracelets and murmured coolly, "They are graced by the one who wears them, Madame." ·

Robin rolled her eyes at Stephanie in a mute appeal for bailout. Rough go, all right.

Robin was boggled at the prospect of making two days' worth of wifey-type conversation with this tower of silence. She felt tongue-tied around her, paralyzed at the whole idea of spinning chitchat from the nightmarish raw material in Stephanie's memo.

Fortunately, Jeanne chose to stick with her husband on his rounds of the Hill committees and TV news shows. The West Wing consensus was that he did as well as they'd hoped—especially helpful since Vietnam, reacting to the increasingly iffy prospects, had cut off press visas. So Larry invited the royals to Camp David for a postconference strategy weekend. *As if it's all going to happen.* . . .

Before the chopper ride on Friday afternoon, Oudong shyly confided "a personal wish" to Robin. He wondered if he might visit "that jolly gathering" outside the fence.

Seizing this as the best excuse to get herself over there too, Robin challenged Jim to rise to the occasion. "If Pol Pot didn't do him in, the Fence won't either." An hour later, inside an edgy ring of agents, she and the royals slipped out the side exit to join the march.

The extraordinariness of it filtered instantly through her crust of guards. She felt a kind of enveloping, benevolent calm, the famous "protective aura." Knots of people milled in the street by the Treasury, talking, arguing, the feel in the air like a county fair.

They rounded the corner, riding the slipstream, smiling at the marchers passing in reverse flow. Posters reflected her Big Pecker revisionist theory of history: "WE ALREADY WON THAT WAR, HANOI LARRY!" "AMERICA KEEPS THE WORLD FREE." But somehow they seemed less obnoxious close up.

She showed Oudong and Jeanne the left-hand gate where Cambodians still came to touch the fence for blessing. A bystander crowed, "We had six arrivals so far today. You wanna try for seven, Prince?" Oudong laughed and patted a rail.

While agents held up the traffic, they popped over to Lafayette Square. Reveling in the rare hookey-playing, Robin remembered a line from Faulkner about "the short walk from the hallelujah to the hoot."

They ran into a double greeting squad of Fence Vets and Fence Kids, the vets with red bandannas on their arms, the kids with variations of green scarves. One of each peeled off as their "personal guides to the waxworks." Robin's were Mac Olsen, "kind of a maitre d' around here," a tall, spruce ex-Marine who walked with a limp, crucifix over his khakis, and Geneva, a 14-year-old elf in white boots, electric-blue jumpsuit and spikey blonde hair, a purple-and-green bow on her arm.

Robin was knocked out by the diversity of the organized chaos. On a platform under Lafayette's statue, a bearded guy in camouflage fatigues lectured on Agent Orange effects. Under Rochambeau a dainty Asian-looking woman in a pin-striped suit talked about being "sold" from her native village at age 13 to work the Saigon bars. Back under Von Steuben, a guy in blue jeans and a Dallas Cowboys sweatshirt wanted to arm a counterrevolutionary militia to "drive the Commies back out of Indochina." The crowd heckled a little; periodically a cowbell clanged a change of speakers.

A shaggy guy in old khakis, bent with grief, weeping, was embraced by two fellow vets urging let it out, bro, you made it back, now let it go. Mac said this "tripwire vet" had been living in heavily defended isolation in an Oregon rain forest, "still fighting his own war. The Fence brought him in. It brings a lot of 'em in."

Geneva said the vets "mostly did policing. The kids are more into stuff like helping people out." She pointed out a half-dozen kids warily circling each other. "There's Tina and Raymond with some stepkids who just met, getting it together."

One seemed part-Asian. Geneva explained that through the Fence his real father had found the kid, who'd been adopted years before, "so now the whole family's finally met up, at least." Her voice leaked pride and satisfaction in that, the Fence Kids deftly facilitating an osmotic linkup, communicating in a wordless language only other kids understood.

Mac pointed out the trees and lampposts where posted messages aimed to reunite families and army buddies. From a sea of cards and photos, Robin focused on a Polaroid of a toothy, grinning, black-haired kid with note attached: "Dave (also name Speedo) from Iowa, 2nd Battalion, 5th Cav April '69 in Danang, here's your son Tommy lives in Enid, Oklahoma." She began to understand that along with an on-going debate over the usefulness of war as a political instrument, this amazing brew was coalescing a healing of the social fabric ruptured by that war.

Robin asked Geneva what had brought her to the Fence. She said she'd wanted to learn about why her father died eight months after she was born. "When I was a kid, see, I always figured it wouldn'ta been so rough if he'd been around. So I came here to find out why he wasn't."

What Geneva found instead was a community. "Like Tina, she's 13, her dad killed himself when she was 5, years after he got back from Nam. Raymond's dad died before he was born, and his stepdad got a drug habit in the war." She said matter-of-factly they found they were good at helping others like the vets "because we know a lot about desperation."

And survival, you amazing little street rat. As the gutsy urchin twitched proudly at her purple-striped armband, cup-sized earrings dangling in the wind, it was all Robin could do not to pick her right up and smuggle her home.

The sight of an elderly Cambodian prostrating herself before Oudong reminded Robin that the prince had been a Sun-King of sorts in his time—although she also heard a young girl with the old woman ask who the little fat guy was.

One of the Fence Kids asked Jeanne where she lived. Jeanne said, "Mostly in China and North Korea. How about you?" The girl said she used to live in an abandoned hotel in Buffalo, but now she lived mostly in a van parked down by the river. Jeanne nodded, saying serenely she guessed it helped to have someplace to go when it rained.

Robin suddenly decided she wasn't the least bit intimidated by that woman after all.

☆

Next day, while the makers and shakers conferred, the two women strolled in the Camp David woods, talking easily now like vets of the same campaign, one pacing royally in ankle-length sarong and silk padded jacket, one scuffing along in jeans and Irish sweater.

The princess peered at the towering pines, remarking on how fortunate Robin was to have such a peaceful place to come to. Did she come here often?

"Not as often as I'd like," she murmured. "But it does have special memories for me." *There but for. . . .*

Jeanne said the scenery resembled Cambodia's Cardamom Mountains, "where we had a small vacation house. I cannot recall now—is it possible you visited us there?" No, but Jeanne had her to tea in the "golden, quite magical" palace.

Jeanne shivered, saying ah, yes. They'd actually lived then in a smaller house, but in many ways her favorite was their mountain home. "Just a 'bungalow,' I believe you call it, two bedrooms, quite American in style, with a little kitchen where I sometimes cooked for my husband and myself." Shy glance. "It may seem strange to you, Mrs. Devlin, that I would take pleasure in that. But some memories I treasure most are those weekends in our little mountain home."

Robin said in that case she was especially glad they were able to visit here, blurting, "Your presence does great honor to this place, Princess Jeanne."

Jeanne softly thanked her for her graciousness. "But it is we who are honored, by the courageous efforts you and President Devlin make to retrieve a future for our country."

As they walked and talked in the odd intimacy that springs up between women at times like this, they touched on the usual wifey topics, kids and travels. Hard to top Jeanne in either department: one son a ballet dancer in France, the other studying in Moscow, stepchildren scattered literally around the globe. She mentioned that her husband's youngest child, Princess Viryanl, commuted between their home in Beijing and her own in southern California: "She has tried hard to improve our English, *mais hélas*."

As Robin protested, praising her fluency, she realized *some* of the prince's children, at least, were younger than Jeanne's. That's how she handled *her* playboy prince—with utter aplomb. Never turned a hair. Robin wished a bit of the knack had rubbed off on her years ago. Might've come in handy. . . .

Or might not, if the price of that peace was to treat your husband like an Asian king. She smiled at her guest, murmuring, "Madame, you make me understand so many things."

☆

That evening they threw a small soirée in the Laurel cabin for the major players, including Cal and Hale Wiley, back from a Phnom Penh "inspection tour" with fresh tales and burnished hopes. Alexis came as a "personal friend of Prince Oudong" to forestall any larger Devlin invasion, though nimble nephew Kevin tagged along as her escort.

In the inevitable toasts, Robin was most moved by the odd little ex-king, who saw "fulfillment of a dream I have carried so long in my heart, that men of good will will waken before the sands of time run through the glass, and commute the death sentence hanging over my suffering country. And now at last I begin to believe that this dream has a chance to become real—that Cambodia will spring to new flowering of life from the bloody roots of recent years."

Larry had graceful words of "welcome and commitment—to this great multinational effort to restore peace in an area where the futility of war as an instrument for resolving human differences has been so amply demonstrated. . . ."

The postdinner surprise was the guitar and electric piano trotted out by Oudong's aides-de-camp. Suddenly the irrepressible prince was warbling to "La Vie en Rose," passable Mel Torme imitation, gesturing for the rest to dance.

Larry ventured out with Princess Jeanne, Robin with Eric Lowenthal, followed by Alexis and Hale Wiley. Eric's old bones turned out to be remarkably spry as he whisked her around the floor, chuckling, "You know, my dear, I think we may be getting the hang of something here."

The music soared on the party mood. Odd pairings on the floor: gorgeous Kevin with 75-year-old Sara Lowenthal. Jeanne with a remarkably animated Cal. Larry with Stephanie, of all people, looking twinkly as his feet. Harley Richmond leaned over Robin's chair. "Fine party, my dear. Now if we could get my committee moving like this. . . ."

She chuckled, tweaked his tie. "Up and at 'em, Harley."

Suddenly Cal asked if she'd "like to take a spin." She tossed up a precautionary *there but for. . .* and joined him on the floor. So strange to feel that lanky body jigging briskly against her. He didn't dance well, but the surprise was that those long, gloomy bones danced at all.

She smiled as they maneuvered a turn, and said in a nostalgic burst, "You know, this is the first we've danced together since. . . Cambodia, at least."

"Yup, I guess." Skipped beat. Then a deep, warm chuckle. She echoed that, leaning back to catch his eye. But he was looking across the room, staring at. . . .

Stephanie, dancing with the prince. Cal laughed again. "Look at that, she's teaching the old thief to boogie. Damn, she never quits, does she?"

The vulnerable, flooded-open look riveted on Stephanie was a caress with his eyes. The kind she hadn't thought was in him. . . .

Ah, so!

She went on dancing, saying nothing. Feeling a twinge of loss, yet also peaceful and somehow eased. That strange, tangled skein of ties that somehow bound you to another body in that way, when you knew their touch. . . . didn't hold up well in the light of ridicule. Not for her, anyway. Not when he was carrying a torch for her hired help. As she felt it unraveling, she realized there'd never been much holding them together except shared sorrow. And an accident of twisted strands.

When the song ended, she plunged into playing hostess, pumping up the party mood. Reminding herself sternly, *this too will pass.* . . .

Midway through "C'est Si Bon," Oudong set down his mike, bowed to her, and crooned the rest of it as they waltzed around the floor. Blushing, entranced, she decided this was the most romantic thing that had ever happened to her.

At the finish he signaled a switch to a tinkling Oriental tune. Leading her by the hand, he linked up with Jeanne and Larry to begin a slow, stately Cambodian dance, a bit like a conga line. "Our traditional *ram vong*," he explained.

Like a flood it all came back, from that nightclub years ago—the simple steps, the graceful hand movements. Cal, Alexis and others joined in, stretching the chain. A moment later she looked down the line and saw the whole room hand in hand, faces alight—friends, family, strangers, allies, dancing out a celebration of hope.

☆

Hours later she slid abruptly from dreamless sleep, feeling washed ashore. She bolted up, heart drumming, eyes darting around the strange room.

Ah sure. Camp David. She rocked in the mussy sheets, patting her chest, calming her breath. Alarm ebbing, she caught the feeling that had tumbled her so suddenly to consciousness. *Moist. Warm. Hot.* . . . Hugging herself, she laughed softly, embracing that waking moonlit sensation, flowing into it.

God. She'd never in her whole life felt so horny.

All through her now like fire to her gut, like soft touch to her skin. She rolled her head, murmuring at this startled pleasure.

She groped her way to the john, shivered at the shock of cold seat on warm skin. Walked back to the bedroom without flushing, thinking groggily *don't wake Larry next door* as a gob of juice rolled out of her vagina.

Soft laugh, hefting the thought. *Cunt wiser than the queen.* . . . *Yes, go!*

Still she hesitated, rubbing her arms, shivering with desire. *Don't think. Go now!*

In the hallway she sniffed for guards. No sign. She opened the adjoining door, feeling eerily like she was stepping back into the magical hotel room in Phnom Penh under the lazy ceiling fans.

His turn to be sluiced from sleep. He rolled groggily onto an elbow, squinting at the door. "Wha'? Who's there?"

"Sssshhh. Be quiet," peeling the gown over her head.

He blinked, eyes still blind. "Rob? Is that you, Rob?"

She lifted off the bedcovers, like slipping under his mosquito netting. "You talk too much," she whispered fiercely. "Shut up for a while" as her warm body moved down to cover him, as her mouth closed over his like a fountain.

A sea.

CHAPTER SIXTY-TWO /

April 25th

Prilla

"That too much pressure, Mrs. Sterling?"

Face against the sheet, she mumbled, "No, no. Go hard as you can." Strong hands dug into her shoulders, hammered at her spine, kneaded her arms. She blocked her resisting pain. *Let go, let it all go. . . .*

The woman told her to roll over. Soothing hands stroked her shoulders, her neck, loosened her face. Softly: "Now I want you to just lie here and relax for a while, Mrs. Sterling. Let the good effects of the treatment sink in."

She murmured, "Thank you, Ingrid." The Valkyrie blonde slipped out of the cabana.

She drifted in a hazy languor, afterglow of the brusque handling. Lulling music on a tape, flutes sighing, chimes tinkling. *Feels so good. Let go, leave it all behind. . . .*

A distant clang of duty nudged her back. Sighing, stretching, she climbed off the massage table and wriggled into her suit. Outside by the 40-foot pool, Ginny waved a glass of iced tea. "Now, darling," she called out, "didn't I tell you Ingrid would fix you right up?"

Blinking despite the sunhat and shades, Priscilla took the frosty glass and stretched out on a padded lounge. "As usual, you're absolutely right. I feel almost reborn."

Finally they'd squeezed in a weekend stop at the Hibbings' fabulous Palm Springs spread. While the men were off playing "golf war," as Mort put it, Priscilla got sunbath-and-catch-up with Ginny, who was "just tickled pink you could finally come by, even just overnight. I'd almost given up talking you into it and here you are, popped down like a gift from the gods."

She chuckled. "Just goes to show, patience brings all things." Wry glance: "That's something I've been telling myself a lot lately."

Ginny said, "Yes, of course. And how's that awful Congress doing? I know Mort's very optimistic, but I'm still so *scandalized* by what they've been pulling. . . ."

Mort had pulled another fast one last week himself, offering the South Dakota Democrat's wife a fat job at Dan's biggest PAC. Phil said Mort sometimes just couldn't help himself, he wasn't used to being hog-tied and stymied like this. Phil wasn't used to it either, of course. And didn't intend to be, he told them right to their face: "We've been held up and hijacked by that crew for long enough, Dan."

God, how they wanted it, nobody more than herself. She'd always thought Phil could get anything he set his mind to. Yet this dragged on and on, Phil still as hog-tied as the rest of them. And Chet hadn't turned up anything worth two plugged nickels yet. The way things were going, sometimes she thought she'd have to peel off the gloves and get the job done herself.

Yet at the same time she was broken, seared by this endless ordeal. Terrified by those swarms they seemed to be living in the midst of— great buzzing crowds wherever they drove, walked, talked for that day's media takes. Loud, angry faces all around them, shouting through that fragile space she tried to seal around him and her, safe from all the snarling craziness out there.

If it went on much longer she'd snap apart like glass. A thousand things could go wrong, could finish them by tomorrow, tonight. And meanwhile, minor footnote, Mort was acting up again and Ginny as usual didn't know beans about it.

She groped for safe ground, veering onto how that ghastly Vietnam business had polarized the House. Stuck in its own mud, Dan said. Now all those demonstrations, practically riots in the streets, and that absurd circus at the Fence. . . .

Catching Ginny's dutiful glaze, like a warning blinker, she abruptly changed the subject. "Well, let's not waste our time on that. Tell me what's up with you and the girls."

Ginny said no, no, darling, she was terribly interested, really. "Of course we're all for peace—*anybody's* for peace, for heaven's sake—but I don't like the way that Devlin is setting himself up like a little Caesar."

"Well, exactly. Or a Nero, Dan calls him, fiddling while the country burns." She said Devlin was predictably playing this for all it was worth, so Dan's men had to hold the line in the committees, keep that bill from getting to the floor. Thank goodness they had a few southern Democrats who weren't about to get roped into giveaways to the Reds and didn't mind the free TV time either. "So overall Dan thinks we're in pretty good shape—at least we're halfway there."

More than halfway, Ginny corrected. "And I haven't a doubt in the world you're going to make it very, very soon."

She sighed, "Ah, let's hope," reaching wearily for the Bain de Soleil.

Ginny felt rather like a cheerleader flapping her pom-poms. Glad to have the chance to do it, naturally, after all the fooferaw Prilla'd been putting up with lately.

But this cheering business seemed to get a bit wearing lately. Just a tad boring, though of course she'd never let on a breath of that to Prilla. The same old lines over and over started to sound like a bad soap. Or the verging-on-white-lie you'd tell a child: When you wake up tomorrow the sun will be shining. Ginny'd noticed that the catchier news items lately, the ones that stuck in your mind, didn't seem to involve Prilla and Dan. . . but she found herself lapping up anything about the Devlin White House.

Prilla was touchy-touchy about that, of course, but Ginny'd had her fill of congressional talk. So she slid in a sly mention of the appalling gall Devlin had shown in trying to make "a regular royal visit over that weird little Cambodian prince. And that princess wife of his, who looks as Western as Dale Evans, for heaven's sake. . . ."

Sour-pickle mouth on Prilla. Ginny added hastily of course it was all so overblown about Oudong's exile, his boneyards, his murdered children and so on. Then last night his visit to the Fence, another fast one. She didn't say she couldn't keep her eyes off *that*.

Prilla slathered on lotion, saying curtly, "Fat lot of good that's done them. All that sob stuff hasn't make a dime's worth of difference in the committees."

She wanted Prilla to unload and get into the good stuff. She purred, "So darling, tell all. How's it going for you, *really*?"

Priscilla grimaced. "Well, it's pretty. . . tiring, actually. I've just about. . . ."

In the nick of time she remembered anything confided to Ginny went straight back to Mort. "Of course we're making very rapid, solid progress." Ginny never bothered with the grim details, thank god. "So we're keeping our chin up, but when I stop to think how we *should* be living now instead of still out of the suitcase, camped in the plane—well, sometimes I do get a teeny bit. . . discouraged."

"Well darling, you *mustn't*," Ginny insisted. "I know it's been harder than we bargained for, but Mort's absolutely sure the end of this folderol's right around the corner. You just wait till your fabulous Forum rally, that'll turn it right around, you'll see." Rattling on about that show. . . .

Which was already more headache than Priscilla could've imagined when she dreamed it up. Looking over the pool, giant shimmering aquamarine, she heard herself blurt, "Sometimes I feel I've aged ten years since last fall."

Instantly: "Prilla Sterling, that's absolute nonsense. Darling, you don't look a day over 40. In fact, you've hardly aged a week since we met."

She smiled gratefully. "That's a terrible lie, and you know it. But thanks anyway, dear."

"Well, I mean every word of it. You'll see, darling. With just a *little* more patience, it's going to turn out every bit as glorious as we thought."

Ruefully fingering her arm flab, Priscilla admitted, "Just between us, it doesn't get any easier, you know. Just—keeping it all together."

Confiding laugh. "Darling, isn't that true for us all. Gad, keeping up my looks is practically a full-time job. But I don't know *anyone* who does it better than you, Pril."

She could almost let herself believe it, in the healing glow of that massage. "Thanks, dear," she smiled. "But enough of me—what's happening with you?"

Burst of prattle about that good-for-nothing son of hers, "a regular lounge lizard Billy's turning out to be. . . ." On and on about Billy and his impossible wife, until she laughed, "Prilla darling, it's such a relief to see you. There's *nobody* I can talk to like this, you know."

She patted Ginny's arm, saying she felt just the same. "Speaking of kids, did I tell you the latest on Natalie?"

Ginny waved crossed fingers. "Not pregnant, I hope?"

"Worse, maybe. She showed up last night at a Stars Shine for the

Peace Initiative rally—in her time off from filming that ghastly TV movie."

Whispered: "The one about the boys who. . . ?"

"Mm-hmm. Of course we're glad she finally found something to keep her busy, but *this*. . . ." Ginny wanted to know if the men actually took off all their clothes.

"So I gather. Down to their G-strings, at least. In front of crowds of howling women."

Mutual suffering in their shared glance. Ginny murmured, "Darling, what *will* they think of next?"

Priscilla soothed more lotion over thighs already pink from the California blaze as they chatted about the Group: Suzy Laubert's latest war with her Japanese houseboy, who'd chopped down every rosebush on the place after he was "attacked by thorns." And Mindy Bradburger's gorgeous new silver Rolls. . . .

Ginny got around to the royal wedding. "Such an absolute *smash* it will be. Best fun ever, don't you think?"

Warily, feeling that tummy knot again: "Oh, for sure."

Ginny's acute radar picked up that slight hesitation. Sternly: "Pril, you *are* going to the wedding, of course?"

She said they hadn't decided. "Of course, it was dear of Raine to have us invited. Danny and I were thrilled."

"*Well*, then!"

She admitted she'd hate to miss that "marvelous, absolutely perfect wedding. But quite honestly, dear, with that awful House vote dragging on so, I don't see how we can plan on anything that far ahead."

Ginny hissed, "Darling, I know just what's bothering you. If Dan's president by then, of course, you'll be a *terribly* honored guest." For a moment Priscilla let herself slip back into the Let's-Pretend game. "As First Lady you'd rank practically right up there with the Queen. But even if that hasn't happened *yet*, Prilla dear, you're going to the wedding anyway, and that's that. I couldn't enjoy one bit of it without you there to share it. And I *will not* let you pass up such a glorious party just for that wretched Congress."

She sighed. "Well, we'll see. You're such a good pal. Whatever would I do without you?"

"Well, good! That's settled, then," Ginny said briskly. "And there'll be such a mob, I'm sure there's no chance we'd run into those Devlins, even if they were there."

When she got her breath back, Priscilla excused herself to take a dip, stretching a bathing cap over her head. *But Bernardo's coming soon.* . . . She tossed the cap aside and dove in, feeling the water unleash her hair, wishing she could stay down there forever.

That evening the Hibbings threw a marvelous, glittery party in honor of the visit, inviting all the Group and some of the stars lined up for the Forum rally. Ginny said Frank was horribly sorry he was out of town, but Bob had promised to drop by, and Wayne Newton was trying to fly in.

Priscilla worked the room so busily, at Dan's elbow, that she lost track of new arrivals. But as she chatted with Phil Laubert and Dodge Phelps, a big Nevada contributor, she sensed a prickly magnetic shift. *Star-alert.* . . .

Bingo: Bob Hope sailed in with a six-man entourage.

They hurried over with a warm greeting. Dan thanked him for agreeing to do the Forum rally. Bob said he was glad to help out. "It's about time some of us stood up to be counted on that shameful mess going on in the Congress. That's just what I was telling that army of reporters you've got camped out there, Dan." Thumb jerked toward the driveway.

Dan said that would help "light a few fires under those cushy Washington armchairs, and get the people's voice heard again." Someone in the crowd shouted hear, hear. "I always tell Prilla, one sure way to spot a good patriotic American cause is if Bob Hope comes aboard. And thanks to you and our other good friends, we'll get that message out across the country on May 15th."

Bob only stayed long enough for one quick drink, but promised them to "start letting the American people know what's really going on in this great country of ours."

Magnetic tug again when he left, slight shriveling of the room's excitement, like a punctured tire hissing air. Of course Dan was still here, in his way as big a star now as Bob. Almost. . . but not quite. Not yet. . . .

The Nevada lawyer told her heartily, "With Bob and Frank headlining the ticket, it'll be one crackerjack show, Mrs. Sterling. And I'm proud to say we're contributing a substantial amount to the overhead fund."

She purred, "Thank you so much, that's terribly generous of you, Mr. Phelps." She'd learned long ago that advance thanks often helped get the check in the mail.

Around ten she slipped off for a pit stop and makeup repair. It occurred to her that Bob actually seemed a bit jealous of the press-gang outside. He should sample the wild crowds hounding her and Dan most days now, dogging them around the country, roaring for this highway robbery to be *over*. Finally. And when it was over they wanted payback, someone's head served up on a platter. . . *but it mustn't be Dan's!*

Back at the party she couldn't find him. He was gone too long for a pit stop. She circulated and chatted, struggling to hide her mounting concern. When he finally showed up, she snapped quietly, "For heaven's sake, where were you?"

He said he'd tell her later. Just then Mindy Bradburger swooped down, cooing about "that scrumptious dress. I just bet Suzy it's a Nipon. . . ."

The party broke up on the stroke of midnight. Mort was never one for late nights. She and Dan pumped out front-door farewells, parting strokes: "So grand to see you both." ". . . counting on your support, now!"

Finally alone in their guest-wing suite, she let him ramble on about the party. "Great seeing Bob again, by gosh. He's the same as ever, never changes a lick. . . ."

She agreed it was "a productive night. Worth the trip, I think. Now, what was your little vanishing act all about?"

He said Mort had urged him to talk to Dodge Phelps. "He thought that fella could do us some good."

Instant alert. "Well? *Can* he?"

Sure sounded like it. "He says he's got a chit from Bill Pickett, the Nevada congressman, and can't conceive of a better use for it than hauling this country out of the hole that damned House has been digging."

Wheels spinning. "Well, my goodness. What's the chit?"

He didn't know. "Phelps just said Pickett 'owed him a big one.' He seemed pretty sure he could bring him around."

She beamed, radiant with relief. "Oh, that's wonderful news! Number six. Danny, we'll be two-thirds there!"

Frowning, he sat on the bed, looked at his feet. "Yeah, sure," he said slowly. "But he did mention some young U.S. attorney who's been 'stirring up a pack of trouble' in Nevada. Phelps hinted he'd like that guy canned."

"Lord, if that's all he wants. . . you'll be putting in your own people anyway." Chattering brightly against his gloom. "Danny, I knew this was a good idea, coming out here. But I didn't expect such quick results. Look how fast things can happen away from that swamp on the Hill."

But he said, "Nah, I can't go along with that, fooling with U.S. attorneys." He looked straight at her. "Pril, I'll bet you dollars to doughnuts if we turned Chet's boys loose on Phelps, we'd find out he's hooked up to some investigation he's trying to squash."

Heart sinking, she said carefully, "Now we don't *know* that, Danny. Phelps is a very respectable lawyer, a big contributor all these years. Just because he wants to help out in this terrible pinch is no reason for you to start maligning the man's character."

"Yeah, but you know Nevada, you know Vegas. One heck of a lot that goes on there is mob-connected one way or another."

Her breath froze in her throat. "Danny, for heaven's sake! You're not suggesting that Dodge Phelps is. . . ."

"Well, I don't know. But I've sure got some questions."

Deliberately calm, she slipped out of her dress. "Hon, let's sleep on it. If you want, we can have Chet look into it, just to reassure you that Phelps is okay."

But he shook his head and reached for the phone book. "I won't let it get that far. This smells like day-old fish, and I'd be a damn fool to have any part of it." Thumbing pages, muttering, "I think he's staying at the Desert Inn."

While she stood there creaming makeup from her face, sick with dismay, he actually picked up the phone and called the hotel. "Say, Dodge, I didn't want to leave any misunderstandings about our chat tonight. Of course, I'd be mighty pleased to see Bill Pickett come over to the right side of the fence here, but I want to make it clear I can't agree to any quid pro quo. . . ."

CHAPTER SIXTY-THREE /

May 1st

Robin

At dinner Robin upbraided Larry over the pro-initiative Viet vet march on Philadelphia's Liberty Hall, bushwhacked that afternoon by hard-hat and VFW brawlers. "Now why can't you do something about those street mobs?"

Abruptly, in a leave-it-alone tone, he said that was up to local authorities to handle, he wasn't about to call out the National Guard. Feeling his tension like a ticking fuse, she turned off the nag by mentioning her run-in with Barbara Walters at a Democratic women's do. "She wants to show everybody the real White House Devlins. Including my delightful children, she says."

"Sure! Why not?" "Hey, great, Mum."

B. W. was a code name in Tish's rants, as in "next thing you know you'll be doing Barbara Walters and Merv Griffin." She looked at Larry. He shrugged: "What the hell, Rob. . . ."

She smiled. "Okay. We'll see."

After dinner the boys went to a school awards ceremony. Heading to his office, Larry asked if she was hanging out.

Hanging in, she guessed: "A free workroom night's like a present." She asked impulsively if he by any chance wanted a quick tour. Blinking, surprised, he said, "Well, sure."

Misgivings rising with each step upstairs, she chattered, "Oh, this is probably a very bad idea. Don't expect much—it's only my dabblings, you know." He said that was fine, he'd just like to see what the hell she'd been up to.

She saw the familiar room freshly: furniture cluttered against the walls, paint supplies littering every surface, dustball nests in the snarl of cables linking her machines.

He walked in slowly, looking around. Silence thundering in her ears, she babbled, "I suppose it wouldn't hurt to get a maid in to sweep. Or I could do it myself. . . ."

He pointed at the strewn canvases. In transparent disbelief: "That's what you've been doing up here?"

"Well, sure. What'd you think?"

Jolted astonishment. "Hey, this stuff's incredible."

"Ah!" She gripped the door handle, giddy with relief. "Thanks. That's nice of you to say."

"Nice? Shit, Rob." He grinned. "I was, ah, planning to like it anyway, but I thought you were still doing flower bunches. Damn, that's first-class work. Good as a museum."

Groaning in mock dismay, she said please don't go overboard, babe, she'd settle for "pretty good."

"No, I mean it. What's this,"—he pointed at the easel—"some campaign thing?"

"Hey, very good." She said it had started out as Prilla Sterling with some doper kids, although she was pleased he couldn't tell that. She kept the background cameras as a frame of reference. "Stick with what you know best, like they always say." Pottering happily, she explained the half-dozen canvases. How she'd shifted gears from the old street lady to the press mob that caught her at the airport coming to the Inaugural. . . .

"Shit, you really got the feel of that. That's just how it is out there, actually."

She'd found some eye-of-the-storm incidents on video-tape, like Prilla hugging a child with flowers. "I'm looking for a moment with emotional echo, see. And I want lots of cameras so you see them shooting, reflecting each other. . . ."

His astonishment ebbing, he took in the audio-video battery. "And what the hell's all this?"

She chuckled, lighting up the big screen with a slow-motion echo of the fractured image on the easel, Prilla Sterling with ex-dopers, hugging a girl with flyaway blonde hair.

"Christ, Rob! That's fantastic," he muttered as she danced the echo-figures in frame-by-frame freezes.

"See, there's sort of a spark connecting them. A spontaneous, poignant gut feeling she's giving off. That's what I'm trying to capture, anyway. You get the idea."

"I guess." Startled wariness in his look. "Hey, real interesting. Thanks for the show, Rob."

"Thanks yourself. For coming by." She stayed by the easel as he moved distractedly toward the door.

"Okay then." Halfway out, he turned back, flashed a grin. "Good job, Rob. Don't work too damn hard tonight."

She changed into work clothes and put on Marvin Gaye and Rod Stewart. Spirits dancing like those video images, brush slapping canvas, she moved into her private world.

☆

At eleven she knocked off work, showered and stretched, and tucked herself into bed. Then she discovered that sleep wasn't what she craved after all.

Laughing softly, she pulled on a silk dressing gown and slipped barefooted down the stairs. Dimly lit hall. No one in sight. She crossed to Larry's bedroom, tapped on the door and boldly pushed it open, streaking light across the rug. A slow, deep chuckle came from the dark.

"Hey, lady. Come on in."

She shed the robe and gown as she crossed the rug. Climbing up into the massive four-poster bed, she murmured, "Good god. Is this what they mean by the ship of state?" And rolled, warm and laughing, into his open arms.

As he floated back into his head, "Wichita Lineman" wailed softly from the clock-radio. Except for that, a weird trick of memory almost made him think they were back in the old hotel room in Phnom Penh where the geckos scampered on the walls and the ceiling paddles waved flower-scented air over their horny sweat.

They lay on their sides, bodies tangled, flexing spasms of residual pleasure. In the green digital glow he lightly traced her face. She murmured, "Mmm. You smell so good."

"You too. Feel good, too."

"Mm-hmm. Ahhh, delicious. . . ."

That night so long back, when they'd made love fifty different ways till the sun finally nudged them into sleep, was the most romantic time he could recall in their marriage. . . until now. He'd been amazed by the passion, sweet fire that poured out of her. God, but he'd loved her that night. Felt like she'd brought him home to his best, real self.

He'd thought then they could maybe start all over, make it turn out differently. But it hadn't lasted. Back home the same old pressures ground them down, drained out the juice. What had happened over there seemed like a freak moment, a random spark snuffed out by a cold dose of real life. . . .

Gone for good, he'd thought. But tonight this sure as hell felt like a second chance.

He'd been almost shy with her a few hours ago. Those paintings! Christ, sometimes he felt like he hardly knew her at all. Hardly knew what was in her.

She stirred languidly against him, murmuring, moving his hand to her swollen breast. He felt a tender urge to fill her to overflowing with the tidal seas surging in him.

The best times they'd ever had in bed, at least before Phnom Penh, were those months before they were married when they'd skirmished around the goddam family flaps to roll in the sack every chance they could snatch. Ahh, good times. . . .

Yet after the four-star wedding, Babs and Harry Swann's Broadway opening, those peaks had quickly flattened out somehow. Once she'd said something sour about him always wanting "the forbidden fruit." He'd pretended not to hear because it struck him she was probably right. He just seemed to be built that way, and didn't see what the hell he could do about it.

But now he wanted her like he never had before—wanted all of her, wanted to touch those secret places she'd kept hidden from him. With a longing that was almost an ache, he loosed his unsprung tensions into a wave of loving. Her body felt like the matched half of a slow-rolling wheel. The lost half of himself.

He chuckled against her neck, thrusting langorously. Wheel turning faster, he slid again into that wild, private refuge of their pleasure.

The green glow spelled out 1:04 as she lay, head nested on his hip, one hand twined with his. Ahhh, how she loved slipping into these uncharted oceans of sensation. She murmured happily, "Damn. This really *was* a great idea."

He kissed her fingertips. "The best, kiddo."

The room seemed bathed in magic. . . or maybe just their own afterglow. The draperies of this crazy old boat of a bed enclosed them in a tent of enchanted netting, almost like. . . .

She chuckled, "Nice digs you've got here, babe. So pretty and silvery in the moonlight."

"That's not the only thing that is." He stroked the hair that spilled across his belly. "Pretty, I mean."

She smiled at his crinkled eyes. "Why, thank you kindly, sir."

She wondered if anyone knew they were doing this. Carmen or the agents. Or Hamilton. . . hard to put anything past Hamilton. Yet she sensed no one *did* know, and maybe Larry wanted as much as she did to leave it that way, this fragile different new connection. . . .

She had no idea how long this sudden bloom would last. Their first honeymoon had somehow seemed to peter out almost as soon as they'd gotten past the altar, and this present dip into delight might not last much longer. She sensed a tender sort of urgency coming out of him, but she had no idea how that would—*if* it would—change how their situation ultimately got resolved. And right now she felt a warning, intrusive need to clarify that much, at least, between them.

Stroking his chest, she said she hoped he understood this real nice interlude didn't necessarily change "how things finally work out for us, babe. I just don't want us to have any misapprehensions on that score."

He stiffened. "Shit, Rob." His fingers combed her hair, cradling her skull. "What's this, more divorce talk?"

Soft laugh. "Nah, not tonight, babe. Farthest thing from my mind, actually, right now."

"Mmmph. That's more like it."

She kissed his warm belly, marveling at how long it had taken them to rediscover the great time they could have at this. "You know what makes me sorry, babe? All the good time we wasted getting back to here."

He chuckled. "What's that they say? Never too late?"

She shook her head. "Ah, but—'taint necessarily so, Dev. A pretty idea, but don't bet the farm on it."

Dry, wary: "Dead sure of that, Rob? Fixed in cement?"

She said lord, she wasn't sure of anything, except that he sure wasn't an easy man to walk away from. She kissed his open palm, cradled it on her cheek. Softly: "But a big part of my head's already gone, you know. That's why the painting's finally working for me, Dev. I'm just—freed up."

He nodded, belly muscles tight. She sensed that he wanted to argue, but chose not to risk it.

A lot of her was tied up with Cambodia too, which was part of what was cooking between them now. "It's like we're sharing this amazing trip together. But we can't count on that to last. Don't you see, babe? *This* is the Shangri La. Now, for us. And damn, aren't we lucky for that?"

"Ah." His head jerked, fending off that odd logic. He asked stiffly if it was unreasonable to ask why she was so hell-bent on getting out.

"I'm not hell-bent. How can I put it?" She pressed his hand between her fingers, saying sadly, wistfully, "I just can't fit the box anymore, Dev. When this fling's over, back in real life—see, I finally know who I am, what I need to keep my life on keel. And that's definitely not" —she waved at the moon-silvered room—"this."

"Or me, apparently. . . ."

"Correct, sir," she smiled. "You're a terrific man in some ways, Dev. And a terrific father, and lots of other things. But damn, you're a rotten husband."

Uneasy laugh. "Hey, that could change, Rob."

"Ah, sure. And the mountains could move."

She said god knows she didn't mean to lay all the blame on him. She claimed at least a good share of that. But *all* politicians made rotten husbands. "And that game's in your blood like corpuscles, Dev. You couldn't change it if you wanted. That's who you are, bless your ornery hide." She stroked his tangled chest hairs. "I'm just not up for living with it, sooner or later. But my lord, you do make a golden lover. . . ."

Abruptly, he sat up and bent over her, cradled her head. Whispering intensely, "God, I want you," he lifted her to his fierce kiss.

CHAPTER SIXTY-FOUR /

May 4th
Prilla

Flipping through a *People* magazine while her hair dried, Priscilla saw the 60s recycling of Alexis Devlin: riding elephants, touring Cambodian temples with Prince Oudong, a "rare interview" rambling on about the priceless art heritage that peace-conference gimmick could somehow "rescue from the devastations of time and war."

Extraordinary, the publicity rockslide that family had engineered lately. More today with Robin Devlin's standing-room-only lunch for the Fence People. Just when the TV focus was coming off its Vietnam binge, that rag-a-bag mob around the White House had exploded into a hit. "National theater," "live democracy in action" they were calling that parade of losers hung up on yesterday's war. Everybody and his uncle getting air time, while Priscilla and Dan got the short end of the media stick. And the big all-star show she counted on to turn this around was still eleven days off.

As Jean-Marc combed her out, a gofer brought news that Congressman Diamond, a Colorado Democrat, had collapsed in his House office. A major stroke, they said. He was conscious but couldn't talk. If he survived, he'd be sidelined for a few weeks at least.

She beamed. "Well, good news for a change." Colorado, five-four for Talbott, would tie without Diamond, knocking Talbott down to twenty-three. Back to three votes short!

Like a sign, almost. A lucky omen that all this could turn around *very soon*. Maybe when she least expected. . . .

She set out for Bunny Montague's luncheon rethinking her strategy. Trying *not* to think of that festering hotbed just two blocks south of the Carlton on 16th Street, a scene their drivers had standing orders to avoid. Robin Devlin's free-meal extravaganza today would guarantee more fanning of that already dangerous mob. Yet her husband was letting them camp in the streets, egging them on to bail out his riverboat gamble.

The Montagues' sprawling red-brick mansion looked grander than she recalled from their Inauguration night "consolation party." Odd lot of cars on the curved drive—kelly-green Rabbit, battered Buick wagon. Not one Mercedes. . . .

Ginny had pushed for this lunch with a few of Bunny Montague's "old friends." The BOTs, Ginny said. "The Beautiful Old Things, dear. D.C. version of our Group. A very different kettle of fish, of course, but they'll be a *huge* help to you."

Oddly nervous about this lunch, wary of breaking new ground, Priscilla fell back on her old trick of imagining a movie role: *Guest at an English castle, cool, crisply witty, comfortably "at home".* . . .

Waiting with the butler at the front door, Bunny Montague wore an old tweed suit and linen blouse. Feeling suddenly overdressed in her Nipon silk print, Priscilla chattered nervously, "Mrs. Montague, how delightful to see you again! And how sweet of you to ask me over."

She said please, call her Bunny. "After all, my dear, we'll be neighbors of a sort rather soon, won't we?"

"All right, if you promise to call me Prilla. My, what a pleasure to see this lovely house again." Marble foyer big enough to throw a party in, Constable landscapes, exquisite Aubusson, Chinese jardinere with blooming orchids on the antique demilune table. "We had *such* a charming evening here last winter. . . ."

In the opulent parlor, ten women were a blur of cashmere, pearls, old tweeds and clunky old-gold jewelry. Stout shoes, figures to match. And more silver hair than in all of L.A. *Yes, definitely overdressed.* . . .

"Matron" was a word she never used for her own crowd—they spent too much time and money staying glamorously young—but it summed up this droopy-bosomed upper-crust bunch. She matched faces to Ginny's rundowns. "Mrs. Ingram, so nice to see you again." Husband an "old-money lawyer," former ambassador to some dinky European country. "Mrs. Bendell, what a pleasure to meet you." Married a cereal fortune, big in the fox-hunting set.

But the point of this cozy lunch was the smiling young woman in a prim navy silk suit, discreet pearl pin, looking surprisingly at ease. Her presence was a calculated risk, but that suit somehow reassured Priscilla. They wouldn't expect *her* to dress out of Grandma's cedar chest either.

Bunny said, "And I believe you know Carla Florian. . . ."

"Oh, yes. So pleased to see you again, Miss Florian."

Carla allowed herself a small, ambiguous smile as she shook the old starlet's limp paw. "How nice to see you looking so well, Mrs. Sterling."

What a hoot this little chow-down was shaping into. She was trying to absorb every morsel to play back to Kittyhawk in their pillow talk, but she'd already gone into overload as the genteel old Georgetown babes waited for the guest of honor. These pillars of old Washington society mostly got their inside ticket by marrying rich, privileged men, the sort who'd run the country for years on end. They somehow matched this heirloom-littered house: They were classic, expensive, and beyond caring how they looked. Yet before the star attraction arrived, they were dithering and twittering like 50s teenagers waiting for a peek at Elvis.

They scrambled to their feet as she sailed in, her plastic smile locked on, expression as flexible as her oversprayed hair. But any face was bound to be tight if it'd been lifted as many times as this one. Probably the best knife jobs California bucks could buy, but Carla spotted the telltale hairline, the tiny traces behind the carefully-combed-over ears.

In the cocktail chatter she picked up an edgy apprehension in Prilla's mannered patter. When it dawned on her that *this* old babe was quietly dithering as much as the rest of them, she decided to sit back and enjoy the show.

"High time we had some elegance and good taste injected into this dreary social scene," one piped up. "We're all too aware, Mrs. Sterling, of how much the tone is set by the White House, like it or not."

"Heavens, yes." Patsy Bendell was "counting on you and your husband to rescue us from the blue jeans and country music we've been deluged with for the past four years. I won't mention the last few months, since we have the mercy of knowing *that's* not going to last." Maude Ingram said she'd learned over the years not to expect much from Democrats. "But at least Norleen Talbott didn't consider herself a hippie, 'free spirit,' whatever we've seen lately. . . ."

These cookies knew how to dish out the soft soap, at least. Gloating at that music to her ears, Prilla said she did think as the national show-piece the White House should be "a lovely, elegant home, with a lifestyle to match. And I hope my husband and I will soon be sharing that with you."

No mention of anything so vulgar as the House vote. Wayne would laugh some when she acted out *this* routine for him. The complex game he was playing could probably be described as mischief making, and she played his Scheherazade, spinning him antic Washington tales to percolate his nights. Yet for herself Carla couldn't help but wonder if any of these dames had ever scrubbed a bathroom floor. Or mended patches, or wrestled a drunken husband into bed. . . .

At lunch, overlooking terraced lawns, the conversation revolved around gardens, grandchildren and charity balls. Prilla chimed in with reminiscences of her L.A. volunteer work, and the "exquisite" Biedermeier secretary she'd once unearthed in a Sacramento knickknack shop.

Carla smiled and nodded, hefting the Georgian sterling. Two centuries old, give or take a few decades, and heavy as lead sinkers. She wondered if you wound up with silver like this, in a dining room wallpapered with antique tapestries and Chinese screens, would your life somehow become as stuffy and boring as these women's seemed to be?

All the while that Florian girl sat prim as a schoolmarm, quietly taking it all in. Her aplomb suggested a self-assured familiarity with surroundings like this, but Priscilla knew through Chet that she was one of seven kids, with steelworker parents left jobless in their fifties. After a brief marriage to an Ohio hometown boy, she'd come to Washington and the Hill for eleven years of relentless, upwardly mobile drive.

When Dan's team learned she'd once worked in Speaker Whalen's office, Chet put her on the enemies list and brooded over ways to "minimize her influence" over Kittyhawk. But Priscilla sensed from their first meeting, when Florian had crashed the Marsden dinner party, that her fierce ambition was quite apolitical. The little lady wanted in and she wanted up: That much was crystal clear. *How* she'd get what she wanted still seemed negotiable. And Priscilla had sensed enough of a kindred spirit to gamble on including her in this lunch.

So far it was paying off: Florian was a model guest, docile and charmingly well-behaved. Now if Priscilla could just engineer a few minutes alone with her. . . .

Over coffee in the 'sun room'—an orangery with a museum-quality Oriental jade collection scattered among vines and trees—Priscilla asked if Bunny would mind if she "took a peek at your gorgeous flower beds?" Certainly not, Bunny said. Several joined her, including Florian.

On the manicured grounds, Florian stuck close by. Priscilla trotted briskly down the paths. "Look at that lovely wisteria! And the rhododendrons. . . ."

At the hedgerow they left the rest behind. Florian murmured, "Thanks for having me invited here today, Mrs. Sterling. I'm enjoying it very much."

Out of the madness all around, here finally was home ground. She wasted no time: "Carla, you strike me as a young woman with great potential, who might profit from exposure to this kind of gracious life-style. So different from the ordinary hurly-burly." Like a trout fly dropped into a shimmering stream. "The sort of life someone like Mr. Kittyhawk might lead, if he were so inclined."

Slight, enigmatic smile. Florian said she couldn't quite see him ensconced in this sort of situation. "But then, he's a man of many surprises."

Ah yes, she agreed. "A brilliant, talented young man. Perhaps a little lacking in direction. But a man like that could go far. . . with the right woman behind him."

Again the cryptic smile. A murmur about Kittyhawk's "rather unpredictable nature."

She tapped Florian's arm. "You know, Carla, sometimes great men need a little help understanding themselves. Which creates an opportunity for a woman sensible enough to seize it. On this House vote, for instance, I can't for the life of me comprehend why Kittyhawk still waffles when he could be making a real name for himself. And profiting considerably from the situation, if he'd only *decide what he wants.*"

Risky words, but she trusted her instincts. If worse came to worst, she'd deny she ever said it.

"My point is, Mrs. Sterling, I don't think the Congressman is entirely clear on what he *does* want." Florian added softly, "Unlike some of us."

Ah, yes. And you want plenty, tootsie. . . . She joked that as far as she could see, Kittyhawk mainly wanted "to be a star, somehow." Florian surprised her by agreeing with that. Priscilla snapped impatiently, "The question is how he's going about it, Carla. If he plans to do it through this vote, *you* know it won't do him any good to hold off till the train's pulled out."

"Quite right, Mrs. Sterling. Nelson Diamond's stroke is certainly a great break for your husband. That gets him back the momentum, and I understand you have another switch coming up tomorrow."

Uh-oh, watch out, she's fishing. . . . "Oh, yes?" Priscilla asked lightly. "What switch is that?"

Nevada, she said. Bill Pickett. . . .

Rattled, astonished, she wondered how Florian had gotten onto that.

And how much else she knew. "Goodness, we'd certainly welcome Mr. Pickett's vote, of course. But I can't. . . ."

Stone-faced, Florian said she understood Pickett was "concerned about the country's increasingly ugly mood. And after all, Nevada did vote for your husband last fall. Of course that still leaves you three short—in other words, even with Talbott. If you'll excuse an unintended pun, it would seem you're all a bit hung up on the Fence right now."

That zinger whizzed by her before she'd even shot down the Pickett trial balloon. She plunged ahead. "In any case, Carla, your man better make up his mind before it's too late to matter. What's this I hear about him wanting to run PBS?"

Florian said that was last week. Now he was more interested in developing a coalition-type government.

Like trying to pin a raw egg to the wall. "Yes, I heard him talking about that on *Good Morning, America*. Now that's a subject my husband also has great interest in, so you might encourage the Congressman to think in terms of a cabinet post perhaps, if that's where his ambitions lead him. . . ."

God help her if the bushes were bugged. "I hope you catch my drift, Carla. I'm thinking of *your* future as well as his. I'd like to see a young woman of your talent and enterprise get ahead, *but there's no more time to waste*."

That leaked more desperation than she'd intended. So she tucked a hand under the girl's elbow, saying lightly, cozily, "Well, Carla, what a nice talk. We'll keep in touch. Feel free to call me anytime you want to chat. But right now, let's get back to this delightful party."

CHAPTER SIXTY-FIVE /

May 15th
Robin

By mid-May the House vote was still tied at 23-23-4-1. The Vietnam resolution stayed stuck in the committees, and the Fence ran along on its own steam—while the lilacs and magnolias came and went.

A week after Jason's eighteenth birthday, Robin decided to take the boys on a New York overnight to check out Jason's college for next year. Jim tried to talk her out of it, but she was hell-bent on a "rare escape from the old plantation," as she put it.

So Jim mapped out the whole move to keep the press off their tails. The unmarked cars slid off the grounds through the west exit where the Fence People were kept away, Robin slouched out of sight in the back seat. While a private jet whisked them up to Princeton Airport, she felt like a sailor on shore leave. Jason was fussing and fidgeting, plucking at his seldom-worn suit. She reminded him this was only a college they were looking at, not jail or boot camp.

She relished this rare chance to play Mom to him. She hadn't been around much when Melissa went off to college, so this gave her a chance to catch up on some pleasant maternal duties.

It made her smile a bit to see Jason so antsy, acting like he thought he might not get in. Princeton University was probably turning ass-backwards right this minute to welcome this latest Devlin, the President's son, but Jason was sweating as if he were about to go over the cliff.

☆

Robin's mood was still high and light when she and the boys finished their tour of Larry's old dorm suite, Jason's for next year—the rooms dilapidated enough not to've changed much in the years between. But strolling out into the sunshine, they ran smack into two TV crews. A Groucho Marx mustache pushed a CBS mike into her face: "What brings you to Princeton, Mrs. Devlin?"

She glanced at her watch: 3:35. The dodg'em game had lasted three hours and twenty-five minutes—about three hours and twenty-four minutes longer than she'd expected.

"Oh, this is just a private visit," she said. Unfamiliar second-stringers, but bigger guns were probably speeding to the scene. "Jason plans to attend next fall, so we dropped by to check things out."

A blonde woman, ABC mike, asked for comment on the Senate Foreign Relations Committee voting out the Vietnam resolution with a recommendation for "prompt action" on the floor.

Glowing at that welcome bombshell, Robin called it "a small transfusion of hope for a desperate country. And I hope the House acts promptly as well. The Phnom Penh peace conference will open in just five weeks, and our wholehearted participation is essential to its success. Please, all of you, don't let's risk jeopardizing this conference, and compounding an already overwhelming tragedy. . . ."

☆

Melissa and Thad turned up to join the overnight campout in Robin's apartment, a bonus to her twenty-four-hour parole. Puttering happily, Robin snipped off dead leaves, drank in her Central Park view. In the street below, press hawks roosted in ambush. But up here she was safe and secure, nested in her own world of browning leaves and greening hopes.

She took a Tab from the near-empty fridge. Missy said she'd have one too. As Robin popped the cans, she glanced at her daughter. "Say, are you going skinny on us?"

Melissa beamed. "Hey, thanks for noticing." Proudly, she flattened her T-shirt. "Eight pounds—almost."

She said terrific, bravo for you, Miss Skin-and-Bones.

Melissa shared the credit. "I got so fed up with people raving about my gorgeous Mum, I decided to compete."

Smiling, Robin said since Mother Hubbard's larder was empty, they'd better order in Chinese or make a Zabar's run. Melissa called into the living room, "Kev, Mum says are we eating Zabar's or Chinese."

"Ah, shit. I guess we better tell her."

"Tell me what?"

Kevin said "a few cousins" were throwing a dinner in her honor at his apartment. "Shelley and Frannie are over there cooking right now. With any luck it'll be fit to eat. I mean, how much can Shelley do to spaghetti? So get your glad rags on, Rob, we hit the big town tonight."

No, no, not a chance. "You kids go do whatever you want, but I'm definitely staying put."

Chorus of protest. "Come on, Mom," Melissa said, "it's Friday night in Neewww York City."

She said it was no fun going out with that mob downstairs, why didn't they bring the spaghetti over here?

"No way, Rob," Kevin chuckled. "The name of the game is give-'em-the-slip. Like you did today—how long was it?" Three hours, she admitted. "Well, we'll beat that tonight. We've just gotta smuggle you out like the last time, you remember, Rob. . ." *Just barely. A hundred years ago, last January*. ". . . so go put on your high-heeled sneakers."

Jason urged, "Come on, Mum." Melissa crooned happily, "East Side, West Side, all around the town. . . ."

So much for the quiet family night at home. Kevin organized the escape. "Mel, Thad, Jason, you go out the front and head them off. Rob's the one the buzzards are after. . . ."

After the decoys and their agents left, Sean, Kevin and Robin's agents slipped her down the freight elevator, out to the back alley. As they loped past garbage cans she laughed softly, Sean shushing with mock indignation. Cars waited in the next garage. As they gunned up the ramp, she gasped, "Lord, Jim, don't tell me it worked again!"

He said sourly, "So far, anyway."

Kevin patted her knee, ear-to-ear grin. "Like I told you, Rob. Just stick with me, kid."

They giggled and goofed across the park to Kevin's East 74th Street apartment house, where a freight elevator whisked her up fifteen floors to Kevin's back door. Shelley and Frannie waited by dented trash cans, laughing, "Aunt Robin! How awfully nice of you to drop by!"

She greeted Kevin's brother Liam, Billy Sedgwick and Ken Talley, plus assorted dates. The decoy crew blew in, to loud applause. Melissa said, "You should've heard the new Princeton jock, asking the buzzards what they wanted from Zabar's. . . ."

They sat on the floor eating Shelley's "gourmet treat" from unmatched plates. Kevin plunked down beside Robin for a one-armed hug. "Kevin, you old devil, such elegant digs! Don't tell me you're finally getting civilized?"

He hoped to god not. "So how goes it down there, Rob?"

So-so, she decided. It was pure fluke, after all, that Larry had lasted this long, and having this major Vietnam thing come along was "more than he could've bargained on. But the big clock's running out. Five weeks to go, and if he can't pry the resolution loose by then. . . ."

Kevin said piss on Congress, Larry shouldn't let those clowns screw up the works. She said he couldn't be a one-man band, and without at least rubber-stamp support from the House, they were left "high and dry for the conference. If it even comes off. . . ."

Feisty Devlin reflex: "Hey, what's the doom and gloom, Rob? Of course it'll come off. Larry can't let those Hill jokers shoot down an opening like this."

She told him it was already happening—China increasingly wary, Vietnam backpedaling more every day, even Thailand ready to pull out. "The whole deal's coming unstuck."

Kevin brought up the approval ratings Larry *and* the initiative were getting: 73 percent, 76 percent was "no one-man band." She said tell that to Dan Sterling.

Bristling response: "Ah sure, Cowboy Dan. That cocksucker's trying to ride this over the top, boy. Feeding that go-get-'em shit to his right-wing goons. And those goddam Dixiecrats tying up the resolution for him—they should've had their balls clipped a long time ago. But at least the infighting's pushed Roy Bob off the scope. So it comes down to a power struggle between Uncle Larry and the Cowboy. . . ."

Sighing at that glimpse of Kevin as Devlin-on-his-way-up, she mused about what she'd learned from all this: "that you have to fight as hard for peace as for war. I don't know why that comes as such a surprise, actually. But *wanting* it so badly unfortunately doesn't guarantee it'll happen. So what hell-raising have you been up to lately?"

Over ice cream served from an ironstone chamber pot, Shelley and Liam launched a pet family game, "Quotes from Granny." Shelley opened, in high-pitched imitation of Mother Devlin: "Ladies never chew gum on the street."

From Liam: "Gentlemen always wear shoes to church."

Melissa's pet: "Ladies don't sweat, they perspire."

Robin added, "Don't forget ladies never, never spit."

She insisted on doing the dishes, taking inordinate pleasure in this once-familiar drudgery, listening to Shelley and Melissa on the White House. "You got Cupid's bed? Oh god, I always wanted to sleep in that. . . ."

Scouring a scorched saucepan, she thought dreamily, *It's simple, really. Good times, good kids, good life.* . . .

Back in the living room, Kevin was asking, ". . . Xenon or Magique?"

She covered her stab of disappointment. "What, are you guys going out on a toot?"

"Correction, Rob. We're all going out on a toot."

She said no way, no chance, but Melissa insisted, "Mum, it's all settled, your only vote is Xenon versus Magique."

Kevin waltzed her in brisk circles around the floor. "Game's no fun, Rob, unless you give 'em a moving target."

Sean piped up, "She votes for Xenon. Right, Mum?"

In the end they talked her into it, after she extracted a promise to "be on your best behavior, as Granny would say. No funny stuff up your nose or anything."

"That's right, guys." Kevin mock stern, bringing her jacket and purse in from the bedroom. "Stash the snuff boxes tonight, we're painting the town with the President's lady."

Jim kicked up a major stink over this last-minute foray to "that fancy honky-tonk," but he was no match for Kevin's resolve. In the car Robin asked fretfully if any of them had checked this out with their father. Melissa said he'd just be jealous he missed it.

"Well, if the cowchips fly, I'd like someone to remember this whole thing wasn't my idea." She moaned that Sean was probably too young to get in legally, "so we're breaking the law on top of everything else."

"Ma, come on," Jason chided. "Brooke Shields goes all the time, and she's younger than Sean."

She asked what was in Kevin's shopping bag. "A record. Lay off it, Rob. I had enough shit on this from your shadows. You've gotta take what you can get, girl, and we're gonna have ourselves a fine old time."

Hustled in through a back alley, she watched the club owner brusquely empty three ringside banquettes, thinking in a daze, *This must be what it's like to be Frank Sinatra.*

She kept Sean next to her, but the pounding, hypnotic music drove out other cautions. Foot tapping, she watched the fancy choreography, aware of the flashes of recognition, the hungry stares, Jim glowering in "close protection," wearing his Cotton Mather face.

But for once she didn't give a damn. Her acute ex-alkie radar recognized that the infectious high came from drink and dope as much as music. But the shared warmth, the sense of celebration were real, and she rode them past the chemical buzz into her private ecstasy.

She smiled at Kevin and Shelley twinkle-footing. Kevin the king of the roost, handsome and cocky-assed, obviously a regular here. She'd tried hard to disapprove of this racy nephew with his nightlife habits and unshakeable self-assurance. But, in fact, he was her favorite in-law.

Soon the rest were dancing too—Melissa with Thad, Frannie with Ken, Jason with Liam's date. Now Kevin hoofed by with Brooke Shields in skintight silver pants and 6-inch heels. Nose dusted by that incredible head of hair, he winked at Robin. She poked Sean: "Look who Kev's after now!"

"Yep." He startled her with, "You want to dance, Mum?"

"Sure! Love to, honey."

She shucked her jacket and stepped onto the floor, flowing to the beat of "Can You Feel It?" Sean threw himself about with coltish gusto, grin plastered to his shiny face.

Kevin whirled by, shouting, "Way to go, Rob!" Jason mouthed approval from the middle of the floor. They stomped and shook and sweated through two long numbers, laughing all the way. Just as she was about to suggest a break, the music shifted abruptly into a tinkling Asian rhythm.

As the dancers looked uncertainly around them, Kevin suddenly lifted her hand, leading her into the steps of the gentle, courtly *ram vong* that Oudong had taught them at Camp David. She reached back to link up with Sean. Kevin bent toward her. "Whatcha say, Rob? Glad we came?" Laughing, she lifted her face to the lights, shaking loose her hair.

Shelley took Sean's free hand; Jason hitched on behind her. Then Melissa and Thad, Brooke Shields and Liam. The steps were so simple, so free-form, that other dancers quickly joined in. Looking down that magical line, she saw hands linked, faces aglow. Jason added some basketball footwork, Melissa a few kicks. And it was all perfectly right.

She danced in this dark New York night-cave for the soul of Cambodia, moving in an echo of centuries, pierced by the moment's startling joy. And she was still dancing when the TV lights found her a few minutes later.

CHAPTER SIXTY-SIX /

May 15th
Prilla

Dan was riding high tonight. He'd hit cloud nine somewhere around the opening number of their show, and was still floating at Frank's post-gala 'cast party.' He wanted to shake every hand, rehash every joke and song. Trying to personally thank "every one of you great people who put on this wonderful heartwarming show," he made sure all the women got kissed.

Prilla tugged at his arm. "Danny, please let's go. . . ."

He spotted someone he'd missed. "Jimmy! By gosh, you outdid yourself tonight. Never seen you in better form. . . ."

He could almost swear he was back at one of those fabulous old MGM premieres. The Century Plaza ballroom was wall-to-wall with stars, decked out with an elegance and style you hardly saw anymore. Everybody who was anybody seemed to be here. In one corner he spotted Gloria Swanson, regal as Queen Bess in a black velvet dress he thought he remembered from *Sunset Boulevard*. And Chuck Heston beaming ear to ear, looking like Ben Hur and Moses rolled into one. "Great show!" "Fabulous show!" drummed like rain on a roof. Ginny Hibbing called out, "Très gala, Dan! Quite a smash."

Ginny was a good pal in her way, but to her this was just another party—like the sixty-four she went to every week. To him it was one night in a million, when the old Hollywood came shining back to life and poured on him all the love and applause he'd hankered for all his years in this tinsel town.

And by gosh, he was lapping it up. Storing up memories of this night that had always seemed out of reach, to warm his cockles in whatever rough times—or good times—lay ahead. Right now, right this minute, he guessed they'd never get much better for him than this bath of glory tonight.

"Say, Dino! Thanks for the great number, boy, that golden voice sounds better than ever. . . ."

Like trying to pry the boy out of the candy store. . . .
Coming over from the Forum show, Priscilla had reminded him that everyone had just put in a long, hard day. Got him to promise he'd "just pop in and say our bit. Twenty minutes, max."

In one of her better scheduling ideas, she'd suggested they leave the party before the show tape was aired. The Secret Service seized on that, jumpy as they were about the huge crowds trailing Dan now, the sour, volatile mood on the streets. They wanted him off-stage "the sooner, the better."

No easy job getting him to agree to that, but she promised on their first night off they'd watch the whole tape at leisure, backtracking all he wanted. So finally he'd gone along with it, thank goodness. The last thing they needed now was coverage of Dan reacting to the show, chortling, guffawing, choking up over the valentines. . . .

Her radar read it differently: *too late for this. Timing all off. . . .* A day when fifteen supporters were arrested in Texas and a bunch more hospitalized in Alabama was no time for Dan to be seen whooping it up with his Hollywood pals.

Now this black-tie reception, a grand party, Frank's generous treat—but off, off, all wrong in terms of image. Ginny was fluttering nearby, trying to catch her eye, but she waved her off. She needed all her grim concentration to keep calm in this hurricane eye, keep steering Dan straight.

Her eyes darted to the huge screen filling one end of the room. They *had* to get out of here before. . . . Suddenly the young Mormon pipsqueak cornered Dan. "You don't mind if I call you Danny? You can call me Donny."

Enough! She pulled Dan aside, hissing in her now-hear-this voice, "Come on now, it's time to go home."

They slipped away with no fanfare, limo gliding silently from hotel basement, ducking the mobs for once. She sank, exhausted, into the grey felt seat, as if somebody'd just pulled her plug. Dan checked his watch: "By gosh, eight minutes to go. Good thing we've got TV-on-wheels."

She'd planned *that* too, of course. But not how let down she'd feel, squinting at the grainy little set, seeing the family arrive at the hall, their daughters properly dressed for once, Yvonne's bosoms tamed under navy sequins. The net effect seemed spoiled by the twins with their three peculiar children. She'd fretted all night that one would throw up on the rug and walk off with the show.

Yet she was pleased to see the calm, polished radiance she herself projected—no hint she was running on automatic pilot, choked and brooding behind that fixed smile. And the dress she and Adolfo had agonized over looked exactly right. Watching herself intercut with the acts—Debby Boone in a blue Virgin Mary robe, Ethel Merman's spangly purple knit like an old sock on a lumpy foot—she decided her Elizabethan-style scarlet taffeta had been a *perfect* choice.

Dan purred cheerily, "By gosh, nobody can put one together like Frank."

Dutiful murmur: "Absolutely, hon. Top form he was in." She'd wanted this two-hour special to be a swelling chorus to the patriotic brushfires smouldering around the country. To get the audience off their fat fannies to *do something*. But what came across was Oscar-night-warmed-over, old-boy soft-shoe celebration of a victory not yet won. Too slick, too chummy. Too much stand-up love-fest, not enough bugles to the barricades. . . .

But she should've known that! These stars were trained for inaugural galas, royal benefits—just what they were pumping out tonight—so who could she blame but herself?

All the way home he chuckled happily, calling plays. "Here's where Jimmy chokes up. Boy, that sure got to me." He said Ethel could belt 'em to the balcony still, by gosh. Reveled in Bob's jokes, marveled at

Frank's voice: "Good as ever, and they say he does it now on pure technique."

Lord, he did love to watch his old pals perform. As the car turned down their Brentwood street, she reminded him Chet was coming by for a *short* meeting. He said testily that damn well better wait till after the show.

She summoned a last smile and a wave for the two lonesome cameras that had trailed them to the door. Inside the house, Chet leapt up from his chair by the living-room TV.

Dan waved him down. "Stay put, Chet. How's it playing?"

"Oh, great show, Governor! Great show."

Dan joined Chet by the TV as Consuelo hustled in with drinks and cheese. Priscilla took a few stiff belts and went to change that Elizabethean rig for a silky nightgown and robe, then came back to hold hands and watch TV with Dan.

In the windup to the drumbeat finale, she deliberately suspended her judgment, ignoring that inner nag: *too slick. . . too Hollywood. . . .* After an off-key Frank-and-Dean duet, Frank exhorted them all to "get behind this great national effort, each and every one of you out there. . . ." Feeling that pinch of stage fright again, back in the wings. "Help us win this crucial campaign to 'Invest in a Strong America' through the leadership of the man forty-two million Americans elected last November 4th—the next President of the United States, Daniel. . . ."

Roaring cheers as they swept onstage, waving and beaming to the millions. *Well, maybe it works, after all. . . .*

Seizing the triumphant mood, Dan deftly wound it higher, hotter. "We say to those 435 members of our House of Representatives, give us back the country we lost last November 4th. Give us back the America where true freedom and democracy still reign. . . where every man's vote counts and the president is elected by the vote of the people, not by a few politicians in smoke-filled rooms. . . ."

She was glowing up at his face as he hit his stride, no sign of the crick in her taut neck. He was performing beautifully, with no cue cards. *Looks good. Sounds right. . . .*

Cranking up the rolling finale: "My fellow Americans, I invite you tonight to join in this sacred crusade to set America back on the path of justice and righteousness. With the help of Almighty God, and your strong voice and prayers, we can redeem the promise of our Founding Fathers by ringing in a new era of peace, liberty and democracy throughout this great, broad land we love."

Drum-and-trumpet fanfare as the kids swept out to join them and the glittery all-star cast. When Dan picked up the smallest grandchild, Priscilla nudged the other two up front, all bowing and waving as the credits rolled.

Chet exploded with praise; Dan beamed like a kid at a circus. As she turned down the volume, thinking *all this to get back what they stole*, she snipped, "Chet, I hope this will be short and sweet—we've had quite a day."

He said he realized that, but wanted to tune them into a promising development with Ralph Brogan, Iowa's Democrat governor, who was fed up with his job and hankered to "retire" as ambassador to Ireland. His old friend and Democrat ally, Congressman Doug Kosters, was hankering to be Iowa's new governor.

"So the deal is, Kosters would agree to 'go fishing' and skip a presidential vote. He means that literally—as an avid fisherman, he figures he could get lost in the woods, plead outboard-motor break-down, something like that. The beauty of the plan is it won't be traceable to you, sir, since Kosters will stay Democrat. He anticipates that with Brogan off to Ireland he'd be a shoo-in to succeed as governor."

Dan's fatigue showed as his high wore off. Slow nod, looking glazed: "Sounds good, Chet. Sounds pretty good."

Chet said the hitch was they had to hold this card till the final vote, "since Kosters won't consider jumping the party fence. The most he'll go for is getting himself lost for, say, two, three days. But on the other hand, all you'd have to trade away is ambassador to Ireland."

Dan said he wouldn't pin himself down. "But Brogan's a good fellow. With that name, he might do fine in Dublin."

Slight sheepishness in that look he turned on her. She said quietly, intensely, "I say yes."

Face kinked into a tired half-smile, he said, "Well, let's say Brogan would have a good shot at the job, anyway."

They both knew better than to press him further. Chet said Brogan wouldn't insist on "a face-to-face meet, since he knows your constraints, but he'd appreciate a call."

On to those last two votes. Chet said Speaker Whalen's threat to move against any questionable campaign funding was "pretty empty, but it seems to've nudged a few wavering Democrats back in line, momentarily at least. . . ."

Dan broke off to watch the excerpts of "our show" on the late news.

As if he couldn't get enough of it. "Well, that looks pretty good, don't you think, Pril?"

"Wonderful, sweetie," she said flatly.

Chet said the House pressure was running so high that one Alabama Democrat had postponed open-heart surgery until the vote was settled. Suddenly, Robin Devlin flashed bizarrely onto the screen, doing some weird kind of dance.

Priscilla shushed them. ". . . out on the town with her three children at Xenon, a popular New York disco. . . ." Shivering, Priscilla turned her head. But her eyes still watched. *Beautiful, so beautiful. Shaking that fire-hair into the light, moving like a snake. . . .*

Devlin explained she'd learned this *ram vong* from Prince Oudong and Princess Jeanne on their recent Washington visit. "It's a lovely traditional Cambodian dance, like a conga line, that anyone can learn quickly and easily. . . ."

Dan huffed, "Well, my gosh. What'll those guys come up with next?" Chet remarked on that "unsavory nightclub, certainly no place to take your children to. . . ."

She quietly excused herself and took her purse to the powder room as Dan was asking if the House committee could hold the line on that resolution with the Senate gone.

She swallowed two Valiums, splashed on cold water. Sternly talked herself out of the aching flutters in her chest.

Back in the living room, a familiar tirade: "Four hundred thirty-five guys, and we can't crank out two votes? Dammit, Chet, you fellows must be slipping up somewhere."

Eyes darting between her and Dan, Chet murmured that they'd gotten some "confidential input" on Harley Richmond, who was a swing West Virginia vote as well as Foreign Affairs chairman. "But you probably don't want to hear it, Governor."

Dan frowned, then looked away. "That's dead right. If it's more of that—stuff. Like I told you, Chet."

She said briskly, "Absolutely. Chet, what's happening with South Dakota, what's his name, Spatz?"

Spaetz. Chet's windy answer added up to "nothing much." When she caught Dan yawning, she urged him to turn in. "That was a long day, sweetie, and we're still jet-lagging."

He said wearily, "Okay, Mommie. Chet, that's good news on Kosters. So let's get cracking on those two votes."

"Right, absolutely, Governor."

Chet took the cheese tray and glasses to the kitchen as Dan walked slowly down the hall to their bedroom, stooped with fatigue. *He's wearing out.* Chet ran on about the show: "Sure to get top ratings, with that cast. A very dramatic presentation of the Governor's strong—"

"Chet, could that 'going fishing' ploy really work?"

"Oh, no question it's do-able, Mrs. Sterling, if it's done right. With no fallout."

She slapped a sheet of Saran wrap around the oozing Brie. "So what's this about Harley Richmond?"

Voice hushed, he talked of a young man who worked in Richmond's congressional office years ago. Shot to death in his town-house bedroom one afternoon in '64—an unsolved case. But his brother now said he was present in the basement at the time, and so was Richmond—in the bedroom. It wasn't entirely clear if the man was shot "by Richmond or an intruder. Or possibly killed himself. The point is, Richmond's the only one who knew. And he never came forward."

She asked what Richmond was doing there. Chet said, "I understand they were. . . umm, romantically involved."

Rinsing glasses at the sink, she peered at him, wondering why he'd call *that* "romantic." "What's the proof, besides what this brother's saying seventeen years later?"

He said there was "corroborative evidence" of generous unsecured loans Richmond made to the brother over the years: "Obviously the price for his silence." Plus personal correspondence between Richmond and both brothers.

She said slowly, "So what're you talking about? Obstruction of justice, something like that?"

Chet said that was one possibility.

"Well, you were right not to mention this to the Governor, Chet. Under no circumstances should he hear anything like that." She squeezed the sponge, suds spilling over the glass. She felt like glass herself lately, fragile, transparent, resonating to all the rising decibels, waiting in fearful trembling for that pitch that could shatter her to bits.

She mused, "We can't have any slipups now that we're so close. But the Governor needs our help, our protection. He counts on us to do what's right for him. . . ."

He said quietly, "I think we're finally getting on top of this thing, Mrs. Sterling."

No reaction to his words. "We need to win this soon, Chet. Very soon. Before that wretched conference in Cambodia grabs off all the media. . . ." A few days earlier, in a flash hunch, she'd realized if they didn't win this before Devlin got his grandstand play in Phnom Penh, they might not win it at all. Dan said she was just borrowing trouble, talking like that, but she couldn't shake the hunch.

She set the glass on the drainer, watching the drips spill off. Softly: "Do what you think you should, Chet. Just make sure you're doing what's good for *him*—and do it right. But I don't want to hear anymore about it."

For him. For him. . . .

When she got to their room Dan was already in bed, drowsing off. As she creamed off her makeup, he asked sleepily, "Chet have anything else to say?"

"Nothing much. Mainly how much he liked the show."

"Mmmph. He say any more about Richmond?"

"Oh, that's a big fuss over nothing. Apparently some pansy who used to work in his office got himself shot years ago. It's certainly nothing we'd want to hear about."

"Damn right." He yawned. "You coming to bed, Mommie?"

"Yes, sure."

He was already dead asleep when she slipped between the sheets a few minutes later. She kissed his forehead, whispered, "Sweet dreams, Danny." Spooned, cuddled against his warmth, until he rolled away from her in his restless sleep.

Then she lay tensely curled on her side, blinking into the darkness, waiting for the blue pills to work.

CHAPTER SIXTY-SEVEN /

June 2nd

Robin

Jolted awake, dream still raw. Napoleon's coronation, from the French brandy ads. But Roy Bob wore the royal robe, grinning, snatching his crown from the kneeling lackey. . . Larry.

Choked with foreboding, Robin blinked at the lavender ribbons floating over the bed, anchoring her panic. So long since she'd thought of the inevitable coup de grâce. The longer the deadlock had stuck, the more she'd forgotten how fast it could change. Tied at twenty-three, Talbott somehow slid from focus, as Balch had earlier. So it seemed more like a dogfight between Larry and Sterling—and how could Larry *not* win that?

Yet the dream reminded her it could be over quick as a car crash. If Sterling *or* Talbott got lucky, he could cop three votes in an hour. . . and where would that leave Cambodia?

Sheet pulled over her head, she pushed past her dread to negotiate a deal: *Just get us through the conference, lord. That's all I ask you, not such a lot. . . .*

A few hours later she did the royal greetings bit herself for Barbara Walters in a state of red alert, although Walters had claimed she only wanted "some relaxed, spontaneous family footage." She'd seen too many people make asses of themselves trying to be "spontaneous" for Walters.

☆

At dinner the kids were congratulating themselves on how "A-one terrific" they'd performed with Walters. Larry said they'd better catch the show before they doled out reviews, and anyway it was on hold for the time being; some "Citizens for America" outfit had enjoined any airing by ABC until Sterling got equal time.

Loud raspberry from Jason. The talk drifted to questions Walters might've put to other presidential families. Sean thought she'd ask Washington about his wooden teeth. Jason said maybe how Jefferson liked sleeping with slaves?

Hoots all around. "Foul ball, buddy," Larry declared.

"Okay then, how he invented tomatoes, and that other stuff he fooled around with in his greenhouse." Robin said my, my, she had no idea he was so up on old Tom.

Sean figured Walters would've wanted Lincoln to take her along to the war front, or to visit soldiers in the hospital. That sounded to Larry like "a good bet, pal. And what would she ask his boys?"

How they beat the draft, Jason suggested. Sean said Lincoln was "my favorite one of all those guys. I always wanted to see how that statue of him looks in the dark."

Great idea, Robin said, why not check it out tonight? Larry sheepishly decided that was fine for *them*, but without more lead time, he'd humor the Secret Service and "stay put."

Jason protested that Nixon had done it, "one night when he was real nuts. What good's being president if you can't even go where you want?" But Larry couldn't be shamed into it.

The mischief mood was back as they scampered up the broad white steps of the Memorial, giggling like trick-or-treaters, a half-dozen agents fanned discreetly around them. Deserted except for a handful of startled tourists, Lincoln sat in a luminous glow, projecting a field of calm. Sean murmured, "He looks like he was waiting for us."

She hugged his shoulder, so grateful for these snatched moments. Tiptoeing, whispering like in church, they read the quotes on the wall: "Let us strive to finish the work we are in to bind up the nation's wounds. . . ."

Melissa whispered about "Daddy walking now in Abe's big shoes." Robin wished he were there to share the moment. *Damned agents anyway.* . . . Hearing a clatter of steps, she flashed him grinning, booming, *Okay, troops, little change of plans here.* But the agents' instant snap-to doused that fantasy. She turned and saw Nelia Wingo, NBC's Robin-watcher, sprinting toward them with a three-man crew.

The magic switched off, agents closing protectively around her. As they swept her toward the stairs, Wingo wailed, "Ah, have a heart, Mrs. Devlin! First you give Barbara Walters a whole day, now you've gone and ruined my nice steak dinner."

She laughed. "Okay, Nelia. We were just leaving, but you can walk us down to the car."

Wingo knew by now how to get her talking. After asking what they were doing at the monument—"Lincoln came up at the dinner table, and Sean suggested. . . ."—she slid onto the prospects for Larry's Indochina project.

"Well, the resolution of support is still tied up in the House. And the Phnom Penh conference opens in just three weeks. I can't believe any American would willingly sabotage this chance for peace in Indochina and a national future for Cambodia. But that may be the net effect, unless we unite soon behind this broad international effort. . . ."

☆

"And I got in a whack at Pol Pot, too." Brushing her underarm across Larry's chest. "Told her they should go bird-dog him for a change instead of us."

He chuckled, asked what old Abe had to say for himself.

Tracing his face, she whispered a field-trip report. ". . . just hunkered down, looking so sad. And wise." On the lumpy Lincoln Bedroom mattress they could feel bumpy crochet through the sheet stripped from her bed upstairs. Tucked against him, smiling into the dark: "Wished so much you were there with us, babe. I kept thinking what Abe would say about Cambodia, how much he'd be for what you're trying to do. Like it says on those stones, 'That these dead shall not have died in vain. . .' "

"Ah, shit." He lifted her hair to his cheek. "That guy could write. But talk's cheap, Rob."

She touched his lips. "Have faith, babe. It'll happen." Urging him to believe what she herself didn't. "It can't've come this far just to flop, Dev."

With rarely vented bitterness, he mulled the jeopardy from Sterling having "turned this into a home-grown football." She sensed his hunger, his rage that they might go empty-handed to the conference cooked up from his own guts.

He said Trudeau and MacGuigan kept calling from Canada, "trying to figure out what the hell's going on down here. Why this government can't get its act together." Now the U.N. was dickering to horn in on the peacekeeping force—kiss of death, hooking up to that goddam arthritic bureaucracy, but he might not need them to finish it off, since New Zealand and Sri Lanka were already balking on sending in troops.

"But they don't count for much anyway, Dev. As long as the Viets are still ready to move. . . ."

He said god, don't count on Hanoi either, those old politburo gents were antsy as hell over how this was coming down. Wiley was working on damage control, but they were just about convinced we wouldn't come across. . . .

She said a lot might work out once the conference started. Or Cal would come up with something: "He's in this too, don't forget, babe, so screwy with hope—he can't believe what he's started. Cal must have spare aces up his sleeve."

Sarcastic laugh. "Yeah, well. Keep on dreaming, Rob." To stop the sad words, she plugged his mouth with a kiss.

Sweet shots volting between them. She whispered, "D'you think Abe and Mary ever had half as good a time?"

"Not a chance." Sprawling, laughing, they slid into one more dizzy romp on Abe and Mary's bed.

———

As he drifted back they were lying across the mattress, still locked together. He felt the bursting contentment flowing out of her, echoed back in his languid moves.

Ahhhh god he felt good.

They lay for a while, stirring in quiet rhythm, steeped in feeling. Then she nibbled his neck. "Hate to break this up. But I've got to pee."

Chuckling, he edged free with slow moves. As they came apart she sighed, "Ahhh!", pulling his face into a kiss.

When she went in the john he was already missing her. Way back when they were dating, friends would ask every so often was he getting serious about Rob. He always said no, no, no. Sometimes, just to prove it, he'd stop calling for a while.

He'd always wound up dropping the dime again, but thought Rob was too simple for him, too goody-goody for the long run. Christ, what an ass he'd been. With brains like that, he'd needed real Irish luck to wind up where he had.

Question was, would the luck still hold. . . ?

When she came back he was strutting, naked, glowing cigar clamped in his jaw, brandy glass in hand. These past months the sour suet had boiled off him; he was back to that bronzey-gold leanness she used to find so sexy in him.

He waved the cigar. "I like the digs, Rob. Nice idea."

"Thanks, m'lord." Leaning on him, slipping her hip along his. "But I guess a few others had it first. Including Michael. Some of his better naps were here, n'est-ce pas?"

"Bitch." He smacked her rump.

She twirled away, spun down on the bed. Feet propped against the carved headboard, she laughed about Dennis Darien's tour of the room. "Out of line as usual, he speculated on how many First Couples did it in here. The mind boggles—Pat and Dick, Ike and Mamie, Eleanor and Frank. . . ."

He said Dennis was definitely in the wrong line of work. She supposed she might not be surprised if Mel and Thad had checked it out too. Bristling paternal reflex: "Hey, is Mel sleeping with that pipsqueak?"

Guilty twinge. "Oh, for lord's sake, Larry. I don't know, ask her yourself. I'm not playing cop."

"Okay, okay." He flopped down beside her.

She said softly, "Melissa's okay, you know. I used to worry quite a lot about her, but she's turning out fine."

He rolled over and seized her belly, puckering it together. "You used to sing to Mel when she was in there, remember? Back when I called you Birdy Pumpkin."

She said he never ceased amazing her.

He grunted. She watched his care lines ease as she lightly traced his face. "Well, damn," he said happily.

"Oh, yes."

They lay quietly for a while, stroking, nuzzling. Suddenly he said, "Tell me about September 17th."

She asked blankly how he'd remembered that date—she forgot she'd even mentioned it.

He said tell him what happened. So she talked about coming home dog-tired from a three-day campaign swing, catching a TV rerun of *The Misfits*, ". . . and the next thing I knew I was totally into it. Especially Monroe, wailing about those damn mustangs. I remembered Michael once compared me to her, which I found flattering at the time—my 10-inches-above-the-knees phase, you remember that, babe."

"Ahh, yes." Vestigial grievance flicked across his face.

But that night Robin had been riveted by other similarities: "Like that mewling they passed off as compassion. But mostly by Monroe playing herself, the sexy dishrag, such a doormat for those guys. The terrible, visceral need shimmering out of her. I kept remembering Marilyn was one of Michael's scores—for all I know he had *her* up here too."

He shook his head. Wary, nettled smile.

"Well anyway, just from that movie I could see why she tumbled for him. Such a born victim. . . like me."

She'd slept very little that night. Next morning, still tasting that movie, she'd canceled her campaign schedule and gone to an AA meeting where some woman was "bitching about her husband. How much trouble they'd had since she went off the sauce—an old tune around AA that I'd heard a hundred times before. But this time it hit like a fire alarm. I just finally recognized, Dev, that if I was ever going to be well—stay well—I probably couldn't stay in this marriage."

Before he could challenge that, she slipped off the bed and picked up her Perrier, swigging agitatedly as she prowled the ugly floral rug. "I just hadn't ever seriously considered that, see, Dev, because I was so sure it was the other way around: I was trying to stay dry so I could stay married. In an odd way, that's why I moved out, you know, way back when. . . . To break the old cycle we were stuck in—too much boozy penance from me, too many ladies and late nights from you." She shot him a sad smile. "Not much fun, was it, babe?"

He cleared his throat. "Ah, boy. Pandora's box. . . ."

"That's right, Dev. But we can slam it shut right this minute if you want."

Face tight, neutral, he flipped a go-ahead gesture.

Cold bottle pressed between her breasts, she said she'd also realized what a lousy love life she was settling for, "waiting for Mr. Five-Minute-Wonder to come home damp from his shower at Miss X's. Wasting so damn much time and energy trying to figure out which ones you were fucking then, and did they do it any better than me."

"Is that question or indictment, Rob?" Watching her like a hawk from the bed. "Because I sure—"

"Oh, question, babe. Old, dead question." The whole mess was at least as much her fault as his. She'd finally gotten that much sorted out on her trip to France.

Bristling, he said sure, he figured France would come into this somewhere. "The minute you're home from that trip, next thing I know you're packing up, moving out, moving to New York. Shit, it had to be you met some guy. . . ."

"Not the way you think." She hesitated, sure she'd regret this impulsive candor. Plunging anyway: "But I did have my first real affair. Actually just a four-day fling."

He asked sarcastically who was the lucky guy, that fag actor she was dancing with in *Newsweek*?

No, no, that was a publicity ambush. The man was "just a tubby Italian, grey and half-bald. Nobody I'd look at twice. But a warm, caring person who I guess turned around my life."

She was editing out her astonished discovery of the terrains her unlikely friend—lover—had opened in her. "And I don't mean that in any crude, obvious way, Dev. What I remember most is the last time I saw him, when he apologized for not being able to 'take away that sadness' in my eyes. Somehow I knew the minute he said it that nobody could do that but me. I also knew I didn't want to—couldn't—live like that much longer, so I'd damn well better try to do something about it, better late than never."

So she had, and she'd mostly stuck it out since, except for a few early jolts off the wagon. Arms crossed defensively, she turned back toward his pensive face. "So now you know all my deep, dark secrets."

He said dryly, "Very interesting."

His head still went mercifully blank, trying to imagine her with some other guy. *That* other guy. It almost hurt more to know it was a dumpy old Italian, "nobody I'd look at twice." That meant she hadn't done it for any easy reason, but because the guy had touched a part of her where he'd been shut out for years. . . where he hungered now to get to.

If it wasn't already too late.

She swigged nervously from the bottle. "And since you're polite enough not to ask, I might mention that you're the only one I'm sleeping with these days."

His crooked finger beckoned her back. She sat behind him on the bed, her nails trailing on his back. He grunted, "Well, since you didn't ask. . . me too."

Soft laugh, bending to kiss his shoulder. "Ah, ain't we the pair, babe. Marooned together in this leaky dinghy."

"Mmmph." He pressed her hand to his stubbly cheek. "Damn right, Rob."

She whispered, "Ever since Cal showed up I've been feeling so. . . *ferocious*. About things—about life."

He nodded. Grinning, she said in an odd way Larry had turned out to be her "first big adventure, P.C. Post-Cambodia." Spoken like a lover's name. "But what a treat, Dev, that it turns out to be *you*, of all people." Cupping his cheek, stroking his eye crinkles. "I feel so lucky getting to know you this way, babe, after all the years we wasted. Such a special time it's been. I'll always be so glad we had this."

He stiffened in defensive reflex. "Hey, listen, Rob, I'm not writing anything off."

Sad smile. "Fair enough, babe. Just so you realize none of this detour through Wonderland's going to last. Us, or here." She gestured toward the walls. "So just don't start counting on it, Dev. It's like wartime. The Blitz. Such a hell of an experience we've been through together. But sooner or later, babe, when 'real life' hits again. . . ."

That coiled snap echoed his drive to make things happen. "Fuck it, Rob. I'm not giving up on you, or any of it. I'm damn well gonna dent the waxworks, at least."

"Oh, you sure will. Real big dent." Crooning with pleasure, stroking his chest. "You'll see, Dev. Guaranteed."

"Okay. So listen, Rob, how about"—fingers laced with hers—"you come along for the ride. Give it a try."

"Ah babe, don't you get it yet?" She shook her head, hair spilling over his gut. "This is *our* Shangri La, Dev. Our little piece of jungle magic. Here in the dark and the warm. But don't forget how that old story ends."

He pulled her down against him, leg slipping over hers. "Ahhh, shit. Good times, Rob."

"Yesss yes." Embracing him with her skin, herself. Before they moved past words she whispered, "Are you thinking much about Michael lately?"

He paused, lost in thought. Then: "Sure. I always do."

"Me too. But especially tonight. . . ."

"Aaarrhhh." He rolled above her, nuzzling her lips. "You think Mike's keeping score?"

Soft laugh. "I'd bet my socks."

"Well, what the hell. Let's keep him busy." And off they slid, sailing in Abe and Mary's bed.

CHAPTER SIXTY-EIGHT /

June 2nd

Prilla

Priscilla told herself—told Dan, anyway—that they were two votes shy and closing fast, counting Chet's "fishing expedition" as good as done. Yet it had been four weeks since they'd picked up Nevada—and neither of them cared to dwell on that one. Dan just said he was glad Pickett had "seen the light and come over the fence."

Washington seemed gripped by a peculiar mood, part exhaustion, part frustration—part spring fever, maybe. She kept thinking of Rhett Butler's parting shot: "Frankly, my dear, I don't give a damn."

Dropping Dan off for a stag Heritage Foundation lunch, she murmured through a parting kiss, "Give 'em hell, Harry." On to the Carlton. As she crossed the lobby, spirits light and jaunty for a change, a few reporters nailed her: Was she satisfied with her husband's progress on the House vote? "Encouraged, but certainly not satisfied. This election should've been over and done last January, and here we are rolling into summer, still without a real president."

Any estimate on when they'd reach the magic twenty-six? "Not a clue. How about you?"

They asked about her next antidrug special, the "President Dan" rally in Chicago, and Robin Devlin, until she waved them off at the elevator. Upstairs she spent four hours phoning wives of swing congressmen—pure penance, hard work.

While Laurie Pendergast dialed out, Priscilla chattered, 3-by-5 in hand: "Ellen, I just wanted to tell you what a pleasure it was to see you last week at. . . ." Or Marie or Virginia. "Pity we didn't have more chance to chat about. . . ." Skim through kids, weather, whatever, down to, "You know, Patsy,"—or Sheila or Jan—"I've felt since we met that you're the kind of woman who appreciates the seriousness of the crisis this country's going through. And what a major leadership role your husband could play in resolving this terribly dangerous impasse. . . ."

Finally she sent Laurie out and called Kittyhawk's office herself, letting her urgency spill over. "Carla, I hope you realize this isn't just a job you have now. It's a rare opportunity to *make something important happen*—something as good for the country as it could be for you, and how many times do you get that kind of chance?"

Every time a cold spark of hope fired: Maybe Florian would drop the tease and come across.

"I think he's getting ready to move, Mrs. Sterling." Choking on disappointment, knowing in her gut *you could make him do it, girlie.* "But it'll take more time."

"We've just about run out of that," she said tartly. "I don't like to think my confidence in you is mistaken, Carla. But if you let him shilly-shally much longer, you'll blow any advantage you could get. I've taken a quite personal interest in you, you know, and I'd like to see you do something smart and useful *for yourself.* . . ."

That got her a vague promise to "keep in touch." She hung up the phone thinking bitterly, *and pffft to you too, cookie.*

Dan turned up at four after taping a half hour for CNN. She asked how it had gone. "Too damn much harping on Vietnam," he said wearily. "I wish to hell they'd concentrate on that House vote." She mentioned her thirty-two calls, betting him they'd made a thousand for every blasted vote they got.

Edgy chuckle. "Well, don't quit while we're ahead. Maybe a couple thousand more will turn the trick."

For two hours they pressed the flesh one-on-one with a handful of swing congressmen corralled by Chet. Even as she twinkled through the familiar ritual, she sensed its stale flatness. Maybe she was reading in her own battle fatigue, but it seemed to her they were *all* fed up with this endless crisis—even the gasbags most responsible for it.

The last of them was broomed out in time for her and Dan to catch the evening news. An ABC reporter outside a bamboo gate was talking about Pol Pot, "the mysterious leader of one of this century's bloodiest purges, who maintains his defiant isolation. . . ."

She snapped that it sure must have been a slow news day. On NBC, a Cambodia "exclusive," Tim Crispen interviewing a gloomy young woman she recognized from that famous Girl-on-the-Crutch photo, "a survivor of the 500 orphans marched to jungle death camps. . . ."

She broke a fingernail changing channels. Dan said they'd sure got plenty of yardage out of that Farragut tearjerker. She caught a note of envy in his voice that didn't please her one tiny bit. On CBS she found Norleen Talbott at a jock tournament for handicapped kids, being asked what she thought of Robin Devlin's performance as First Lady.

Pricked to alert for the routine answer: "Doing a fine job. . . valuable contribution to this difficult interim period before my husband is returned to the presidency. . . ."

Then she saw herself against the Carlton's potted palms, fending off the same question: "I'm sure Mrs. Devlin is trying to do the job as she sees fit. But maybe we could all do with hearing a little less about foreign countries with self-inflicted problems that are really no concern of ours." Fixed smile not matching her words. "If she wants to get involved in politics, she might pay more attention to the constitutional crisis right here at home—the *real* threat to America's future."

He could hardly believe what he was hearing. With the roof still caving in all around them, Pril had to go blow off her gaskets on Robin Devlin. Picking that cat fight he'd warned her not to. Damn women with their bitch grudges, just couldn't keep their claws to themselves! Now how in hell was *that* supposed to help out with this endless mess?

She turned to him with a guilty simper, her naughty-schoolgirl look, like she damn well knew she'd come up with the wrong answer but would see how far wheedling got her anyway. "Sorry, hon. I know that wasn't what I should've. . . ."

"Dammit, Prilla." He drilled her with a furious glare. "What the hell did you do that for?"

She jumped like he'd slashed her with a knife. "Oh Danny, honey, I'm so sorry. I only meant—well, I'm just so fed up with what she's been getting away with. So I just—Danny, please don't be mad at me, hon."

He guessed she'd only done it out of worn-out pique, but by god, he was pretty worn down himself, and that blooper was the last straw. Glowering, he said he thought they'd agreed she wasn't going to get into personal attacks on Devlin. "Pril, that stuff doesn't do us any damn good at all."

Babbling her contrition: "I know, I know." Oh god, what if she'd hurt him. *Like Jane Muskie. . . .* "I won't let it happen again, I promise I won't, never a peep, Danny."

Still stiff with anger, he headed for the kitchen. "I'm getting a drink. You want one?"

"No. Yes, sure. Whatever you're having." She trailed him, cooing remorse. "I won't even mention her again. Strictly 'no comment' from here on out. . . ."

The one cross she could not bear was any hint of rejection from Dan. His approval was her oxygen, her essential sunlight. Yet she sensed his cold, punishing withdrawal even as she snuggled up to him, frantic to undo that rebuff, purring anxiously, "Oh please, sweetie. You know I never, ever mean to hurt you. Let's kiss and make up."

"Okay, okay." She pressed against him, clinging, lifting her face for that forgiving benediction. He pecked her cheek brusquely and turned away to pour the drinks.

Glancing peck. Barely that.

Damn her!

CHAPTER SIXTY-NINE /

June 4th

Robin and Prilla

Robin promised Jim she'd stay in the woods, running her variable figures-eights today among blooming fruit trees, bursting carpets of blossoms arcing over her head. A lone saxophone down at the Fence wailed

"Hey Jude." Now guitar chords. Patchy voices floating, song snatches to remind her of the party she was missing out on. From the trees she saw the spurting fountain—but not the soul-mate choir.

Spotty applause. Then crisp, piercing sax notes of "Jumping Jack Flash." Stretching her figure-eight, she added another loop to the edge of the trees beyond the tennis court. That fountain's perpetual orgasm, constant climax, fit nicely with her Big Pecker theory of history, she decided. Suddenly, on impish impulse, she lit out over the grass.

The vets unrolled a jubilant welcome, leaping, hanging off the Fence, fists punching air, "RAH-BIN! RAH-BIN!" Banners whipped, dipped in salute, sax stuttering a horse-race opener, dat-dat-da-dah, wings to her feet. Laughing, waving, she stretched her stride to the rhythmic chant, "RAH-BIN! RAH-BIN!"

Near the cover of shrubbery, she heard sudden backfire: pop pop —THWACK! A tree trunk just ahead of her threw off a giant splinter, burst a pale raw jagged wound.

Jim's trained hair-trigger reflexes reacted to that sound he'd heard so often in troubled dreams. Hurtling forward to push her down, minimize the target, he saw one bullet strike a tree, so he knew before they hit the ground this was real. His head screamed *No, no, not her!* as he pulled out his gun and yelled into the radio, and all the time he wasn't even sure the little lady underneath him hadn't taken one like the tree.

Whump! Body-tackled from behind, she pitched into the grass, face first, a ton of someone on top of her, crushing out her air. She struggled to lift her face from the grass, gasp for breath. Feet darted around her in noisy confusion. Lots of shouting. She wanted to tell them she couldn't breathe, but no sounds came from her throat.

Like slow-motion double take, her stark terror caught up with her. She heard a sound. Herself whimpering with fear. Suddenly three guys grabbed her, hoisted her up. Ran her, feet paddling air, to the van suddenly there in the drive.

They tossed her in, piled in behind. As the van zoomed up the drive, she still didn't know what had happened. Jim said somebody "apparently took a potshot at you, Mrs. D." She wondered if she looked as rattled and pasty-faced as he did. "Real sorry about that tackle, I hope I didn't break your face."

Knees going like marimbas, she insisted she was fine, not a scratch on her. But they took her to the doctor's ground-floor office, where

Stephanie was waiting. Slipping into aftershock, Robin fought the impulse to burst into tears. Somehow the sight of Stephanie pale and bug-eyed stifled the urge.

Robin told her for heaven's sake cool the fuss, she was perfectly all right. Larry sailed in, shaken past his usual cool, choking on a lousy joke. "Rob, that's not, ah, the kind of constitutional I'd recommend."

An operator buzzed through: Would Mrs. Devlin care to take a call from Mrs. Varner? *Got 'em trained right on priorities, at least.* . . . She said please tell Mrs. Varner she was absolutely okay and would call her back shortly.

Melissa, from the family compound at Bar Harbor: "Mum! What's going on, are you really okay?" All the family nightmares stirred alive in one TV bulletin. Robin said of course she was, fit as a fiddle, please don't worry dear, it was all a big fuss over nothing. Larry got on the line, talking in the same vein, and Melissa seemed to settle down a little when she realized he was there.

The doctor found two scratches and a chin bruise—not much damage. Stephanie asked if she'd do a brief bit for the cameras, "just to reassure your public." She said no way, absolutely not.

Larry told her the perpetrator was one Herbert Holland, age 37, apparently a whacked-out ex-adman from Boston, 4-F in the Vietnam war on a psychiatrist's letter, his recent history a mix of odd jobs and cocaine abuse. After the shooting, some tripwire vets at the Fence had literally tried to kill him with their bare hands, and in the process, put several agents out of commission. Safely in custody, Holland wasn't coherent about much, including any motive. He kept babbling about the voices telling him to "shoot the bird."

Robin decided on a nap and urged the rest of them back to work. En route to blessed privacy upstairs, she had to fend off everyone she saw, including Hamilton, shrill with distress, and Carmen, all mother-hen solicitude.

She got rid of Carmen by swearing she was going right to sleep. Then she called Tish and argued against her coming down. "No, no, I'm fine, hardly a scratch. I didn't even know what was happening till it already hadn't."

Tish said if some nut had been target-practising on *her*, she'd want to talk it out. Robin said well, different strokes for different folks; right now all she wanted was a long, fat nap.

Brief chat on some bit of trivia. Later Robin couldn't remember what.

After hanging up, she locked herself in the john and turned on water for a shower. As she peeled off her shorts, her knees unexpectedly buckled. She crumpled to the mat, pouring out her terror juices—tears, sweat, phlegm, stink. Seeing that splintered tree, feeling the bruising tackle. Imagining herself split like that trunk, bleeding wood sap. *There but for the grace of. . . . God help me, god help me. Thank you, lord. For my life.*

After the purge, she felt free and clear, freer than she could remember. Not afraid anymore, of whatever was to come. She took a brisk shower and slept like a zombie until Carmen woke her at six, saying the boys had been waiting to talk to her since they got home from school.

Lord, the boys! She rushed out to find Sean waiting in the hall, crumpled in a chair, staring at her door like a little lost boy. She crunched him in a hug, saying see, look, honey, she was absolutely fine, he shouldn't worry for a minute. They went downstairs to find Jason, arms twined like moonsick lovers. Jason's reaction was cooler than Sean's, but no mistaking the relief that flared in his eyes.

Sean still didn't let go of her as they watched the news, curled on a solarium couch. Without any new footage of her, the nets ran any-and-everything else. She was numbed by the shock waves the incident touched off, the Fence People especially carrying on like she'd been a DOA. "Here, of all places!" one anguished vet kept saying. "That psycho draft dodger violated everything the Fence stands for, man."

At dinner they stayed off the subject, but the kids were sweet, on their best behavior, Sean reaching over every now and then to pat her hand.

Later that night Larry came upstairs and cradled her for a long time, rocking her to his tick tock "Thank god, Rob, thank god." She felt a bit like letting go, crying it out again, but decided to be brave for him instead.

They talked for a while. Pillow talk, happy talk. He was still holding her when she drifted asleep.

☆

Priscilla and Dan heard about the attempted shooting from an agent, while they were driving from the Des Moines airport to some kind of farm rally. Her first reaction was it must be a joke—in extremely poor taste. But of course agents didn't joke about something like that.

Dan said right away, "Well, thank goodness she wasn't hurt. Paul, you get off a telegram. Flowers too, I guess. Say Prilla and I are distressed at the news, but thankful to God that she came to no harm and so on.''

She felt she ought to say something. But the words stuck in her throat. Her choking emotion wasn't really for the Devlin woman, although god knows she'd never wish her that kind of harm. But if it could happen to *her*, inside the ironclad security of the White House, it could happen to any one of them.

Clutching Dan's hand, she looked out on the solid walls of people they were speeding through. *To us, too. Any one of those maniacs out there could go after us, anytime.* . . .

She cleared her throat, said yes, she thought the flowers were a good idea. "Not too extravagant a bunch, but something to convey the idea. Lord knows I've never had much use for her, but certainly nobody would want her to be. . . .''

Paul remarked on what a disgraceful sign of the times it was that someone would attack "a woman." Dan reacted with a start, tuning in—a little late—to his wife. He hugged her to his chest, saying softly, "Pril, don't you worry. I'm not letting any of those bozos get anywhere near you."

As if he could stop 'em. . . . They were swimming in a sea of bozos now, thumbing their nose to danger every day, way out on the high wire without a net, cranking higher all the time. And the only thing she knew for sure was if those nuts ever got Dan they'd better get her too, because she'd never make it through without him.

CHAPTER SEVENTY /

June 5th

Robin

When Robin woke at 6:20, he wasn't there. She yawned and put her nightgown on for Carmen, who brought the coffee and papers at 6:45, beaming, "Sure is a good morning to see you safe and smiling, Mrs. Devlin!"

"Top of the morning to you, Carmen." She unfolded the *Post*, found herself at the bottom of page one. "What kind of day is it out there, anyway?"

Carmen looked out the window. "Well, a bit cloudy, Ma'am. The weather is. But the strangest thing happen, I swear I don't know what to think. . . ."

Robin peered curiously at her. "Carmen, what are you muttering about?"

Carmen said she wouldn't find it in the papers, tapping the glass. Robin got up to see. The view outside was postcard-pretty, same as usual, except. . . . the Fence was bare.

Scraps of flotsam littered the Ellipse, like after a holiday concert. But no people. As if they'd melted, vanished in the night.

She asked angrily if they'd been arrested, shipped out, or what? Carmen said no Ma'am, apparently they just "went back where they came from. Wherever that be."

CHAPTER SEVENTY-ONE /

June 9th

Prilla

When the media spotlight finally went back on Congress after that bizarre Fence sideshow folded its tents, Priscilla realized that wasn't such good news after all.

What had started out as "intense scrutiny" was now House-bashing, a contact sport. The papers were open sieves, riddled with leaks, idle rumors, mostly involving money. Each fresh exposé, print or TV, shot more paralysis into the system.

Some House members claimed they didn't have a shred of privacy left. Montana Democrat Tyler McCotter, for instance, complained that the *L.A. Times* had published his tax returns, the *Chicago Tribune* had fine-tooth-combed his three mortgages and his father's debts, and now *The Wall Street Journal* was investigating his kids' college tuition payments. McCotter said sometimes he wondered why any sane, self-respecting man would run for Congress these days.

A few swore they'd never do it again. Like Jolson, the Pennsylvania Democrat roasted for his travel vouchers by *Newsday*, although he'd been "glued by duty to my office chair these past five months, grappling with this national crisis." Seventeen of his official trips the previous term, including Pago-Pago, Rio at carnival time, and the Paris air show, were made with his female scheduling assistant, "an innocent and entirely reasonable coincidence." Jolson said if he'd known this kind of indignity was involved in public service he'd've stayed in the fertilizer business.

The more the media poked, the tighter Congress froze in its glacial indecision. Sometimes Dan's troops made guerrilla war on the House, keeping it open all night so one member after another could talk to the TV. "I've seen the sacred processes of this chamber tattered and dragged in the *dust*. . . ." But by morning nothing would've changed.

Meanwhile the next circus, the one scheduled for Phnom Penh that Priscilla prayed would never open, was warming up off-stage, Canadian Air Force flying in air conditioners and so on. The TV preparations in themselves guaranteed the conference would be puffed into a big deal, ABC flying in its own earth-station satellite link-up rented from the Brits, and god knows what other extravaganzas in store.

When she heard a rumor that the British Prime Minister and French Premier might fly over to beef up the opening ceremonies, she realized with a sickening jolt that if Devlin managed to get away with this, Dan might just wake up and find himself dealt out of the game.

She tried to put that over to him, in a "pure conjecture," what-if scenario. He told her not to borrow any trouble, they had plenty already. But her gut instinct was still saying, *Stop the circus now, while you still can.*

CHAPTER SEVENTY-TWO /

June 19th

Robin

Legal skirmishing from the pro-Sterling PACs kept the Barbara Walters special off the air for over two weeks. When they settled for ABC agreeing to "proceed with" an hour special on the Sterlings and Talbotts but airing the Devlins now, Larry decided to combine the Friday-night screening with an early eighty-seventh birthday party for his mother.

Robin voiced no objection. Lord knows five dozen Devlins weren't her ideal company for watching the show, as she'd hashed out with Tish the night before. This Mother Devlin birthday blast was also a fourth anniversary of her last terrifying slip, from champagne toasts to waking up on a ward in one precipitous three-week slide.

But of course he should invite them. They had their own deep roots in this White House, and it seemed right to gather them here before his acting presidency reached some kind of crescendo with the opening of the Phnom Penh conference.

Before she went down to her AA meeting under the marble stairs, she got a call from Harley Richmond. She tried tactfully to sniff out why. "Harley, it's always such a delight to hear your voice. Is there anything I can do for you?"

He said no, not particularly. Sounded pretty drunk. "I just wanted you to know, my dear, that these trials we've all been enduring will come out right in the end. You tell your husband that for me, will you?"

Swackered to the gills, she gathered. She said he could say it himself, soon enough—she expected him and Wynona next week for the Medal of Freedom dinner.

He said ah yes, Wynona. "You know, I think it wasn't until you happened along the way, my dear, and made your difficulties so bravely evident, that I fully realized what a sorry lot you wives were expected to put up with. Now there's another thing I have to thank you for."

Harley rambled on a while, aware he wasn't making much sense. Finally he apologized for "interrupting your day. I wanted to pay my respects and pass along those thoughts."

He hung up realizing he hadn't been strictly truthful with her. At another, earlier time he'd seen stark evidence of Wynona's pain, seen the steel and suffering under her fluttering magnolia skin. He'd learned that day what she was willing to pay for love. And tried ever since in his own way to make it up to her, but time was never enough for that. Ah, those extraordinary Southern women. Wynona was made like his dear mother, lovely as lace, strong as oak. He'd picked well the day he decided on her.

He poured another stiff one, musing on the good fights he'd fought along the way. Now he was up against the Johnny-come-lately types like Daniel Sterling, new-style flash-in-the-pan concoctions of the tinselly public-relations boys—a vicious, know-nothing lot made hungrier by their desperation. They had few scruples, and no gut comprehension of what real tradition meant. Or real strength of character. To them the sacred processes of this government were mainly opportunities to fatten their cronies' pockets.

He'd spent a career fighting blind, grasping ignorance like that, and by god he wasn't about to knuckle under now.

Robin didn't know what to make of that rambling, boozy, somehow disquieting call. She thought of calling Larry, then decided not to. *Come on, Harley's fine, just having a little toot. The one you need to get a handle on is you.* . . .

At the AA meeting she found herself talking about the ripple effects of smother-mothers.

☆

A blasting preparty shower reminded her what it felt like being trapped at these mass family events, sprayed by the collective energy of that congenitally overachieving bunch. *Nothing casual about tonight. But take it as lightly as you can, there but for.* . . .

Melissa wandered in, asking if her geometric silk was okay for the tribal blowout. Robin said, "Sure. Looks great. You're getting svelte as a stick, Missy."

Melissa moaned about falling into the birthday cake.

Mock indignant: "Come on now, where's the do-or-die party spirit, have a fine old time if it kills us?" She tucked a hug around Melissa's waist. "*Avanti*, kiddo. Let's jump aboard for the latest spin on Granny's merry-go-round."

Pauline was holding court on a hall couch, drawling yarns about "your Uncle Michael, the first Devlin President" to the kids. The salty grande dame made a model grandma. Mother-in-law was another story, of course. . . .

Robin asked if there was anything she could do for her. Brusque brush-off from Gran: "Not a thing. Hamilton's seeing nicely to that, aren't you, Hamilton?"

He beamed, cock of the roost in his party glow. "Yes ma'am, Mrs. Pauline."

Robin drifted down the hall, greeting the various relatives roaming the quarters like flea-market regulars. Only one missing was Alexis, who ducked the tribal shivarees whenever she could. And here came the star attraction: "Evening, troops. Sorry I got held up. Where's the birthday girl?"

They flocked around like pigs to the trough. Cecily mooning like a cheerleader beholding the star quarterback. Brian kept slapping Larry's back, saying, "Hanging in good there, boy. Hanging in real good."

It occurred to her, hearing Tim Brandt explain to Kevin the differences between the Chinese and American banking systems, that this really was an interesting family. She liked seeing them, even en masse, now that she finally had one thing straight: She didn't give a damn what they thought about her, the red-headed alien, "that Swann girl," Larry's "tragic mistake." The one Devlin who couldn't sail worth a damn, let along hold her liquor.

Okay, she preferred to be liked. Even hoped sometimes to be understood, at least by the kids. But her gut was finally convinced that she neither expected nor required the approval of this family.

At 7:45 Larry and his mother led the parade down to the State Dining Room. The seating plan for Granny's dinner had been drawn up by Jason and Sean. For once, the inevitable sniping and bickering couldn't be blamed on Robin's table arrangement.

Delighted to find herself between Kevin and Billy Sedgwick, she got to settle a '50s-trivia argument on the name of Buddy Holly's original band: "He only *had* one. The Crickets, of course." And stumped them on who'd given Buddy his seat on the fatal plane ride: "Hah! It's Waylon Jennings," she crowed from triumphant memory.

Halfway through the meal, Larry toasted "the significant breakthrough we honor tonight, Mother's eighty-eighth year. May it be as full and rewarding as all the rest rolled into one."

Cries of "Hear, hear!" as they rose to drink, Robin gripping her Perrier in both hands. The other speeches were mainly by the kids. Shelley read a funny poem about "the Granny Game." Kevin warbled his best Sinatra version of "You Did It Your Way." Billy reached for eloquence: "To the gallant lady who stands unique in American history—the only mother of *two* Presidents."

Tough act to follow, but Melissa took a shot. Gulping nervously, she noted "a lot of talk these days about women needing good role models and so on. I guess I'm pretty lucky in that, 'cause I've got two of the best, both gutsy and terrific—my mother and my grandmother."

Good god. What's this. . . ? Brief, startled silence.

Kevin stood up, saying loudly, "I'd like to second that." Guiltily murmuring that this was Mother Devlin's night, Robin lifted her glass along with the rest. But Kevin took it from her. "Nothing doing, Rob. This one's on you."

Larry noted, "Mother always says the only present she wants is attendance at Mass, especially from her ungodly grandchildren." Hoots, laughter, applause. "But we thought of something she might like anyway, as a token of our enduring love and respect." In sudden darkness, a huge cake rolled in—a miniature White House, roof ablaze with candles.

The grandkids grouped for what Kevin called "the moment of truth, Gran. Don't forget the wish!" Bing McCarthy captured the instant when Pauline puffed, and dozens of lungs doused the candles. Lights, cheers, popping corks. . . .

At 9:45 they trooped to the East Room to watch the Walters show on a large projection screen. Larry and his mother got front-row center, the rest fanning around them. Robin stayed on the move, making sure everyone was taken care of, until raucous applause greeted "An ABC 20/20 Special: Barbara Walters Visits the Devlin White House."

Slipping into a back seat, she was too nervous to take much in. The opening clips of Michael and Alexis included the scenes burned into memory: his Inaugural Address, the funeral. . . . Glimpses of herself and Larry were like peering down a tunnel of time. *A hundred years ago, at least.* . . .

In the recent footage stuff she was thrilled by how well the kids came across, making the starchy old house come alive. She choked up at Sean showing Walters the heart he'd carved on an oak tree with PEACE & LOVE, S. P. DEVLIN, explaining in his soft voice, "I wanted to leave a souvenir of the special time we spent here, and my Mom said that was okay if it didn't cost the government any money. So I thought of this."

Walters gushed that this "might well have been the tree that took the bullet aimed at his mother two days later." *But it wasn't, dope!* In-laws craned to catch Robin's reaction.

In his Oval Office interview Larry surprised her with a tribute to "my wife Robin's great courage in confronting and dealing with medical problems aggravated by the pressures of public life." From the audience, an anonymous "Yeah, Rob!"

In her Truman balcony interview, the Fence People marched in the background, like ghosts from a long-gone dream. She came across less nervous than she'd felt, talking about Cambodia as "a child we see by the roadside, wounded and sick, very close to death. There isn't one among us who wouldn't stop to help that child if we could, and bring it back to this miracle of life we all share. . . ."

She remarked that she and Barbara were both reaching their middle years—and so was America, in a sense. "One interesting thing about middle age is how you become less willing to waste time on careless mistakes or half-baked choices. You decide what you really want to be, want to do, and you get on with it. In that way I think countries are a lot like people. So isn't it time we decided what kind of people we Americans want to be? What we want this special country of ours to stand for. . . ?"

The rest whizzed by in a bright-imaged blur. Suddenly the lights came up, audience standing, clapping, whistling lusty cheers. Kevin was first to reach her. "Goddam, Rob!" Wet smack on her cheek. "You were terrific, girl."

"Ah, come on," she murmured, feeling her blush.

"Kid you not, you're a natural-born star. Every time little old self-effacing Rob hit the screen—boom!" He snapped his fingers. "You lit the damn thing up."

In the triumphant buzz she sensed a subtle, slightly fawning shift toward her, tacit agreement she was "the goddam star of the show." Lord, how this bunch did love a winner. Now the grande dame herself approached, head tilted in beady appraisal, like a bird checking out the worm. She half-expected thanks for stealing my birthday show. . . .

"Ah, Robin." Head pecking forward to deposit a leaf-dry kiss on her cheek. "Very nice, my dear."

Peggy, the prime Devlin busybody, drifted up. "That went quite nicely, Robin, don't you think?"

"Oh, quite. Great souvenir for the family scrapbook."

She thought the kids handled themselves very well.

"Ah, they were terrific. Absolutely."

Peggy cleared her throat—not a good sign. "Although I must say, Robin, if you don't mind me mentioning this, that all that unfortunate business about the drinking and so on happened a very long time ago. So it doesn't do any of us much good for you to harp on it still, when people might be more inclined to just forget it, don't you think?"

Okay. Nothing changes, after all. . . .

She surprised herself by saying sweetly, "Peggy dear, why don't you mind your own damn business?"

Glancing away from Peggy's spluttered apology, she saw Ben Boylan draw Larry aside for whispered consultation. Her radar locked on as Larry reacted with a snap of his head, bending closer to hear Ben's message. Breath caught in her throat, she watched Larry turn to the crowd, ashen-faced. "I'd like your attention. . . ."

Instant silence. Voice battling emotion, he said he had "a distressing piece of news. Harley Richmond's body has been found on the steps of the Jefferson Memorial, shot in the head." Finding her eyes. "Apparently by his own hand."

CHAPTER SEVENTY-THREE /
June 19th
Prilla

Priscilla had taken three pills already—one an hour before the show, which they were watching with Chet and Paul so they could "squeeze in some business" at the breaks. Yet when Dan turned it on, she could barely make herself look.

She'd been braced for a Walters treatment: gushy, breathless, kid-glove. What she wasn't prepared for was Robin Devlin's impact. From her stroll-on to a fatuous intro—"the charming, determinedly original mistress of America's most historic house"—the woman was riveting. Even with kids tripping over the dog, she stole every scene.

Walters' whole approach, letting them treat that national showcase like some kind of jock barnyard—sock races in the Grand Hall, for heaven's sake!—showed an appalling lack of dignity and respect. "Oh, cute. I'd like to know who wrote *this* script," Priscilla hissed as the women changed into sneakers at the tennis court, Walters burbling, "Do you do this to all your visitors?" Galloping slow-motion around the court, sweating up their silk dresses, the dog bouncing on the sidelines like a Dallas cheerleader.

She looked across at Dan. "Well, honestly, now. Can you beat this for tacky?" Paul muttered something about scraping the bottom of the barrel as Larry Devlin popped up at a picnic lunch, Walters simpering, "Mr. President, could I interest you in a barely used tennis racket?"

Worst was Robin's balcony interview, overlooking what Walters called "the best view in the house"—staged to play up the bobbing propaganda posters along the Fence, of course. Walters had no trouble coaxing shockers. On those abandoned children—"difficult to ask about, since we've seen your happy family life"—Devlin talked of making that hardest-ever decision "quite literally to save my life."

More on her boozing problem, so gooey-sweet, so sincere. Trusting her kids to "be strong and mature and loving enough to understand why I had to make that choice." Claiming the main joy of these last months was the chance to "share this very special time with them. But when I was living away, I felt just as much a 'mom' as I do here. That central reality of my life never changed, never will."

The supine way Walters played right to her! Let her run piously on about appreciating now "what I'd heard from other First Families about the importance of keeping a sense of privacy, nurturing a personal life apart from the fishbowl limelight." Coy coaxing about her painting hobby: "You mean we're *never* going to see these famous 'dabblings'?" Robin smirking like a cat: "Not if I can help it, Barbara."

Now an especially fawning, booby-trap question: "Other First Families had found it "so difficult to move out of this magical house. Will it be the same for the Devlins?" But Robin skipped nimbly by: "We take things one day at a time around here, Barbara. . . ."

Then off on the usual toot on Cambodia.

Priscilla couldn't sit still for that. Wouldn't, anyway. She carried the ice bucket out to the kitchen for a refill.

Out of the room, away from Dan, she realized how hard she was fighting to keep control. Body strung tight as piano wire, trembling from that assault. . . .

She drowned out the TV chatter in a rattle of fresh ice. Some idiot had left crackers open on the counter, where they'd be soggy before morning. She sealed them in Ziplock, put them in the fridge where they belonged.

Voices still drifted in. Leaning on the fridge door, cheek pressed to that flat coolness, she waited out the end.

As she took the ice back to the room Paul was saying, ". . . mixture of Brentwood and here, if we can work out two locations. You'll want the family included, of course."

Dan's first choice was the Malibu ranch. "Forget that phony tennis game—we'll get Barbara up on a horse, give her a tour in the Jeep. That'll be a good excuse to get back there ourselves." That damn ranch again. Sometimes, when the heat was on, she thought he wished he'd never left it.

But she was grimly fixed on the Walters "sequel." *Lumped with the Talbott also-rans? Paired up with Norleen to follow an act like THAT?* She snapped briskly, "I'd say scrap the whole idea."

Paul said something about the hard-fought deal with ABC, but she slapped back, "If you *think* about it, Paul, you'll see it'd just play up the fact that Dan isn't *where he belongs*. And that won't do us any earthly good at all.''

Mild protest from Dan: "Shoot, Pril, I can't see handing back an hour of network time." While they thrashed it out, a phone in the sunporch office rang. Chet went to answer it.

". . . all for letting the people out there see what's really going on, by gosh." "Besides, you'd just be lumped on equal footing with that has-been Talbott. . . ."

Suddenly Chet was in the doorway, face pale as milk. "Governor, I'm afraid we've got bad news." Stammering, avoiding her eyes. "Congressman Richmond's body was found on the steps of the Jefferson Memorial. With a note—and a gun."

She grabbed her throat. "Oh, no. No, no."

Dan and Paul together: "Gosh, that's terrible news. A damn shame." "Certainly unfortunate, Governor. Great loss to the Congress. . . . Of course, West Virginia is a split state."

She choked out, "Are they sure? No one else. . . ?"

He said he didn't know much more than he'd told them.

She felt Dan's eyes, his questioning frown, but couldn't look at him. She went abruptly to the john and threw up.

No thought in her head but *Clean up! Clean up!* She flushed the toilet and rinsed her mouth. Gargled with mouthwash, brushed her teeth. Tremors shot through her. Skin clammy, teeth chattering, breathing rapid. . . .

Fighting off the warning signs, she saw behind her closed eyes, like a TV rerun, Richmond at the House podium conferring with Whalen. That peculiar purple tie, rakishly tilted under the kindly old face, frowning, concerned. . . .

She doused her face, shakily repaired her powder and lipstick. Eyes in the mirror like burnt holes. Dry.

But floating like a shadow on the mirror, she also saw that other face. Wondered if she always would. . . .

At least she knew now how much she loved Dan. This much, even this. *But he must never, never know*. . . . She took another pill, prodding, *Get out there! Before they leave.* . . .

The TV already had it. ". . . sixteen terms in Congress, rising to chairman of the powerful House Foreign Affairs. . . ." She stood behind Dan's chair, hands on his shoulders, leaning on his strength. Drawing calm from that touch.

Her shaky voice asked Paul how this should be handled.

"I recommend sincere regrets, that sort of thing. But beyond that, regardless of your commendable reluctance to exploit this situation, Governor, I think we're obligated to press ahead with whatever advantages this opens up."

Patting her icy hands, Dan said he and Chet had "brought Paul into the picture on that fella we've got set up to get lost fishing. But we can't play that card till we're sure we've got all our ducks lined up."

They talked out other prospects for a roll. Chet said Richmond couldn't be replaced without a special election. He'd have to check the West Virginia election laws, "but if the Republicans on that delegation can hold the line, we should have a clear field for several weeks, minimum."

Dan mused to himself on the timing. "Okay, this is Friday night. That gives us two days till the next vote. Now we don't want to tip our hand, play that Iowa ace too soon."

She pressed on his shoulders. "No, no, Danny—he's got to get lost *tonight*. Before he's supposed to've heard about Richmond." *This must be worth the price!*

Paul thought that scenario would have "significant advantages—if we can count on a ninth vote." Back to the list of possibles: South Dakota, Arizona, Vermont. . . .

She said softly, "All right, get working. Flat out. Any stone you can budge. I have some ideas myself." The strength of her pain poured into her grip. "But it has to be now. That's what you're saying, really, Danny. It's got to be now."

He nodded, stirring in the chair. "Right. It's about time to fold this traveling circus." Finger stabbing between Paul and Chet. "And you guys damn well better know there's no room for slipups. This time around, just make sure it gets done right."

CHAPTER SEVENTY-FOUR /

June 20th

Robin and Prilla

The Irish wake began with Harley's death.

In her agony of grief Robin went over and over that odd last phone call from him. If she'd only taken time to tell Larry. If she'd only *heard* what he was saying! *Lord forgive me, there but for.* . . . Larry tried to say he wouldn't've heard a cry for help either. But her grief was a huge, hot stone in her gut, searing, pressing out other feeling.

At 10:30 on that Saturday morning Larry appeared in the West Wing press room, while she and the kids watched on the solarium TV. "All of us are profoundly shocked and saddened by the untimely death of Congressman Harley Richmond. . . rare gifts of character, scholarship and intelligence fused to an extraordinary devotion to this country and what he called its 'great democratic engine,' the Constitution. . . ."

He slipped a sheet from his pocket. "Two handwritten letters were found with Congressman Richmond, one addressed to his wife Wynona and one to me. Under normal circumstances I would maintain the confidentiality of such a communication from a man I consider a good friend as well as a colleague. But I believe Harley Richmond intended this to be shared with the American people, whose best interests were the guiding principle of his distinguished career. Accordingly. . . ."

She'd already seen that letter, wept over it. But she felt its brutal impact again as he read flatly: "Dear Mr. President, I ask you to forgive a tired old man for quitting the field before the battle is won. The personal toll exacted in the struggles of the past months has finally exceeded my capacity to weather the storm, but I hope that in choosing to fold my flag, I do not fail the trust and responsibility you and so many others have placed in me.

"A great American writer, James Baldwin, once said he was 'worth more dead than alive, unfortunately.' I pray this may be so in my case, Mr. President. The most profound regret of my life is that the Congress in which I have proudly served for thirty-one years, and the House committee which I have chaired, have not yet approved the joint resolution of support for the Indochina peace initiative. My earnest hope is that my removal from the arena of often rancorous debate might in some manner help to advance that historic goal.

"If my life could be exchanged for the peace that now struggles to take root and breath, I would consider it an enduring memorial to the America I love and have tried to the best of my humble abilities to serve.

"With respect and affection, and abiding gratitude for the many rich and full blessings that have been bestowed on me, I remain, your friend, Harley P. Richmond."

She honked into a Kleenex as Larry said curtly, "That letter speaks most eloquently for itself. I have no further comment, except to express again my sense of deep personal loss at his passing and my profound condolences to Mrs. Richmond and the family."

Melissa said if *that* didn't blast out the resolution Daddy better send in the Marines. Robin winced: "Missy, don't joke about that, please."

Walter Cronkite was saying gravely, ". . . eloquent deathbed statement from the colorful sixteen-term West Virginia Congressman known for his purple bow ties and the fluent Shakespearean quotations that peppered his conversations. . . ."

She wondered briefly why Cronkite, not Rather. ". . . a remarkable intensity to the grief evidenced in these halls today. There's also much guilt. Many congressmen privately agree with Richmond's chief aide, who claims that Richmond was killed by the long, bitter committee fight over that stalled resolution. Now Speaker Whelan is trying to muster enough zero-hour support to rescue it, as Richmond's dramatic suicide note clearly intended."

God, she hoped Charlie was up to this one.

She couldn't deal with the flip side of Harley's death: Sterling just two votes short of the magic twenty-six. Somehow that *two* seemed geometrically more ominous than *three*, so close it was almost home. But Talbott had been that close for a while, and *he* hadn't made it. So she clung to what Tish had told her that morning: Hang on tight, lady, because anything can still happen, and probably will.

The kids shared her subdued, elegiac mood. As if a fire bell were clanging and you rummaged through your head, deciding what to grab if the alarm turned out to be real. . . .

Her shadows hadn't let her out on the grounds since the shooting, but today she insisted on "one last run, maybe, Jim." She'd make it short, but wanted to tuck in the feel of these woods again, just in case.

Running through the Children's Garden, past the tennis court, she felt the drizzling rain, softly hissing on the leaves. She lifted her face to the drops, soaking up that sense of privacy she always took from these runs—ignoring the four shadows slogging noisily around her. *Some day I'll have woods back to myself, somewhere. . . .*

Trying not to think that the Phnom Penh conference might have died with Harley. Or think of Harley's fine, fragile brain splintering, splotting like the tree trunk. Trying not to moon over everything she'd miss if—when—they moved out. She groped for plucky optimism over what was happening, so fast now. But nothing helped stem the grief.

On her way back to the house she detoured through the Rose Garden, acknowledging to herself as she plucked one perfect, peach-colored rose what a bald lie she'd told Walters about leaving this house. *Lord, but I'll miss old Hamilton popping up everywhere. And Carmen, and the wake-up coffee steaming from the silver pot. . . .*

Impossible to recall now how much she'd dreaded coming here, how passionately she'd wanted to trade these imperial comforts for "real life." *Time to move on, kiddo,* she reminded herself sternly. *Hit the road, Jack, before you start thinking all this is real too.*

She spent the rest of the day painting, furiously trying to finish up "Prilla and Ghosts." In the scene of Prilla trapped by an angry crowd outside a factory gate, she'd finally found a way to make it work: In place of the workers, she was painting in Cal's orphans. Those hungry faces reaching out, like an echo of the Fence People.

☆

The stereo was crooning "Let It Be" when the wake-up call came at six. The painting wasn't quite 'there'—but getting close, she decided when she stepped back to look.

She changed and went downstairs, where she discovered that tonight's game plan was a family picnic and swim, "just us, nobody else," said Sean. "Okay by you, Mum?"

"Terrific. Whose first-class idea was that?"

Jason snorted, "Take a bow, jerk."

In the crisp June night air, over burgers and hot dogs around the pool, they debated the last time they'd picnicked like this, just the five of them—"the original nuke family," as Melissa put it. And nudged loose memories of other good times. "Hey d'you remember when. . . ?"

Larry drifted into a string of yarns about "your Uncle Mike," who'd died before either of the boys was born. Holding the floor with those tall tales the kids had all heard before but loved hearing again. Always stories of Michael's life, she noticed—never of his death.

Larry was at his unmatchable best at moments like this. The thought came to her as she watched Sean's shining face: *They'll remember this night for as long as they live. . . .*

After dinner they all took on the pool, even Kilkenny. Slipping through the cool, night-black water, she felt soft and sad and somehow close to tears. At the other end Larry and the boys noisily played "Devlin water polo."

She jackknifed gracefully to the bottom, rolling belly-up to watch the lights filter through the water, rippled by the thrashing legs down the pool. She stayed down in that dreamy wet-blue world like the Little Lady in the Glass, humming, turning in languid circles, feeling the swirl of mermaid hair around her shoulders. When her lungs seemed about to burst, she kicked up with powerful strokes and exploded into the light.

Melissa floated by, squirting a small gusher in her direction. "Hey, Mum, that wasn't half bad. A little more practise and you might walk on water."

She said happily, "Later for you, kid."

Right now, right this minute, it seemed to her it was worth it all, worth anything just for this one night.

☆

While the word about Richmond was still going public, Dan's Congressional operation burst into high gear, pushing every likely combination of moves. Priscilla watched, listened. . . wasn't reassured. Dan said those Democrats were "so traumatized by the way old Richmond did himself in that they're afraid to get off the pot, let alone jump the fence." She wanted to spur him on, put fire in his belly, but the ritual words stuck in her throat.

She tried to keep busy, avoid the TV. Yet echoes seemed to seep from the sockets, walls: Police interviews. Stately wake. Highlights from the "long and distinguished career." Funeral arrangements for grieving colleagues. *No no no.* . . .

She heard from another room Devlin reading that letter. Afterward she caught one staffer's remark that they'd've preferred a natural death, since the Democrats were "playing this like a papal funeral. But it'll have to do. . . ."

She went to their bedroom, took another pill, and called Florian. Sharp tone etched by her acid grief: "Carla, *there's no more time.*" Kindred spirits talking now. "We're one short and closing fast. If you want him to get any credit for putting us over, you'll have to jump *now.*"

"Wait a minute, he's coming in. Let me talk to him."

"Well, make it fast, Carla. This is his last shot."

CHAPTER SEVENTY-FIVE

June 22nd

Robin and Prilla

Over the weekend Robin struggled for an even keel, praying her mantra a lot, venting her anxieties with calls to Tish and Bella. Now, while the family gathered in the Oval Office with the peace-initiative team to watch the Monday morning House session, she found herself wrapped in fatalistic calm.

For once the rest seemed more jittery than she did, though the men's moods were obscured by stiff upper lips. Hale Wiley drummed a rat-a-tat on his knees. As conference delegation chief, he probably had as much at stake as any of them—except Cal, who shredded his cuticles as Eric Lowenthal talked quietly to him. *Like a doting uncle.* . . .

Seeing Cal the old Buddhist philosopher in that state somehow revived her own nervousness. She caught his eye, fingered a V sign. He threw her a slow, sad, luminous smile that stirred memories of. . . .

Tish's voice rasped in her ear: *Leave it alone!* Anyway Stephanie had the squatter's right there, if anyone did.

As Ben bustled in and out with bulletins, Larry was. . . inscrutable. Except the slight tic under his left eye. The 9 a.m. session would be covered live on two networks—"a positive sign in itself, Mr. President," Eric suggested. "Those fellows don't preempt for a no-news event."

She murmured, "Don't count any chickens, Eric."

"Damn right," Larry agreed. "Harley's dealt up a new hand, but it could play either way."

On-screen, John Chancellor talked about "Richmond's dramatic suicide on the steps of the memorial to the man he often called 'our noblest American,' an event which seems likely to shake up the stalled peace conference vote. But it could also finish the acting presidency of Laurence Devlin, architect of that bold initiative. . . ."

Jason muttered, "Bullshit. What do those faggots know, anyway?" She silenced him with a glare. Loyalty she understood, even the tribal loyalty built into these kids, but they had to roll with the punches now like everyone else.

After the opening prayer, Charlie Whalen recognized "the honorable gentleman from Missouri, the ranking minority member of the Foreign Affairs Committee."

Gravely solemn at the podium, Anthony Curreri waited in silence, head bowed, till every rustle stilled. Then: "A good and wise man once told me, 'Tony, the thing to remember is not so much why we fallible mortals choose to act, but how.' That man was Harley Richmond, a revered colleague who was also my close personal friend, whose passing I mourn with a grief surpassing my poor powers to give it voice."

The orgy of eulogy was launched. Curreri said his whole committee had been subjected to strong pressures, and perhaps "in that highly charged atmosphere we were less sensitive than we might have been to the effects of that stress on our colleagues. I was certainly—tragically, as it turns out—not aware that the Chairman was more severely afflicted. . . ."

Robin shivered in empathy with that breast-beating grief. *See, you weren't the only one. . . .*

He heaped praise on Harley's wisdom, his foresight, his "rare ability to penetrate to the heart of an issue with a single phrase, a single skillfully crafted thought. In one hearing he borrowed the words of a young musician, an adopted American: 'Give peace a chance. And from those tendril roots we might yet see a towering oak of human possibility grow.' I resisted that optimism at the time, out of my profound concern for safeguarding our national interests.

"But I cannot turn a deaf ear to Harley Richmond's final plea: that these United States should lend their full voice and resources to the international effort to stabilize a lasting peace in southeast Asia. When our committee convened in special session less than two hours ago, I moved for approval of House Resolution 137, the Phnom Penh International Peace Conference Act, as a living memorial to our late esteemed Chairman. At this critical conflux of history, I believe we must find in ourselves the courageous vision and abiding faith with which Harley Richmond lived a long life in the service of the country he loved. I believe we must rise to his final challenge, and give peace a chance."

Dramatic pause. "Mr. Speaker, distinguished colleagues, at the request of the interim chairman, the honorable gentleman from New Mexico, I am privileged to report the results of our committee's deliberations. The Foreign Affairs Committee voted this morning by twenty-eight ayes and eight nays with no abstentions to approve House Resolution 137 and urge its immediate consideration by this House."

Tidal applause as Charlie recognized the House Rules chairman, to report that his committee had "within the hour voted to recommend waiving the three-day rule so the full House may immediately consider House Resolution 137.''

Harley's last hurrah rolled to inevitable triumph. Member after member rose to heap praise and urge prompt adoption of the resolution. As Wiley noted this "fresh evidence that nothing more instantly enhances a man's reputation than his untimely demise," Larry took a call from the House Whip.

Robin tuned to his cryptic "When was that?. . . Yep, okay." Worried frown on Ben. "Understood. Jack, let me know if. . . . Right. Looks that way. Cold trail."

He hung up and said, "Troops, we have a problem with one of the Iowa Democrats. Doug Kosters and his wife are unaccounted for. His staff say they haven't a clue where he is, but a neighbor thinks he went fishing over the weekend."

Ahhh!

She'd thought she was ready for this, but that arithmetic came at her like a mugger's knife: Iowa a split state, like West Virginia. *No please, not now, not like this.* . . .

Jason wanted to know how a guy like that could just disappear. "Beats me, Jase," Larry said cheerfully. The FBI and state police were combing the woods, but so far no trace.

Jason muttered angrily about "goddam shit-faces."

Stern compassion in Larry's glare. "Jason, back in January, how long did I predict we'd be here?" The boy mumbled a couple days. "That's right, a few days. 'Maybe a week at the most.' Okay, so we got five months more than we bargained for, and one thing we've accomplished is what's going on in the House right now. So simmer down and shape up, Jase."

The final vote was almost anticlimax: H.R. 137 passed by 319 ayes, 106 nays, 8 abstentions. Larry's secretary rolled in chilled champagne and a Perrier. He did the ceremonial uncorking, spraying foam over his desk.

The toasting was a tournament in eloquence, but no one topped Cal's "To life. . . to Cambodia."

Midway through Eric's third toast, to "the President whose tenacious vision in the face of much disheartening adversity has brought us to this propitious hour," NBC switched to Chris Wallace at the Carlton with Governor Sterling.

The old ham stepping from the limo, reaching for Prilla's hand. "Any comment on the House vote, Governor?"

He paused on the sidewalk, letting more cameras catch up. "Chris, I want to commend the House of Representatives for its action this morning. The great goal of world peace is shared by all Americans. It seems fitting that our national commitment to pursue a just and lasting peace in southeast Asia should be reaffirmed on this day of tribute to the memory of the distinguished leader who gave such articulate voice to that cause, Congressman Harley Richmond. . . ."

Mixed reaction—mainly surprise—in the Oval Office. But watching Larry's grimace, Robin caught his quiet mutter: "Okay, cowboy. You think you've got it. . . ."

Priscilla stood beside him, reaching for composure as he said, ". . . one of the finest public servants this country has produced. . . wise counsel will be sorely missed. . . ." Struggling to keep from sliding into her usual frozen-smile face.

The drive in from the farm had been perfectly timed, for once. Dan got first crack at reacting to that farce in the House. *All right, enough of that. Let's get down to it. . . .*

Asked about the presidential vote, he said with one major logjam out of the way, he was "fully confident the House will promptly do what I've been urging for the past five months and two days, and that's exercise its constitutional duty to *elect a president.*"

Darn right!

Up in the suite, the mood was high and rosy, staff bustling with upbeat bulletins, speech writers polishing his "address"—she was superstitious enough not to let anyone call it anything else. Talbott was on a living-room TV: ". . . full congressional support, we can proceed to the Phnom Penh negotiations, which will have my strong support as president. . . ."

Dan chortled, "You tell 'em, Roy Bob. Make the most of your last hurrah, fellow."

"Don't you get too cocky, Dan Sterling," she teased. "Is that your feet I see trotting 2 yards off the ground?"

He laughed. Paul said, "Looking good, Governor. You should have it wrapped up in within a few hours."

Dan patted his belly contentedly. "Well, better late than never, I always say."

Trying hard not to think how easily this could still fall apart, she went to the bedroom and unpacked her royal-blue linen suit, wrapped in voluminous tissue paper. For so long she'd been meticulously plotting every detail of this day. Now that it was finally in reach, all she could think of were the hundred things left undone.

Ticking off her mental checklist, fighting emotion, *organize, organize.* . . . Jean-Marc had done her hair already; he'd be by for touch-up after the vote. She wished she'd paid more attention to the swearing-in plans coordinated with the White House and House brass months ago. In the House chamber, they said. Roughly two hours after the vote. In her skitter of chagrin battling anticipation, that face still floated in her head. Whatever Chet had done, she mustn't ever know. . . .

Most of all, Dan must never, ever find out.

He called her in to catch Larry Devlin in the Oval Office: ". . . can think of no more fitting tribute to honor the memory of Harley Richmond. . . gratified by Governor Sterling's strong support for the peace initiative. . . ."

Dan chuckled, aglow with satisfaction. "Nice touch. Going out in style, aren't you, Larry boy?"

Devlin introduced key members of "our delegation" to the Phnom Penh conference, Wiley and Lowenthal—"*your* delegation, buddy. For as long as *that* lasts," Dan muttered. Then Calvin Farragut, "who helped many of us see what was at stake through his internationally acclaimed film on Cambodia. And my wife Robin, who has contributed so much to the success of this effort. . . ."

"Well, listen to that," Dan said. "The guy said something nice about his wife, for a change."

She patted his arm and went back to the bedroom. All she wanted to hear now were the roll-over speeches.

She still felt bad about the lovely shocking-pink wool outfit she and Adolfo had worked so hard on for the "original" Inaugural. But after exhaustive consultations with Ginny, she'd decided on the royal-blue linen, an Adolfo she'd worn twice already. She told herself firmly, *Never mind, it'll do. Just focus on what matters.* . . .

She wished with all the force of her battered iron will for this ordeal to finish *now*. But the bitterness still rankled, under her desperate hopes. She couldn't shake that sense of being aggrieved. . . cheated of her due.

This wasn't the way it was supposed to be.

Robin raced around her workroom, wrapping up all the canvases except the one on the easel. If Sterling got his votes there'd be no time, and she already worried these paintings might get left behind in the rush, like hostages.

The Sterlings wanted to move in "as close as possible to immediately after the swearing in," as one flunky had put it. And she knew how obsessively Prilla would comb the house. *Tant pis* who poked through her underwear drawer, but she had to make sure the workroom was cleaned out.

Sharp rap at the door. Larry, tie dangling at half-mast, face oddly frozen. She pulled him inside. "Oh lord, Dev. What's happening?"

Wry smile. "Charlie called. Says the word's out they've got it. He's not sure who's rolling but they only need one."

Arrow to her chest. "Ah, damn. So it's the boot, finally. I'm so sorry, babe. Today of all days. . . ."

"Well, that's the breaks." He looked vacantly at the easel. "Hey, that's coming good. Are those Cal's kids?"

"Yes, right. Never mind that. Are you okay, babe?"

"Sure. Hell, can't say I didn't see it coming." He leaned his rump wearily on the dresser, hands jammed in his pockets, sad smile. "So. . . I guess the ride's over, Rob."

She asked softly how he felt about that. Absorbed in the toes of his shoes, he rolled the question, kaleidoscope reaction flicking on his face. Slowly: "Okay, I guess. Sure it hurts, but there's no point racking your brains with what-ifs. . . ."

She was thinking of their stillborn, Michaela. Feeling a bit like that now, but this time the grief was shared.

As she poked it out of him, the fizzled confusion in his head started to come clear. "At least I got a good shot at it—which I guess is more than I ever expected, just between us." He hesitated. Then, rapidly, words tumbled out: "And I think I did about the best goddam job with it I could, Rob. Sure I screwed up some, maybe plenty." A light peacefulness washed over him. "But overall I think I did. . . about the best damn job I could."

She beamed. "Ah, better than best, Dev."

He shot her a faint grin, conceding that when he'd got dumped into this, he really thought of it as Michael's turf and what the shit was he doing here anyway. "And all that—you know. Then after Cal turned up, when I got a handle on something that might make a difference. . . ."

She burst out, "Now what happens to the conference?"

His face darkened. Curtly: "Who knows? That dumb shit cowboy. . . but we got the resolution, Rob. At least we tied his hands that much."

Smiling, nodding. "Oh yes, Dev. You did indeed."

Damn if it didn't almost feel like victory glow. "Hey, at least they'll know I was here. And I seem to remember a promise to somebody that I'd settle for that."

Bell sounds of laughter as she crossed the room to fold him into a chaste, almost ceremonial embrace. Murmured against his ear: "Bravo. Bravo for you, babe."

He gripped her hand as she stepped back. Cocky grins, like two kids celebrating some obscure, uncharted rite of passage. He touched her face, tracing her chin. "Real glad you were along for the ride, Rob."

"Me too. I wouldn't've missed this for anything."

He pulled her into an exulting kiss. A minute later they were laughing, tossing the litter off the narrow bed pushed against the wall. Got half their clothes off before they rolled into their goodby to Shangri La.

The ringing phone attacked the languid tangle on the rumpled bedspread. She stirred, muttered, "Damn." Blinked at the offending instrument across the room. "They're probably chasing you down, babe. You want to answer it?"

"Hey, it's your phone."

"Okay. Just don't go away." Rolling free, she smacked the naked rump jutting under the T-shirt he hadn't shucked.

"Yes, hello. . . Hang on, Ben." She waved the phone.

He snatched up clothes getting off the bed. She dressed with record speed while he pulled on shorts with a phone pressed to his shoulder. "Okay, I'm on my way." He hung up. "Well, here goes nothing. You coming to watch the hanging?"

"Sure, of course." As he zipped up his pants, she tossed a sheet over the painting on the easel, knotted a cord. Sure enough, it *did* feel like the house was on fire. *Get Jim to move the paintings.* . . . "Okay, all set, babe."

Suddenly he pulled her back to the bed. "What the hell. Let 'em wait." They tumbled down, his eyes so close, so vulnerable. She cradled his face. For a long, private moment each savored, stored up the look, the touch of the other. She murmured, "We sure came a long way, babe."

He rocked her gently. "Ah, damn. That's a fact, lady."

"No regrets, then?"

"Not many." Pause. "Not yet, anyway."

"Ah, sure. Give it five minutes. . . ." Lazy chuckle. "Maybe the trick is to find something to laugh about, Dev."

"Yep, I guess." He rolled onto his back, avoiding her eyes. Flatly: "Listen, Rob, I'm not out of a job yet, you know. This vice-president thing. . . ."

"Yes, sure, I understand." She rubbed his chest, asked what color the old Naval Observatory was.

He peered at her. "White, I guess. What's. . . ?"

She said maybe her promise to stick around might cover living in a white veep house too. "That's not to say I'm signing on for a four-year hitch, mind you. But I'll hang in for a while. At least until it's. . . the right time to go."

Smile like a sunburst. "Mmmph. Okay by me." He buried his face in her spilling hair, whispering so softly she almost missed it, "Thanks, Rob. For—everything."

"My pleasure, sir." She patted his rump. "Enough said, Mr. P. Ass in gear, let's move it out."

He stood up and shrugged on his jacket, tie dropped on like a noose. For one teary moment she peered around, cramming her head one last time with the look, the feel of this very special room. *Don't forget to give Jim the key. . . .*

Suddenly she laughed. "Well, there's two good things out of this, at least. Norleen gets her damn furniture back. And Prilla gets to go to the Royal Wedding instead of me."

"Yeah, well. Take it where you find it, kid."

She locked the door and walked with him to the Oval Office, ignoring the curious stares they drew from Ben and the other staffers. One TV was already rolling with the one-minute floor speeches opening the afternoon session. Third one up was Wayne Kittyhawk, who started off, "Mr. Speaker, the time has come to ring down the curtain on this farce."

Larry said quietly, "Okay, there it is. Number nine."

He reached for the phone on his desk.

CHAPTER SEVENTY-SIX

June 22nd

Robin and Prilla

As the rest of them watched Kittyhawk, Paul put his hand over the phone receiver, saying in an oddly excited voice, "Governor, d'you want to talk to the White House?"

Dan looked up, blinking irritation. "What? Who is it?"

"She says it's Devlin."

Priscilla beamed at Dan. He grunted his surprise. "Well, my gosh. He's not wasting time, is he?" He got up, hitching his pants, squaring his shoulders.

Holding the phone to his ear, waiting for Devlin to come on the line, he caught the end of Kittyhawk's brief, fiery ". . . the job the people of Alaska elected me to do. And after we've finally elected a president in the person of Daniel Sterling, this House should immediately set about its equally grave responsibility to find the guts and means to make itself a functioning body again."

Dan cleared his throat. "Good to hear from you. . . . Well, thanks very much. And I look forward to sitting down with you soon to work out the important role you'll be playing as my vice president." She caught his eye, smiling at that whopper. Devlin calling in his congratulations somehow made this whole moment of triumph a little more real.

Now Dan was frowning, surprised. Cryptic phrases: "Unh-huh. Well, I can understand that. . . . No, certainly not. . . ."

What's this? Jangled to full alert, she tried frantically to decipher Dan's face. *Should've picked up the extension before he came on. . . .*

"Well now, that would obviously require some consultation between us. . . . All right, thanks for calling. I'll give it some thought, let you know my decision."

As he hung up she burst out, "What was that all about?"

He looked blankly at her. "He says he's going to Phnom Penh. With or without my okay."

Bursts of protest: "No way, no way." "Outrageous, Governor!" "Ridiculous, preposterous. Way out of line, sir."

She snapped, "Dan, that man obviously hasn't got it through his head that *you're* going to be president, not him. And you'd darn well better set him straight on that, starting *right now*."

They pressed him for details. "Well, he said he couldn't go to the conference as long as he was still filling in, but now he thinks he could make a significant contribution over there, keeping things on track."

Paul called that "absurd on the face of it. The man will have absolutely no authority on his own, not to mention resources, staff, facilities. What's he going to do, fly over there Pan Am tourist class? Set up a bootleg delegation of one? It's pure bluster, pure blackmail, sir. And of course you can't go along with it, not for one minute."

Dan said dubiously that he knew it was crazy, but Devlin was "a crazy guy from word one, and he's sunk all his chips into this Cambodia thing. I wouldn't put it past him just to take off and go."

Chet pointed out one advantage to "your sending him there, Governor, with orders to act on *your* authority—you'd get him out of the picture in this turnover period."

"Out of the picture? Hardly!" she snapped. "He'd be all over the news night after night, lapping up media time."

Dan shook his head. "Listen, the bottom line is who's running the show. The last thing I need right now is mutiny aboard ship. As long as we're stuck with this Cambodia thing, we didn't just lick 'em, we joined 'em. So we'd damn well better do it right, come out looking good."

They argued out pros and cons. "At least he'd be over there, not breathing down our necks. . . ." "But if he gets away with this, god knows what he'll be pulling next. . . ."

Finally Dan barked, "Okay, enough. This is my decision to make." He walked toward the second bedroom, calling out, "Barney, where the hell's that latest draft?"

Robin's teary mood was back as the limo glided to the East Gate, heavy with a cargo of gloom. She sensed that Larry was bleeding too, behind his front of determined cheer. But the kids were beyond pretending. Jason asked dourly if they'd get the fender flags going home. Larry said, "I guess not, sport. Better start getting used to it."

Rolling into the defiant roar from the packed sidewalks, she saw the crowd was mostly Vietvets, leaping, waving. Some crying. *Fence People back for a last hurrah. . . .*

Melissa craned her neck for a last look at the house, murmuring, "Gosh, it's all just so sad."

Jason said bloody rotten of the Sterlings to boot them so fast too. "At least the Talbotts got a night to pack."

Solid walls of people, grieving faces jumped out at Robin from the crowd. She couldn't look at them and keep her own lid on too. "Sean, honey, see what's on the tube."

He switched on the built-in TV. Sterlings walking to their car, waving to noisy crowd—click, click. Dan Rather in a wooden armchair, talking to a plump Oriental man. "Could you tell us about your future plans, Mr. Chairman?"

In the pause for translation, she peered at the screen. "My god, it's Pol Pot. Dan Rather's found Pol Pot!"

Jason said, "Yeah, Dan! Way to go." Larry popped a broad grin, said well, score one for Rather and CBS, as the interpreter piped up, "I intend to live in China, and pursue my goal of assuring the territorial integrity of Kampuchea. . . ."

She stared at that smooth, serene face. "Good lord. He looks. . . like the little old man inside the Wizard of Oz."

Roars fell away as they rolled into the empty Capitol grounds. Pulling up at the wedding-cake steps, she murmured, "Does anyone get the feeling we've seen this movie before?"

No answer as they stepped out into the swirl. Charlie and his escort committee waited, hand out. "Mr. President, an honor to receive you in this House, sir." He crushed her to his chest. "Robin, you're a sight for these Irish eyes."

Marine guards whisked them inside, where Larry was peeled away into a clump of dark suits. She barely had time to straighten Jason's Princeton tie and remind Sean to smile before the kids were routed off by their own escorts.

Heart riding in her mouth, she followed two gold-braided Marines down the hall to the "Distinguished Ladies" holding pen. Gertie Whalen waited in the doorway, with a small squad of congressional wives. "Robin, dear." Gertie folded her into a warm hug. "Always so good to see you."

"You too, Gert. Although I can't say I expected the pleasure tonight. . . ."

They shared a rueful, knowing laugh. She shook hands with the other three, managed some gracious chat about the weather. Three TVs were set up, cueing machines for the ceremonials. She pointed to CBS. "Have you been watching that? Dan Rather's tracked down Pol Pot."

"Yes, so I see," Gertie said. "An odd bit of timing."

"Well, as the saying goes, you takes what you can get." She calmed herself with deep breaths and small, deliberate motions, pressing her shaky hand to the waist of her red silk dress, pushing a stray hank of hair behind her ear.

The Marines snapped to, and suddenly Priscilla was there, looking so much frailer than Robin remembered. With a sense of circles closing, she reached out her hand, saying softly, "Hello, Prilla. Good to see you."

Her hand limp as a leaf. "How are you, Robin?" asked the thin piccolo voice. Glittery and impeccable as ever—but tense and strained behind that packaged crust, looking years older than last January.

"Very well, thanks. And you?"

"Fine."

The others leapt in with small talk. But she was only aware of the thin little woman in the deep-blue suit, nervously patting that swoop of spray-plastered hair.

As if they were rarified sea animals who had unexpectedly come upon their mirror selves somewhere in the deep. As if there were no one else in the room.

The deliberate calm Priscilla had stoked all day unraveled at the sight of That Woman. In a glance she took in the blazing, flyaway hair, the spotlight red dress. Here she'd dressed down to fit the funereal overlay of the day, and that one came decked out like a bullfighter.

She seemed to be talking about, of all things, Pol Pot, pointing at one of the TVs against the wall. Priscilla said, "Yes, well, how nice for Dan Rather. I'm sure that's quite a coup, isn't it?"

Now she was saying something about the Wizard of Oz. Here was Priscilla finally come to the end of this long, terrible trail to their brief moment of glory—and it was dribbling away with small talk on Pol Pot.

She went to the bathroom to check her makeup. The woman followed, smiling into the mirror as she opened her purse. "Odd how these things work out, isn't it, Prilla? I certainly never thought the last time we ran into each other that it'd take this long to get back for the next go-round."

She said coolly, "Nor did I, Robin. Nor did I."

Fiddling with that fire-alarm belt. "That's the game for you, I guess. Often so different from what you expect."

"*Game?*" Priscilla boiled over, voice quivering, reedy with too-long-swallowed rage. "You call it a game? Maybe that's all it is to you, but let me tell you it's. . . ."

She broke off, tilted perilously close to the edge. Terrified for one awful moment of slipping past her controls.

Robin stared at her, murmuring something about "a manner of speaking. . . didn't mean to imply. . . ."

She stood quite still for a moment, pulling herself together. Then she whirled around, fists clenched at her sides. "You've ruined it! You've ruined it! You've gone and made a mockery and a laughing stock of it all."

Stunned by the frontal assault, the icy fury in those eyes, Robin was about to lash back. Suddenly she flashed on her own tantrum in her apartment bedroom, Dennis purring, "It's all right, darling, they all felt that way at the beginning—Eleanor and Pat, Betty Ford, even your sister-in-law Alexis."

Ah, sure. . . .

Smiling, riding an impulse, she reached out and patted that thin arm. "It's all right, Prilla. It always feels that way at first, you know. Every First Lady starts out scared to death of the job, even the ones who really wanted it. We all felt absolutely swamped, thought we couldn't possibly cope. But you'll see—it'll work out fine, much better than you think."

As Prilla stared into the mirror, Robin chattered on about what a "lifesaver" she'd find in Chief Usher Fletcher. "He's really a miracle-worker, the answer to every First Lady's prayers. It's kind of an odd, exclusive club you're coming into now, you know, stepping into Martha's shoes. But you'll take to it like a duck to water. I've said for months you'd make a much better First Lady than me—you know just how to do it, Prilla."

Stiff, wary nod. "Well, thank you. That's kind of you."

But Robin couldn't let it go at that. She was too raw with her hard-won understanding of the wrenching, bizarre experience just opening up now for Prilla Sterling.

With a sad, wistful smile she reached out to squeeze those tight-clenched hands, reassuring her softly, "It's all right, Prilla. It'll be okay. It's your turn now."

☆

The ceremony sped by in a merciful blur. From her front-row seat in the House well, tucked between the Cabinet and Supreme Court,

Robin was mainly absorbed in that extraordinary sight of Charlie and Larry perched in matching chairs above Dan Sterling's head.

As the old ham's golden tongue unrolled his Inaugural Address, running on for about half an hour, she was mainly watching Larry maintain his politely blank expression for the audience of millions, thinking prayerfully, *Don't yawn, please, babe. Don't even blink. . . .*

Winding up, the old boy paused for a calculated moment of dramatic effect. *Okay, hang on. Here's where he parades out his elephants. . . .* Then, firmly, ringingly: "America has set its house in order. And we can turn our attention now to that great goal that has always been an essential part of the American dream—lasting peace in the world.

"Accordingly, I am asking my Vice President, Laurence Devlin, who has served our nation so well in these past difficult months, to shoulder a new and demanding assignment as leader of our delegation to the peace conference which opens four days hence in Phnom Penh."

He turned and craned up at Larry in the vice-presidential roost next to the Speaker. "Larry, I know I'm asking you to tackle a tough job. But I'm confident no man is better qualified to undertake it. With the help of almighty God and the prayerful support of this nation and this government behind you, I have no doubt of our ultimate success."

From the tumult of her reaction, two thoughts shook out: *Lord, they can't wait to rush him out of town. . . .* And then:

Cambodia! We're going to Cambodia!

Turned out Larry and she were the elephants. Applause was still pouring as Dan and Prilla led them at the head of the grand march out to the Capitol's east lawn, where a big Marine chopper was parked. As TV crews scrambled ecstatically around them, Dan rattled away at Larry: "They tell me the White House staff will have your luggage aboard Air Force One at Andrews. . . keep in close touch. . . every confidence you'll do a great job. . . ."

Parading out through the wildly cheering crowd, Robin spotted Stephanie and Cal and beckoned them forward, agent ranks parting to let them through. Last burst of Sterling oratory at the red carpet leading to the idling chopper: "You carry with you the hopes and prayers of all Americans. Good luck and godspeed, Mr. Vice President!"

Cal managed to be the first one up the chopper steps, trailed by Wiley, Lowenthal, Stephanie, the kids and Ben. Dan bussed her cheek, saying heartily, "Bon voyage, Robin. Make it a good trip."

Priscilla offered a cordial, dignified handshake. "Goodby, Robin. And good luck."

She echoed back the smile. "Good luck yourself, Prilla. It'll work out fine—you'll see." *Funny thing, we both get what we wanted most. Astronomical odds against that. . . .*

Up the chopper steps, turning to wave from the door. As she buckled into the seat beside him, Larry said above the engine roar, "Hey, lady, didn't I promise you some fun?"

Laughing, she turned to wave at Prilla, who waved back, clutching Dan's hand, twinkling cheerily into the lights as the prop wash tore up her hairdo. They lifted off in a cloud of dust and circled around the gorgeous floodlit monuments, lighting their souls on those candles to Washington, Lincoln and Jefferson. With one last spin around the kindled White House, they flew off to the tragical, magical land of Cambodia.